पुरातत्त्व
पुरातत्त्व
PURĀTATTVA

Bulletin of the Indian Archaeological Society

No. 18 1987-88

Editor
S.P. Gupta

Jt. Editor
Makkhan Lal

D.K. Printworld (P) Ltd.
New Delhi

Cataloging in Publication Data — DK
[Courtesy : D.K. Agencies (P) Ltd. <docinfo@dkagencies.com>]

Purātattva : bulletin of the Indian Archaeological
Society, no. 18, 1987-88 / editor, S.P. Gupta ;
jt. editor, Makkhan Lal.
p. cm.
Includes bibliographical references.
ISBN 812460293X

1. Archaeology — India — Periodicals. 2. India
— Antiquities — Periodicals. 3. India — Civilization
— Periodicals. I. Gupta, S.P. (Swarajya Prakash),
1931 - II. Indian Archaeological Society.

DDC 934 21

First Published in 1989
First Reprinted in 2005
ISBN 81-246-0293-X
Price for volume 18 (1987-88): Rs. 800 US $ 40

Reprint authorised by
Indian Archaeological Society
New Delhi - 110 016

The Editors are not responsible for the opinions expressed by the Contributors.

Purātattva is published annually.

Manuscripts (whether in the form of articles or notes or book reviews) offered for publication should be sent to the Editor, Purātattva, Indian Archaeological Society, B-17, Qutab Institutional Area, New Delhi - 110 016.

Published and printed by:
D.K. Printworld (P) Ltd.
'Srikunj,' F-52, Bali Nagar
New Delhi - 110015
Phone : (011) 2545 3975, 2546 6019 Fax : (011) 2546 5926
E-mail : dkprintworld@vsnl.net
www. dkprintworld.com

PURATATTVA

CONTENTS

BOOK REVIEWS

PURATATTVA

NUMBER 18 1987-88

Editorial

We are very happy to place *Puratattva* No. 18 in the hands of readers. It gives us great satisfaction that for the past 10 years we have been able to Publish our Journal in time and there has been no backlog. More : we now plan to make *Puratattva* a biannual Journal. We hope that our readers and contributors will extend their help in this undertaking.

We greatfully acknowledge the financial help by the Archaeological Survey of India and the Indian Council of Historical Research which has made the publication of this volume possible. We are heopeful that their financial help will continue in future.

We deeply mourn the untimely death of Dr. Devahuti.

For the help in bringing out this issue the editor's special thanks go to Dr. Salahuddin, Dr. Q. S. Usmani and Messrs Anis Alvi, and N.H. Zaidi of the Archaeology Section, Department of History, Aligarh Muslim University.

Editors

Dr. DEVAHUTI (1929-1988)

DR. DEVAHUTI 1929-1988

Dr. Devahuti (born May 22, 1929) did M.A. in History from Punjab University in 1950. In the same year she married Sri Damodar Prasad Singhal. In 1956 Devahuti obtained her Doctoral Degree from the London University. Soon after, along with her husband she moved to Singapore where Dr. Singhal was to serve as a lecturer at the University of Malaya. In 1961 she accompanied her husband to Australia where the latter took up the position of Reader at the University of Queensland, Brisbane. The lure of Motherland and the Indianness in her was so compelling that she could not but return to India. She joined the Delhi University in the seventies; initially, as a Reader in Department of History and subsequently accepted Professorship in South Campus of the same University.

Prof. Devahuti was a stuanch Indian and admirer of Indian Culture, Civilization and Arts. This admiration of things beautiful urged her to travel widely, in India, as well as abroad. She and her husband, keen travellers as they were, had visited almost all the major civilizations of the world from Egypt, Greece, Rome to China and Peru.

After the untimely demise of her husband, Prof. Devahuti assumed the Directorship of the Centre for Research and Training in History, Archaeology, and Palaeo-Environment, New Delhi, in the establishment of which she and her husband were the nuclear force.

Prof. Devahuti is the author of several books and research papers. A few selected ones are as follows:-

1. *Harsha: A Political Study.* (Clarendon, 1970)
2. Ashoka's Dissent from the Hindu and the Buddhist Goals and Methods of the Chakravarti, the Great Conquerer, in S.C. Malik (ed) *Dissent, Protest and Reform in Indian Civilization* (Simla, Indian Institute of Advanced Study, 1977).
3. *India and Ancient Malaya,* (Singapore, Eastern University Press, 1965).
4. 'Prehistoric Links Among Australia, South East Asia and India', *South East Asian Review 1(1)*
5. Some Impressions of China, *China report,* (jointly with D.P. Singhal);
6. Possibilities of Research on the Indian Elements in the History of Early Borneo; A study of Sabah, *Bulletin of the Institute of Traditional Cultures* (Madras 1973);
7. 'Mauryan Art and the Episode Theory', *Annals of the Bhandarkar Oriental Research Institute, 52 (Poona)* 1971.
8. Harsha : A Hindu-Buddhist King, Hemisphere Contacts and Cultural Synthesis, in Sita Ram Goel, et al. (ed.) *India's Contribution to World Thought and Culture,* (Madras, 1970)
9. India and Malaysia--Ancient Heritage and Modern Attitudes, *Cultural Forum 11* (3.4)
10. The Coins of Harsha Siladitya; A Reappraisal, *Journal of the Numismatic Society of India. 26* (Banaras, 1964).
11. Role of Architecture as Revealed by Early Indian Art, *Indo-Asian Culture 12* (2)
12. Singificance of contemporary Dharmasastras and Indigenous Historiographical Literature for Shidyor Hindu-Muslim Encounter in Early Middle Ages,
13. The Problem of Political Paradigms-A factor in Early Hindu-Muslim Silriatron in Devahuti (ed). *Historical and Political Prospectives,* (New Delhi) 1982.

BIO-STRATIGRAPHY OF THE CENTRAL NARMADA VALLEY WITH SPECIAL REFERENCE TO HEXAPROTODON SPP.

Salahuddin*

In the present work *Hexaprotodon* spp. which are being considered as the marker of 'Upper' and 'Lower'groups in the area have been taken up for a detailed morphological study. Different measurements on skull, mandibles, incisors, canines and cheek teeth have been taken to see the similarity and differences between the two species and also individual variation in the species. The variation have been compared with that of Siwalik *Hexaprotodon siwalensis* which shows a very wide range of individual variation within the species.

The river Narmada, one of the largest rivers in India originates from Amarkantak(22°45'N: 77°45'E) on the Makiala range in eastern Madhya Pradesh and passes through a lineament between the Vindhyan and Satpura. It passes through various geolgical formations like cretaceous Deccan Trap, Crystaline Dolometic limestone of Dharwar system, fluvial tract and sandstone and quartzitic rocks of Vindhyan and Satpura, and after flowing for about 1310 km. through Madhya Pradesh and Gujarat, debouches in the Gulf of Cambay near Broch.

Previous Work

Strech between Bhedaghat and Handia which forms the trough, preserves about 152 m. thick alluvial deposits (Khatri, 1966), forming the central region of the Narmada Valley. It has yielded one of the richest cultural and faunal materials. In its richness of fossil fauna it stands second after the Siwaliks in the Indian sub-continent.

In the Narmada Valley the credit for discovering the first fossil remains of *Elephas sp.* and *Equus sp.* goes to Sleeman in 1830, which were published by Princep (1832). Spilsbury (1837 & 1840) added the species of *Elephas sp.*. *Equus sp.*, *Hippopotamus sp.*, *Bubalus sp.*, *Bos gaurus*, *Palaeotherium* and *Cervus affinis* to the faunal list of the Narmada, but without any stratigraphical control. Theobald (1860) for first time started scientific exploration in the valley. He discovered, *Elephas hysudricus*, *Elephas (stegodon) insignis*, *Elephas (stegodon ganesa*, *Equus sp.*, *Rhinoceros* sp., *Hippopotamus (Tetraprotodon)*,*Hippopotamus (hexaprotodon)*, *Bos namadicus*, *Bubalus palaeindicus*, *Cervus sp.*, *Cervus stylocerus*, *Rusa* sp., *Cervus duvauceli*, *Axis* sp., *Sus* sp. *Hystrix* sp. *Mus* sp., *Trionyx and Emys namadicus*. Theobald on the basis of the molluscs and lithology came to the conclusion that there has been a change in species and lithology from 'Lower' to 'Upper' deposits and thus he divided the deposit into 'Lower' and 'Upper' group.

In the early years of the twentieth century main emphasis was put on the palaeontological and geological studies of the Narmada deposits. Pilgrim (1905) gave the first faunal list of *Elephas namadicus*, *elephas (stegodon) insignis*, *Elephas (stegodon) ganesa*, *Equus namadicus*, *Rhinoceros unicornis*, *Hippopotamus namadicus*, *Hippopotamus palaeindicus*, *Bos namadicus*, *Bubalus palaeindicus Leptobos frazeri*, *Cervus duvauceli*, *sus* sp., *Ursus namadicus*, and *Pengsura tectum* from the Narmada Valley and on the basis of similar fossil fauna like *Elephas antiquus (namadicus)*, *Hippopotamus pala-eindicus* and *Equus namadicus* from the Godavari Valley, he assigned a Middle Pleistocene age to both the deposits. Later H. De Terra and Paterson (1939) explored the valley and on the basis of lithology divided the deposits into 'Younger Alluvium' and 'Older Alluvium' and assigned Middle Pleistocene age to the deposits on the basis of fauna, *Elephas namadicus*, *Equus namadicus*, *Hexaprotodon namadicus*, *Bos namadicus*, *Bubalus palaeindicus*, *Sus* sp., *Trionyx* sp. and *Emys* sp. They questioned the authenticity of *Leptobos* and

* Department of History, Aligarh Muslim University, Aligarh 202001.

Stegodon reported earlier by Pilgrim (1905). Colbert (1942) added two more fossil species namely *Holarctos namadicus* and *Palaeoloxodon namadicus* to the faunal list and supported the chronology proposed earlier by Pilgrim (1905). After a lull of nearly two decades Khatri (1966) explored the area and collected numerus fossils like, *Elephas namadicus, Elephas maximum indicus, Equus namadicus, Hexaprotodon namadicus, Bos namadicus, Bubalus palaeindicus, Bison* sp., *Cervus* sp. and *Sus* sp. and postulated that the fauna recovered from the area are ranging from Middle Pleistocene to Halocene period in age.

In the meantime Sen and Ghosh (1963) explored the area and came up with a new hypothesis of vertebrate faunal change in 'Upper' and Lower' groups of Theobald and H. De-Terra & Paterson's 'Younger' and 'Older' alluvium on the basis of Hooijer's (appendix Sen and Ghosh, 1963, with the fauna of *Elephas namadicus, Elephas maximus indicus, Equus namadicus, Hippo-potamus namadicus, Hippopotamus palaeindicus, Bos sp. Bubalus sp., Sus sp.) remark which was based on the single isolated molar of Hippopotamus sp.* Hooijer oppined that the 'Lower Group' might have had primitive *Hippopotamus namadicus* as compared to the 'Upper Group' which has advanced form of *Hippopotamus palaeindicus.* Supekar (1968) explored the area and collected few mammalian fossil like *Elephas sp., Elephas hysudricus, Equus caballus, Hippopotamus namadicus, Bos namadicus, Bubalus bubalis* and oppined that there is no faunal change in the area. In the subsequent years Khan (1968) explored the area and listed a few mammalian fossils like, *Stegodon namadicus, Palaeoloxodon namadicus, Equus namadicus, Hexaprotodon palaeindicus, Bos namadicus, and Sus namadicus.* He also doubted the presence of *Bison* as reported by Khatri (1966).

In 1979 Badam under took detailed Palaeontological study of the area and on the basis of fossils, *Elephas hysudricus, Stegodon insignis ganesa, Elephas maximus indicus, Equus namadicus, Hippopotamus palaeindicus, Bos namadicus, Bubalus bubalis, Cervus duvauceli, Crocodylus sp. Gavialis sp. and Trionyx sp.* established a relative stratigraphical time scale for the 'Lower' and 'Upper' group. He supported the view of faunal change proposed by Sen and Ghosh on the basis of presence of *H. namadicus*, in the 'Lower Group' and that of *H. palaeindicus* in the 'Upper Group',. In 1978 Dassarma and Biswas proposed three fold faunal chage in the area. They reported for the first time three species of the genus *Hippopotamus, namely H. Sivalensis, H. namadicus and H. palaendicus* from basal, middle and upper alluvial deposits respectively. However, later they clarified that only *H. namadicus and H. palaeindicus* had been collected. The former from the lower and middle and later from the upper group of the Narmada. (Biswas and Dassarma, 1981). The detailed faunal list as given by some of the workers is summarised in the table No. 1.

The presence of *Hippopotamus namadicus* (six incisored Hippo) and *Hippopotamus palaeindicus* (four incisored Hippo) in the Narmada Quaternary deposits has been treated as index of evolution in the genus since 1847 by Falconer and Cautley. They considered *H. palaeindicus* as an evolved form and similar to the present day *Hippopotamus amphibius* of Africa. The only difference from that of the present hippo was attributed to the bigger size of 2nd pair of incisors instead of the first one. this was supported by Theobald (1860) giving a new name *"Tetraprotodon"* (?) to *Hippopotamus palaeindicus*. In the later years the identification of both *H. namadicus* and *H. palaeindicus* was made on the basis of differences in the mandibular symphysis index and some other minor differences in the cranial parts, rather than the number of the incisors (Hooijer, 1950; Deraniyagala, 1969; Biswas and Dassarma, 1984).

H. palaeindicus has also been reported from the Gangetic alluvium (Pilgrim, 1904), Godavari Valley (Pilgrim, 1905), Belan and Son Valleys (Alur, 1980; Blumenshine and Chatopadhayay, 1983), Ghod Valley (Badam and Kajale, 1977) and Manjra valley (Joshi et. al. 1981 and Badam et. al. 1984) and that of *Hippopotamus namadicus* from godavari Valley (Tripathy, 1967).

The fossil remains from these places except Narmada Valley are representated by isolated molars and parts of post cranials which lack diagnostic characters for identification upto the specific level. In all these cases geological context of the finds has been taken into consideration for identification rather than the morphology of the species. Since all the specimens in other parts of India have been found in geologically younger deposits than the Narmada, these have been treated as *Hexaprotodon palaeindicus (Hippopotamus palaeindicus).*

In the present paper, the fossils collected by the author and some previous researchers (Supekar, 1968; Badam 1979), housed in Deccan College have been studied. Before discussing the identification of two species of *Hexaprotodon* in the Narmada Valley it would be profitable to discuss some other probalems regarding its genus and evolution.

Genus

The family *Hippopotamidae* which represents several extinct (six incisored, four incisored and two incisored) and extant (four incisored and two incisored) forms posed a great problem for its classification into generic and specific levels. There are several schools of thoughts regarding the classification. Taking their incisor number into consideration falconer and cautley (1836) put them into two sub-genera under the genus Hippopotamus which was accepted by Pilgrim (1941) also. Owen (1845) considered incisors as a tool for generic classification and separated them into two genera, *Hexaprotodon and Hippopotamus. Lydekker* (1882) considered incisors as the basis for the species classification and treated the two genera proposed by Owen as *Hippopotamus* only. This classification was followed by Hooijer (1950) and Biswas and Dassarma (1984). Mathew (1929) hypothesized that except incisors there is no difference between six incisored *Hexaprotodon* and four incisored present day *Hippopotamus* and therefore, he gave them sub-generic status. He gave the generic status to the two incisored pygmy hippopotamus *Choeropsis.* But he was not sure whether it can be separafed generically from *Hexaprotodon* and *Hippopotamus.* Colbert (1935), who laid much emphasis on the cranial bones rather than incisors, regarded *Hexaprotodon* and *Tetraprotodon* as separate genera.

In recent years Coryndon (1977), who worked on Hippopotamidae for long time accepted Colbert's (1935) criteria of differences based on cranial and Long bones, separated *Hexaprotodon* and *Tetraprotodon* into different genera. She also put *Choeropsis* into *Hexaprotodon* on the basis of similarity of cranial bones. According to Coryndon both the genera *Hexaprotodon* and *Hippopotamus* exhibit the following differences :

	Hexaprotodon	*Hippopotamus*
Facial bones	Nasal only slightly expanded posteriorly.	Nasal wide posteriorly.
	Lacrimal small.	Lacrimal broad.
	Frontal with anterior extension in contact with maxillary.	Frontal not in contact with maxillary.
Orbit	Post orbital length near 1/2 Cranial length	Post orbital length very short.
Pre-maxilla	Incisors set in a shallow arc	Incisors set at 45° to midline
	Terminal wear-facets.	Lateral wear facets.
	Median suture closed.	Median suture open.
Upper canines	Posterior groove deep.	Posterior groove shallow.
Lower canines	Smooth enamel.	Ridged enamel.
Pre-molars	Row long and more complex in structure.	Row short and comparatively simple.
Limb bone	Gracile, longer.	Robust, short.
Astragalus	Slender, elongate	Robust, broad
Pes	Median toes approaching digiti grade.	Splayed, plantigrade.

Taking the evidence from other animals, extinct as well as extant into consideration it seems logical to accept Colbert's (1935) and

Coryndon's (1977) classification on the basis of cranial bones rather than incisors.

Evolution

Regarding the evolution of the family there have been varied opinions. Falconer (1868) and Lydekker (1876) hypothesized that Hippopotamidae might have evolved from Anthracotheride. this hypothesis further gain support from Andrew (1896), who considered *Merycopotamus* as an ancestor of Hippopotamidae. Pearson (1923) postulated that the family has evolved from Suidae, a view supported by Mathew (1929). Later Colbert (1935) on the basis of the studies on the family suidae, Anthracotheridae and Hippopotamidae suggested that the Anthracothereidae and Hippopotamidae probably had a common ancestor in Miocene (?). this conclusion was based on the similarities between the premolars, skulls and mandibles of the two families.

Recent studies (Coryndon, 1978) on the materials from Africa have not revealed any affinity of Hippopotamidae with Suidae and Anthracotheridae. However, both Anthracotheridae and Hippopotamidae show week hypocone in molars.

In India the family first appeared in Dhok Pathan (Pilgrim, 1913) of Middle Siwaliks in north-west India. It then spread in different parts of India and survived till the terminal pleistocene period.

As far as the specific evolution in India is concerned, it is thought that the *H.sivalensis* has given rise to the *H. namadicus* which in turn evolved as *H. palaeindicus.* (Lydekker, 1882; Hooijer, 1950; Biswas and Dassarma, 1984). The above scholars thought that the tetraprotodonty was achieved through the elimination of the second incisor. The discovery of a fossil from Pinjor (Sahni and Khan, 1961) with five incisors, short diastema, single rooted P_1 steeper slope along the mandibular symphysis and irregular circumference outline of the incisors gave some support to the hypothesis postulated above (Prasad and Satsangi, 1964). But as said earlier it was a solitary specimen and was given the name of *Pentaprotodon sivalensis* . However, the abnormality in the taxon can not be ruled out as Coryndon (1970) has argued and in that case the fossil belongs to *H. sivalensis* and not a new species, *Pentaprotodon sivalensis.*

Researches carried out by Coryndon gives the idea that tetraprotodonty might have evolved from *Hexaprotodon* about 5—4 millions years ago, but the Pleistocene *Hexaprotodon* was not the ancestor of the *Tetraprotodon* (Coryndon, 1967, 1976), as the evidence from the African sites: Chemeron in Kenya and Kaiso in Uganda suggests (Coryndon, 1978). In the Chemeron deposits tetraprotodon is probably similar to *Hippopotamus Kaisensis* from the Kaiso formation in Uganda, (Coryndon, 1978). She says, "*Hippopotamus* as known includes no species with other than four incisors in each jaw; this genus now includes several species in Africa and Europe, the earliest known being *Hippopotamus Kaisensis* from the Pliocene of Uganda, but it is so far not known from Asia", (Coryndon, 1977; p.69)

As far as the ancestory of *H. sivalensis* is concerned, it is not clear. In certain characters like 3rd incisor, premolars and molars *H.siavalensis* is similar to African species *H. harvardi.* However, in *H. sivalensis* the 4th premolar is more advanced and molars are more trefoliate as compared to the *H. hardvardi.* On the other hand the *H. sivalensis*, except in size and divergence of premolars series at P_4 (it is at P_1 in *H. iravaticus*, from Burma) is similar to the *H. iravaticus.* the difference between African species *H. harvardi* and *H. iravaticus* are more promienent than between the *H. sivalensis* and *H. harvardi,* (Coryndon, 1977). According to her *Hexaprotodon* evoluved from the African ancestor in the early Pliocene and might have migrated to India from Africa via Arabian peninsula in Mid Pliocene. It seems logical to accept that the *H. sivalensis* and *H. iravaticus* might have evolved from the same ancestor. The slight differences in size and morphology could be due to the different habitat and long geographical isolation, (Coryndon, 1976).

In the case of *H. namadicus* it is possible that it might have evolved from the *H. sivalensis.* But there is no direct evidence to substantiate this statement.

With brief introduction about the genera and its evolution in the previous pages now I will

Princep, 1833
Spilsbury, 1837
Theobald, 1860
Pilgrim, 1905
Deterra & Pat
Hooijer, 1963
Khatri, 1966
Supekar, 1968
Badam, 1979
Khan, 1972
Biswas & Dass
Badam & Salah
Present Collect

NOTE : For
indivi

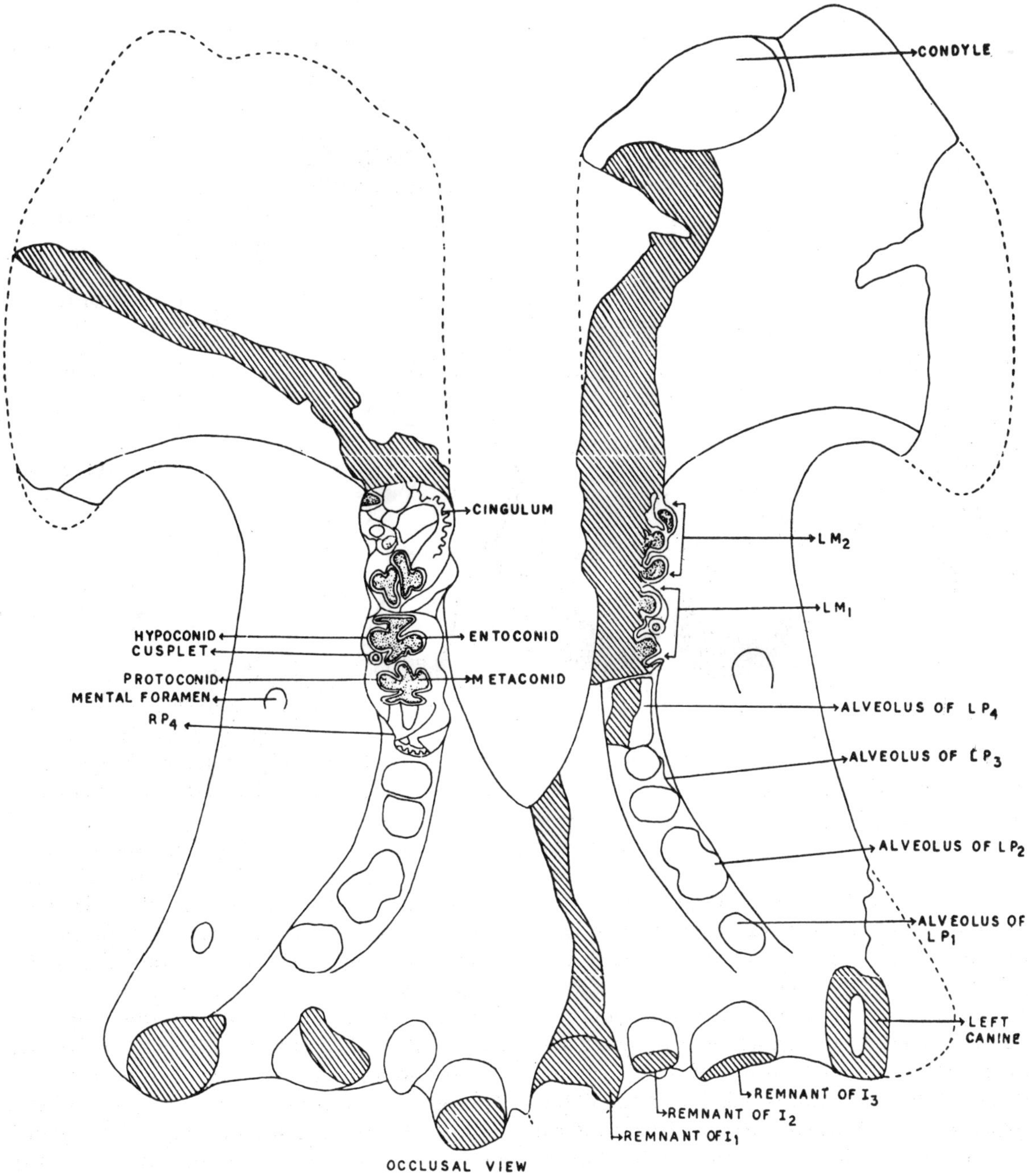

OCCLUSAL VIEW

HEXAPROTODON NAMADICUS: MANDIBLE; NMD/231/DC

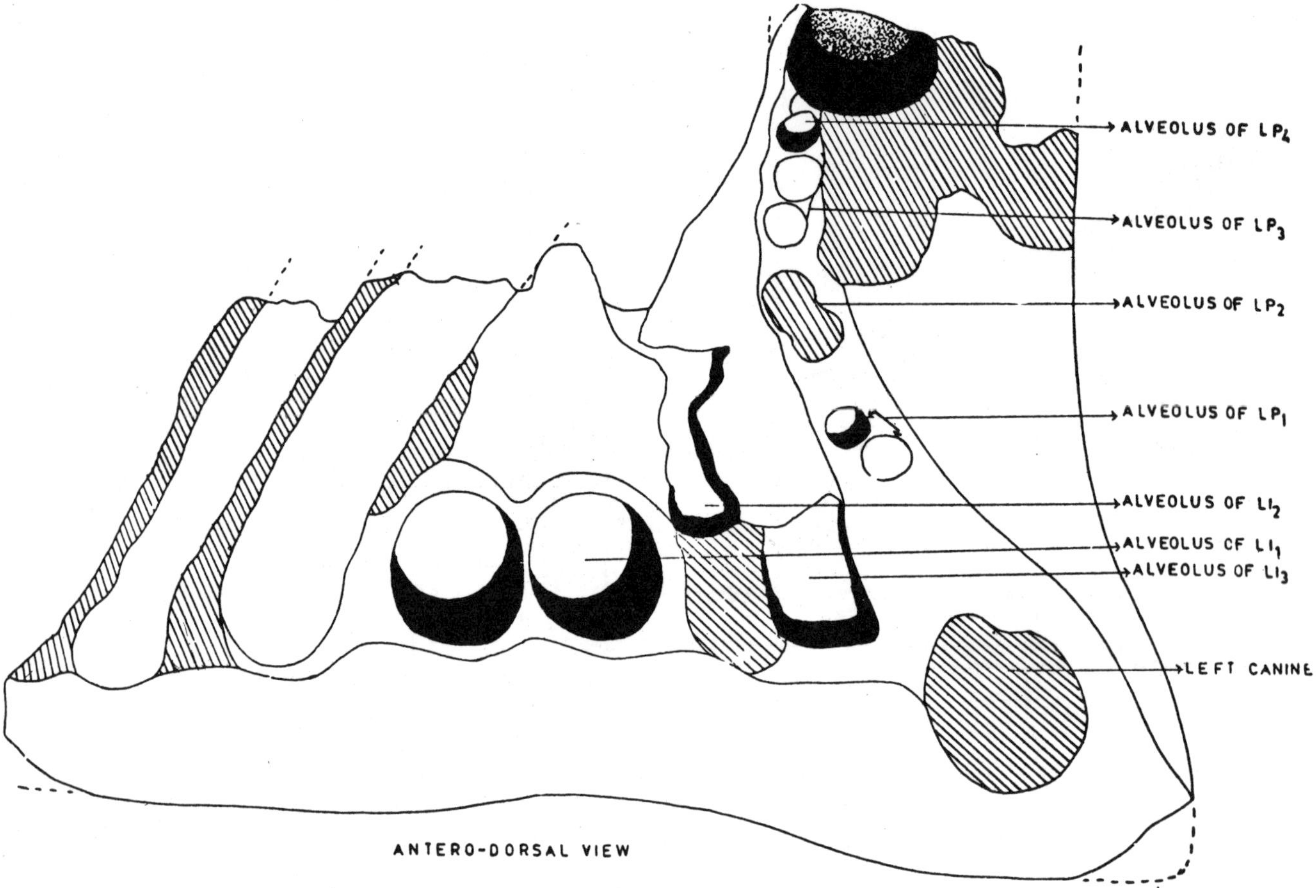

HEXAPROTODON PALAEINDICUS: MANDIBULAR SYMPHYSIS: NMD/232/DC

describe the Narmada specimens.

Hexaprotodon Falconer and Cautley, 1836.

Diagnosis

Presence of three pairs of incisors in each jaw, long mandibular symphysis; small prominence of the Orbits; elongated astragalus; lacrimal bone extended from orbital rim by frontal, touching maxiallary bone. (Falconer, 1849, p. 237; Lydekkar, 1882, pp. 28-33; Mathew, 1929, p. 556).

Remarks

The family represents several extinct species in Europe, Africa and Asia. Two living monospecific genera, *Hippopotamus amphibius* and *Hexaprotodon liberensis (Choeropsis)* is confined to sub Saharan Africa and Central Africa (costal plain from Guinea to Ivory coast) respectively.

From the Indian subcontinent several extinct species like *Hexaprotodon sivalensis, Hexaprotodon platyrhinchus and Hexaprotodon magagnathus* (from Dhoku Pathan to Pinjor in siwalik hills) and *Hexaprotodon namadicus and Hexaprotodon palaeindicus* (from Middle to upper Pleistocen diposits of Peninsular India) have been reported. However, Lydekker (1884) doubts the identification of *Hexaprotodon platyrhincus* and *Hexaprotodon magagnathus.* In the present paper only *Hexaprotodon namadicus* and *Hexaprotodon plaeindicus* have been taken up for detailed morphological study.

Hexaprotodon namadicus Falconer and Cautley, 1836.

Systematic Palaeontology

Order	Artiodactyla Owen, 1848.
Family	Hippopotamidae Gray, 1821.
Genus	*Hexaprotodon* Falconer & Cautley, 1836.
Species	*Hexaprotodon namadicus*, Falc & cautley, 1836.

Synonymy

1836 *Hippopotamus namadicus*, Falconer and Cautley, *Asiatic Research*, Pl. I, fig. 1-5, Pl. II, Fig. 1-5.

1847 *Hippopotamus (Hexaprotodon) namadicus*, Falconer and Cautley, *Fauna Antiqua Sivalensis*, Pls. LVII, LVIII (name & figures; Lydekker, 1884, Pl. Ind. (x) *III*, p. 43.

1929 *Hexaprotodon namadicus*, Mathew, *Bull Amer. Mus. Nat. History*, Vol. *LVI*, Pt. VII p. 557.

1969 *Hippopotamus namadicus*, Deraniyagala, *Spolia Zeylonica*, Vol. *31*, Pt. II, pp. 1-5.

1950 *Hexaprotodon namadicus*, Hooijer, *Zool. Verhand.*, No. *8*, pp. 1-124.

1984 *Hippopotamus namadicus*, Biswas and dassarma, *Rec, Geol. Survey of India*, Vol. 114, Pt. 2, pp. 19-24.

Diagnosis

Size large; orbits high; brain case large post dental part of calvarium short; mandibular symphysis short as compared to its width and high in relation to its length; 2nd incisor two third of the size of Ist incisor; 2nd and 3rd incisors subequal. (Hooijer, 1950; Biswas and dassarma, 1984).

Type

Not specified, No. 36838, 36839 and 36840 are co-type. (*American Mus. Nat. History*)

Horizon and Locality

Narmada (Narbuda river bed).

Present Specimen (Pl. I & Fig. I)

During the course of exploration in district Narsinghpur, Madhya Pradesh I collected two specimens of *Hexaprotodon namadicus* from the Narmada river section. The details of provenence, accession number, identification etc. are as follows:

Specimen	Lower jaw
Catalauge No.1	NMD/231A/DC
No.2	NMD/231B/DC
Horizon	Sandy pebbly gravel
Locality	Talayyaghat, river Varurewa.

Both the specimen belong to a single jaw and can be joined together to form a complete jaw. The specimen is among a few complete jaws in India and is fairly good state of preservation.

The part of right jaw is complete except for the ascending ramus. M_1, M_2 and P_4 are well preserved. The alveoli of P_3, P_2 and P_1 are present alongwith the remnants of incisors and canines. The horizontal ramus is short and stout and more are less sagittal with the vertical axis of the jaw.

The posterior part of the jaw is thinner than the anterior. The molars are more or less in straight line while the premolars diverge on the right side due to which the labial side is concave and the lingual side convex. The symphyseal part which bears the canine and incisors is very high and wide. The length of the symphysis is less than its width. Superior border of the symphysis protrudes outward making a shallow depression on the anterior part. Inferior border is more are less rectangular in shape. The symphyseal depression has several foramina.The body of the ramus has several pits and cracks which is an indicator of sub-aerial exposure of the specimen before burial.

The canine which is the largest tooth is broken at the base and is more are less oval in cross section with a slight depression on the dorsomedial side. The incisors which are unequal in size are broken. I_2, the smallest tooth, is represented by an alveoli. The inner border of incisors placed between canines in a transverse fashion is more are less even, while the outer border is not even as the I_2 is placed at a higher elevation.

The lower part of the angular ramus is blunt and somewhat rounded. The angle between the horizontal and angular part of the vertical ramus is of the order of 60° or 90°

The description of the promolars and molars is as follow:

P_1 to P_4

P_1 and P_3 are represented by the alveolii of the bifurcated rounded roots whereas the P_2 is represented by the remmants of the bifurcated roots. P_4 is complete. As compoared to molars it is simple and conical. It is *quatrefoil* in cross-section. Cingulum is very weak.

M_1

The tooth is complete and slightly worn. The anterior cusps are fused and make a single median cavity with irregular enamel layer. Posterior cusps are also fused and have an irregular enamel layer. The development of cingulum not uniform. At the buccal side between the valley, a small cusplet with a small cavity is present.

M_2

The tooth is complete. The anterior cusps proto-and metaconids are mildly worn showing trefoil structure. The septum between the two cusps is not fused. The enamel layer is irregular, Hypoconid, trefoil in nature and shows very mild signs of wear while the entoconid has none. The cingulum is well developed at anterior and posterior sides but weak lingually and buccally. The upper part of the posterior cingulum is converted into cusplet without any sign of wear. The left jaw has partly broken ascending ramus. Outer border of the symphysis is also broken. The ascending ramus is devoid of coronoid process while the condyle is well preserved and elongated Labio—lingually. It is slightly higher than the crown of the molar line. Towards lingual side the condyle is more extended. The angular part of the ramus is blunt and round where as the lower part makes 60 degrees angle with the horizontal ramus.

Horizontal ramus is short and stout. The posterior portion is comparatively thinner than the anterior. Molars are situated in a straight line while the premolars diverge towards the Labial side. The divergence gives a concavo—convex shape to the ramus.

Mandibular symphysis represents the left half of the total breadth. The length is less than the breadth. The height of the symphysis is nearly equal to the length. The mandibular foramen, situated just 7 cm. below the anterior part of the condyle is quite deep.

Canine is broken, its remnant exhibit oval cross-section. The incisors which are unequal in diameter and size are placed in a transverse line between the canines.

I_2 is smaller than I_1 and I_3. The inner border

uneven because the I_2 is placed at a higher elevation.

The superior border of the symphysis is protruded while the inferior border is slightly retracted. Four foramina are present in the symphyseal depression, almost in a straight line and parallel to the incisors.

Description of teeth is as following:

P_1 to P_4

P_1 and P_3 are represented by alveolii of their roots. P_2 and P_4 are represented by the bifurcated roots.

M_1

The tooth is represented by the meta-and ento-conids. Cusps are moderately worn. The pattern of the metaconid is not clear while that of the entoconid is trefoil. Between the valley a small worn cusplet is also present. The cingulum at the central portion is well developed as compared to that on the anterior part.

M_2

The tooth is represented by inner cusps only. Both the conids, meta and ento, are slightly worn. The cusps are trefoil in nature. Cingulum at anterior side is strong as compared to that near the central portion.

Hexaprotodon palaeindicus Falconer & Cautley, 1836.

Systematic Palaeontology:

Order Artiodactyla Owen 1848.
Family Hippopotamidae, Gray 1821.
Genus *Hexaprotodon* Fal. & Cautley, 1836.
Species *Heaxaprotodon palaeindicus* Fal. Cautley, 1836.

Synonymy

1836 *Hexaprotodon palaeindicus*, Falconer & Cautley, *Asiatic Research*, Vol. 19, pp.39-53.

1847 *Hexaprotodon palaeindicus*, Fal-coner and cauntley, *Fauna Antiqua Sivalewis*, Pt. 7, Pls. 59-60.

1950 *Hippopotamus palaeindicus*, Hooijer, *Zool. Verhand*, No. 8, po. 1-124.

1969 *Hexaprotodon palaeindicus*, Deraniyagala, *Spolia Zeylonica*, Vol. 31, Pt. II, pp. 1-5.

Diagnosis

Skull short and wide; mandibular symphysis short as compared to its width and higher than its length; jaw squarish, six sub. equal incisors; braincase small; sagittal crest well developed. Orbits high; 2nd incisor situated at higher elevation as compared to Ist and 3rd incisors. (Hooijer, 1950; Deraniyagala, 1969).

Type

A lower jaw (Falconer & Cautley, 1847), No. 19743. (*Amer. Mus. Nat. History*)

Locality and Horizon

Narmada Alluvial deposits, pleistocene,

Present Specimens

1. Right jaw with broken teeth
2. Mandibular symphysis

Description

1. Specimen (Pl. 2)

Right jaw with half symphysis

Catalange No.	NMD/28/DC
Horizon	Sandy pebbly gravel
Locality	Talayyaghat, river Varunewa

The specimen is represented by the horizontal ramus and a part of the half mandibular symphysis. All the teeth are broken except M_3 which is also partly broken. However, the remnants of their roots are present.

The jaw is slightly elongated and twisted. The molar line is diverted on the right side, thus making the labial side concave. Symphysis is represented by half of the total width which bears the remnants of oval shaped canines and rounded to sub-rounded alveoli of three incisors. The outer border of the transverse line of incisors is not even as I_2 is placed at a higher elevation as compared to I_1 and I_3. Protrusion and retraction of the superior and inferior borders of the symphysis is not marked and the depression formed in between is shallow.

Distance between canines and P_1 is short.

2. Specimen (Pl. 3 and Fig.2)

Mandibular symphysis

Catalouge No. NMD/232/DC.

Horizon Sandy pebbly gravel.

Locality Devakachar, river sher.

The specimen is represented by the mandibular symphysis along with the alveolii of incisors and remnants of canines and aleveolii of premolars. The width of the symphysis is large as compared to the height and length. Height is slightly more than the length. Superior as well as inferior borders are not protruded and retracted but seem to be at the same level. Consequently depression between the superior and inferior border is not marked. Outer and inner borders of the transverse line of incisors are not even. Pair of I_2 is placed above the I_1 and I_3. However, the pairs of I_1 and I_3 are also sub-equal. The diameter of I_1 is more than that of I_3. The cross—section of the canine is oval with a slight depression on the latero-posterior side. The diameter of the canines are more than that of the incisors. Diastema between canine and P_1 is short.

In the above pages we have discussed morphology of mandibles of *Hexaprotodon sp.* in somewhat great details. We shall now turn our attention to some of the salient features that can be deducted from the above detail description regarding these species. We shall also deal with problem whether there were two species of *Hexaprotodon (H. namadicus* and *H. palaeindicus)* are just one and the scholars here made a mistake in identifying two species.

Discussion

In the present study both the species *(H. namadicus and H. palaeindicus)* have been studied metrically and non-metrically to observe the differences if any. The observations are given below:

Metrical Observations

Canines

In the present collection only three manadibular symphysis (one *H. namadicus* and two *H. palaeindicus)* with four broken canines are present. In all the cases the dorsoventral width is more than the bilateral width (Table No. 2). In *H. namadicus* both these measurements are slightly smaller than the *H. palaeindicus*. However, the measurements of the right canine do not tally with those of the left canine in the same individual of *H. namadicus*.

Table 2

Measurements (in mm) of mandible of *Hexaprotodon* spp. from Narmada Valley.

	H. namadicus NMD/231A&B/DC	**H. plaeindicus** NMD/28/DC	NMD/232/DC
1. Length of mandible	410	-	-
2. Length of Mandibular symphysis	144	135	142
3. Width of mandibular symphysis	316	324	333
4. Height of mandibular symphysis	133	140	150
5. Dorsiventral width of canines	R 46 L 50	53	61
6. Bilateral width of canines	R 36 L 38	52	44
7. Dorsiventral width of incisor I	R 33 L 36	39	37
8. Bilateral width of incisor I	R 30 L 32	-	34
9. Dorsiventral width of incisor III	41	—	—
10. Bilateral width of incisor III	34	—	—
11. Diastema	R 26 L 26	32	44
12. Depth of mandible at M_2	130	—	—
13. Length of molar and Premolar series	R 247 L 247	255	—

Incisors

In both the species the incisors are sub-equal in size. I_3 is larger than I_1 which is larger than I_2. In the case of incisors also both the sides have different dimensions. The dorsoventral width in all the cases is greater than the bilateral width (Table No. 2). But differences in both the species are not significant. The index of I_2 in *H. namadicus* is 6.1 while in *H. palaeindicus* it is 6.6 and 5.8 (Table No. 3). The indices do not show any significant difference and indicate, that in both the species I_2 is reduced equally. P.E.P. Deraniyagala (1969) also gives 7.4, 8.2 and 4.8 indices for *H. namadicus* and 11.6 and 11.8 for *H. palaeindicus*.

TABLE 4 : Width/Length Ratio of Upper and Lower Cheek Teeth of *Hexaprotodon* spp. taken from the publised sources (Deraniyagala; 1969, Nanda 1978 and Biswas & Dassarma, 1984) and present collection

I_1 which is the second largest tooth has indices of 4.5 and 9.5 in both the species respectively which show size reduction in *H. palaeindicus*.

I_3 is the largest tooth in both the species. However, in the present collection *H. palaeindicus* does not have I_3 but the alveoli show very wide diameter. In *H. namadicus* it has an index of 3.9 which shows that the tooth is large with slight reduction in lateral width. As a whole the fluctuation of indices in both the cases and other Asiatic species are quite evident.

Table 3

Indices of I_2 in *Hexaprotodon* spp.

Sl. No.	Species	Bilateral width (in mm)	Dorsiventrall width (in mm)	Symphyseal width (in mm)	Index
1.	H. sivalensis S/136/DC	23	26	240	4.8
2.	H. namadicus NMD/231A&B/DC	21	30	295	6.1
3.	H. palaeindicus NMD/28/DC	25	30	324	5.8
4.	H. palaeindicus NMD/232/DC	23	27	333	6.6

Index : $\frac{\text{Symphy sealwidth}}{\text{Bilateral+dorsiventralwidth of incisors}}$

Molars

The molars in the *Hexaprotodon spp.* show slight unstandardized measurements (generally length is more than the width, but sometimes width is more than length). Further, the vriation within the species are so much that it is very difficult to reach at any conclusion on the molars. The measurements are given in the Table No. 4.

Statistical observations on cheek teeth

The statistical observations made on the available cheek teeth show the following results (Table No. 5,6,7,8,9 and 10).

1. The differences of standard deviation in length and breadth of *H. namadicus* and *H. paleindicus* are very less and show the normal deviation as compared to the Siwalik species: (Table No.9).

2. The standard deviation for length and breadth indicates that the Narmada group is different from Siwalik's *Hexaprotodon sivalensis*, Table No. 9).

3. Width/Length ratio in the case of Siwalik and Narmada specimens is generally very close to each other. (TableNo. 4).

4. The standard deviation in length and breadth of *H. sivalensis* is very high as compared to that of the Narmada group Table No. 5, 6, &7.

The statistical study is based on a meagre data. However, the number of specimens of *H. sivalensis* are larger which lower the average than the Narmada group (which has less effect on the average). Inspite of that, the standard deviation in Narmada group is less than in *H. Sivalensis*. If there is more data in the Narmada group then the differences between *H. namadicus* and *H. palaeindicus* may be even less.

Metrical Observations on Mandibular Symphysis

Only three mandibular symphysis are present which show the following metrical results. However, some more data have also been substantiated from the published sources.

In *H. namadicus* the width and length are slightly smaller than the *H. palaeindicus* (Table No. 11) with symphyseal indices which ranges between 182.8—242.3 and 220—263.2 respectively (Table No. 12).

Both the species overlap with each other in indices. However, in the case of *H. sivalensis* the indices are very less as compared to *H. namadicus* and *H. palaeindicus*. The indices for *H. sivalensis* range between 121.4—192.7 with an everage of 165.8.

But in the case of indices differences *H. sivalensis* show very wide range of variation as compared to *H. namadicus* and *H. palaeindicus*. The differences between the *H. namadicus* and *H. paleindicus* are of the same order as in the *H. sivalensis*.

Observations on Skull Measurements

In the collection of Deccan college only one partial skull is present which could not be taken up for a comparative study because of its very fragmentary nature. The data discussed here has been published by Hooijer (1950) and Biswas and Dassarma (1984).

Thirteen parameters have been taken into account to study the skull measurements. These are:

6. Breadth of parietal.
1. Length from the condyle to posterior border.
2. Lenth from sagittal crest to posterior tip of nasal bone.
3. Length from occiput to anterior border.
4. Zygomatic width.
5. Distance between orbits.
6. Breadth of parietal.
7. Elevation of orbits above alveolus of M^3.
8. Elevation of orbits above frontal.
9. Elevation of frontal above palatine.
10. Height of occiput.
11. Width of occiput.
12. Width of condyles.
13. Distance of M^3 from posterior border of palate.

These measurment (Table No. 13) show much variation within the species. The differences within the *H. sivalensis* are of great order as compared to that of Narmada species.Therefore, the minior differences in skull measurements in *H. namadicus* and *H. palaeindicus* can not be taken as the specific characteristic features. The differences are very small and could be attributed

Table 5

Statistical values of molar measuraments of Hexaprotodon sivalensis.

	M^1			M^2			M^3		
	L	W	W/L	L	W	W/L	L	W	W/L
Ɛx	198	197	5.05	508	512	11.15	469	469	9.98
Ɛx^2	7990	7767	5.20	23690	23978	11.44	22105	22097	10.00
x^-	39.60	39.40	1.01	46.18	46.54	1.01	46.90	46.90	0.99
σn	5.46	1.01	0.14	0.56	3.65	0.11	3.30	3.17	0.06
σn-1	6.10	1.14	0.16	4.79	3.83	0.11	3.47	3.34	0.06
n	5	5	5	11	11	11	10	10	10

	M_1			M_2			M_3		
	L	W	W/L	L	W	W/L	L	W	W/L
Ɛx	281	239	6.80	652	477	10.25	749	444	7.12
Ɛx^2	9993	7261	5.87	30710	16437	7.60	47309	16510	4.30
x^-	35.10	29.87	0.85	46.57	34.07	0.73	62.4	37.00	0.59
σn	3.91	3.88	0.10	4.96	3.63	0.08	6.82	2.61	0.08
σn-1	4.18	4.15	0.11	5.15	3.77	0.08	7.12	2.73	0.08
n	8	8	8	14	14	14	12	12	12

Ɛx =Sum of all the variables

Ɛx^2 =Sum of squares of all the variables

x^- = Mean

σn = Standard deviation

σn-1 = Standard deviation with n-1 variables

n = Number of variables

Table 6
Statistical values of molar measurements of *Hexaprotodon namadicus*.

	M_2			M_3		
	L	W	W/L	L	W	W/L
Σx	186	125	2.69	82	61	1.49
Σx^2	8678	3983	1.86	3394	1861	1.11
$\bar{x}$	46.5	31.25	0.67	41.00	30.50	0.74
σ n	2.69	4.38	1.11	4.00	0.50	0.06
σ n-1	3.10	5.05	0.10	5.65	0.71	0.09
n	4	4	4	2	2	2

Table 7
Statistical values of molar measurements of Hexaprotodon Palaeindicus.

	M^1			M^2			M^3		
	L	W	W/L	L	W	W/L	L	W	W/L
Σx	81	75	1.84	158	124	2.34	126	81	1.28
Σx^2	3281	2871	1.69	2332	5234	1.84	7988	3293	0.81
$\bar{x}$	40.50	37.50	0.92	52.66	41.33	0.78	63.00	40.5	0.64
σn	0.50	1.50	0.05	1.88	6.01	0.08	5.00	2.5	0.01
σn-1	0.70	2.12	0.07	2.30	7.37	0.11	7.07	3.5	0.01
n	2	2	2	3	3	3	2	2	2

Table 8
Standard deviation comparision, between Hexaprotodon spp.

Group	M^1			M^2			M^3		
	L	W	W/L	L	W	W/L	L	W	W/L
H.svalensis	5.46	1.01	0.14	4.56	3.65	0.11	3.3	3.17	0.06
H.namadicus	-	-	-	-	-	-	-	-	-
H.palacindicus	0.5	1.5	0.05	1.88	6.01	0.08	-	-	-
Isolated molars	-	-	-	3.12	2.4	0.1	2.12	2.06	0.02

Group	M_1			M_2			M_3		
	L	W	W/L	L	W	W/L	L	W	W/L
H. Sivalensis	3.91	3.88	0.10	4.96	3.63	0.08	6.82	2.61	0.08
H.namadicus	-	-	-	2.69	4.38	1.11	4.00	0.50	0.06
H.palacindicus	-	-	-	-	-	-	5.00	2.50	0.01
Isolated molars	-	-	-	0.81	3.09	0.08	4.14	1.65	0.03

to the sex and age factors. It is very much common in *Hippopotamidae* family (Hooijer, 1950; Coryndon, 1970).

Non-Metrical Observations

Skull

In the Deccan College collection there is only one partial skull. Therefore, most of the observations have been made on the data published by Hooijer (1950), Deraniyagala, 1969, and Biswas and Dassarma (1984).

In both the species (*H. namadicus* and *H. palaeindicus*) there are altogether thirteen non-metrical differences, (observed by previous scholars) out of which nine differences like height

Table 9
Measurements (in mm) of isolated upper and lower teeth of *Hexaprotodon sp. from Narmada Valley.*

Sl. No.	Catalogue No.	M^1 Length	M^1 Width	M^2 Length	M^2 Width	M^3 Length	M^3 Width
1.	NMD/301/DC	--	--	38	41	50	43
2.	NMD/40/DC	--	--	46	41	50	39
3.	NMD/40/DC	30	30	43	41	45	38
4.	NMD/402/DC	--	--	46	41	47	38
5.	NMD/32/DC	--	--	46	35	--	--

Sl. No.	Catalogue No.	Length	Width	M_2 Length	M_2 Width	M_3 Length	M_3 Width
1.	NMD/27/DC	--	--	44	37	54	32
2.	NMD/38/DC	31	30	46	31	51	28
3.	NMD/36/DC	--	--	45	30	--	--
4.	NMD/33/DC	--	--	--	--	58	30

Table 10
Statistical values of isolated molar measurements of *Hexaprotodon* sp.'

	M^2 L	M^2 W	M^2 W/L	M^3 L	M^3 W	M^3 W/L
Σx	21[illegible]	199	4.56	192	158	3.27
Σx^2	9641	[illegible]349	4.2	9234	6258	2.67
$\bar{x}$	43.8	39.80	0.91	48.00	39.5	0.81
σn	3.12	2.40	0.10	2.12	2.06	0.02
$\sigma n\text{-}1$	3.49	2.68	0.11	2.44	2.38	0.03
n	5	5	5	4	4	4

	M_2 L	M_2 W	M_2 W/L	M_3 L	M_3 W	M_3 W/L
Σx	135	98	2.17	225	122	2.15
Σx^2	6077	3230	1.59	12725	3732	1.15
$\bar{x}$	45.0	32.66	0.72	56.25	30.5	0.53
σn	0.81	3.09	0.08	4.14	1.65	0.03
$\sigma n\text{-}1$	1.0	3.78	0.10	4.78	1.91	0.03
n	3	3	3	4	4	4

Table 11
Measurements (in mm) of mandibular symphysis of *Hexaprotodon* spp. and their indices.

Sl. No.	Species	Length of Symphysis	Width of symphysis	Index $\frac{Width}{Length} \times 100$
1.	*Hexa. sivalensis* S/136/DC	140	240	171.4
2.	*Hexa. namadicus* NMD/231 A&B/DC	133	295	221.8
3.	*Hexa. palaeindicus* NMD/28/DC	135	324	240.0
4.	*Hexa. palaeindicus* NMD/232/DC	142	333	234.5

Table 12
Variation in mandibular symphysis indices in *Hexaprotododn spp.*

Species	*Hexaprotododn sivalansis*			*Hexaprotodon namadicus*			*Hexaprotodon Palaeindiucus*		
	Derani-yagala, 1969	Biswas & Dassama 1984	Present	Derani-Yagala 1969	Biswas Dassarma 1984	Present	Derani-Yagala 1969	Biswas Dassarma 1984	Present
Indices	172.9 192.7	121.9 174.1 162.5	171.4	218.2	182.8 219.3 214.2 242.3	221.8	263.2	259.3 220.0 233.3 234.5	240.0
Range	192.7	to	121.4	242.3	to	182.8	263.2	to	220.0
Variation	71.3			59.5			43.2		

of orbits, space between orbits, frontal contact of nasal with Lacrimal and orbitis, shape of nasal bone, heavyness of zygomatic process, width and height of occiput, width of occipital condyles are relative terms and all the differences can be because the age, sex and health, and to some extent abnormalities. The sex, indeed plays a major role in osteolgical differences in animals (Coryndon, 1970; Grigson, 1982 a).

The remaining four differences the extension of maxilla bone above M^3, V shape of posterior nasal choanae length of palate beyond the M^3 and shortness of post-dental part of the Calvarium in *H. namadicus* which are not noticed in *H. palaeindicus* are of some morphological importance. But as we scan the literature on the *H. sivalensis* (Lyddeker, 1882; Mathew, 1929; and Colbert, 1935). We come across such variation in *H. sivalensis*, Colbert (1935: p. 280) has given the following description, "In view of the variation of the skull characters in *H. sivalensis* it seems quite likely that certain of these characers which both Falconer and Lydekker considered as of special rank, are of actualy of variational magnitude or even more like, are but individual variation. Naturally with only a limited series of fossil specimns to study, certain variations that were probably quite typical within the species would not appear. It is certain that the several skulls in the American Museum collection show some differences in the species described by Falconer and Lydekker. Therefore, it may be well to present a list of distinctive dental and cranial characters of *H. sivalensis* as shown by the specimens in the American Museum, not only to review and give additional informations about this species, but also to evaluate, if possible, what characters may be considered as of real work in the establishment of taxanomical distinctions". Similar opinion was also expressed by Mathew (1929).

Regarding the posterior nasal Choanae which Lydekker (1882) also thought as a specific characters, Colbert (1935: pp. 283-284) remarked as follows:

"There is a great deal of variation shown in the development of the posterior nasal choanae....... The examination of the several skulls in the American Museum collection shows that while for the most part of the choanae are situated at a considerable distance back of the 3rd molar (M^3), they do not at times (as in American Museum No. 19784) reach as far forwards as the last molar. Thus this character would seem to be of little specific value. On the whole the choánae are narrower and more V shaped in the fossil form than in the recent species".

A close examination of specimens and the various studies like that of Collert (1935) we can say with some degree of certainity that the minor variations between *H. namadicus* and *H. palaeindicus* are not of great value or significance. The scholars proposing these differences are, infact, overemphasizing the evidence to establish two species theory which could well be the variation within a single species.

Mandible

In both the species *H namadicus* and *H. palaeindicus* the mandibles do not show any marked differences in shape except the slight robosity in the case of *H. palaeindicus*. The anterior part of the symphysis in both the cases has vertical as well as slight depressed surface formed due to retraction and protraction of the border of the mandible. The divergence of the premolar series and straightness of molar series in both the cases are of same order. The ascending ramii in both the species are wide and low with blunt rounded angular part. As far as the incisor line is concerned it is considered that in *H. palaeindicus* the inner as well as outer border are uneven because of the elevation of the IInd pair of incisors (Deraniyagala, 1969). But similar situation has also been noticed in some specimens of *H. namadicus* (Lydekker, 1882; Biswas and Dassarma, 1984). According to Hooijer (1950) the two species can be distinguished on the basis of the depth of the mandible at M_2. But this may not be true for the specific variation as it may depend on the age and sex of the animal. The observations made on three mandibles in present collection (housed in Deccan College) classified as *H. namadicus* (one specimen) and *H. palaeindicus* (Two specimen) can be summarized as below:

H. namadicus	*H. palaeindicus*
1. Length of the symphysis is less than its width.	1. Length of the symphysis is less than its width.
2. Shallow depression present on the anterior side of the symphysis	2. Depression on the anterior side of the symphysis is less prominent
3. Canines elliptical in cross-section with depression on the postero-lateral side.	3. Canines more or less oval with depressionon the postero- lateral side.
4. Dimension of canine is less than in the *H. palaeindicus.*	4. Slightly larger thanthe *H. namadicus.*
5. The inner border of the incisor teeth are even, but the outer border are uneven.	5. The incisor teeth line is uneven on both the borders because of the evlevationof IInd pair of incisor.
6. Dimensions of I_1 are more than I_3.	6. Dimensions of I_1 are more than I_3.
7. Jaw elongated.	7. Jaw elongated.
8. Ascending ramus low with blunt angular part.	8. Ascending ramus low with blunt angular part.

Cheek Teeth

Some differences in upper molars with outwardly directed posterior lobe of paracone, which extends beyond the anterior lobe of the metacone; thick enamel and large cingulum in upper molars of *H. namadicus* and thin enamel layer in lower molars of *H. palaeindicus* are taken as the criteria for distinguishing *H. namadicus* and *H. palaeindicus* (Biswas & Dassarma, 1984). But in the present study this criteria has not been found useful, as in the single specimen with two molars, the cingulum and enamel layer are found variable. Further it is not safe enough to rely on the isolated dental remains for identification of the species (Hooijer, 1963; Nanda, 1978). The slight variation in enamel pattern is an effect of feeding habitat rather than the morphological

Table 13
Variation in skull measurements in Hexaprotodon spp. data taken from Hooijer, 1950 and Biswas and Dassarma, 1984.

Parts	*H. sivalensis* Range	Variation	*H.Namadicus* Range	Variation	*H.Palaeindicus* Range	Variation	Range variation between *H.palaeindicus & H. namadicus*
Length from the condyle to posterior border	185-219	34	185	–	195-197	2	Between *H. palaeindicus*
Length from sagittal crest to posterior tip of nasal.	220	–	160	–	165	–	5
Length from occiput to anterior border	222-245	23	190	–	190	–	0
Zygomatic width	325-390	65	365	–	345-400	55	Between *H. palaeindicus*
Distance between orbit	176-200	24	285	–	250	–	35
Breadth of parietal	90-177	87	140	–	115-130	15	25
Elevation of orbits above alveolus of M^3	131-186	55	175	–	165-205	40	Between *H. palaeindicus*
Elevation of orbits above frontal	12-14	2	50	–	28-42	14	22
Elevation of frontal above palatine	126-151	25	120	–	158-160	2	Between *H. palaeindicus*
Height of occiput	164-186	22	190	–	176-195	19	Between *H. palaeindicus*
Width of occiput	205-263	58	280	–	255-290	35	Between *H. palaeindicus*
Width of condyles	112-147	35	145	–	142-144	2	3
Distance of M^3 from posterior border of palate	10-18	8	16	–	13	–	3

characters (Corydon, 1966; Geist, 1981) and variation within a species is considered perfectly normal, (Coryndon, 1970). Further more, the *Hippopotamidae* teeth are conservative in development and are positively the least useful element for diagnosis (Coryndon, 1977).

The morphological and metrical observations with indices of different parts of the cranium and mandible show some ambiguous results as they overlap with each other. All the specimens of so called species of *Hexaprotodon* except in a few cases of *H. sivalensis*, exhibit a similar range of measurements of various indices. The variations in the measurements are never so great that we could group the specimens in different categories and give different names.

It shows that the metrical and non-metrical observations are of very insignificant value in separating the *H. namadicus* and *H. palaeindicus*. However, the metrical and non-metrical observation show some difference in craniums, mandibles, canines and incisor. But in the absence of any standardisation the variation could be individualistic, (Colbert, 1935).

The variations are of relative type and may be due to the sexual dimorphism and age. Such variations are very much evident even in the present *Hippopotamus* (Hooijer, 1950; Corydon, 1970). The fossil *H. karumensis* shows very clear sexual dimorphism in the cranium and mandible, (Coryndon, 1977). The male has heavy and robust parts as compared to the female. This type of dimorphism is common in other animals like Cattle, Elephant, Deer, Pig, Horses also (Leithener, 1927; Hooijer, 1950; Geist, 1981; Grigson, 1982a and 1982b) .

In the case of *H. namadicus* and *H. palaeindicus* the minor differences in the skulls, mandibles, incisors, canines and molars can not be taken as representing various species and their evolutionary trend. In Africa the evolutionary process took about 12 m. years and three stages have been demarcated, (Coryndon, 1978). In India if it is to be accepted that *H. palaeinicus* has evolved from the *H. namadicus* then the billion dollar question that has to be answered is : whether it is possible that a new species can evolve within a span of just a few thousand years?

Secondly, the fossils of *H. namadicus* and *H. palaeindicus* are found in the same strata of the Narmada deposits. Thus, it is not possible to put the line of demarcation for biozonation of the deposits and also of the course of evolution.

Thirdly, if elimination of the second pair of incisor is the critria for the evolution then the *choeropsis liberiensis* must be the most advanced form as compared to the *Hippopotamus amphibius*. But this is not the case. *Choeropsis liberiensis* is more primitive than the *H. amphibius*, (Coryndon, 1977).

Conclusions

Metrical and non-metrical observations made on the skulls mandibles and dentition can be summarized as below:

1. Metrically the skulls of *H. palaeindicus* and *H. namadicus* show less variation as compared to the *H. sivalensis*.
2. Non-metrical observations height of orbits, space between the orbits, frontal contact of nasal bone with lacrimal and orbits, heavyness of zygomatic process, width of occipital condyle etc. reveal that the differences in both are relative.
3. Indices of mandibular symphysis in both *H. palaeindicus* and *H. namadicus* show less degree of variation than that of *H. sivalensis*.
4. The canines in the *H. namadicus* are slightly smaller than those of *H. palaeindicus*.
5. The cheek teeth measurements (length, width and width/length show no dfference.
6. Based on the metrical study the 2nd pair of incisor in both the species do not show any marked difference as opined by earlier scholars.
7. *H. namadicus* and *H. palaeindicus* do not possess any significant morphological characters to ascertain the evolution of the *H. palaeindicus* from *H. namadicus*.

On the basis of our observations it is opined that both the species do not show any marked differences. The minor differences are because of individual variation.

It seems that both *H. palaeindicus* and *H. namadicus* are synonym of each other. The robust form *H. palaeindicus* could be the male while the gracile one so called *H. namadicus* could be the female of the same species. Therefore, it is suggested that both the species may be considered one and be known as *H. palaeindicus namadicus* same as in the case of *stegodon* where earlier known species *Stegodon insignis* and *Stegodon ganesa* are now known as *tegodon insignis ganesa.*

Acknowledgement

I am grateful to Prof. M.K. Dhavalikar, Director, Deccan College and Dr. G.L. Badam for permitting me to study the material housed in Deccan College. Thanks are also due to Prof. V.N. Misra, Prof. S.N. Rajaguru and Mr. R.K. Ganjoo for their help in various ways.

References

Alur, K.R. 1980

Faunal remains from the Vindhyas and the Ganga Valley. Appendix, in: G.R. Sharma, V.D. Misra, D. Mandal, B.B.Misra and J.N. Pal : *Beginning of Agriculture*, Allahabad : Abinash Parakashan, pp. 201-227.

Andrew, C.W. 1896

A descriptive catalouge of the Tertiary Vertebrata of the Fayum, Egypt, London.

Badam, G.L. 1979

Pleistocene Fauna of India, Pune: Deccan College.

Badam, G.L. and M.D. Kajale 1977

On the occurence of *Hexaprotodon palaeindicus* from the Ghod Valley, Western India. *Journal of University of Poona (Science & Technology)*, 50: 209-219.

Badam, G.L., V.G. Sathe and R.K. Ganjoo 1984

New fossil finds from the Manjra Valley, Central Godavari Basin, India. *Journal of the Geological society of India*, *25* (4) : 245-251.

Biswas, S, and D.C. Dassarma 1981

a new species of *Stegodon* from the alluvial deposits of the Narmada Valley in Peninsular India, *Proceedings of Neogene/Quaternary Boundary Field Conference, India*, 1979, pp. 15-20.

1984 Fossil *Hippopotamus* from Quaternary deposits of Narmada Valley in Madhya Pradesh. *Record of Gological Survery of India*, 114, pt. 2: 19-24.

Blumenschine, R.J. and U.C. Chatopadhyay 1983

A Preliminary Report on the Terminal Pleistocene Fauna of the Middle Son Valley. In: G.R. Sharma and J.D. Clark (eds): *palaeoenvironments and Pre-history in the Middle son Valley*, Allahabad: Abinash Prakashan, pp. 281-84.

Colbert, E.H. 1935

Siwalik Mammals in the American Museum of Natural History. *Transactions of American Philosophical society*, (N.S.), 26: 1-401.

1942 The Geological Succession of the Proboscidea in India, In: H.F. Osborn: *Proboscidea, American Museum Natural History*, 2: 1421-1521.

Coryndon, S.C. 1966

Preliminary Report on some Fossils from the Chiwondo Beds of the Karonga, Malawi. American Anthropologist, 68(2), Pt. 2:59-66.

1967 *Hexaprotodon* Hippopotamidae of East Africa and the Phylogeny of the Family. *Congress Pan-African De-Prehistore*, Dakar, pp. 350-352.

1970 The extent of variation in fossil *Hippopotamus* from Africa. *Symposium Zoological Society, London.* 26: 135-147.

1976 Fossil Hippopotamidae from Plio-pleistocene succession of the Rudolf Basin. In Y. Coppens, F. C. Howell, G.L. Isaac & R.E.P. Leakey: *Earliest Man and Enviroments in the Lake rudolf Basin.* chicago: University of Chicago Press, pp. 238-250.

1977 The Taxanomy and Nomenclature of the Hippopotamidae (Mammalia, Artiodactyla) and a description of two fossil species. *Proceedings of the Koninklijke Nederlandse akademie Van wetens Chappen*, Amsterdom, Series B, 80 (2) : 61-88

1978 Hippopotamidae In V.J, Maglio and H.B.S. Cooke(eds.): *Evolution of African Mammals*. Cambridge: Harvard University Press, pp. 483-95.

Dassarma, D.C. and S. Biswas 1978

fossil *Hippopotamus* from Madhya Pradesh. *Geological Survey of India, News*, 9(6) : 7.

Deraniyagala, P.E.P. 1969

Relationships of the Fossil Hippoptamus, *Hexaprotodon sinhaleyus, Spolia Zeylanica, 31*, Pt. II; 1-5.

Terra, De H. and .T. Paterson 1939

Studies on the Ice Age in India and Associated Human Cultures. Washington: Carnegie Institution Publication No. 499.

Falconer, H. 1859

Descriptive catalouge of the fossil Remains of Veretbrate from the Siwalik hills, the Nerbudda, Perim Island, etc. in the Museum of Asiatic Society of Bengal, Calcutta.

1868 *Palaeontological Memoirs*, Edited by Murchison, I:1-556.

Falconer, H. and P.T. Cautley 1836

Notes on the Fossil *Hippoptamus* of the Siwalik Hills. *Asiatic Research, 19:* 39-53.

1847 Fauna *Antiqua Sivalensis Pt. 7, Hippopotamus*, London: Smith Elder & Co.

Geist, Valerius 1983

On the Evolution of Ice Age Mammals and its signficance to an understanding of speciations. *ASB Bulletin, 30* (3): 109-33.

Grigson, C. 1982a

Sex and Age determination of some bones and teeth of domestic cattle: a review of the literature. In: B. Wilson, C. Grigson & S. Payne (eds.): *Ageing and Sexing Animal Bones from the Archaeological Sites.* BAR British Series 109, pp. 7-23.

1982b Sexing Neolithic domestic skulls and horn cores. In: B. Wilson, C. Crigson & S. Payne (eds.) : *Ageing and*

Sexing animal Bones from Archaeological Sites. BAR British Series, 109, pp. 25-35.

Hooijer, D.A. 1950

The Fossil Hippopotamidae of Asia with notes on the recent species. *Zool. Verht. Leiden, 8*: 124

1963 Preliminary identification of some fossil mammals from Narmada Valley, India. *Rivista Di Scienze Preistoriche, 18* (1-4): 20.

Joshi, R.V, S.V. Chitale, S.N. Rajaguru, R.S. Pappu & G.L. Badam 1981

Archaeological Studies in the Manjra Valley, Central Godavari Basin. *Bulletin Deccan College Research Institute, 40*: 67-94.

Khan, E. 1968

Narmada Alluvium and its equivalent. *Proceedings of the Indian National Science Academy 38* (3-4), Pt. A: 89-96.

Khatri, A.P. 1966

The Pleistocene mammalion fossils of the Narmada river valley and their horizons. *Asian Perspectives*, 9: 113-133.

Lydekker, R. 1876

Notes on the osteology of *Merycopotamus dissimilis. Record Gelogical Survey of India, 9*: 144-154.

1882 Siwalik and Narbada Equidae, *Palaeontologica Indica*, Series 10, 3 (2): 35-104.

1884 Siwalik and Nàrmada bunodont Suina. *Palaeontologica Indica Series 10, 3* (2): 35-104.

Mathew, W.D. 1929

Critical observations upon Siwalik Mammals. *Bulletin American Museum Natural History, 56*: 437-560.

Nanda, A.C. 1978

Hexaprotodon sivalensis, Falconner and Cautley from the upper Siwalik sub-group, Ambala, Haryana. *Recent Researches in Geology, 5:161-174.*

Owen, R. 1845

Odontography, London, pp. 543-72.

Pearson, H.S. 1923

The hinder end of the skull in *merycopotamus* and in *Hippopotamus minutus . Journal of Anatomy*, 63 : 237 - 41.

Pilgrim, G.E. 1904

Pleistocene Fossils from the Ganges Alluvium. *Record Geological Survey of India*, 31, Pt. 5: 176-77.

1905 On the occurence of *Elephas antiquus (namadicus)* in the Godavari Alluvium with remarks on the species, its distribution and the age of the associated Indian deposits. *Record Geoloical Survey of India, 32* (3) : 199-218.

1913 The correlation of the Siwaliks with mammal horizons of Europe. *Record Geological Survey of India, 43*(4): 264-326.

1941 The dispersal of the Artiodactyla. *Biological Reviews, 16*: 150.

Prasad, K.N. and P.P. Satsangi 1964

A note on the mandible of *Hexaprotodon sivalensis* from Siwaliks of Punjab. *Bull. tin Geological Mineral and Metalurgical Society of India, 31*: 1-6.

Princep, J. 1832

Note on the Jabalpur fossil bones. *Journal Asiatic Society of Bengal*, I: 456-58.

Sahni, M.R. and E. Khan 1961

On the abnormal dentition of *Hexaprotodon sivalensis* Falc. & Cautley. *Research Bulletin Punjab University (N. S.), 12* (3-4): 257-258.

Sen, D. and A.K. Ghosh 1963

Lithic Culture-complex in the Pleistocene sequence of the Narmada Valley, Central India. *Rivista Di Scienze Preistoriche, 18* (1-4): 3-23.

Spilsbury, G. G. 1837

Notice of new sites of fossil deposits in the Narbuda Valley. *Journal Asiatic Society of Bengal, 6*: 487-489.

1840 Notes on various fossil site on the Narbuda illustrated by specimens and drawings. *Journal of the Asiatic Society of Bengals, 8*: 950-52.

Supekar, S.G. 1968

Pleistocene stratigraphy and Pre-historic Archaeology of the Central Narmada Basin. Ph. D. Thesis. Poona University, Poona.

Theobald, W. 1860

On the Tertiary and alluvial deposits of the Central portion of the Narbuda Valley. *Memoirs Geological Survey of India, 2*: 279-298.

Tripathy, C. 1967

The Pleistocene alluvial deposits around Nevasa, Ahmad Nagar district Maharashtra. *Record Geological Survey of India, 95* (2) : 355-366.

Leithner Von, O.F. 1927

Der Ur. Ber. int. Ges. Erhaltung Wisents, 2 :1-140.

Puratattva No. 18; 1987-88

THE ARCHAEOLOGICAL BACKGROUND AND IRON SAMPLE FROM HATIGRA

N.C. Ghosh and Arun K. Nag*
Pranab K Chattopadhyay+

The ancient site at Hatigra (Lat. 22.49;)Long 87.35) District Birbhum, West Bengal on the right bank of the river Bakreswar is nearly 24 km. north-west of Bolpur (Santiniketan), Railway Station. Roughly over an area of four acre (21.00 sq. m.), black and red ware, red ware, buff ware analogous to West Bengal Chalcolithic and early Iron age type were found strewn over the surface. It is a low imperceptible mound which rises upto 2 m. above the general level of the surrounding area. The abondoned settlement is distinctly marked by dark ashy colour of the soil in the midst of redish brown alluvial land-scape. The mound is bad, distrubed by the local inhabitants and its northern side is being eroded by the river. As many as four ponds of varying sizes dot the surrounding area. The river, except in its turbulent spurt during monsoon, just meanders with low discharge. The antiquity of the ponds at Hatigra is doubtful. Nevertheless, the significance of the ponds in the pattern of the settlement of Indian villages or towns may not lost sight off.

Reverting back to the theme - the archaeological background' which has emerged from the excavation at Hatigra[1] and the archaeomatullurgical studies' which has been carried out on an iron sample from the same excavation are presented here. In the field operation only four trenches were laid at potential spots of the site but the actual digging was restricted in one or two quadrants of each trench measuring 5 x 5 m. It was mainly directed to collect well-documented samples for analysis, comparative study and to enlist technical reports on the samples from excavation viz., flora, fauna, soil, metal and material for c-14 dating, which have been amply rewarded. We have planned to undertake such small-scale excavation at different sites of comparable chrono-cultural horizon to collect such data to unravel the past.

The excavation unearthed the Black and Red ware at the earliest level. The cultural remains have been encountered in all the quadrants except HTR-2 located almost in the middle of the site (fig. 1). Apart from two successive floor-levels and nearly 0.65m., thick habitational deposit (figs 2 & 3), there is no other evidence of their permanent dwelling at this place. the bulk of the pottery is black and red bowls. The paintings are in white pigment and are confined to dots and dashes. The number of painted sherds are small . Besides, the red ware and black-slipped ware are represented in lesser number. Non-occurrance of copper from the limited area of the dig may be an obvious reason. Though stone blade is not recorded from the dig but several waste flakes have been found from the surface.

The rest of the cultural reportoire recovered from the period, though a few in number, furnish an insight into various facets of their life. Among them mention may be made of large terracotta convex disc decorated with notched design, terracotta beads, hopscotch (?) of potsherds, spindle whorl, stone saddle quern (?), and pestle. From the collection of faunal remains at hatigra only twenty-six bones could be identified[2] and eight of them belong to the period I. The majority of the bones recognised from the period belonged to *Bos Indicus* (Linn), *Bubalus bubalis* (Linn) and *Sus acrofa cristatus* wagner of the suidae family. Only one fragment of rib of a humped cattle show chopping mark and a few of them including the unidentified one show marks of roasting in fire. The higher percentage of *Bos Indicus* even in the then limited collection demonstrates that rearing of the cattle was widely practised. The evidence is not at variance with the known archaezological evidence recovered so far from nearly half a dozen excavated sites from this region[2A].

Six dates[3] are available from Hatigra of which only one pertains to the period I. The sample no. (H/C 6) PRL 1191 which provides 2950 + 120 B.P. (1000 B.C.) was recovered from the Tr. HTR-4AL, Qd1, layer 7, depth 1.92 from the surface. It marks the top-most level of the period I and below there is a habitational deposit of 0.63 m, devoid of any

* Visva-Bharati, Santiniketan
+ Alloy Steels Plant, Durgapur.

structure. The early dates of the Chalcolithic levels from Bharatpur (PRL-15, 1435±140 B.C.), and Mahisdal (PRL-391, 1380 ± 105)[4] may indicate the initial phase of this culture in south-west Bengal. In this time-bracket the C-14 date (PRL-886, 2850 +150 (900 B.C) from Bahiri[5] relating to the early level of the period I (Chalcolithic) appears to be erratic and the published depth in the locus of the sample appears to be out-side of the archaeological context.

The cultural change from the period I to II at Hatigra was not very distinct. One of the variations is noticed in the relative frequency of the pottery types. The dominant five basic types of the earlier period viz. convex sided bowls in black and red ware and vessels with out-turned rim in red ware etc., were proliferated by variety of shapes in different ware in Pd. II (fig. 4). there was minimal increase in the frequency of the black-slipped ware which was a scarce commodity in the preceeding

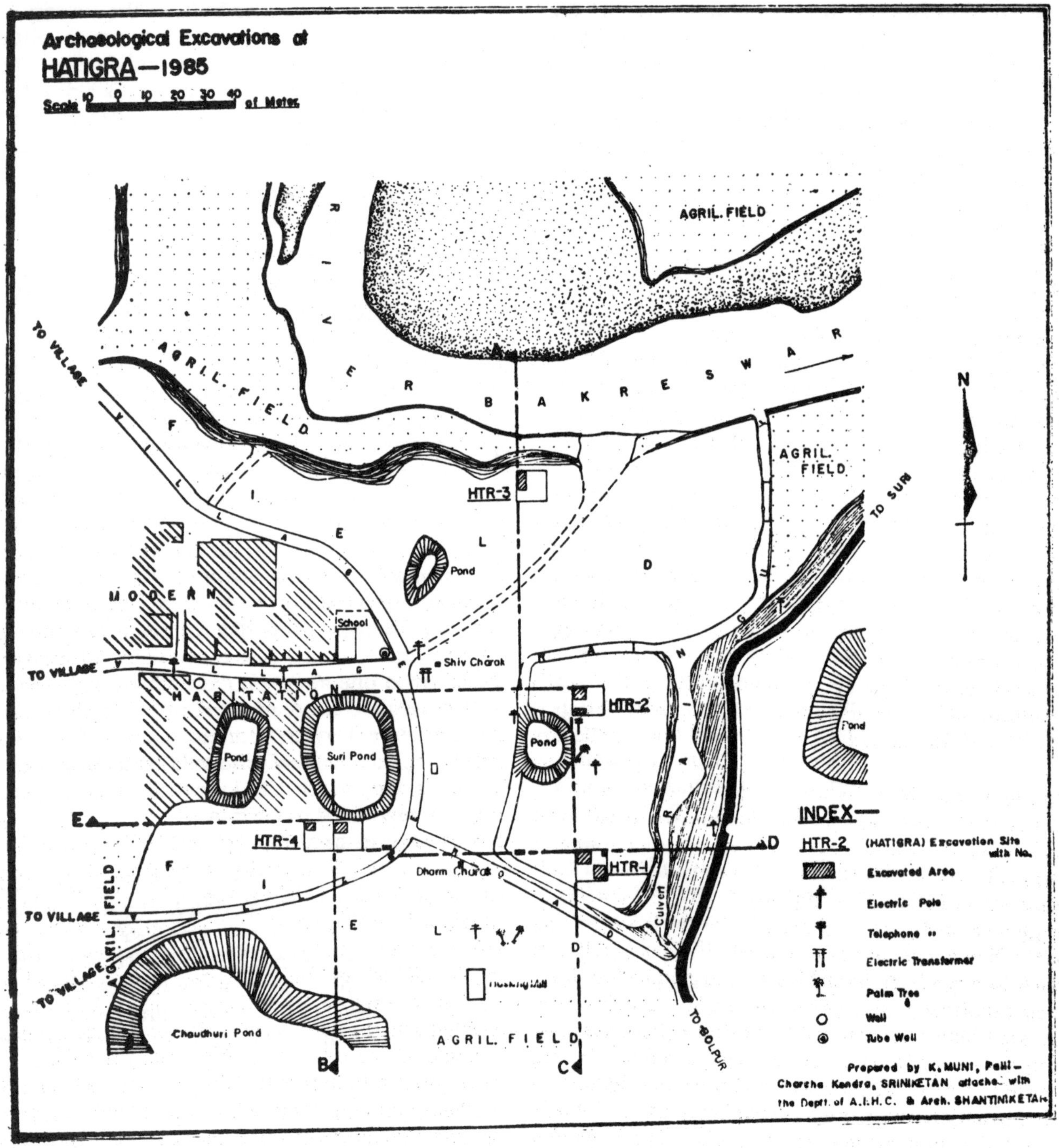

Table - 1
Analytical data of the Soil Sample from site Hatigra Dist Birbhum

Sample No.	Depth in m	PH.	T.S.S. (m mhos/ cm)	$CaCo_3$(%)	Org. carbon (%)	Total N_2 (%)	Total P (% ppm)	Remarks
1.	0.20	7.2	0.14	0.50	0.47	0.056	996	
2.	0.40	7.4	0.14	1.00	0.39	0.042	1245	
3.	0.60	7.6	0.16	2.00	0.42	0.049	1494	
4.	0.80	7.7	0.15	1.50	0.40	0.042	1992	
5.	1.00	7.6	0.18	2.00	0.41	0.045	2490	
6	1.20	7.8	0.10	2.00	0.30	0.035	2490	Iron
7.	1.40	7.7	0.11	2.50	0.38	0.039	2988	HTR XA1 QD I
8.	1.47	7.6	0.13	2.00	0.31	0.032	2490	Period II
9.	1.60	7.8	0.11	2.00	0.16	0.017	2490	Period II
10.	1.80	7.7	0.10	2.00	0.11	0.014	1992	
11.	2.00	7.7	0.09	2.00	0.11	0.012	1494	C14-(1000BC) HTR-4, A1QdI
12.	2.20	7.6	0.09	2.00	0.10	0.011	1992	Period I
13.	2.40	7.5	0.10	1.75	0.09	0.010	1494	Period I

level. It has smooth texture, thin section, grey core and unlike other ware its slip does not peel-off easily. The dominant type is bowl. The fabric, texture and finish of the pots are better in comparison to other ware. Its better finish and scarcity not only at Hatigra but also in several sites from the area may signify its 'de-luxe' nature. Black slipped ware in comparable shapes are recovered from the Chalcolithic level and the early Iron age sites from south-west Uttar Pradesh[6] and the date neolithic level at Chirand[7]. The channel-spout-bowl in black and grey ware is recorded from the mid-level. The type in different ware is found in similar circumstance at Pandu Rajar Dhibi, Mahishdal, Nannur[8] and Bahiri[9]. It is noteworthy that the iron at the site is available from the top of the lower level of the period II onwards.

Only eight fragments of iron ware recovered. Two of them, a dagger (?) from the mid level and a rod from the top level of the period II can be recognised, the rest were reduced to shapeless lumps. Its unimpressive record is in general consonance with the known evidence from the excavated sites from the region. Iron slage from the layer 2 of the TR HTR - 4, depth 28 cm. below surface suggest black-smith's fire place in the vicinity.

Remains of modest dwelling is represented by mud-rammed floors with thrash-hold facing east in one of them, post-holes and burnt and half-burnt clay-chunks with reed impressions. It is also significant that the settlement, judged by the occurrence of the remains of this period from all the excavated trenches including HTR-21, (which did not yield any sign of occupation in the earlier period), was enlarged. this observation also supported by the analytical data of thirteen soil-samples [9] tabulated (Table - 1).

The phosphrous value at Hatigra varies from 996 ppm to 2988 ppm in a vertical (0.20 to 2.40 m), profile. The behaviour is plotted in a graph, the peak (2988 ppm), and flanking plateaus (2490 ppm) are formed between 1.60 and 1.m of the profile. The higher values are indications of intensive human activity during this phase of occupation at the site, implying also increase in population at that time. it corresponds to the mid-level of the period II of the site.

The animal bones[9a] from the period II include *Bos Indicus* (Linn), *Bubalus Bubalis* (Linn), *Capra hircus aegagrus* Erxl, *Bos* sp, *Bovid* and *Chitara Indica* Gray of Reptila class. The bones of *Bos Indicus* (Linn) are comparatively less in quantity than the *Bubalus Bubalis (Linn)*. *Bos* sp. *Bovid* and *Capra hircus aegagrus* Erxl are not reported from the earlier deposit. At the same time *SusS crofa Cristatus* wagner is not available in the later accumulation. A distal end of metatarsal of *Bos* sp. and two shafts of limb bones of two different *Bovids* and a humerus of a third one bear cut mark. Mud-chunks with impressions of rice-husk is a noreworthy evidence of grain from the

HATIGRA—1985
HTR—4, TR—XA1, QD-1
SECTION LOOKING WEST

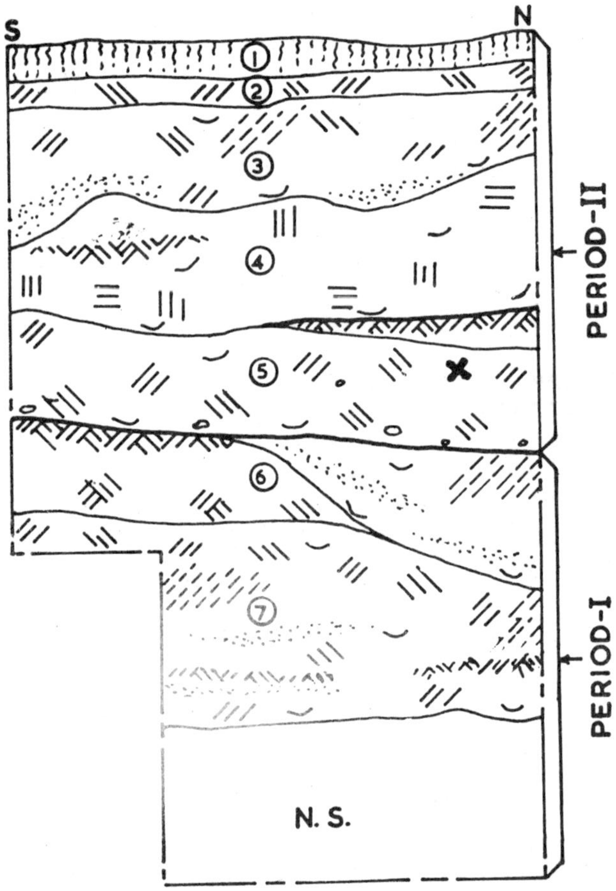

C-14 ——
IRON OBJECT—✕
SCALE 1:20 MTS.

period II. the imprints of rice husk is being studied to identify it, wild or cultivated.

Thanks to the multidisciplinary approach the faint contours of the cultural profile of the village community in West Bengal is coming out in bolder form. The outline glides over the time without any discordent note. it may not be late now to ask! Is it necessary to differentiate the proto-historic culture of West Bengal including Hatigra in period I (chalcolithic), and period II (Iron Age) merely on the presence or absence of the 'black-metal' or on the evidence of ill-sorted pot-sherds. We may review and divide the period in early (copper-stone) and late (copper-stone Iron), phases. In that period they carried out cultivation, practised animal husbandry, engaged in mass production of wheel-turned earthen pots and made use of semi-precious stones and other luxury items. Neverhteless, one should not run-away with the idea about them other than of an improvised community whose life remained stagnent in all respect over the centuries inspite of the introduction of Iron. It is also significant that most of the protohistoric villages in this part including Hatigra were abondoned soon after the advent of iron in those settlements. it was a paradoxical situation. Against this economic and cultural situation. Against this economic and cultural back-drop we may now view the iron technology mastered by them.

Morphology of the Object

The present iron implement (HTR 4, XA1, Qd. I - 1.12, 5 Acc No H. 54) under the investigvation is dagger (?) of about 165.1 mm length, 26.4 mm breadth and 16.5 mm in thickness. One end of the implement is rectangular in cross section and the other edge is a pointed one, and almost at the middle of the tool there is a small projection (pl. 1) . The implement was found covered with thick corrosion layer and we are fortunate enough to find a metallic core which could be chemically and metallographically analysed.

Chemical Analysis

We tried to analyse the iron core by the ARL Quantovac - a sophisticated computerised equipment at the Research and Control laboratory of the Alloy Steels Plant at Durgapur. We have taken a small slice of the metal from the flat end of the impement and half of it was used for chemical analysis and the rest for metallographic investigation.

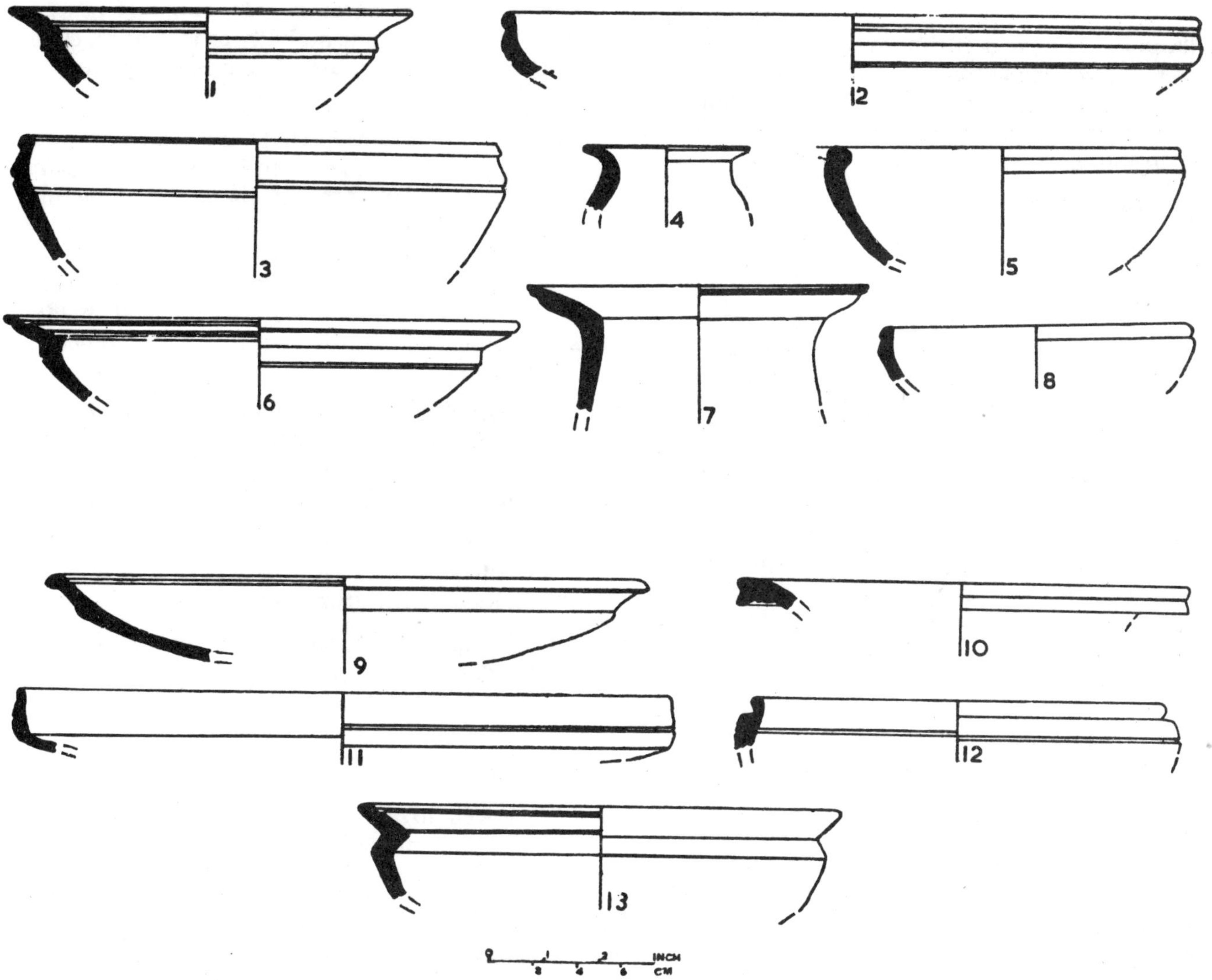

Fig.4. Assorted pottery from different layers at Hatigra

The slice was forged to a thin section. The fire of the forge was attempted from a neutral flame, so that it might not pick up carbon from the flame (i.e. carburisation). We have taken three sparks reclaibration and the results are listed below :

C	Mn	P	S	Si	Ni	Cu	Al	Co	Pb	Sn	Sb	Ti
0.35	-	0.51	.015	.102	.036	.108	.027	.037	-	.001	.016	.008

The Carbon (C) percentage shown in the table above is not from the instrumental value. This is correlated from our experience in metallographic observations. The ARL Quantovac had printed a value of 0.955 which greatly differs with the carbon content normally found in the micrograph for the range of 0.35% to 0.40% of C. The instrumental value as printed is definitely an increased one due to the unavoidable pick up of carbon from the fire during forging into a thinner section. One particular observation that must be commented upon is that the value of carbon in the outer surface of the implement was much higher and that it had been lost in thikly corroded Zone. We cannot determine this amount but guess that it was nearer to the printed value.

The other peculairity of the composition is that the metal was found to be free from mangnese. Nickel, silicon etc. are of 'trace' amount which directly came from the iron ore.

Krishnan (1955 : 75)[10] has mentioned that the limonitic iron ore of Birbhum contains 1.5 percent of P_2O_5. We know that phosphorus (P) of ore are picked up to the metal itself while smelting. Our analysis of .051% P here indicate the possibility of using similar type of iron ore.

Metallographic Studies

As mentioned earlier one portion of the implement was considered for metallographic observations.

The specimen was found to contain a trace amount of silica inclusion - as slag, and no presence of sulphur could be detected in polished condition.

For revealing the metallic matrix of the metal a 3% Nital etchant was used. Microstructure revealed was quite non uniform a very common feature to all bloomery iron. The crystallised grain size in the ASTM standard was found from fine - 7 to 8 external surface to coarse - 2 to 3 at the central region (Figure 3). So far as carburisation is concerned a concentration of carbon was noticed more at the edges. The structure found was a normalised equixed one consisting of mostly ferrite and pearlite. (Ferrite is the structure of an almost pure iron and the pearlite is the aggregate of ferrite and cementite - a chemical compound of iron carbide).

Near the edges a typical structure called Widmanstatten was found to be present along with pearlite. a photomicrograph was taken at a magnification of 100 later optically magnified to 1.5 times (Plate 2). the pearlites appeared to be 'broken lamellar' at higher magnification of 500. The photomicrograph in this region was later magnified to 1.5 times (Plate 3).

Here we must mention that when hypoeutectoid steels are heated to temperatures considerably exceeding the Ac_3 point in the iron - carbon diagram austenitic grain growth is quite common. here on subsequent cooling in addition to austentic grain growth excess ferrite precipitates as long plates or needles cutting across the pearlitic grains. This unusual feature is probably owing to the stability or formation of co-occurrence of nitride needles in ferrite plates.

From the metallographic observation it is conclusively inferred that the metal under investigation is a *low carbon hypoeutectoid steel.* The manufacturing process indicates a long time exposure in either the smelting furnance or at the smithy forge at a temperature around 1200°C. This peculiar superheated normalised steel indicates that the metal was cooled in still air after final forging. The microstructure further indicates the following :

1. The implement was first shaped into a 'bloom' (the porus iron which is formed after the melting of the ore, is preimarily forged to form a bloom).
2. Next, the implement was manufactured from that bloom in its own shape, again by another charcoal hearth furnance.
3. Subsequently, carburisation of the surface was done causing prolonged heating at around 1200°C - as evidence by an Widmanstatten structure.

Observations

The well advanced manufacturing skill of the analysed implement makes us confronted with a few obvious questions (i) Is it possible to assign such a highly developed iron technology in the material milieu of the period ? (ii) has it got any parallel in eastern Indian early iron age ? (iii) Is there any evidence of different "stages" of this achievement? (iv) Is it the object, an import ?

The first question deserve serious consideration from the archaeologists as well as Sociologists (ii) and (III) : Most of the early iron implements discovered from eastern India were not subjected to metellurgical analysis and from the known specimens, we could not find any parallel. Regarding the last question of the series, it is difficult to give a definite yes or no. antiquity of iron, however in this part of our country is linked with these issues.

Acknowledgement

The authors acknowledge the help received from the Physical Research Laboratory, Ahmedabad, Zoological Survey of India, Calcutta, Indo-British Fertilizer Education Project, Durgapur. We are obliged to Dr. Anil Dey, Professor of Chemistry, Visva-Bharati, for going through the manuscript, and for his suggestions. Shri Kapil Muni, has drawn the line drawings incorporated in the paper. We are thankful to him. Lastly, we thank our colleagues in the Department for their suggestions and help.

References

1. *Indian Archaeology A Review* 1985-86
2. S. Banerjee, Paleozoology Division, Zoological Survey of India, Calcutta. His study (1985-86), on the animal bones from the excavation will be included in the report under preparation.

2A. S. Banajerjee, Animal Remains from Bharatpur District Burdwan, West Bengal Rec. Zool, Surv. India 79 : 193-201 1981, p. 193-201.

3. Dr. D.P. Agrawal, Physical Research Laboratory, Ahmedabad.

4. D.P. Agarwal Radiocarbon and Indian Archaeology' *Physics News*, vol. 6, No. 4 Dec. 1975 p.9

5. Dr. D.K. Chakrabarti and S. Jamal Hasan, 'The Sequence at Bahiri (Chandra Hazar Danga), District Birbhum, West Bengal, *Man and Environment, IV, 1982, p. 111-149; Indian Archaeology* A Review, *1982-83, p. 145.*

6. *Jagannath Pal, Archaeology of Southern Uttar Pradesh* (Allahabad 1986) p. 139-140, fig 19-20; G.R. Sharma et. el., *Beginnings of Agriculture*, p. 140, fig. MGR-7

7. N.C,. Ghosh, *Purattava,* No. 5, 1971-72, p. 33-34; VibhaTripati, *The painted Grey* Ware - *An Iron Age Culture of Northern India* (Delhi, 1976). H.P. Sinha, 'Black Slipped ware - A study', *History and Culture,* (Delhi 1987) p. 55-578.

8. The pottery form Pandu Rajar Dhibi, Bharatpur and Nannur personally studied and also see D.K. Chakrabarti, op. cit. 91982).

9. Soil analysis carried out by the Indo-British Fertilizer Education Project, Durgapur.

9A. S. Banerjee, Op. Cit. (1985-86)

10. M.S. Krishnan, *Iron Ores of India* (Calcutta, 1955)

11. Two iron samples from the recent excavation at Pandu-Rajar Dhibi (1987-88) *are subjected to* archaeometallurgical investigations. The sample no. 1 is from the period I (C. 1000 B.C.), while, the present studies revealed that iron objects introduced in Period II and maturity reached in period III at Pandu-rajar Dhibi.

Puratattva No.18; 1987-88

KHAIRADIH - A CHALCOLITHIC SETTLEMENT

Birendra Pratap Singh*

About twenty five years back, Chirand in northern Bihar presented hitherto unknown horizon - the Neolithic - chalcolithic complex taking back the history of this region by about one thousand years beyond NBP period. In our bid to find the northern extention of the Chirand complex, we concentrated on exploring the banks of Ghaghra - it may be recalled that Chirand is situated near the confluence of Ghaghra and Ganga. Our explorations lead us to the imposing mound of Khairadih on the right bank of Ghaghra. Its extensive size and location impressed us and as a result the mound of Khairadih was subjected to excavations. The lowermost levels revealed a substantial pre-NBP deposit yielding cultural material comparable to chalcolithic phase of Chirand and recently excavated site of Senunar in district Rohtas, Bihar. The present paper seeks to highlight the significance of the results of Khairadih excavations particularly the period relating to the pre-NBP deposit.

Khairadih (Lat 26° 10'N, Long. 83° 51' 30"E) is a small village located in the Ballia district of U.P. The ancient mound covers an area of 710 mt from east west and 510 mt north south, and rises to a maximum hight of about 11 mt above the river bed. The mound is partly occupied by the villagers, a Vaishnava math and partly under cultivation.

The five seasons (1980-81 to 83-84 and 85-86) work under the joint direction of Prof. K.K. Sinha and the present author, provided cultural assemblage of three successive periods - I -III.[1]

The earliest Period I was represented by a maximum deposit from 2.40 to 0.80m. In the cuttings located away from the river the Period I deposit was missing. It is, thus, possible to assume that the early inhabitants who settled directly over the vergin soil were confined to a small area along the river bank. These people lived in mud-huts as evidenced by the remains of post-holes, reed marks in burnt clay lumps and fragmentary remains of a mud wall in the earliest level of the period. The available hight and width of the mud structure was 1.06 m and 0.62m. respectively. It may, however, be mentioned that no exact plan either of the post-holes or the mud structure could be ascertained due to limited area undertaken for digging.

The ceramic types are wheel turned and available in fine, medium and coarse varieties. The pottery of the Period I consists of the following categories.

1. Black and Red ware, both plain as well as painted, recalling the corresponding ware from Chirand,[2] Taradih[3], Senuwar[4], Narhan[5], Manjhi[6] etc.
2. Black-slipped ware, plain as well as painted.
3. Red ware consisting of both slipped and unslipped variety and a limited number of painted specimens as well.
4. Black ware, distinct from the black slipped ware on account of its core and surface treatment. Usually the exterior of the pot had a smoothened surface indicating some sort of burnishing. Though occurring in a limited quantity the importance of this ware at Khairadidh lies in its possible link with the burnished black ware which is commonly associated with chalcolithic assemblage in Bihar and Vindhyan regions.

The pottery of group (i) is further divisible into four categories; i.e., A,B,C, and D. The sherds under category 'A' are without any surface treatment and ranged in fabric from medium to coarse. The shapes mostly represented are bowls of varius types and vases with long flared-out rim having carination at the neck.

The pottery of category 'B' showed an improvement over the preceding one in surface treatment and levigation of the clay. The exterior of the pot is treated with dull red slip which at times gives an impression of wash also. The inner surface, however, is treated uniformly with a black slip. Shapes in this category are basins, perforated legged bowl, pedestalled bowls and bowls with various profiles (figs 1 & 3).

Category 'C' represents further improvement over the preceding ones. As a rule this class of pottery is treated with slip both externally and

Department of AIHC and Acrchaeology, Banaras Hindu Univeristy , Varanasi 221005

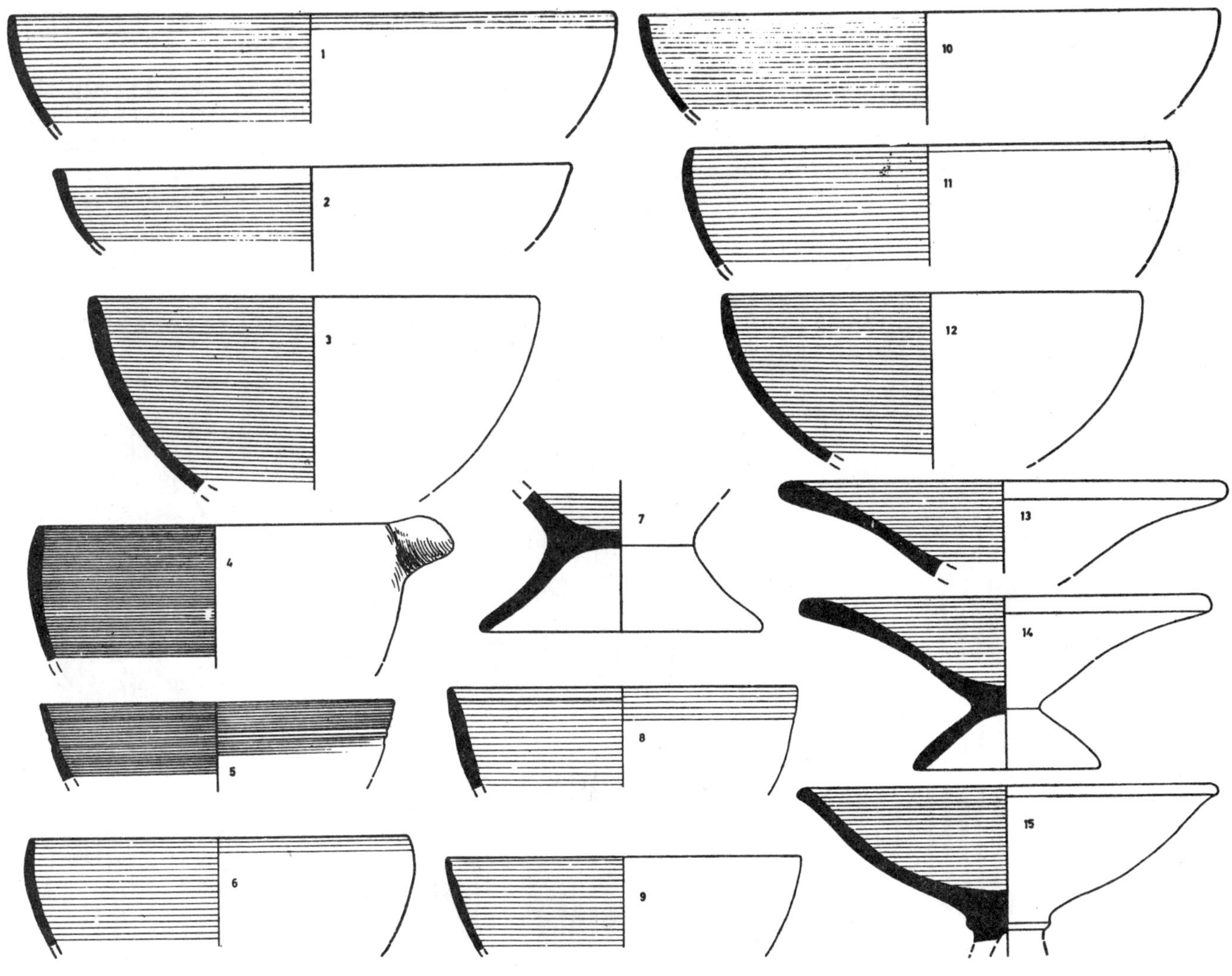

Fig.1. Black and Red Ware from Khairadih, Period I

internally. Specimens with smoothened surface suggesting some sort of burnishing have also been noted. Among the new shapes introduced in this class are dishes, ring based bowls, lipped and small channelled bowls (fig.3). The number of pedestalled bowls increased as compared to the preceding class. Besides, the size of the bowls has also increased and further variety in their shapes have been noted. An interesting feature noted in this class is the absence of vases. The general observation about this class of pottery is that smaller shapes for eating and drinking purposes were made.

Category 'D' is represented by limited number of sherds. The characteristic features of this class of pottery are the use of well levigated clay without any admixture, compact core and controlled firing. As a result, when struck, it gives a metallic sound. Only bowls are represented. It may, however, be mentioned that pottery of this class is noted towards the closing phase of the period.

Barring the specimens of category 'A' the painted designs have been noted in the remaining categories. The pigment used for the motif is white although some pieces are in red paintings also.

The painting is executed on both the surfaces, the designs included a row of uniformly thick vertical lines, wavy line, oblique strokes, semi-circles (fig. 2,1-13). Besides, there is also evidence of incised designs represented in form of leaf pattern.

Among other notable feature of the black-and-red ware mention may be made of some cord impressed sherds.

The black slipped ware belonging to group (ii) is divisible into three groups viz., A,B, and C. The pottery of group 'A' is represented usually in thin fabric with an application of thick uniform black slip. In the same class of pottery specimens with reddish soft core have also been met with, in such cases a very thin slip has been applied which in most cases has come out from the surface.

Sherds of medium fabric represent group 'B'. Further two sub-divisions on the basis of surface treatment have been done. One group represents the use of thick black slip covering the entire body surface, while in an other an inferior type of thin paste has been applied, which in majority of the cases has come out exposing the grey surface. There are quite a few sherds in the group which are rusticated. The outer surface is partially roughened or rusticated by the application of a

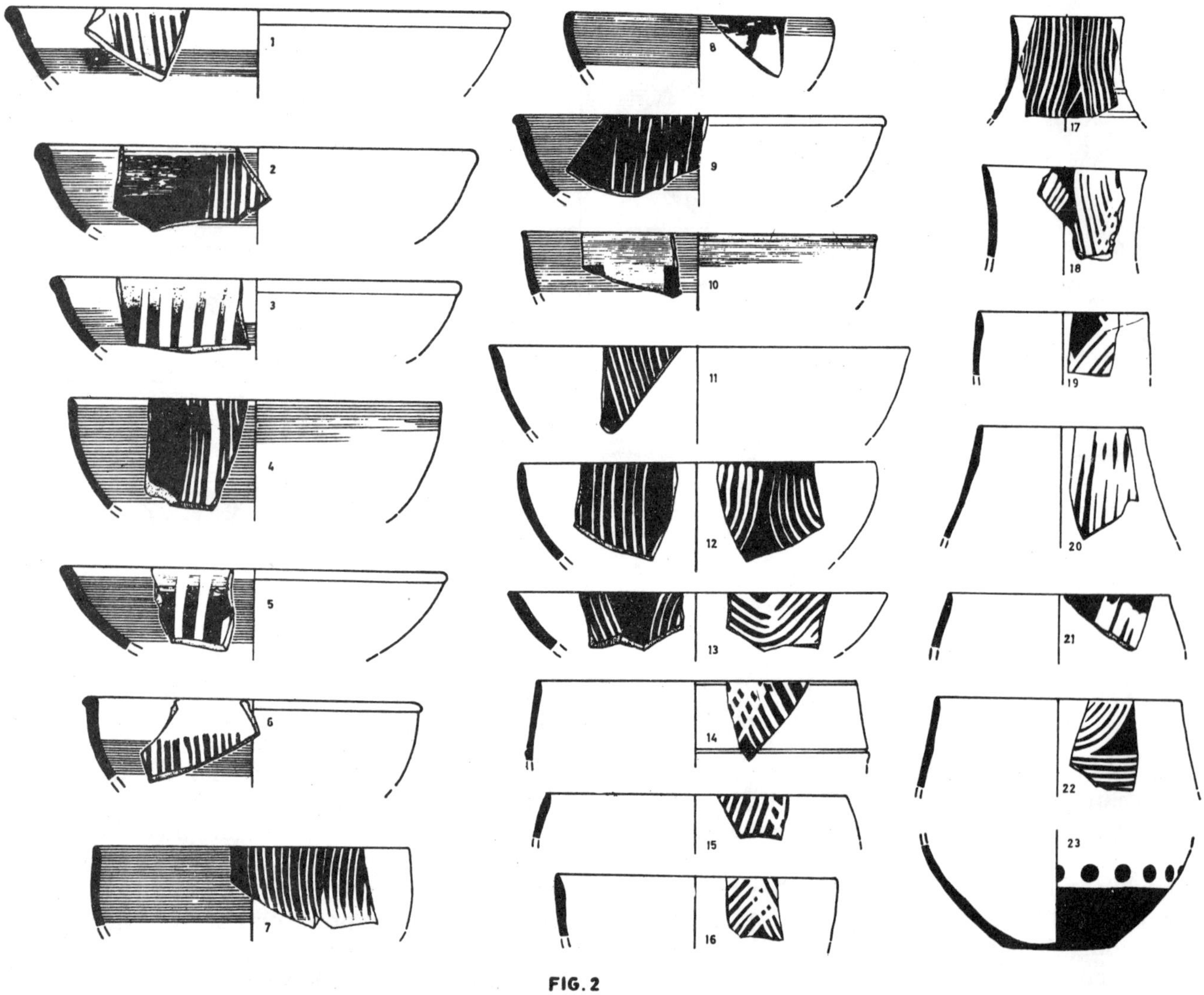

FIG. 2

Fig.2. Black and Red Ware 1-10; Painted Black Slipped ware 11-23

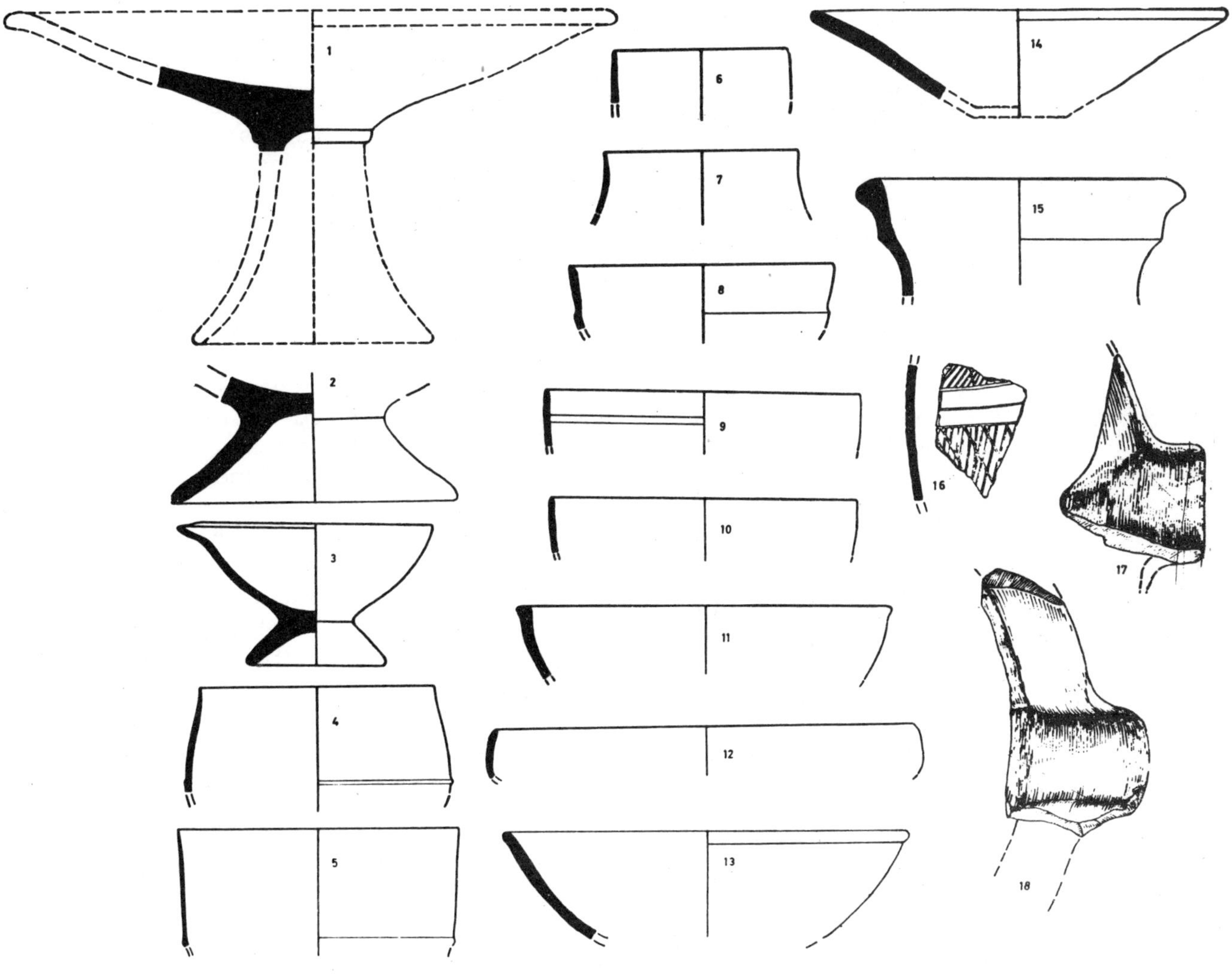

FIG. 3

Fig.3. Red Ware 1-2, Black Slipped Ware 3-12, Red Ware 13-15; Incised Sherds of Red Ware 16.

thick coarse grained solution. This feature of roughening the surface of the black slipped ware has also been noted at Senuwar.

The specimens belonging to group 'C' are coarse and thick in fabric having porous core. The pots in this class of pottery are treated with a thin slip. Variety of shapes has been noted in the above classified groups of black slipped ware such as corrugated bowl, flat based bowl, carinted bowl, flanged bowl, straight sided bowl with everted featureless rim or featureless rim, hemispherical bowl, convex sides bowls and bowls with internally levelled rim (see fig. 3,4-10). Some types of black-and red ware have also been incorporated in the black slipped ware such as pedestalled bowl, channelled spouted bowl etc.

The painted motifs in creamish white over a black surface included lattice, group of slanting or oblique lines, concentric arches and solid dots applied by finger tips (fig. 2,14-23 also pl. III)

The red ware is the dominant industry. Generally the fabric of the ware ranged from medium to coarse, but specimens of the fine fabric are also present. Two classes of pottery have been noted, one without any surface treatment and the other with surface treatment. The latter has usually fine thick slip ranging from bright red to light red or orange in colour. Presence of cord impressed and rusticated sherds in this ware was a noteworthy feature. Some specimens of red ware showed applique design such as twisted rope and incised designs executed after the pots had been fired. Besides a few painted sherds in the ware have also been recorded. Here particular mention may be made of a pot-sherd painted in cream colour with a design which included a group of multiple vertical strokes (Pl.1). There are quite a few red slipped sherds over which a thick coarse grained paste of brownish colour is applied in the form of thick bands. A variety of shapes has been noted in the red ware and include (a) Vases with flared out rim with carinated neck (b) perforated legged bowls (c) bowl with a pedestal base (d) channelled spouted bowl (e) bowl with globular or ovoid body (f) small sized bowls with several variants (g) deep and shallow basins of various types (h) large sized *kundas* etc. (fig.3).

It has been observed that certain shapes in red ware, particularly bowls bear close resemblance with their counterpart in the black slipped ware. This feature continues from the beginning of the period but gets prominence only towards its closing phase. The principal types in the black-and-red and red wares are the bowls and basins of various profiles and capacity. Next in order of frequency comes the vases. In the black slipped ware bowls are mostly represented. Out of the eight major types classified in the red ware just referred to above, four (A-D) have been copied from the black-and-red ware suggesting their importance in the entire ceramic range. It may, however, be mentioned that the number of dishes are less in comparison to other types in all the wares.

The use of copper is attested by the occurrence of a socketed arrow-head having two perforations on the socket (pl.II) and an indeterminate object. But iron in any form was not encountered in this period.

Among other notable finds mention may be made of tanged and socketed arrow-heads of bone (pl.II) akin to the type just mentioned above. Bones of animals and birds were frequently met with from the strata of this period. Some of them were charred. The bones, showed cut marks caused by sharp instruments. All these suggest that the meat also formed the part of diet of the people.

Agriculture was known to them. Rice-husk has been found mixed with clay on some of the potteries. Cattle breeding formed another important occupation of the people as is suggested by the discovery of the remains of animal bone.

Among other finds of the period mention may be made of disc shaped beads of steatite of varying sizes, beads of cernelian, agate, chert and chalcedony mostly cylindrical in shape, hop-scotch, dabber, whirl-wind of terracotta and a large sized handmade terracotta figurine most probably of an animal.

Though limited in number, the occurrence of cord impressed pottery, rusticated ware, burnished red and black wares, are important as they have been noted in the neolithic and chalcolithic cermaic assemblage of the northern and southern Bihar and Vindhyan region. The cord impressed pottery has been treated as the 'fossil type' of the Vindhyan neoliths and on the basis of its occurrence at other places particularly at Sohagaura in the Gorakhpur district and sites in adjoining district of Basti a separate Neolithic horizon has been suggested by scholars.[7] It may, however, be suggested that presumption of neolithic culture on the mere occurrance of Cord impressed pottery would be misleading. In fact, a more appropriate approach would be to consider other cultural traits also instead of giving prominence to one feature. We know that this pottery is associted with chalcolithic and in a limited number with NBPW deposit as well.

The exploration conducted by the author in Rohtas district, Bihar, has brought to light several neolithic, chalcolithic and NBPW settlements, where aforesaid wares have been found.[8] The ceramic assemblage and other cultural traits of some of these sites provide comparable horizon with the other neolithic and chalcolithic sites of Bihar, eastern U.P. as well as vindhyan area. The fabric and form of the ceramic assemblage of Khairadih showed striking similarity with those of the particularly excavated sites like Chirand,[9] Senuwar,[10] Taradih,[11] Chechar, Kutubpur,[12] Oriup,[13] Maner,[14] Narhan,[15] Eran,[16] etc. on the one hand and sites explored in Rohtas district in Bihar on the other. Common shapes enountered at the above mentioned excavated and explored sites and at Khairadih include dish-on-stand, bowl with globular or ovoid body, lipped bowl, bowl with pedetal base, chancelled bowl, vases with flared rim, perforated footed bowl, basins with splayed out rims etc. Other associated finds include beads of steatite, semiprecious stone and terracotta, socketed and tanged arrowheads of bone etc.

Paintings in linear pattern in cream or white pigment on the black and red and the black slipped waves, pin hole decoration are other common features codmparable to those noted earlier at Chirand, Taradih, Oriup, Senuwar, Narhan etc., The above evidence clearly suggests that the chalcolithic cultures of Bihar and Ghaghra basin, apprently are closely related to each other. The presence of common elements on the above mentioned sites and in Period I deposit of Khairadih is in keeping with the general trend of the occurrence of material remains and chronology of the region. However, there is one discordant note i.e., the complete absence of lithic tools at Khairadih. But the presence of copper, ceramic assemblage represented by both painted and unpainted variety and material remains testify to the existence of a comprable chalcolithic phase at Khairadih.[17].

Only a limited area in the lower levels was brought under excavation at Khairadih. Yet the excavation brings to light important data about the chalcolithic culture din the earliest Period I. The duration of the Period I must have been reasonably long as is evident from the occupational thickness of over 2 m. The earliest settlement at this site goes back to C.1100 B.C. as revealed by the combined testimony of Radio Carbon determination and comparative study of cultural assemblage from other excavated and explored sites. The dates for the period I are:

BSIP	3070 ±	90	B.P.
PRL-1049	1030 ±	160	B.C.
	940 ±	150	B.C.

It is thus clear that the C-140date of Khairadih is also in an agreement with the chronology suggested for chaloclithic cultures of the east. Particular mention in this regard may be made of sites like Pandurajardhibi which has yielding a date 1012±120 B.C., Mahishdal 855±100 and Chirand provides a span of Rs.1300-700 B.C.

Notes

1. The period I deposit was superimposed by successive deposits of Period II (C.600-200 B.C.) and Period III (C.200 BC-300 A.D.) yeilding a continuous sequence and remains of early historical period preliminary details of which have been reported elsewhere (See *IAR*-80-81, pp.69-70, 81-82, pp. 67-70, 82-83, pp 92-94, 83-84, pp. 86-87).

2. *IAR*, 1981-82, pp. 13-14, Sinha B.P.,*Archaeology and Art of India*, pp. 34, ff also Verma, B.S., 'Excavations at Chirand: New light on the Indian Neolithic Culture-complex', Puratattva, Vol 4, 1970-71 pp. 19-22.

3. *IAR* 1981-82, pp. 10-11.

4. The site is situated on the right bank of the river Kudra in the Rohtas district, Bihar. The recent excavation done during the session 1986-87 by the author, under the auspices of the department of Ancient Indian History Culture and Archaeology, BHU, brought to light deposits of four cultural periods-Neolithic, Chalcolithic, N.B.P.W. phase and Kushan. The black-and red ware recovered from the Chalcolithic phase is similar in fabric and pottery types from those recovered from Khairadih I. AT both places plain as well as white painted black-and red ware is found.

5. Singh, P. and Lal M., "Narhan 1983-85: A Preliminary Report' *Bharati*, New Series, No.3, pp. 120, ff.

6. Personal observation.

7. Chaturvedi, S.N. 'Advance of Vindhyan Neolithic and chalcolithic cultures to the Himalayan Tarai: Excavation and Explorations in the Saryupar region of Uttar Pradesh'. *Man and Environment.*, Vol. IX, 1985, pp. 101-108, Sharma, G.R. *Bharatiya Samaskriti Puratatvika Adhara; (1985).*, pp. 71-73. also Pal. J.N., *Archaeology of Southern Uttar Pradesh Ceramic Industries of Northern Vindhyas (1986).*, pp. 91 ff. The cord impressed pottery has been reported in the Ganga valley from sites like Koldihwa, Mahagara in the Allahabad district, Lalhania, Kunghun in the Sidhi district (M.P.), Chirand, Senuwar and Chechar in Bihar, Susipar, Ramnagar ghat, Gerar and Lahuradeva in Basti, Sohagaura and Narhan in the Gorakhpur district. Besides its occurrence in the eastern neolithic complex has also been reported.

8. The field survey was conducted during the session 1985-86 under the auspices of the department of A.I.H.C. and Arch., BHU. The exploration resulted in the discovery of several Neolithic, chalcolithic and NBPW settlements. Of particular mention in this regard are those of Sakas, Daindih, Senuwar, Raja Ki Akorhi, Akorhi, Kusuridih, Madhuri etc., Recently a site named Shaharidih in Vikramganj tehsil has also been explored by Shri N.K. Singh research scholar of the department. The assemblage of the cultural material as a whole betrays Neolithic and chalcolithic character in its earliest level. Among surface finds, pottery constituted the most prominent trait. It included black and red ware both plain as well as painted, black slipped ware, black burnished ware, red ware with bright red slip, coarse red ware, burnished grey ware and cord impressed pottery. Among noteworthy shapes met within red ware and black-and-red ware, included bowls with rounded base, perforated footed bowl, vases with flared rim, basins, chanelled spouted bowl, lipped bowl etc. The tools are made on locally available rocks like basalt, chert, chalcedony, and included bladelets, blades, flakes, together with fluted cores and debitage.

9. *IAR 1968-69, pp. 5-6 pl. V A, 70-71, p. 7 1971-72* p.6 B.S. Verma excavator of the site saw the material of Khairadih. He is of the view that there is a great affinity in fabric and typology between ceramic industries of the Chalcolithic phase of Chirand and the pre-NBP deposit of Khairadih.

10. Period II, at Senuwar is chalcolithic. The ceramic industry of the period, is represented by black-and red ware (plain as well as painted), burnished black ware (plain and painted), black slipped ware, slipped and unslipped red ware and black painted red were commonly known as black-on-red ware. Among other objects of the period mention may be made of microliths, copper, beeds of semi-precidous stone, bone tools etc. The occurrence of black-on-red ware is not only the first of its kind to have been noticed in this region but shows a resemblance with the chalcolithic ware of central India suggesting some kind of contact. Leaving aside the black on-red ware, which is absent not only at Khairadih but in the entire region of eastern U.P. the remaining wares have close parallels in fbaric, typology and other details with the Khairadih pottery. The difference is noted in the painted sherds. The black slipped ware of Khairadih is both plain and painted whereas at Senuwar it is plain. Similarly the burnished black ware of Senuwar is plain and painted both whereas at Khairadidh it is plain only.

11. *IAR*, 1981-82; pp. 10-11, 1983-84, pp. 12-13.

12. *IAR, 1977-78, pp. 17-19.*

13. *IAR, 1966-67, p.6, pl. IIIA.*

14. The excavation conducted at Maner by the department of Ancient Indian History and Culture, Patna University, brought to light chalcolithic culture in its earliest level. The fabric and form of the black-and-red ware industry showed affinity with those of the chalcolithic phase of Chirand, Senuwar and pre-NBP deposit of Khairadih

15. Singh P., and M. Lal op.cit.

16. Prof. U.V. Singh, excavator of Eran site, had seen the pottery of Period I of Khairadih. He pointed out the affinity between the chalcolithic black and red ware of Eran and black-and-red ware of Khairadih. In fact a detailed study of the materials of these sites is necessary.

17. In the absence of lithic tools, the use of the term 'Chalcolithic' for Khairadidh may be disputed by some scholars. However, since the assemblage has many identical features noted at other sites like Chirand and Senuwar etc., where microliths are present, the term is being retained to convey the status of the assemblage. (See Sankalia H.D., In Deo, S.B., (ed.) *Archaeological Congress and Seminar papers* Nagpur 1972. pp. 157 (ff).

Puratattva No.18 ; 1987-88

POPULATION DISTRIBUTION AND ITS MOVEMENT DURING THE SECOND AND FIRST MILLENNIA B.C. IN THE INDO-GANGETIC DIVIDE AND UPPER GANGA PLAIN +

Makkhan Lal*

INTRODUCTION

The archaeology of the Indo-Gangetic Divide and Upper Ganga plains attracted the attention of scholars since late forties only. The result of last four decades of archaeological researches have been extremely rewarding. While in the Indo-Gangetic Divide the existance of Harappan Culture could be established and its phase of decline could be understood in greater details, the antiquity of Upper Ganga plains could be pushed beyond the Buddhist period i.e. 6th century B.C. It could be very firmly established that Harappan culture did not die out suddenly as it was held in late twenties and thirties but its decline was very slow and it spread far beyond the areas that could have been imagined in the early period researches. In the Gangetic plain it could be established that the cultural antiquity of the area goes to early second millennium B.C. and atleast from 1300 B.C. the legacy of cultural development is uninterrupted.

Our main concern here in the present paper will be the study of spread of human population during the second and first millennium B.C. in the Indo-Gangetic Divide and Upper Ganga plains. This spread will be viewed in the context of the then ecological conditions. I would like to mention here that the words settlements and sites have been used interchangably, indicating the units of villages, towns or cities i.e. the human habitation.

The paper is divided into two parts. Part I deals with the ecology of study area, while Part II with the distribution of human settlements over the landscape during second and first millennium B.C. In this we shall be dealing with only the late Harappan and Painted Grey Ware settlements.

I. GEOGRAPHICAL FEATURES AND THE ECOLOGY OF THE AREA

Indo-Gangetic Divide

The region is bounded by the sharply rising and straight Siwalik hills in the north, the Yamuna in the east and in the south it grade into the Thar and its limit here may be taken as the Ghagghar and in the south east the low broken Aravallis ridge which reach out to Delhi. With same violence to strict geographical logic the northern most portion of Bari doab, where Indian territory extends west of the Sutlej around Amritsar, is included for the convenience.

Geologically speaking much of the plain is of a very recent age and its surface has been built up by the silting action of its upward streams during the pleistocene.

Although over the greater part of the plains the general relief is marked by high prominance, yet the topography may be defined as slightly undulating. The existing and extinct courses of the streams provide somewhat lower areas which are interspread by the interfluvial regions of slightly higher elevation which are termed locally as *bhangar, Dahia or Nardak,* At places sand dunes and sand ridges occur in these interfluvial zones.

Apart from a few scattered and broaken Arvalli outliners in the south east, and the topographical discontinuities of the river courses, the terrain is simply usual alluvial monatory. Between Beas and Sutlej the Siwaliks are on the whole more sharply defined than they are in the west, and for climatic and historical reasons more deforested than they are in the east. The result has been the

+ The first draft of the paper was presented at Discussion Meeting on "Ecological History of India" held at Centre For Ecological Sciences, Indian Institute of Science, Bangalore 9-11 Feb. 1988

* Department of History, Aligarh Muslim University, Aligarh-202001

erosion on a large scale. In about 130 Km. of the Siwaliks in Hoshiarpur district nearly 100 streams debouch on to the plains. These are known as *Chos*. These *Chos* are dry except in sudden spates, when they came down armed with masses of sand and are agents of rapid erosion on the plain below, itself sandy and with a perceptile slope near the hills. Each *Chos* is a broad river of sand, with a shallow ever shifting bed, and with banks which, where defined at all, "are composed of ustable sand...... or of scarped cultivation liable to be washed away by any flood". (Hamilton 1935:95). Except in the salt range *Khuddera* and the great Yamuna-Chambal ravines, nowhere in India has erosion been so divastating.

Southeast of the Sutlej none of the streams except the Yamuna is perennial. The only river of some importance traversing the middle of the extensive part of the plains is the Ghagghar, which though perennial in upper courses, becomes dry after flowing for a short distance from the hills. In fact, this entire plain forms a major region of rather inland drainage. The Yamuna which flows almost due south fails to receive the streams coming down the Siwaliks with the exception of the Saub Nadi and its tributary, the Boli in the extreme east of the hills. All other streams which flow in a south-westerly direction have broad sandy courses scarcely below the surface of the country. They vary in width from less than 90 m. to 1600 m. (Spate et al. 1977:535). They are dry during the greater part of the year but become a formidable bady of water during rainy season. This character they maintain for nearly 32 Km. below the hills as in the Bist doab after which they gradually tame down into sluggish streams with wells defined clay banks and a volume much diminished by absorption in sands. Almost all units in Ghagghar which from the commencement is the most important river and which alone pierces the Siwaliks between the Sutlej and Yamuna. The Ghaggar contains a lot more water during the rainy season and at that time it normally flows upto Hanumangarh, a distance of about 465 K. from the source. Beyond, its course is represented by the dry bed of Hakra.

The Indo-Gangetic divide enjoys a semi-arid monsoon type of climate. It is charaterised by the deficiency of rainfall over its greater part, high summer temperatures and evoporation more especially in the southern parts exhibiting as a whole a transition between the arid desert of Rajasthan and moderately humid upper Ganga plains. The annual average temperature ranges from 23.1°C to 25.1°C showing an almost uniform condition in the region.

Although temperature conditions are more or less uniform yet it is not so with rainfall which, in general decreases from north-east to south-west. The submontane tract receives, on an average about 75 cm. of rainfall annually, while in the extreme south-west it decreases to less than 30 cm.

The vegetation in Indo-Gangetic divide is rather thin and when we move from north to south we see that it rapidly diminishes, approaching extinction in the Indian desert. Over the whole region a low herbacious vegetation of plants, common to most parts of India, is spread with thickest of shrubs and a few trees. With a few exceptions all have deciduous leaves. The Chief arboreous vegetation consists of isolated groups of trees in the outskirts of the western Himalayan region and on the banks of the rivers... The principal indigenous trees are *Tamarix articulata, Bombax malabaricum, Sterculia urens, Grewia salicifolia, Balanites Roxburghii, Boswellia serrata, Balsamodendron Mukul and pubescens, Pistacia integerrima, Aegle Marmelos, Odina Wodier, Moringa pterygosperma and concanensis, Dalbergia Sissoo, Butea frondosa, Prosopis spicigera, Acacia arabica, Jacquemontii leucophaea, Eburnea, modesta, and Rupestris, Dichrostachys cinerea, Salvadora persica and Oleoides, Anogeissus pendula, Cordia myxa and Rothii, Terminalia tomentosa, Tecoma undulata, Olea cuspidata, Ficus infectoria and Palmata, Morus indica, Celtis australis, Alnus nitida, Populus euphratica and Nigra, Salix tetrasperma.* The only indigenous palms are *Phoenix sylvestris* and Nannorrhops ritchieana. The only bamboo is *Dendrocalamus strictus.*

Of shrubs, among the most conspicuous are isolated clumps of the *Columnar*, almost leafless *Euphorbia royleana* and *neriifolia.* Other more or less prevalent shrubs and undershrubs in certain districts are *Capparis aphylla, horrida,* and *spinosa, Flacourtia Ramontchi, Tamarix dioica* and *gallica, Grewia* (seven species), *Fagonia arabica, Rhamnus persica* and *virgata, Zizyphus nummularia vulgaris, and Oenoplia, Dodonaea viscosa, Alhagi maurorum, Sophora mollis, Cassia auriculata, Tora,* and *Obovata, Mimosa rubicaulis, Pluchea lanceolata, Reptonia buxifolia, Carissa diffusa, Rhazya stricta, Nerium odorum, Orthanthera viminea, Periploca aphylla,*

Calotropis procera and *Gigantea, Withania coagulans, Adhatoda Vasica, Calligonus polygonoides, Pteropyrum olivieri, Salsola foetida,* and species of *Kochia, Suaeda, Anabasis & c.*

Of special interest as shrubs of this region are three species of Cotton *(Gossypium)*, a genus unknown as native in any other part of India. These are *G. Stocksii* in Sind, *G. wightianum* in the Aravallia forests, and *G. herbaceum (?)* in the Ambala District of the Punjab.

The Upper Ganga Plain:

The Upper Ganga Plain mainly consists of gently inclined alluvial plain dipping towards south-east. It is an extremely difficult task to delineate regional divisions in this featureless plain. For hundred of Kilometres the only reliefs seen are buffs leaves, dead arms of river channels and existing rivers. In contrast to the nominal relief to the north of the Ganga drained by sluggish rivers like Ram Ganga, Gomati and Sai, the Ganga Yamuna doab exhibits a more prominent *bhangar* land rising upto 15-60m. The slope is generally less than 30 cm. per Km. Because of a very gentle slope the movement of water is very slow. The steams like Kali, Hindon, Rind, Pandu and Sengur run parallel to their master streams for quite a distance before emptying themselves into the large rivers. The area south of Bulandshahar and north of Etah consists of silty or clayee *bhangar* tract. Sand ridges alternated by depressions in Bulandshahar, Mathura Aligarh and Etah make this portion of the Upper Ganga plains more diversified than its counterparts in the north and south. The patches of saline and alkaline efflorescene which are the result of excessive quantity of soluble salt in the alluvium are the main characteristic features of the *bhangar* land.

A very different topography is seen in the lower Yamuna tract. Due to the erosional effect of the rain water on the soft alluvial soils along the banks, deep and intricate ravines have been formed. These extend from 3 to 5 km. away from the banks.

The alluvial deposits, which are upper and post Tertiary Himalayan debries filled in a deep basin, are of two types: *Bhangar* and *Khadar.*

The *bhangar* or the older alluvium, occupying the zone above the existing flood plain, belong to the middle ot Pleistocene. Its general levesl is 3.4 m. above the highest and 15.20 m. above the lowest level of the bed of the Ganga. The calcium carbonate nodules *(kankar)* are found everywhere in *bhangar* land, from the surface down to 10.15 m. depth.

Khadar on younger alluvium occupies the flood plains. Its source lies partly in the erosion of the *bhangar* land and partly in the fresh sediments brought from the Himalayas. It is free from *kankar* and *reh* (alkaline soils).

Only the Ganga and the Yamuna originate from the Himalayas, all other rivers rise from marshy plains. The Ganga and Yamuna are mighty rivers and carry large quantity of water throughout the year. Both these rivers have wide courses and large flood plains, sometimes extending upto 5 Km. The other rivers like Kali, Sai, Gomati, Hindon, Rind, Sangur etc. rise from the marshy plains and only some of these are perennial. A few like Pandu and Sasur Khaderi are almost dry or carry very little water after the rains.

The soils of the Upper Ganga plain tend to became heavier from north-west to south-east. In the middle of plain districts of Aligarh, Agra and Mathura which are very near to the arid zone, large patches of alkaline soils (*usar*) as well as windborne sand are quite common. Alkaline soils occur in patches in the districts of Etah, Manpuri, Farrukhabad, Kanpur, fatehpur and Allahabad. On weathering, the alkaline soils liberate large amount of sodium, calcium and magnesium salt and sulphurous acid as a result of which the soils became unfertile and support only grassy growth with little or no tree vegetation.

The *khadar* soils are found in the areas of flood plains and are quite rich in nutrients. The p^H value ranges between 6 and 8. It has been observed that locally the Ganga *khadar* soils have an immature profile with sandy to silty texture, contain high percentage of lime and are alkaline in reaction. On the other hand the Yamuna *khadar* soils have a sub-mature profile with a predomdinance of clay concretion. The *bhangar* soils are more extensively spread. The percentage of soluble salts except in the soils of low lying areas where water logging takes place is low and the soils are neutral to slightly acidic in reaction. The calcium carbonate content generally increases at lower depths and are generally poor in phosphoric acid, nitrogen and other organic matter.

The climate of the Upper Ganga plains is sub-hunmid in contrast to the dry Punjab plains and humid middle Ganga plains. A microlevel there are variations in small measures which have effected the human settlement patterns in the past as well as in present (Lal 1984a: 107-139; 170-237).

The area falls between 600 and 1000m. isohytes. It may be pointed out that nearly 80% of this rainfall comes in the month of July and August. The average temperature during winter ranges from 12°C to 19°C and during summer from 35°C to 42°C with extremes of 45-50°C.

The vast alluvial plains, as we see them today are the result of continuous deforestation from second millennium B.C. to the present, especially during the last two centuries. Across the bare plains of today there once existed a dense, moist and luxurient forest of Sal (Stebbing 1922; Calder 1937). In the traditional literature we have ample evidence for the area being a dense forest. *Satpath Brahmana* mentions that the land between Saraswati (modern Ghagghar of Haryana and Rajasthan) and Sadanira (modern Gandak) was a dense forest and Aryanization of this area was possible only after burning the forests, which was subsequently cultivated also. According the *Mahabharata* Hastinapura, the capital of Kurus was situated in a forested area and the Pandavas, after the division of Kingdom founded city of Indraprastha (modern Delhi) only after clearing the forests. The kingdoms of Panchalas-modern districts of Barailly, Badaun, Pilibhit, Rampur, Farrukhabad, Etah, Etawah and Kanpur in the upper Ganga plains was founded in Kuru jungle. The kingdom of Kuru which occupied the area of upper Ganga-Yamuna doab was also situated in the middle of forest (Law 1954: 40, 115). *Devipurana* mentions nine sacred forest in India of which Kuru jungle, Nimisa and Utpalarange covered the area of Upper Ganga plains.

The pollen records from Hastinapura excavations show the presence of *Pinus, Dalbergia sisso, and Holarrahena antidysentica* (Chaudhury etc. al. 1977), Lal 1954-55: 120). Samples of charred wood from OCP to NBPW levels (1800 B.C. to 100 B.C.) from Atranjikhera belong to *Pinus roxburghii, Dalbergia sisso, Tectona gradis, Boehmeria platyphyla, Cedrus deodara, Cupressus torulosa, Terminalia tomentosa, Tamarix articulata, Dendrocalamus strictus, Acacia nilotica and Acacia arabica* (Chaudhury et. al. 1977). The presence of these species, some of which are now confined only to the *Tarai* regions shows that the plain was quite densely forested during the second and first millenium B.C. Pant says (Agrawal 1971: 225) that in the past the fauna of Siwaliks included carnivores, monkeys, elephants and ungulates suggesting that the Indo-Gangetic plains must have had a thick forest cover like that of *Tarai* and *Bhabhar* regions. In fact the forest cover was so thick even in 15th and 16th centuries A.D. that wild Elephants, Buffaloes, Lions and Tigers were hunted in the Upper Ganga plains (Abul Fazal, Ain-i-Akbari, pp.283-93; Habib, 1982; map 8B). But now, once rich and varied fauna has been reduced to a small number of few species like dear, antelopes, bears, hyenas, wolves, foxes, jackals and monkeys.

The ramnants of early forest can be seen in the patches and the vegetation includes *Butea frondosa, Caserica tomentosa, Alienthus excelsa, Woodfordia floribunda, Acacia laucophoria, Terminalia belerica, Tamarindus indica, Basia latifolia,* and Species of *Bauhinia* and Eugenia (Puri 1960: 212). *Bombax malabari cum, Adina cordifolia, Lagerstroemia parviflora, Lannea gradis, Gmelina arborea, Cassia fistula, Mallotus philippinensis* and *Callicarpa microphyla,* are now confined to the sub-Himalayan tract only. (Puri 1960: 251) In the Central part of the plains mainly in central Ganga-Yamuna doab thorny shrubs such as *Caparis aphylla, Prosopis spicizera, Tecoma undulata* and *Acacia* which farm an extention of semi-arid vegetation of Rajasthan.

In fact, no other part of India has undergone such a drastic change due to tillage of jungle land in the past two centuries. Considerable damage to the forest was done by railways also which obtained their fuel supply directly from local timber until a century ago (Whitecombe 1972; 95). The intensive colonization and large scale deforestation has brought the balance between man and vegetation to a very delicate stage. Mukharjee (1938: 97-103) sums up:

"Nowhere is this interaction between man and vegetation so vividly illustrated over an extensive area than the Gangetic plains.

The balance between the progressive tendencies of vegetation and retrogressive influence of man is nowhere more evident than in the vegetation of this region. Throughout, the Gangetic plain the vegetation may be said have attained an apparent equilibrium in relation to variation in rainfall and temperature which at any moment is liable to be upset...... On the plains the vegetation is rather delicately balanced against the man at about thornscrub state. The soil over most of the Indo-Gangetic plains seems to be supporting all the human and bovine life that is possible under existing methods of exploitation."

Thus it is very clear that the upper Ganga plains were quite densely forested right from early times. The presence of lions, tigers, elephants etc. even until 16th century A.D. indicates that forest were fairly dense and well preserved. As a matter of fact forest disappeared rapidly only in the last two centuries.

HYDROLOGICAL FLUCTUATIONS IN INDO-GANGETIC PLAINS

The region of Indo-Gangetic divide has witness one of the major shifting of river channels during 2nd and 1st millenium B.C. This has attracted the attention of scholars' right from the 2nd half of the last century. (Oldham 1874, 1893; Oldham 1886; Siddiqui, 1944, 1945; Ghosh 1952; Erikson 1959; Allchin and Goudie 1978; Ghosh et. al 1979; Pal et.al. 1980; Pande 1977, Misra 1984). It is not our intension here to review all the data. In fact, it is almost impossible to do a better job on it that done by Prof. V.N. Misra. What is intended here is to briefly summerize these fluctuations as these have affected the course of cultural development, spread and decline.

One of the widest and mightiest dried river channel that has been explored in the subcontinent is that of Ghagghar-Hakra. In the upper coarse, the bed of this river runs in a more or less north east to south-west direction upto the Indo-Pakistan border and is known as the Ghagghar (Ghosh 1952). From this point onwards, it takes south-west course to Bahawalpur and is known as Hakra or Wahind. After entering Sind, it turns southward and flows in that direction right down to its mouth in the Runn of Kutch and is known variously as the Nara, Hakra, Sagara, Wahind and Dohan.

The width of Hakra bed varies from 3 to 10 Km. in different parts of its course. It was obviously a very large river during its life time. The large number of settlements found along its course dating broadly to a period 4000-600 B.C. also shows that it must have been a perennially flowing mighty river. A detailed analysis by Misra (1984:475-81) shows that earlier several rivers were flowing in the Ghagghar-Hakra river filling its large bed with large volume of water.

Now the question is which were these rivers that flowed into the Ghagghar river?

The question has attracted the attention of geographers, historians, and archaeologists for more than a century (Oldham 1874, 1883; R.D. Oldham 1886; Stein 1942; Ghosh 1952; Erikson 1959). Scholars opine that beside the several smaller rivers, Sutlej and Yamuna were also flowing into Ghagghar. A number of dry river beds between Haryana, Punjab and Rajasthan represent nothing else but the various abandoned channels of the rivers Yamuna, Sutlej and probably Beas. A study of landsat imagery pertaining to the period 1972-77 of Punjab, Haryana and Rajasthan area shows that earlier the entire drainage between the Yamuna and Sutlej, including both the rivers was flowing in the Ghagghar (Yashpal et.al 1984). It has been concluded that since 2000 B.C. there has been considerable change in the river channels of the Punjab, Harayana and Rajasthan resulting in the drying of the lower course of the river Ghagghar and also the capturing of Sutlej by Indus and Yamuna by the Ganga.

II. THE POPULATION DISTRIBUTION

Late Harappan Culture

In the last six decades our knowledge of Harappan culture has increased substantially. The continuous efforts towards understanding the various aspects of this civilization has thrown considerable light on the over all personality of Harappan Civilization. One of the results of these efforts is that now more than 800 Harappan sites are known in India and Pakistan. More than three-fourth of the above total came to light in the last three decades. We owe this important addition to our knowledge to a number of archaeologist working in the field both in India and Pakistan.

However, the term late Harappan now is widely used but little of variously understood. In the recent past there have been attempts to define this term (Possehl 1980, 1984; Ghosh 1982; Gupta 1982; Joshi 1984; Misra 1984). It has been noticed that during the late phase of the Harappan culture the regional variations and local characteristic features came to dominate the earlier homogenous cultural traits of the core area. Perhaps because of the collaps of political system, if there was any, the standardization and homogeneity of material cultural of mature Harappan phase disappeared. It was replaced by the regional styles in ceramic shapes and designs as wells as other aspects of material culture (Misra 1984: 470). The regional styles are represented by Lustrous Red Ware complex in Gujarat; Jhukar complex in Sind; Diamabad complex in Maharashtra; Cemetry 'H' culture in Bahawalpur and part of Punjab; Mitathal B complex in Haryana; Late Bara complex in Punjab and Haryana; and Hulas and Alamgirpur complex in the Ganga-Yamuna doab. Each culture complex is different from other in pottery as well as in many other associated cultural items. Yet all of them share some mature Harappan elements, such as a few inscribed seals and sealings, or potsherds; agate, and carnelian beads and bangles; a few and thick and sturdy pottery types; painted designs and even copper Bronze objects. However, it may be emphasized that there was a complete abandonment of cities and people reversed to more or less to village life.

The main objective of this paper is not to list the different characteristic features of the material culture of the late Harappan in the above mentioned complexes. I shall deal here mainly with the location pattern of the late Harappan settlements and the general distribution of population in the Indo-Gangetic Divide and the Upper Ganga plains and see how it conforms with the then ecological features, mainly with drainage and the soils. First the Indo-Gangetic Divide.

Indo-Gangetic Divide

The work carried out in the last three decades have proved that the Indo-Gangetic region, especially the Ghagghar-Hakra river system is the most important area of the Harappan civilization. Following the foot steps of Sir Aurel stein (1942) the work carried out by A. Ghosh (1952), K.N. Dikshit (1980), K.F. Dalal (1980), Suraj Bhan (1973, 1975, 1977), Madhubala (1978), Joshi (1978, 1981, 1984, 1986), Punia (1976), Man Mohan Kumar (1978), Amar Singh (1981) and M.R. Mughal (1980, 1982, 1984) has thrown valuable light on the Harappan culture of the Indo-Gangetic Divide. It has now been proved beyond doubt that the main focus of the Harappan civilization was in the Ghagghar basin.

In the lower and middle reaches of the Gagghar i.e. the Bahawalpur state of Pakistan and Ganganagar, Bikaner and Hanumangarh districts of Rajasthan the early and mature Harappan sites are most prolific. the number of early Harappan settlements (including Hakra ware sites) is 147. The succeeding mature Harappan settlements number 202. It may be mentioned that the sites of these periods are quite big and a number of them are city sites-as big as Harappa and Mohenjodaro. However, during the late Harappan period the total number of sites fell drastically. In Bahawalpur region only 50 late Harappan settlements (Cemetry 'H' and related cultures) have been found (Mughal 1982: 93) though in one of the earlier papers Mugal (1980: 94-97) reported 72 late Harappan settlements). No late Harappan settlement has so far been found in Hanumangarh, Bikaner or Ganganagar districts of Rajasthan.

The eastern most late Harappan settlement in this area is Khetwal (site no. 51 in Mugal 1982, map 1), about 20 Km. east of the Yazman town while the western most site is Bhootanwali (site no. 278 in Mughal 1982; map 1). Thus, these sites are mostly between the towns of Yazman and Derawar. After the settlement of Khetwal near Yazman we see another late Harappan settlement on the bed of Ghagghar or its tributary in the east only when we reach Siswal in district Hissar, Haryana, a distance of nearly 350 Km. while in the same length more than 30 early Harappan and 35 mature Harappan settlements have been found.

The settlements located near the Ghagghar-Hakra bed are large in size. Some smaller settlements are located around Derawar where the Hakra river once formed inner delta. Mugal notes that "there is an apparent constriction in Cholistan during the late Harappan occupation as compared to that of mature Harappan". The reason for this sharp decrease in the number of settlements and their size in the comparison to earlier periods is not very far to explain. By the beginning of second millennium B.C. the hydrological fluctuations in the Indo-Gangetic Divide area began to be serious. Due to these fluctuations quite a large proportion of the population moved to comparatively better areas in the upper regions of the Indo-Gangetic Divide and the Gujrat.

When we move further up in the north and northeast of Cholistan desert (after the eastern most later Harappan settlement) we find that late

Harappan settlements have increased considerably. In Punjab their number is 130 in comparison to 37 mature Harappan settlements. Beside the increase in number, their zone of distribution is also different. While the mature Harappan settlements are located mainly in the districts of Bhatinda and Sangrur along the abandoned channels of Sutlej and Ghaggar and a few in the upper reaches like that of Ropar, Bara and Kotla Nihang Khan; the late Harappan settlements are confined mainly to the districts of Jullundur, Roper, Patiala and Ludhiana i.e. in the upper reaches of the then drainage patterns.

In Haryana there are 297 late Harappan settlements in comparison to only 43 mature Harappan. In this area also the general pattern is that the population moved either towards the north i.e. to the districts of Ambala, Kurukshetra and Karnal along with the Ghagghar, Saraswati, Markanda and Chautang or towards the east in the districts of Gurgaon, Jind, Mahendragarh, Sonepat and Rohtak along the river Yamuna and its various abandoned courses.

When we look at the general pattern of the distribution of settlements in Haryana and Punjab most of the settlements are located in between 500 and 700 mm. isohyte zone. Sites generally fall in shalow water tracts in northern Haryana and along the fresh water belts in southern Haryana. The settlements located on the rivers are on high terraces, away from the reach of floods. There seems to have been a constant movement of people from early Harappan times to the late Harappan time from the lower reaches of the Indo-Gangetic Divide to the upper reaches. Most of the settlements of late Harappan followed the line of rivers in the upper reaches. The frequent changes in the river channels and finally the drying up of the Ghagghar river must have forced people to move up. A few mature Harappan sites that we see on the upper reaches of the Sutlej and its tributaries are decidely later than the sites in the Indus and Ghagghar valley proper. The mature Harappan people in this area must have come from west Punjab following the rivers Ravi and Beas.

Table —1

Distribution of Protohistoric settlements in the Indo-Gangetic Divide and Upper Ganga Plain

District	Harappan	Late Harappan	PGW
	Cholistan (Pakistan)		
Bhawalpur	202	50	14
	Rajasthan		
Hanuman garh	28	—	10
	Punjab		
Bhatinda	14	10	—
Sangarur	05	09	06
Patiala	04	37	12
Ludhiana	04	29	28
Ropar	03	14	05
Kapurthala	02	02	—
Faridket	02	03	01
Ferozpur	01	—	—
Amritsar	01	03	05
Jullundur	01	12	15
Gurdaspur	—	09	09
Hoshiarpur	—	02	01
	37	**130**	**82**
	Haryana		
Ambala	01	21	62
Kurukshetra	08	59	72
Jind	09	96	50
Sonepat	02	11	—
Rohtak	02	10	05
Bhiwani	01	03	—
Hissar	20	26	10
Karnal	—	53	53
Mahendragarh	—	04	—
Gurgaon	—	14	10
	43	**297**	**262**
	Uttar Pradesh		
Saharanpur		52	39
Muzaffar Nagar	—	15	22
Meerut	—	09	39
Bulandshahr	—	03	22
Agra	—	—	14
Mainpuri	—	—	26
Aligarh	—	—	15
Etah	—	—	11
Kanpur	—	—	46
Mathura	—	—	08
Bijnor	—	—	09
Farrukhabad	—	—	05
Hardoi	—	—	03
Etawah	—	—	01
Nainital	—	—	02
Almora	—	—	01
Barailley	—	—	02
Lucknow	—	—	03
Moradabad	—	—	02
Unnao	—	—	02
Fatehpur	—	—	02
Basti	—	—	02
Bahraich	—	—	01
Allahabad	—		01
Deoria	—	—	01
	—	**79**	**279**

In the region of Harayana also the movement of People was along the rivers mainly the Saraswati, Drishadvati, Markanda and others traversing through the districts of Ambala, Karnal, Kurukshetra etc. The presence of the settlements in the districts of Jind, Gurgaon, Mahendragarh and Sonepat can be explained by the presence of several abandoned channels of the Yamuna. The presence of these channels indicates that Yamuna was slowly drifting towards the east. A number of sites of the late Harappan period have been discovered along these channels (Suraj Bhan 1973, 1977; Silak Ram 1976).

An analysis of the size of late Harappan settlements shows that in general there was a decline in the size when compared to the mature Harappan sites. The size known from the single culture occupation sites indicates that most of settlements were villages ranging from one to five hect. in size i.e. they had a population ranging from 250 to 1500. Only a few settlements in Haryana and Punjab region have been found which could be classed as town. The known sites like Bara, Kotla Nihang Khan, Dher Majra measures 16.50, 2.06 hect. and 0.95 hect. only (Dikshit 1981-82: 57). A few towns mentioned above are mainly located in Bhatinda district. Here Mr. J.P. Joshi (1986: section V, p. 139) has discovered three town size settlements which measure up to 25 hect. i.e. could have had a resident population between 5000 and 7000. A few settlements in Bahawalpur region measure between 20 and 38 hect., this having a resident population between 5000 and 9000.

The settlements in the Indo-Gangetic plains were spaced between 8 and 12 Km. The spacing was slightly less in the districts of Ambala, Kurukshetra, Karnal, Ludhiana and Jullundur when compared with other districts.

Upper Ganga Plains

Through Mr. Joshi (1984) has shown 31 mature Harappan settlements in his list for the upper Ganga plains, I do not see any reason for the inclusion of those sites in the category of mature Harappan since none of them have the characteristic features so typical of the period. Mr. K.N. Dikshit who has been working on Harappan problems in the Upper Ganga plains now for quite some time observes "there is not one site with all the typical Harappan pottery in this area", (1982: 346). He further notes, "The Pre-Harappan Cultural horizon found northern Rajasthan, and Haryana is absent in western Uttar Pardesh... The mature Harappan sites which are found in southern Sind, the Pubjab, (Pakistan), Bahawalpur, northern Rajasthan and Saurashtra are also not found in this peripheral region", (Dikshit 1982;348). Similarly Mr. Joshi has included all the OCP settlements in late Harappan, thereby taking the extent of Harappans up to Sringaverapura in Allahabad district. I have treated here OCP culture separately.

Of the late Harappan culture nearly 90 settlements have been found in the Upper Ganga Plains. These settlements are confined in the upper part of the Ganga-Yamuna doab, mostly in the districts of Saharanpur, Muzaffarnagar and Meerut. The settlements are located mainly on the tributaries. No settlement has so far been found on the major rivers i.e. the Ganga and the Yamuna. The settlements are generally located on the higher banks of the rivers and are smaller in size. Most of them measure between 1 and 2 hect. indicating a resident population between 50 and 500. A few larger settlements like Hulas and Alamgirpur measure up to 4 hects. with a population up to 1000. In no case any settlement can be classed as town or city.

Average spacing between two settlements is 8 to 12 Km. in the distrticts Muzaffarnagar and Meerut. The spacing was less in Saharanpur district being 5 to 8 Km. (Lal 1984a: 22). The limited thickness of the cultural deposits (1 to 2 Km.) indicates that habitation was for the shorter duration.

Almost contemporary to the late Harappans, though a few sites like Lal Qila, and Saipai are older, are the settlements of Ochre Coloured Pottery (OCP) users. Nearly 110 settlements of this culture are known (Lal 1984a;28) The distribution area of this culture is larger than the late Harappan. In contrast to the late Harappan which are confined to the upper doab only, OCP settlements are found in the middle doab as well. (sites: Atranjikhera, Lal Quila and Jakhera). A few sites like Pariar (district Unnao) and Sringaverapura (district Allahabad) have been found in the lower doab as well. Most of the settlements are located on the river banks and in size and spacing they are very much like late Harappan. The Cultural deposit is, once again, very small (0.5 to 1.5m.) indicating that the settlements were of shorter duration.

Excavations at Ambakheri (IAR, 1963-64, 53-55), Baheria (IAR, 1966-67, 43-44), Bahadarabad (IAR, 1971-72, 34), Jhinjhana (IAR, 1962-63, 70) and Saipai (IAR, 1971-72, 46-47) show that OCP depostis at these sites were mixed with brown earth, *Kanakar* and sand which came out in lumps during the excavations. The strata were quite disturbed and no sign of regular habitation was found. In case of Bahadarbad the occupational debries were found 6.5 m. below a deposit of rubble, sand and earth. Considering the nature of deposit B.B. Lal (1968) suggested that a large part of the doab, for some reasons, got submerged in water for a considerable period of time. The scientific studies of the OCP sediments from the sites of Atranjikhera, Nasirpur, Ambakheri and Jhin jhana (Agrawal *et. al.* 1977) indicates that the OCP deposits were affected by the floods.

Painted Grey Ware Culture

The Painted Grey Ware (PGW) Culture occupies a very significant place among the proto-historic cultures of India not only because of its claimed association with Aryans (Lal 1954-55; Gupta and Ramchandran 1976) but also because of the first regular use of iron. The potential for urbanization in the Gangetic plain came with this culture.

Although PGW was first discovered at Ahichchhatra in 1944 (Ghosh and Panigrahi 1946) its full cultural significance was realized only after B.B. Lal's excavations at Hastinapura (Lal 1954-55). Lal not only excavated Hastinapura, but carried out a planned exploration in the upper Ganga and Sutlej basins and located a further 31 PGW sites. Since then explorations in the Indo-Gangetic divide and in the Gangetic plains have brought to light more than 710 PGW sites. The cultural associations in different areas are slightly different but we shall confine ourselves only to the distribution pattern of the population. We shall also see that how in different ecological zones the PGW people adjusted themselves. First we shall take up the Indo-Gangetic Divide.

Indo-Gangetic Divide

In the Indo-Gangetic Divide altogather 370 settlements have found (excluding the sites in Jaipur and Bharatpur distrticts of Rajasthan). Of these 14 are located in Bahawalpur region of Pakistan, 10 in Rajasthan along the Ghagghar 82 in Punjab and 264 in Haryana.

In Bahawalpur region all the 14 sites are located between in India border and the town of Kala Par sarai. The western most site is Gharanwali. The sites are located right into the bed of river Hakra. Similar is the situation on the Indian side of the river i.e. the Ghagghar. Mr. Ghosh has observed that Harappan sites were located overlooking the valleys while the later sites are on the river channel proper where the last bit of dwidling water supply could be used (Ghosh 1952, 37-42).

A size analysis of PGW settlements on the Hakra shows that of the 14 settlements 9 (65%) are below 2 hect., 4 are between 2 and 4 hect. and only one is somewhat considerably big (13.7 hect.) Since no measurement of sites in Rajasthan area is available their size is not known but looking at the data from Bhawalpur region and adjoining Haryana we may reasonably guess that it should not have been any different from the above two areas.

In the region of Punjab and Haryana we see that the districts of Bhatinda, Sangrur, Faridkot, Ferozpur and Kapurthala (in Punjab) and Rohtak, Mahendragarh, Bhiwani, Sonepat and Hissar (in Haryana) were least attractive or not attractive at all during the Painted Grey Ware period. It may be pointed out that a few of these districts were quite densely populated during the Harappan period. For example in the district of Bhatinda in a comparatively small area there were at least five settlements of the size of cities and six towns but in PGW period we find only a few small size villages.

In Punjab most of the settlements are found either in Sutlej catchment areas- district of Gurdaspur, Jallandur and Ludhiana or the Ghagghar catchment area - districts of Patiara Sangrur etc. These sites are mostly located on the river banks, away from the flood areas.

In Haryana of 262 settlements 229 (87%) are located in the districts of Ambala, Kurukshetra, Jind and Karnal. These settlement were mostly on the river banks which are mostly dry now. During this period the *khader* bench of Yamuna and Saraswati were also occupied. Most of the sites fall in 400 to 1100 mm. rainfall zone with a greater concentration in 500-700 mm. rainfall zone. A few

Table-6

Average Population per sq. Km. During Different Cultural Periods

Cultural Period	G-R Doab	Y-R Doab	Mean
P.G.W.	3.34	1.39	2.35
N.B.P.W.	7.88	4.46	6.15
Early Historic	16.13	9.60	12.82

Table — 7

Average Spacing (in Km.) of settlements of Different Culture In the Ganga-Rind Doab, Yamuna-Rind Doab and Kanpur General

Cultural Period	Ganga-Rind Doab	Yamuna-Rind Doab	Kanpur
P.G.W.	11	16	13
N.B.P.W.	8	10	9
Early Historic	6.5	8	7.5

Table - 8

Percentage of Villages and Population in different size categories from second millennium B.C. to the present.

Cultural Periods/ Year	Less than 500		500-999		1000-1999		2000-4999		5000-9999	
	1	2	1	2	1	2	1	2	1	2
P.G.W.	82.60	59.60	15.22	32.92	2.17	7.47	--	--	--	--
N.B.P.W.	78.78	52.51	16.66	27.65	4.44	13.59	1.11	6.26	--	--
Early Historic	59.57	28.49	26.49	34.34	12.05	30.74	1.41	6.43	--	--
1901	63.80	30.00	23.00	30.20	10.70	26.90	2.40	12.40	0.10	0.50
1911	67.25	28.28	20.99	25.16	9.89	22.44	1.82	8.45	--	--
1921	68.60	35.50	21.50	32.40	8.40	23.90	1.40	7.50	0.10	0.70
1931	67.05	26.92	21.85	24.99	8.13	19.12	2.01	8.40	0.05	0.54
1941	61.41	20.14	25.35	21.97	10.45	17.63	2.72	8.90	0.10	0.67
1951	55.60	24.30	27.40	30.80	13.40	27.60	3.60	17.30	--	--
1961	46.30	18.10	30.90	29.50	17.90	32.90	4.05	16.07	0.40	2.80
1971	36.70	12.20	33.00	25.90	22.00	33.80	7.50	22.09	0.80	5.20

1. Percentage of Villages in this class to the total number of villages.
2. Percentage of Population in this class to the total population.

Table - 2
Variation in Population Density per Sq. Km. in Different Tahsils of Kanpur District

Tahsils	1881	1891	1901	1911	1921	1931	1941	1961
Bilhor	212	211	177	162	160	177	190	241
Kanpur	399	448	467	419	421	419	673	1142
Sheorajpur	213	209	209	184	—	—	—	—
Narwal	182	177	166	168	—	—	—	—
Akbarpur	175	163	172	156	158	155	174	239
Derapur	151	148	190	169	168	159	177	238
Bhoganipur	122	135	150	139	137	146	173	228
Ghatampur	130	135	143	138	140	143	171	233
Rasulabad	176	171	—	—	—	—	—	—

(Tahsils 1—4 (from top) are in the Ganga-Rind doab, 5 is spread both in the Ganga-Rind and Yamuna-Rind doab and 6-9 are in the Yamuna -Rind doab. Tahsils 3, 4 and 9 were broken in subsequent years and merged in various tahsils)

Table -3
Average Population Density in the Ganga-Rind doab and Yamuna-Rind Doab

Year	Ganga-Rind Doab	Yamuna Rind Doab
1881	236	151
1891	242	150
1901	238	163
1911	218	151
1921	246	151
1931	251	152
1941	346	174
1961	541	235

Table-4
Average Spacing (Km.) of settlements in Kanpur District (Based on Census of India 1971,Series 21, Part II A).

Tahsil	Spacing
Bilhor	1.80
Kanpur	1.78
Akbarpur	2.05
Derapur	2.03
Bhoganipur	2.02
Ghatampur	2.32

(By taking Akbarpur tahsil common for both the regions average spacing in the G-R doab is 1.8 Km. and in the Y-R doab 2.2 Km.)

Table - 5
Estimate of Population in Kanpur During different Cultural Periods

Cultural Periods	Population in G—R Doab.	Percentage	Population in Y-R Doab	Percentage.	Total Population
P.G.W.	10155	70.0	4354	30.0	14509
N.B.P.W.	23968	66.0	13941	34.0	37909
Early Historic	49045	62.0	30032	38.0	79077

On the basis of physical and chemical characteristics, soils of Kanpur district can be divided into six categories. Each of these include several soils of similar nature with only minor variations (Agrawal and Malhotra 1952). Kanpur type I (recent Alluvium), type II (Ganga Upland) and type III (Ganga Lowland) occupy the whole area between the Ganga and Rind. These are good for agricultural purposes and easily managable. Kanpur type IV (Central Lowland), type V (Yamuna Flat) and type VI (Yamuna Upland) occupy the area between Rind and Yamuna. These soils are yellow to dark in colour. Because of poor drainage, especially in the type IV and V at places water logging takes place. Consequently a large portion of tract has become alkaline. The p^H value ranges from 7 to 11. Along the rivers Sengur due to excessive drainage ravines have been formed. These soils contain very little alluvium and are calcareous. For agricultural purposes these soils are not as good as Kanpur types I, II and III.

The district contains a large number of depressions in which water accumulates during rainly season and shallow lakes are formed. These are found South of Bilhor, central portion of Derapur eastern part of Narwal and northern part of Ghatampur tahsil. The most important ones are at Jahangirabad in Ghatampur; Harnu, Itali, and Naila in Bilhor; Rasulpur and Gogamau in Akbarpur and Rahnas in Kanpur tahsil.

The climate of the district is same as that of the doab. But it is important to mention about the rainfall. Average annual rainfall in the district is nearly 80 cm. Variation from tahsil to tahsil is slight but quite significant when it comes to the pattern. Tahsils in south along the Yamuna namely Dearpur and Bhoganipur receive an average 6-10 cm. less rainfall than the tahsils in north along the Ganga namely Bilhor and Kanpur.

On the basis of soils, rainfall, drainage and other microlevel variations Kanpour district can be safely divided into two ecological zones - the Ganga - Rind doab and the Yamuna-Rind doab, taking river Rind as dividing line. Ecologically Ganga-Rind doab is much more attractive and hospitable for human settlements than the Yamuna-Rind doab.

Present Pattern of Population Distribution

Although the external boundaries of the district remained intact since the separation of Fathepur in 1825, extnsive internal changes that have taken place in the matter of tahsils arrangements, specially in 1860, 1894 and 1911 render it impossible to establish a satisfactory comparison of the results obtained at successive enumerations in various tracts before 1901. In the Census Report of 1853 figure are given for no less than 12 tahsils the total of which comes down to 9 in 1860 and subsequently 8 in 1894 and finally six in 1911. Consequently the tahsils of Bilhor, Derapur, Bhoganipur and Kanpur no longer represent the same area as at the time of 1901 census and previous enumerations. It is, therefore, necessary to keep in mind that the earlier statistics of these tahsils refer to them as they were prior to the reconstitution of their present area. Because of the availability of better data the figures of 1891 have been adjusted according to 1894 and of 1901 according to 1906 adjustment.

Table 2 gives the detail breakup of the population per sq. Km. in different tahsils of Kanpur from 1891 to 1961. The tahsils of Bilhor, Kanpur and Sheorajpur are along the Ganga and occupy the area of Ganga-Rind doab. The tahsils of Derapur, Bhoganipur and Ghatampur are in the Yamuna-Rind doab. The tahsil of Akbarpur is spread both in the Ganga-Rind and Yamuna-Rind doab.

The distribution pattern of population in different tahsils of the district shows that the density per sq. Km. in the tahsils in the Ganga-Rind doab is greater than those in the Yamuna-Rind doab. When we estimate an approximate density pattern in the two areas taking Akbarpur tahsil common for both, we find that right from 1881 the density in the Ganga-Rind doab has been much more than in the Yamuna-Rind doab (Table 3). The density per sq. Km. in the Ganga-Rind doab varied from 218 to 541 while in the Yamuna-Rind doab it was from 150 to 235 only. This clearly indicates that Ganga-Rind doab is much more attractive for the human settlements than the Yamuna-Rind doab.

The distribution pattern of the villages in different categories (Table 8) shows that from 1901 it was fluctuating. But there remained a consistency in the size and number of settlements. Smaller villages were highest in number. They constituted more than 60% of the total and the population living in these villages varied from 28.28% to 35.5%. But after 1941 with the increase in population the size of villages also several well known cities and towns were located on the Ganga. It is important to remember that even in modern times no significant city or town has developed on its own on the bank of the Yamuna in the above mentioned stretch. Thus, it can be safely concluded that the relative unattractiveness of the Yamuna has continued from early times.

The size of nearly 80% settlements remained at the level of small villages with a population less than 500. Only 20% settlements were big enough to accommodate a population between 500 and 1000 or in few cases even more. During the period only a few sites like Atranjikhera, Hulas and Radhan were big enough to accommodate a population more than 1500.

In general, the settlements on the major rivers like the Ganga were bigger in size than on the tributaries. On the Ganga the settlements were as big as 8 hect. While on the tributaries they were 2 to 3 hect. When a settlement on the tributary reached to a size of 2-3 hect. (400 to 600 population) there was a tendency towards fission. They could not grow bigger as the settlements on the Ganga. The fissions of settlements on the tributaries was perhaps due to the non-availability of sufficient good agricultural land in their vicinity. Further, the soils found along the tributaries are not as fertile as along the Ganga. This would not only have given comparatively less yeild but also demanded a longer fallow period to regain the fertility. Smith (1972, 415) explains that the settlements of long fallow cultivation tend to be small, though the total population in the region may be large. The basic concept is that the long fallow cultivation does not so much limits the size of total population (within the limits of environments carrying capacity) as it limits the size of local units. The presence of large nucleated settlements on the Ganga is probably due to the greater availability of good cultivable land and shorter fallow periods.

The average spacing between the two settlements was between 11 and 13 Km. However, the smaller settlements are more closely spaced than the bigger ones.

Relationship Between the Present and Past Pattern of Population Distribution

India is known as the country with many customs and traditions which continue from the earliest times. My interest in palaedemography lead me to study the pattern of population distribution in the Ganga-Yamuna doab in the second and first millennium B.C. at an intensive level and compare it with the present pattern of population distribution in the same area. For this purpose it was necessary to have reliable data both for the ancient and modern period. For this purpose detailed archaeological data was collected for district Kanpur (in the middle of the Ganga-Yamuna doab) which represents doab at a small scale with all its characteristic features. On the comparison of data for ancient and modern periods it was found that in the study area and for that matter in the whole of the Ganga-Yamuna doab the change in the pattern of population distribution is more of quantitative nature rather than qualitative. The data for the early period comes from my own archaeological fieldwork in the study area and for the modern period from the decennial Census Reports of the Government of India.

Before we proceed further it will be helpful to have an idea of the ecology of the area as it has been the major factor in influencing the pattern of population distribution.

Ecology of Kanpur District:

Kanpur district forms a part of the middle Ganga-Yamuna doab and the extremities of the district are marked by the parallels of 25° 26', and 26° 28' N. latitude and 79° 31' and 80° 43' E. longitude. Total area measures 6167 sq. Km.

Kanpur is bounded in the north and south by the rivers Ganga and Yamuna respectively while towards the east by Fatehpur district and in the west by Farrukhabad and Etawah districts. The topography of district resembles very much like doab. Beside the Ganga and Yamuna there are six tributaries - Isan, Pandu, Northern Non, Rind, Sengur and Southern Non, which flow through the district. Except for the Ganga and Yamuna all other rivers rise from the marshy plains of the upper doab. The rivers Northern Non, Pandu and Southern Non carry very little or no water during the summer. Land along the Yamuna and Sengur is badly dissected and this bad land topography extends upto 5 Km. from the banks of the rivers.

The river Rind can be taken as the main water parting line. The water of north of the Rind goes in the Ganga while of the south (including Rind) goes in the Yamuna.

sites located on the Saraswati flood plain in Sirsa district show their extension into 300-400 mm. zone.

An analysis of 28 single culture settlements presented by Suraj Bhan (1977) shows that 13 (57%) were small villages having population upto 500. Seven (25%) measured between 2 and 5 hect. that could have accommodated population between 500 and 1200 people. Five settlements are said to be upto to 10 hect. or even more. This would mean that these settlements had the population over 2000. The spacing of settlements in densely populated areas like that of Ludhiana, Ambala, Karnal and Kurukhsetra was 7 to 9 Km. while in less populated areas it was 10 to 12 Km.

Upper Ganga Plains:

In the upper Ganga plains we are certianly in better position regarding our knowledge about the distrtibution, size, spacing and locational patterns of settlements during PGW period and its relationship with then environmental conditions. This has been due to the detail study carried out by the present author towards understanding the relationship between man and the environment during the first and second millennium B.C. (Lal 1984a, 1984c).

In all 279 settlements of PGW period have been discovered. Of these 256 (92%) are confined in 12 districts of the doab and as a matter of fact, upper and middle part of the doab (upto Kanpur district) was the main populated area during this period. At other palaces (districts 13 to 25 in the table 1) only a few sherds of PGW have been found; without any separate cultural deposit of its own. In these cases at the most we can say that PGW travelled to these sites in its later phase of survival and the contexts in which it has been found confirms this. On the basis of evidences available to us we can definitely say that the core culture area of the PGW people was the Ganga-Yamuna doab.

The PGW settlements are found on the major rivers as well as on the tributaries. Nearly 90% of the settlements are on the river banks, (Lal 1984c). However, it may be pointed out that a very few settlements are found on the Yamuna, especially downstream from Agra. Nearly 10% of the settlements have now moved away from the rivers. We shall now look at these settlements and their environmental locations in detail.

During the PGW period in the Upper Ganga plains also, the rivers played an important role in the selection of habitation site. The settlements in the areas of inundation are on high terraces, overlooking the rivers and its vast flood plain. The terraces vary in height and steepness from a series of undulations to more or less level patches of cultivation. These patches are often inundated, providing fresh alluvial deposit which are rich in nutrients and are extremely good for agriculture. The flooding during OCP period shows that seasonal flooding was quite common. The PGW people seem to have learnt from this experience. This may explain why on the Ganga we find settlements only on the higher bank and not along the flood plain. On the tributaries the settlements are found on both the banks. This can be explained by the fact at tributaries have levees and flood plains on both the banks. When there is a levee on the right bank the flood plain lies in front of it on the left bank. After some distance the position reverses i.e. a levee on the left bank and the flood plain on the right.

The settlements which are away from the rivers during PGW period are near large low -lying areas which were regular lakes in the past. In the Gazetteers and Census reports of nineteenth and early twentieth century the swampy areas near Jahangirabad, Bhadaras, Auron and Uttha in Kanpur district are mentioned as regular lakes. The PGW sites which are away from the rivers are located on such lakes and in the past the doab was full of such lakes. The location of settlements on such lakes must have been due to the availability water, acquatic food from the lakes and the fresh alluvial soil around them. But in comparison to the riverside settlements the habitational deposit on these lakeside sites is less, showing that soon after, the settlers might have realized the disadvanteages on being away from the rivers and deserted the site.

The lack of settlements on the Yamuna, especially downstream from Agra and sparseness on the Sengur can be partially explained by the presence of *Kankary* ravines which extend upto 5 Km. away from the banks. The soils along the rivers are most unpromising and this results in sparseness of settlements even tody. Downstream from Agra only three worth mentioning settlements have been found. These are Musanagar (in Kanpur district), Reh (in Fatehpur district) and Kausambi (in Allahabad district). In fact, no ancient city or town was located on the Yamuna between Agra and Kausambi, a distance of nearly 650 Km., while in the same distance increased to the extent that in 1971 census there were only 36.7% of the total village which had a population less than 500 persons and the population living in them constituted only 12.2% of the total. There has been a steady increase in the size of settlements with the increase in population due to health care and timely relief at the time of famine, drought etc. Beside the population increase since 1941 the reason for the increase in the size of settlements is also the non-availability of hinter land for the growth of new settlements.

Now it would be interesting to have a look at the spacing pattern among the settlements. In the district total number of settlements is 1898 which are classified in different categories and distributed in all the six tahsils.

The average spacing between the two settlements in the Ganga-Rind doab is 1.78 Km. while in the Yamuna-Rind doab it is 2.2 Km. very clearly showing that settlements in the former area are more closely spaced than in the later.

Population Distribution During the Second and First Millennium B.C.

During the PGW period total population of Kanpur district was 14,509 of which 10,155 (70%) was distributed on 31 settlements in the Ganga-Rind (Y-R) doab and 4,354 (30%) was distributed on 15 settlements in the Yamuna-Rind (Y-R) doab. The average population was 2.35 persons per sq. Km. It was 3.34 in the G-R doab. The pattern of population distribution shows that at least on 13 sites the population remained at the level of PGW period. Most of these sites are on the tributaries. Settlements on the Ganga show a remarkable increase in size. Total increase insome cases was more than 250 percent. The mean population per settlement was 383 persons (Table 5/6). The average population per sq. Km. in the district was 6.15 persons. It was 7.88 persons per sq. Km. in the G-R doab and 4.46 in the Y-R doab.

During the Early Historical period total population was 79.077 which was much more widely distributed as compared to the previous periods. The population in the G-R doab was 49,045 (62% of the total as compared to 66% during NBPW and 70% during PGW period). In the Y-R doab it was 30,032 (38% of the total as against 34% during NBPW and 30% during the PGW period). The density per sq. Km. in the district was 12.82. Divided into different ecological zones it was 16.13 in the G-R doab and 9.6 in the Y-R doab.

On the basis of analysis presented above we can say that in general with the increase in population for PGW to Early Historical period there has been not only increase in the number of settlements but also their size grew bigger. Most noteworthy thing is that in the Ganga-Rind doab not only the settlements are more in number but bigger in size as well. Average density of population per sq. Km. is more in the Ganga-Rind doab than in the Yamuna-Rind doab confirming the present pattern of population distribution in the study area (Tables 3,6).

Before we proceed towards a detail analysis of density and the population movement, a few words about the locations of the NBPW and Early Historical settlements. As discussed earlier the settlements of PGW are located along the rivers and lakes. But a significant change took place during the succeeding periods. During the NBPW and Early Historical period the population extended beyond the range of distribution of previous period. A good percentage of population was now living away from the rivers and not necessarily along the lakes. This could be possible because of excessive pressure on the river banks and lake shores and people were forced to clear the hinterland and go in for new settlement in hitherto new areas. The carrying capacity (within the means of exploitation) of the area must have forced people to move out. But it must be emphasized that none of the settlements in comparatively less hospitable areas could develop to a big size. The population pressure in attractive areas during the Early Historical periods can be understood by the fact that completely new territories were opened which were not considered at all during early period.

The spacing of settlements in general during PGW, NBPW and Early Hisorical period was 13, 9 and 7 Km. respectively. But when it is seen at the level of two different ecological zones, the picture is completely different. In the Ganga-Rind doab the spacing between the settlements during PGW, NBPW and Early Historical periods was 11, 8 and 7 Km. respectively while in the Yamuna-Rind doab it was 16,11 and 8 Km. respectively (Tables 4,7).

Thus, the pattern of spacing also confirms a continuity in the area right from the ancient times.

Movement of Population in the Study Area

From the changing pattern of Population size

and density (Tables 5 6) during the second and first millennium B.C. in Kanpur and so in the Ganga-Rind and Yamuna-Rind doabs we can have some idea of the population movement from one area to another.

During the Painted Grey Ware period nearly 70% of the population was living in the G-R doab and only 30% in the Y-R doab. But during the Northern Black Polished Ware and Early Historical period the difference is reduced. The difference which was 40% during the PGW period comes down to 32% during NBPW period and 24% during Early HIstorical period. The narrowing gap in the area can be partly attributed to the people's migration to Y-R doab from Ganga-Rind doab. The Census Reports show that in recent past also the surplus population in the Ganga-Rind migrated to sparsely populated areas of the Yamuna-Rind doab. During the early times this was much more possible since Yamuna-Rind doab was muchless populated then.

Continuity in the size of Settlements

We shall now turn our attention towards a comparison of the past and present pattern of population distribution in different categories, according to size. Table 8 gives the percentage of settlements and population on them in different categories right from PGW period to 1971. The table clearly shows that from PGW to Early Historical period there has been a gradual increase in the size of settlements and the population living on them. The number of settlements in the smaller categories declined while the number of settlements in higher categories increased and so the percentage of population living on them. After the early Historical period's distribution pattern when we look at the Census Reports of this century (the relevant data is not available in earlier Censuses) we find that from Early Historical period to 1941 the pattern of population and settlement distribution did not change much. The stabilization in the ratio of settelements and the population living on them that came in the beginning of Christian era continued upto the first half of this century. This suggests that all through the two thousand years population on the settlements was forced to split to form a new settlement after reaching to a certain size. It was after the second World War due to the health care and timely relief provided by the Governments and other organizations at the time of famine, flood, drought and epidemics, there has been a rapid growth in the population. The unavailability of land for new settlements is resulting in the increase in the size settlements.

CONCLUSIONS

The results obtained from researches carried out in the last four decades show that the area of Indo-Gangetic Divide and Upper Ganga-plain was extremely attractive during the protohistoric period. The remains of Harappan culture discovered in the above area extended the earlier known boundary in the Indus plain. It is now very apparent that the main area of population concentration during the Harappan period was Saraswati-Ghagghar basin in which more than 600 settlements of different stages of Harappan culture have been discovered. However, the main concentration during the early and mature phase was the middle of the basin (From Bhatinda and Sangrur districts in Punjab and Hissar and Kurukshetra district in Haryana to Bahawalpur region in Pakistan). The remains of large number of small villages, towns and cities in the above area show that it was quite well populated. Most of the population was settled along the rivers.

With the fluctuations in the drainage systems resulting in drying of Saraswati-Ghagghar rivers forced the population to move in the then ecologically better areas i.e. the upper part of the Indo-Gangetic Divide and Upper Ganga plain. The presence of large number of settlements of late Harappan period in punjab and Haryana confirms this. Even in the upper reaches of the Indo-Gangetic Divide population was not evenly distributed. It was rather concentrated in a few pockets. At some later stage the late Harappan crossed Yamuna probably near Saharanpur district and colonized the doab.

The smaller size of settlements during this period indicates that villages were of smaller size and perhaps there were fewer towns. Certainly there were no cities. The large number of settlements in Haryana and Punjab may not be due to large population only during the period but also due to constant shifting and drying of several river channels which must have forced people to move in some other areas and established new settlements. It seems certain that in most of Haryana and Punjab the late Harappan people came from Sraswati-Ghagghar basin except in the upper reaches especially along the Sutlej and Beas where people seem to have come from Indus region following the line of Ravi and Beas.

During PGW period the distribution of population is almost in the entire Indo-Gangetic Divide (particularly the area earlier occupied by the late Harappans) and the Ganga-Yamuna doab. It is difficult to pin point the routes of migration/immigration of PGW people if at all they came from outside. But we can definitely have some idea about the internal movement of PGW people.

The evidence from Bhagwanpura, Dadheri, Katpalon, Nagar and Manda show that PGW had an interlocking phase with late Harappan in the region of Haryana and Punjab. Also during this phase iron is not found associated with PGW. Same is not the case with PGW in other areas like Rajasthan and Uttar Pardesh. It appears that a large number of sites in Indo-Gangetic Divide having an interlocking phase with late Harappan are comparatively older. PGW people seem to have migrated in the middle reaches of the Saraswati-Ghagghar basin, which was one of the most densely populated areas during the early and mature Harappan times, from the upper reaches. In the Ganga-Yamuna doab also the PGW sites seems to be younger than in the upper reaches of the Divide. This may explain the absence of any interlocking phase between PGW and late Harappan or OCP settlements in the doab, Rajasthan and Bahawalpur.

The PGW settlements in the doab are located along the rivers and lakes. Majority of them were small village with population below 500. The preference for the areas with better ecological conditions is very clear.

A detail study of past and present population distribution patterns in the Ganga-Yamuna doab shows that right from early times there has been a preference for the areas with better ecological conditions. The area along the Ganga was much more preferred than the area along the Yamuna right from the ancient times. The changes in the pattern of population distribution in the area from ancient times have been more of quantitative nature than of qualitative.

References

Agrawal, D.P. 1971:
Copper Bronze Age in India, Delhi: Munshiram Manoharlal.

Agrawal, D.P.; M.N. Deshpande; S.N. Rajaguru and B.Roy 1977:
The ambient environment of the Gangetic sediment of chalcolithic period. *Proceedings of Indian Academy of Sciences* (E&P Sciences). 87 (A) : pp. 23-28.

Agrawal, R.R. and C.L. Malhotra 1952:
Soil Surveys and Soil works in Uttar Pradesh, Allahabad, Government Press.

Allchin, B. and A. Gaudie 1978:
Climate change in the Indian desert and northwest India during the late Pleistocene and early Holocene, In. W.C. Brace (ed.) The Environmental History of the Near and Middle East, pp. 307-18, London: Academic Press.

Calder, C.C. 1937:
An outline of the vegetation in India. In. S.L. Hora (ed) *An outline of Field Sciences in India, pp. 71-89*, Calcutta.

Chaudhury K.A.: K.S. Sarswat and G.M. Buth 1977:
Ancient Agriculture and Forestry in Northern India, New Delhi: Asia Publishing House.

Dalal, K.F. 1980:
A short history of archaeological explorations in Biskaner and Bahawalpur along the 'lost' Saraswati river, *Indica*. 17 (I): pp. 1-40.

Datt, B.1980:
Settlement Pattern of Painted Grey ware in Harayana, Unpublished Ph.D. Thesis. Kurukshetra University, Kurukshetra.

Deshpande, M.N. 1977
The Harappan settlements in the Ganga-Yamuna doab. Paper presented at seminar on *Indus Civilization: "Problems and Issues."*, Shimla, IIAS.

Dikshit, K.N. 1980:
A critical review of pre-Harappan culture, Man and Environment, 4: pp. 32-43.

Dikshit, K.N. 1981-82
Late Harappan Culture: A reappraisal, Puratattva, 13-14: pp. 55-61

Dikshit, K.N. 1982
Hulas and the late Harappan complex in western Uttar Pradesh, pp. 339-51, In. G.L. Posshel (ed.) *Harappan Civilization: A Contemporary Perspective*, New Delhi,

Erikson, K.G. 1959
The dry bed of the river Ghagghar, pp. 22-40. Hanna Rydh. *Rang Mahal*, Lund (Sweden): CWK Gleerup.

Gaur, R.C. 1983
Excavations at Atranjikhera, Delhi, Motilal Banarsidas.

Ghosh, A. 1952;
The Rajasthan desert: Its archaeological aspect. *Bulletin of the National Institute of Sciences I.* pp. 37-42.

Ghosh A. 1953
Explorations in Bikaner, *East and West* 4: PP. 31-34.

Ghosh A. 1982:
Deurbanization of the Harappan Civilization, pp. 321-24. In G.L. Possehl (ed.) Harappan *Civilization: A contemporary Perspective*, Delhi, Oxford and IBH.

Ghosh A and K.C. Panigrahi 1946:
Potteries of Ahichchhatra, *Ancient India I: pp. 37-59.*

Ghosh B., A. Kar and Z.A. Hussain 1979:
The lost course of saraswati river in the great Indian desert. *The geographical Journal*, 145 (3): pp. 446-51.

Gupta, S.P. 1982
The late Harappan: A Study in cultural dynamics, pp. 51-59, In. G.L. Possehl (ed) *Indus Civilization: A Contemporary Perspective*. Oxford & IBH.

Gupta S.P. and K.S. Ramchandran 1976:
Mahabharata: Myth and Reality, New Delhi, Agam Prakashan.

Habib, I. 1982
An Atlas of Mughal Empire, New Delhi: Oxford and IBH.

Hamilton, A.P.F. 1935
Siwalik erosion, *Himalayan Journal, 7.*

Joshi, J.P. 1981
Movement of Harappans in Circa third mellennium B.C. *Man and Environment*, 5: pp. 64-66

Joshi, J.P. Madhubala and Jasu Ram 1984:
Indus Civilization: A reconsideration onthe basis of distribution maps, pp. 511-31. In. B.B. Lal and S.P. Gupta (eds) *Frontiers of Indus Civilization*, New Delhi, Books & Books.

Joshi, J.P. 1986
Settlement patterns in third, second and first millennium B.C. in India- with special reference to recent discoveres in Punjab. In K.C. Verma et. al. (eds.) *Rtambhara; Studies in Indology*, Section V, pp. 134-39 Ghaziabad; Society for Indic Studies.

Kumar, M.M. 1978
Archaeology of Ambala and Kurukshetra districts (Haryana) unpublished Ph.D. Thesis, Kurukshetra University, Kurukshetra.

Lal, B.B. 1954-55
Excavation at Hastinapura and other explorations in Upper Ganga and Sutlej basins, Ancient India, 10-11: 5-151.

Lal, B.B. 1968:
A deluge? Which doluge? Yet another facet of the problem of copper hoard culture, *American Anthropologist, 70: pp. 857-63.*

Lal, M. 1984a;
Settlement History and Rise of Civilization in the Ganga Yamuna Doab. New Delhi B.R. Publishing Corporation.

Lal M. 1984b.
Summery of four seasons of explorations in Kanpur district, Uttar Pradesh, *Man and Environment* 8: pp. 61-80.

Lal, M. 1984c.
Archaeology of Population, Varanasi: Banaras Hindu University.

Lal, B.C. 1954
Historical Geography of India, Paris: Society Asiatique de Paris.

Madhubala, 1978:
A summary of protohistoric investigation in Punjab and emergent picture, *Indian Anthropologist* 8 (2): pp. 89-118.

Misra, V.N. 1984
Climate, a factor in the rise and fall of Indus civilization - Evidence from Rajasthan and beyond, In. B.B. Lal and S.P. Gupta (eds.) *Frontiers of Indus Civilization*, pp. 468-89, New Delhi: Books and Books.

Mughal, M.R. 1980
New archaeological evidence for Bahawalpur, *Man and Environment* 4: pp. 93-98.

Mughal, M.R. 1982
Recent archaeogical researches in Cholistan desert. In G.L. Possehl (ed.) *Indus Civilization: A contemporary Perspective*, pp. 85-95, New Delhi: Oxford and IBH.

Mughal, M.R. 1984
Post Harappan Phase in Bahawalpur district in Pakistan. In B.B. Lal and S.P. Gupta (eds.) *Frontiers of Indus Civilization*, pp. 499-504, New Delhi: Books and Books.

Mukharjee, R.K. 1938
The Regional Balance of Man: An Ecological Theory of Population, Madras: Madras University Press.

Oldham, C.F. 1874
Notes on the lost river of the Indian desert, *Calcutta* Review, 59 pp. 1-27.

Oldham, C.F. 1893
The Saraswati and the lost river of the Indian desert. *Journal of Royal Asiatic Society* (1893), pp. 49-76.

Oldham, R.D. 1886
On the probable change in the geography fo the Punjab and its rivers; A historic-geographical study. *Journal of Asiatic Society of Bengal.* 55: pp. 322-43.

Pal, Y., B. Sahai, R.K. Sood and D.P. Agrawal 1980
Remote sensing of the lost Saraswati river, *Proceedings of the Indian Academy of Sciences* (E&P Sciences). 89 (3): pp.317-23.

Pande, B.M. 1977
Archaeological remains on the ancient Saraswati. In D.P. Agrawal and B.M. Pande (eds.) *Ecology and archaeology of Western India*, pp. 55-59, Delhi, Concept Publishing House.

Possehl, G.L. 1980
Indus Civilization in Saurashtra, Delhi: B.R. Publishing Co.

Possehl, G.L. 1984
Archaeological terminology and the Harappan Civilization. In B.B. Lal and S.P. Gupta (eds.) *Frontiers of Indus Civilization*, pp. 27-36 New Delhi: Books and Books.

Punia, D.S. 1978
Archaeology of Gurgaon and Mahendragarh District (Haryana). Unpublished Ph.D. Thesis, Kurukshetra.

Puri, G.S. 1960-
The Indian Forest Ecology, Vol.2, New Delhi: Oxford University Press.

Siddiqui, B.1944
River changes in the Ghagghar Plain, *Indian Geographical Journal*, 19: pp. 137-48.

Siddiqui, B. 1945
The physiognomy of the Ghagghar Plain, *Indian Geographical Journal, 20:* pp. 87-92.

Silak Ram 1972:
Archaeology of Rohtak and Hissar District (Haryana). Unpublished Ph.D. Thesis, Kurukshetra University, Kurukshetra.

Singh, A. 1981:
Archaeology of Karnal and Jind Districts (Haryana).

Unpublished Ph.D. Thesis, Kurukshetra University, Kurukshetra.

Smith, P.E.L. 1972
Land Use, settlement patterns and subsistence agriculture: A demographic perspective. In R. Tringham and G.W. Dimbleby (eds.) *Man Settlement and Urbanism*, pp. 409-425. London: Duckworth.

Spate, O.H.K.: A.T.A.Learmonth and B.H. Farmer 1972
India, pakistan and Ceylone: The Regions. Third revised edition, Bombay: B.I. Publications.

Stebbing, R. 1922 *Forests of India*, London.

Stein, Sir Aurel 1942
A Survey of ancient sites along the lost Saraswati river. *The Geographical Journal* 99 (4): pp. 173-82.

Suraj Bhan 1973
The sequence and spread of prehistoric cultures in the upper saraswati basin. In D.P. Agrawal and A. Ghosh (eds.) *Radiocarbon and Indian archaeology*, pp. 252-63, Bombay : TIFR.

Suraj Bhan 1975
Excavation at Mitathal (1968) and Other Explorations in the Sutlej-Yamuna Divide. Kurukshetra University Press, Kurukshetra University, Press, Kurukshetra.

Suraj Bhan 1977
The protohistoric settlement patterns in Haryana. In the seminar on Indus Civilization: Problems and Issues, Shimla: IIAS.

Suraj Bhan and Jim Shaffer 1978
New discoveries in north Haryana. *Man and Environment 2:* **pp. 59-68.**

Whitecombe, E. 1972 *Agrarian Conditions in Northern Indian 1860-1900. Barkaley: Univeristy of California.*

LAND USE PATTERN DURING CHALCOLITHIC PERIOD IN THE TAPI BASIN

Vasant Shinde*

In recent years there has been growing emphasis on attempts of reconstructing economies of the prehistoric cultures. The first such a systematic and scientific approach towards subsistence economies was attempted by Graham Clark (1952) and subsequently a number of important studies have been carried out in this field. The concept appears to have gained much of its popularity over the last twenty years as a result of the work of Vita-Finzi and Higgs at mount Carmel area of Palestine who introduced the concept of "site catchment" (1971:1-37) and also with the introduction of the population pressure theory by Boserup (1965), Smith (1972) and Cohen (1977). The concept of "carrying capacity" plays an important role in reconstructing prehistoric subsistence economies (Glassow 1978).

In India the first such an attempt was made by Dhavalikar and Possehl (1974) and since then a number of well documented studies have been carried out (Chitalwala 1979, Paddayya 1982, Dhavalikar 1985, Shinde 1988, Lal 1984).

As far as the archaeological research is concerned, the Tapi basin has been neglected, save Dr. Sali's pioneering work in the early sixties. I have been working in the Tapi basin for the last several years and in order to study the settlement and subsistence patterns of the early farming communities, I surveyed the entire region and collected relevant data. There exists three distinct ecological zones and each one inflicted significant impact on the settlement and subsistence patterns of the early farming communities. The region not only gave birth to the first farmers of Maharashtra, but also attracted the early farming communities from the adjoining regions. This region served as a corridor for the movement of people from north to south and vice versa. The Malwa and the Late Harappan people in the process of migration towards south and the Jorwe people towards north, made large number of settlements in this ecologically favourable basin.

This paper attempts some preliminary assessments of the economic basis of the early farming communities in the Tapi basin. Data in this respect has been collected by means of site location analysis. The emphasis has also been placed on collection of information of soils, which played an important role in the subsistence of the early farming communities.

Topography

The Tapi basin comprises the present Dhule and Jalgaon districts of Maharashtra and the southeastern part of Surat district of Gujrat. It is surrounded by the Satpuda ranges on the north, Gujarat on the west, the Godavari basin on the south and Aurangabad district on the east. The region falls in the semi-arid zone with an average annual rainfall between 500 to 700 mm. There are three distinct geographical zones; they are as follows.

1. **The Northern Zone** — This zone comprises the hilly region of the Satpuda ranges, a large part of which is covered by a thin layer of stony coarse red soil; it is suitable for an excellent growth of pasture. However, there are patches of black cotton soil.

2. **The Central Zone** — This zone includes the region along both the banks of the main river Tapi, which is covered by the fertile layers of black cotton and alluvial soils.

3. **The Southern Zone** —This is the tributary zone which is well watered and covered by the fertile medium black cotton soil.

The region is drained by the main river Tapi and several of its perennial tributaries.

Soils

There are three distinct soil groups in the Tapi basin.

1. The deep black cotton soil— The Tapi basin is considered to be one of the most fertile units in the country mainly because

* Department of Archaeology, Deccan College, Pune - 411 006

it comprises two types of soils, viz., the deep black cotton and the medium black cotton. The deep black cotton soil occures along the banks of the main rivers. Locally this soil is called *Bhari Kali Mati.* The average thickness of this soil in this region varies from 3 to 7m. The soil is little alkaline with a pH around 8 and contain gypsum and some salt concentration. The soil has a tendency to develop deep cracks during summer.

2. The medium black cotton soil— A major part of the Tapi basin is covered by the medium black cotten soil, which is fertile. It is found in the flat regions of the southern zone and along the banks of small tributaries. It is granular to sub-granular and loamy to clayey in structure. It is alkaline with a pH around 7 and contains calcium carbonate and organic matter.

3. The coarse shallow soil —This type of soil is found at the foothills in the northern and central parts of the valley. It is coarse and stony in structure and is suitable for the excellent growth of pasture but unsuitable for the growth of crops. The soil is poor in organic matter and is acidic with a pH between 5.5 to 6.5 The soil was formed as a result of disintegration of basaltic rock.

Cultural Background

Over 110 Chalcolithic sites have been discovered in this part of the Deccan (Shinde in press). Four different Chalcolithic cultures, viz., the Savalda (c. 2000—1800 B.C.), the Late Harappa (c. 1800-1600B.C.), the Malwa (c. 1600—1400 B.C.) and the Jorwe (c. 1400—1000 B.C.) flourished here of which the Savalda culture originated in the valley whereas the remaining three cultures migrated from the adjoining regions.

A casual glance at the distribution pattern gives fairly good idea about their settlement pattern (Fig.1). In spite of the fact that the river Tapi is a perennial river and that there are stretches of good arable land along its banks, it always discouraged heavy concentration. There are a number of reasons for this but frequent occurrence of heavy floods in the Tapi is the most important one because it causes devastating effects on the settlements located along its banks. On the other hand the tributaries present entirely different picture. Most of the tributaries are perennial and flow through deep gorges, as a result they hardly overflow. It is therefore that this zone encouraged heavy concentration of settlements and they have been found to have located very close to the banks. Most of the settlements are small in size falling in the category of 1 to 2 hactare. Prakash, located on the confluence of the rivers Tapi and Gomai can be identified as a regional centre on the basis of its extent and thickness of habitational deposit.

The Tillage Potential

The black cotton soil, being fertile, is the most important single factor in the formation of the early farming communities. Considering the hardness, stickyness and clayeyness of the black soil, Kosambi (1963: 309—318), argued that the Chalcolithic people, in the absence of iron implements, might not have cultivated it. Therefore Agrawal (1982) seems to have argued that the Chalcolithic people might have cultivated only the alluvium patches along the river banks. But this does not seem to hold good as the observation made by Panikkar is contradictory. He observed "no river in central India and Deccan can develope alluvial land along its banks as they flow through uplands and therefore do not spread their fertile waters on the country side till they reach the delta region" (Panikkar 1959:37). Dhavalikar (1973:142) argued that supposing such alluvial strips existed during the Chalcolithic period and the cultivation took place, it should be borne in mind that they would not have been adequate to support the large population.

In respect of Kosambi's statement it is relevant here to consider the observations made by one British agriculturalist who travelled extensively in this part of the country and who was highly impressed by the characteristic features of the black cotton soil. He has stated "in the black cotton soils of the Deccan, where ploughing is rarely practiced, the interchange of top soil from the beneath goes on mainly owing to natural causes. Black soil has a wonderful power of absorbing water, and during the rainy season it swells, so that the whole surface is raised. Although it continues to retain throughout an abnormal amount of moisture, which is of great value to the crops grown on it, and, in short enables cultivation to be practised without irrigation, at the same time, in dry weather, it loses a large amount of moisture, and shrinks in consequence. The shrinking is in all directions; consequently very deep and wide cracks are formed, which make the land quite unsound and dangerous for riding. By the use of Dutch hoe-harrow, the cracks are filled and closed with the fine soil of the surface and by this means a regular circulation of soil is established. The cracks further fullfill the functions of ploughing, by admitting air freely into the body of the soil. The objects of ploughing are attained but nature is left to do a large share of the work, and, further she provided the means by which man can successfully carry out the remainder of it. The plentiful supply of powdery soil is useful not only for carrying on the circulation processes, but for closing up the cracks to prevent excessive evaporation of moisture from the body of under soil" (Wallace 1888:-180-181). From the above statement it is clear that the black soil ploughs itself and a small handplough is sufficient to cut the fields.

Ploughing Implements

Copper was known to the early farmers but, being scarce, the use was restricted to manufacture small and delicate implements like points, chisels, pokers, and some ornaments such as beads, bangles, anklets. They could not afford to make heavy-duty tools such as ploughshares and axes. It is, to certain extent, true that the Chalcolithic people cultivated the black cotton soil and in the absence of metal implements they might have used wooden ploughs as is done even today in

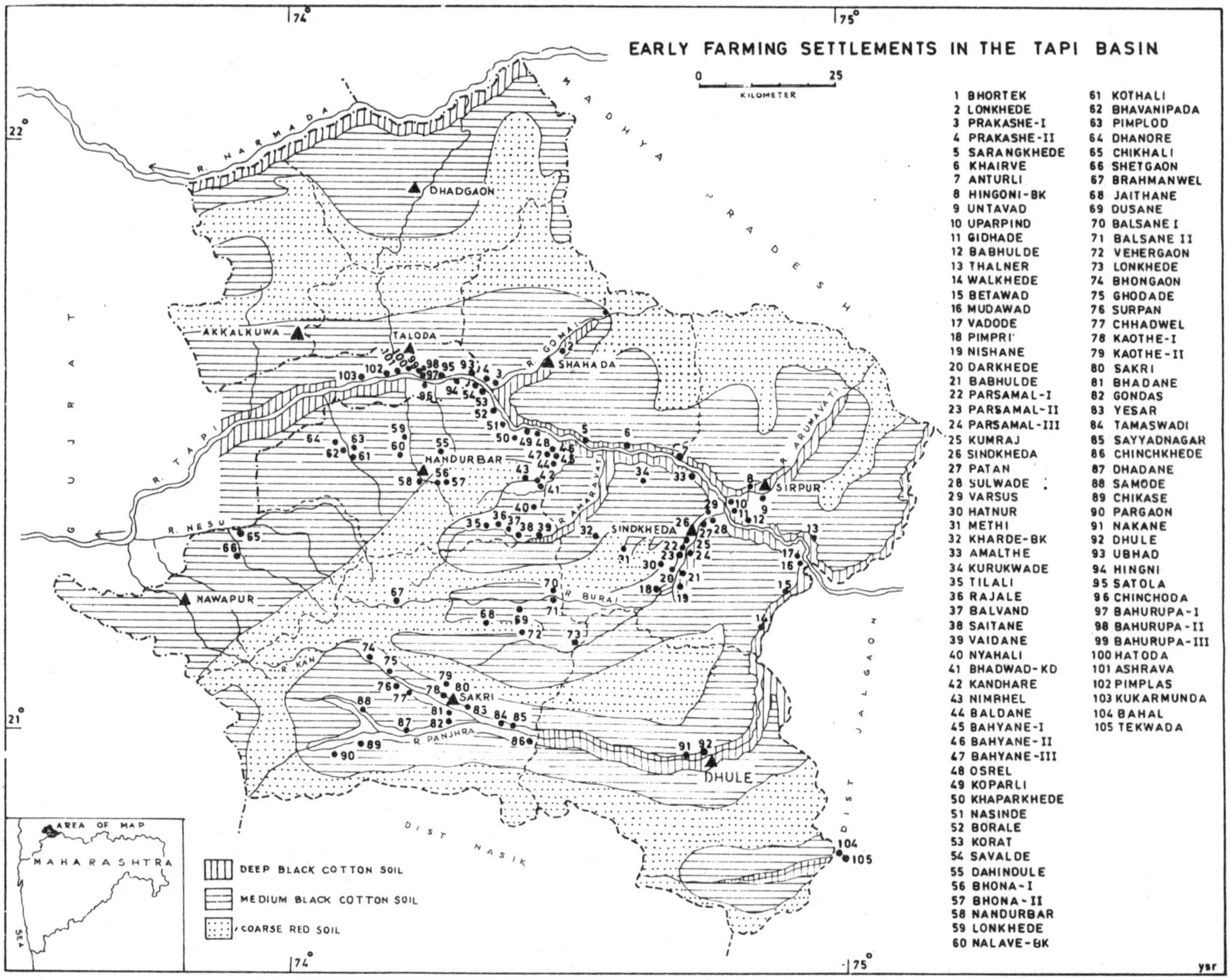

some parts of central India and the Deccan (Wakankar per. com.). The wood of Khair tree *(Acacia catechu Wild)*, which is very hard and withstands rapid wear, is used for making ploughs. A number of Chalcolithic sites have been subjected to large scale excavations, but none of them have yielded positive evidence in respect of a wooden plough, for, wood being organic, would not survive in this hot climate. It is not unlikely that the long chacedony blades, polished stone chisels and even thick antler points recovered from the excavations of many Chalcolithic sites were used as ploughshares (Pl. 1).

The excavations at Inamgaon have yielded two complete specimens of antler picks (Pl. 2), and a number of antler points which are perhaps the broken tips of such picks. These antler picks might have been used for carrying out agricultural operations. Similar antler picks have also been reported from the Neolithic levels in Britain and other European countries, but they have been interpreted as tools for mining flint stone (Clark 1952:177). There was no need to mine chalcedony stone, the chief raw material used by the Chalcolithic people for manufacturing blade tools, as it is available in the form of river borne pebbles. Therefore the use of these antler picks as hand ploughs seems to be appropriate. Even today the Bhils in this region, who have resorted to agricultural rely mostly on hoes for conducting specific agricultural operations. In the Konkan region of Maharashtra, hoes, made of Khair tree *(Acacia catechu*, Wil!d), are still being widely used. It is used more in hilly regions where it is made to work by dragging. It has been described as a missing link between a plough and pick and is most probably the original form of cultivating implement employed by man before ox or horse had been harnessed (Wallace 1888: 168). It has however to be conceded that the area that can be maintained with a hand-plough is considerably smaller than with a plough; it has been estimated to be about 0.5 hac. per head (Oates and Oates 1976:120).

In the beginning the early farmers might have practiced agriculture only along the river banks as they are generally found free from thick vegetation because the recurring floods wash away seeds and small shoots. Slowly they must have cleared the interior area with the help of polished stone axes and more effectively with fire, and expanded the agricultural activities. The use of ploughs become extremely difficult in hilly area and hence the use of digging sticks and hand-ploughs for cutting land is more effective (Dhavalikar 1985:66).

Irrigation

The region falls in the semi-arid zone with an annual precipitation between 500 to 700 mm. However, the rainfall is highly unpredictable and therefore the farmers live under constant threat of famine. In order to overcome such possible crisis, the Chalcolithic farmers practiced artificial irrigation. The evidence from Inamgaon (Dist. Poona, Maharashtra) suggest that the Chalcolithic community was a ranked society. The house of a ruling chief was located in the centre of the mound whereas the houses of craftsmen were located on the periphery. A ruling chief would organize labour, control distribution of water, collect taxes in the form of grains and store it in the public granary (Dhavalikar 1985:69). It has been observed that the construction of hydraulic works implies a central authority not only for mustering communal effort but also for controlling distribution of water (Wittfogel 1959). In India the earliest clear cut evidence for artificial irrigation comes from Inamgaon. An aerial photograph of the ancient site and surrounding area has revealed a small network of irrigation channels (Dhavalikar, Sankalia and Ansari 1988: 248). The main canal dug mainly for diverting flood water and irrigating low lying fields, can be assigned to the Early Jorwe Period which is dated to c. 1400 B.C. The canal runs in north east south west direction and measures 120 m long and 2.5 m wide. Parallel to it was constructed an embankment wall with a view to preventing the canal from silting up. But the most important evidence for the artificial irrigation facility is furnished by wheat, charred grains of which have been recovered from the excavations at Inamgaon and Daimabad. Wheat in this region can be grown only if the artificial irrigation facility is available.

Most of the tributaries in the Tapi basin are perennial and being narrow, are suitable for damming. Hence the Chalcolithic people might have exploited this conducive condition. In the absence of artificial irrigation facility, it is not possible to practice intensive cultivation and therefore the only alternative is to practice extensive cultivation. The Chalcolithic farmers, those settled on the banks of the river Tapi, were most probably compelled to undertake extensive farming, as it is not possible to dam the river Tapi for irrigation purpose. The Gazetteer of 1880 has stated—"the Khandesh valleys are open and level and the small rivers, rising in the Sahyadri hills, flow in shallow beds, blocked here and there by rocky ledges of much service in main masonry weire band *(bandhara)*, while from their flatness or gentle cross slope, large areas of land are easily commended. This irrigation from weir is chiefly practical near the hills on the upper parts of the river courses. As the rivers grow larger and draw near the Tapi, itself their beds are too deeply sunk to be easily dammed. As the Tapi flows more than 100 ft below the level of the plains, is not suited for the irrigation work" (Gazetteer 1880:11).

The river Tapi discouraged heavy concentration on its banks, but the settlements located there were large in size, chiefly due to the availability of good quality arable land. The subsistence pattern of the people living on the banks of the Tapi was also reflected in their settlement pattern. Almost every large sized Chalcolithic village had one or two small sized settlements in the radius of 1 to 3 km. These small sized settlements are located in the proximity of good arable land, however, other determinant factors such as nearness to water, defensive position, etc. were least considered. Almost all the settlements are very small, below 0.5 ha in size and the habitational deposit is very thin suggesting their temporary nature. Considering their location and temporary nature, I have interpreted these sites as "farm encampments", occupied by a group of people from large sized settlements most probably during planting and harvesting seasons (Shinde 1985). Similar pattern is noticed even today in this region. Generally a farm at a distance of 2 to 3 km from a village leads to establish such a small encampment during planting and harvesting seasons. Generally two or three small round huts of thatch and tree brances are raises for a period of 3 to 4 months every year. In the case of such settlements, the survival of evidence is likely to be very sketchy. Thus it is clear that the Chalcolithic people exploited the land lying within their catchment.

On the contrary the sites located in the tributary zone present entirely different pattern. In spite of the fact that the tributary zone encouraged heavy concentration, most of the settlements are medium in size, falling in the category of between 1 to 2 ha. save a few sites like Kaothe, Kholaj etc. It has been observed that very few sites have farm encampments lying within their catchment area, thus suggesting that very few settlement in the tributy zone practiced extensive cultivation. Most of the settlements in this zone are located very close to each other with hardly sufficient space for each settlement to practice extensive cultivation. This peculiar situation is self explainatary and leads one to infer that the Chalcolithic settlements in the tributary zone, with limited arable land at their desposal, might have produced sufficient food grains by practicing intensive farming system. They might have dammed those suitable tributaries for artificial irrigation and resorted to rotation of crops system, which, as is clear from the Inamgaon evidence, was known to the Chalcolithic farmers (Dhavalikar 1985).

Food Grains and Land Requirement

An attempt has also been made to estimate the amount of farm land required for subsistence of the Chalcolithic people. Dhavalikar and Possehl (1974; 37-46) have estimated diet of an individual as follows:

"Minimum requirement for long term survival are about 1700 calories per day, taken within a resonable balanced diet. Good health can be achieved with about 600 calories more. Based on this fact and the ethnographic record of somewhat comparable modern cultures, the estimate presented here is of 2000 calories"

The content of a kilogram of grain is approximately 3350 calories, which will feed 2.5 individuals for one day and multiplying by 365 days gives yearly requirement. The Chalcolithic people, as is clear from the Inamgaon and Daimabad evidence, grew the following crops:

Barley	—	*(Hordum vulgare*, Linn*)*
Wheat	—	*(Triticum* sp.*)*
Rice	—	*(Oryza* sp.)
Lentil	—	*(Lens esculenta*, Moench)
Horse gram	—	*(Dolichos biflorus*, Linn)
Hyacinth bean	—	*(Dolichos lablab*, Linn)
Grass pea	—	*(Lathyrus sativus*, Linn)
Pea	—	*(Pisum arvense*, Linn)
Black gram	—	*(Phaseolus mungo)*
Green gram	—	*(Phaseolus aureus*, Roxb)
Gram	—	*(Cicer arietinum*, Linn)

The total Chalcolithic population in the Tapi basin is estimated on the basis of 200 persons per hectare; the figure is based on the ethnographic record of comparable modern farming community in Nimad district of Madhya Pradesh which was carried out by Leshnik Lawrence (1967:73). The total area occupied during the Chalcolithic period was approximately 1072.138 sq. ha and the total population estimated comes to around 21,455. If considered that 1 kg. of grain is sufficient for 2.5 individuals then the total daily consumption of grain for the total population comes to around 8575 kg. : multiplying by 365 gives yearly requirement of approximately 31, 32, 430 kg.

The area required for the cultivation can be calculated on the basis of 2 ha. per person, based on the ethnographic record of the present farming community in central India. (for details see Leshnik 1967; 73-74). Considering 2 acre per person the total land required for the total Chalcolithic population of 21,455 comes to around 42,910 acre. In the absence of large scale excavations in this region the inference drawn mainly on the basis of surface collection are tentative.

Grazing Potential

Almost the entire northern hilly part of the Tapi basin is covered by the coarse red soil which is suitable for excellent growth of pasture. The evidence from this region suggests that the chalcolithic people exploited grazing potential available, for a number of sites located in the proximity of pasture have been identified as "herding units" (Shinde in press). These herding units are small in size and the habitational deposit and surface collection suggest that they were occupied for a very short period. It is quite likely that a group of people from large sized villages, with their grazing flocks, might have camped near grazing ground for a period 3 to 4 months every year. A study of the shepherd community in Sakri taluka of Dhule district revealed that a group of people from a permanent village set out with their flocks and encamp at a place where ample pasture is available; they raise temporary huts of thatch and tree branches and remain there at least for a period of 3 to 4 months. Thus it will be clear that the Chalcolithic people exploited all the possible resources available in the Tapi basin.

Conclusion

The first farming community of the Deccan flourished in the Tapi basin, the most important river valley in the Deccan. It offered favourable and conducive ecological conditions. The Savalda culture was the first farming community of the Deccan which can be dated back to c. 2000 — 1800 B.C. (Sali 1986:208). The excavations carried out at Daimabad (Dist. Ahamednagar) and Kaothe (Dist. Dhule) have revealed their dependence on domestication. A large quantity of cattle and sheep/goat bones and charred grains of *bajra* (peral millet) (*Pennseutum typhoides*) (Dhavalikar and Shinde in press), have been recovered from the excavations. On the contrary very few bones of wild animals were found. Technologically the Chalcolithic community was advanced. Their agricultural implements and ploughing techniques were infact similar to their modern counterpart.

They must have cultivated the black cotton soil with the aid of primitive wodden ploughs but they being not very effective ploughing implements, the agricultural output must have been badly affected. In the absence of iron implements, they could not raise surplus food grain, and it is one of the most important factors which prevented them from achieving the status of urbanization in this region. The evidence from excavations at Inamgaon (Dist. Poona) and Daimabad (Dist. Ahemednagar) suggests that besides cultivation, the Chalcolithic people depended heavily on plant and animal food. Hunting and fishing also played an important role in their subsistence. The agricultural activities were in full swing as long as the climatic conditions were favourable, but around 1000 B.C. there was a sudden change in the climate which affected the agricultural output. A sterile layer between the Chalcolithic and Early Historic levels at Prakash and Nevasa (Dist. Ahamednagar) suggests that around 1000 B.C. the climate became more arid and there was a decrease in the rainfall (Mujumdar and Rajaguru 1965:252). The Chalcolithic people in the Tapi and Godavari valleys were compelled to desert their settlements. But they could manage to survive for three centuries more upto 700 B.C. in the Bhima valley. The surviving phase of the Jorwe culture has been termed as Late Jorwe at Inamgaon (Dhavalikar 1979). These Late Jorwe people were more dependent on sheep/goat pastoralism rather than agriculture.

References

Agrawal, D.P. 1982

The Archaeology of India. London : Curzon Press.

Boserup, F. 1965

The Conditions of Agricultural Growth. London: Allen and Unwin.

Chitalwals, Y.M. 1979

Harappan and Post-Harappan settlement patterns in Rajkot district of Saurashtra. In *Essays in Indian Protohistory,* (eds. D.P. Agrawal and D.K. Chakrabarti), pp. 113-121. B.R. Publishing Corporation: Delhi.

Clark, J.G.D. 1952

Prehistoric Europe: The Economic Basis. London: Cambridge University Press.

Cohen, Mark 1978

Food Crisis in Prehistory :over Population and the Origins of Agriculture. New Haven: Yale University Press.

Dhavalikar, M.K 1973

Development and decline of the Deccan Chalcolithic. In *Radiocarbon and Indian Archaeology,* (eds. D.P. Agrawal and A. Ghosh), pp. 138-147. Bombay: Tata Institute of Fundamental Research.

Dhavalikar, M.K. 1979

Early farming communities of the Deccan. In *Essays in Indian Protohistory,* (eds. D.P. Agarwal and D.K. Chakrabarti), pp. 247-265. Delhi: B.R. Publishing Corporation.

Dhavalikar, M.K. 1983

Early settlement and subsistence patterns in the Deccan. *In Recent Advances in Indo-Pacific Prehistory,* (eds. V.N. Mishra and Peter Bellwood. New Delhi, pp. 381-390.

Dhavalikar, M.K. 1985

Cultural ecology of Chalcolithic Maharashtra. In *Recent Advances in Indian Archaeology,* (eds. S.B. Deo and K. Paddayya), pp. 65-73. Poona: Deccan College Post-Graduate and Research Institute.

Dhavalikar, M.K. and G. Possehl 1974

Subsistence pattern of the early farming community of Western Indian. *Puratattva* 7: 39-46.

Dhavalikar, M.K., H.D.Sankalia and Z.D. Ansari 1988

Excavations at Inamgaon, Vol-I, Part I. Poona: Deccan College Post-Graduate and Research Institute.

Dhavalikar, M.K. and V. S. Shinde

(in Press) Excavations at Kaothe in the central Tapi Basin. *South Asian Archaeology.*

Gazetteer 1880

Gazetteer of Bombay Presidencey, Khandesh, Vol. 12. Bombay: Government of India Press.

Glassow, M.A. 1978

The concept of carrying capacity in the study of culture process. In *Advances in Archaeological Method and Theory,* (ed. M. Schiffer), pp. 32-46. Academic Press.

Kajale, M.D. 1979

Bioarchaeology of the Ghod Valley. Unpublished Ph D thesis, University of Poona.

Kosambi D.D. 1963

The beginning of Iron Age in India. *Journal of the Social and Economic History of the Orient,* Vol. VI; 309-318.

Leshnik, L.S. 1967

The system of dry farming in the West Nimad district of Central India. *Journal of the South Asian Institute,* pp. 56-74.

Lal, M. 1984

Settlement History and Rise of Civilization in Ganga-Yamuna Doab from 1500 B.C. to 300 A.D. B.R. Publishing Corporation: New Delhi.

Mujumdar, G.G. and S.N. Rajaguru 1965

Comments on soils as environmental and chronological tool. In *Indian Prehistory* (eds. V.N. Mishra and M. S. Mate), pp. 248-253. Poona: Deccan College Post-Graduate and Research Institute.

Oates, David and Joan. 1976

Early irrigation agriculture in Mesopotamia. In *Problems in Economic and Social Archaeology* (ed. G. de G. Sieveking et al), pp. 109-135. London: Duckworth.

Paddayya, K. 1982

The Acheulian Culture of the Hunsgi Valley (Peninsular India)- A Settlement System perspective. Poona Deccan College Post-Graduate and Research Institute.

Panikkar, K.M. 1959

Geographical Factors on Indian History. Bombay: Bharatiya Vidya Bhavan.

Shinde, V.S 1985

Kaothe-a Late Harappan settlement in the central Tapi basin. *Bulletin of the Deccan College Research Institute,* Vol. 45: 173-175.

Shinde, V.S. 1988 Farming in the Chalcolithic Deccan. *Tools and Tillage* (in press).

Shinde, V. S.

(in Press) *Early Farming Communities in the Central Tapi Basin (Study of Settlement and Subsistence Patterns)* Munshira m Manoharlal.

Smith, P.E.L. 1972

The consequences of food production. *Addison Wesley Module in Anthropology,* No. 31.

Vita-Finzi, C. and E. Higgs 1970

Prehistoric economy in the mount Carmel of Palestine: Site catchment analysis. *Proceedings of the Prehistoric Society,* 36: 1-37.

Wallace, R. 1888

. *India in 1887.* Edinburgh: Oliver and Boys Tweedle Court.

Wittfogel, K. A .1959

Oriental Despotism A Comparative Study of Total Power. New Haven: Yale universtity Press.

Puratattva No.18 ; 1987-88

HUMAN SKELETAL REMAINS FROM MEGALITHIC VIDARBHA

S.R. Walimbe *

Peninsular India offers quite a variety of megalithic architectures like dolmens , dolmenoid cists, urns, menhirs topikals, stone circles and the passage graves. So far as Maharashtra is concerned, stone circles with cairn filling appears to be the standard type, mostly restricted to the vidarbha region. This region presents 72 of the known 83 megalithic sites in the state and are concentrated in the hilly, forested regions or wastelands. A noteworthy aspect is that, while there are numerous megalithic burial sites, the number of habitational sites is relatively small. The characteristic material equipment encountered in the excavation of megaliths and habitations comprises of a typical Black-and-Red ware of thin fabric, with a shining surface and with (or without) graffiti, a range of iron artifacts, exotic objects of bronze, gold and electrum, and remains of human and horse. The available archaeological evidence indicates that these people were essentially pastorals who flourished in vidarbha between 8th and 4th century B.C. (Deo 1985). This date bracket is on the basis of several C^{14} dates available from megalithic sites which are not far away from the sites under discussion. The following dates will emphasize the fact that the vidarbha megaliths are homogeneous both from the point of view of cultural set-up and the chronology (Possehl 1988):

Naikund	580	± 103 B.C.
	620	± 108 B.C.
Takalghat	620	± 103 B.C.
	560	± 038 B.C.
Bhagimohari	750	± 100 B.C.
	690	± 100 B.C.
Khairwada	510	± 100 B.C.
	420	± 100 B.C.

From the vidarbha megaliths human osteological evidence is reported from Mahurjhari (Rao 1973, Lukacs 1981, *In press*, Kennedy, et al. *in press)*, khapa (Rao 1970) and Naikund (Kermedy, et al. 1982). The object of this paper is to examine the recently recovered human skeletal material from three megalithic sites of this region, viz., Borgaon, khairwada and Raipur (Fig 1). Of these, the megaliths of Raipur were excavated by Deccan College Research Institute, Pune during the year 1984-85 and in 1987-88; the excavations at Borgaon and Khairwada were undertaken by Deccan College in collaboration with the Maharashtra State Department of Archaeology and Museums, Bombay, in 1980-81 and 1981-82.

Borgaon — (Long 78° 55', Lat. 21° 20') situated 42 km north—west of Nagpur, provides scanty but well preserved human dental data. Forty seven stone circles are located in this area, of which five were excavated. The selection of stone circles for excavation was primarily on the basis of its type, dimension and the thickness of deposit. Besides the material equipment distinctive of the Megalithic phase, one of the excavated stone circle (Megalith 3) yielded a unique stone trough (200 x 80 x 90 cm) at its centre .

Khairwada — (Long. 78° 29', Lat. 21° 0') is situated on the bank of the perennial river Dham, 45 km north-west of the township of wardha. This is one of the few notable occupational sites of the vidarbha region. Khairwada has an area of 1,07,000 sq. mt., largest so far reported in the vidarbha megalithic belt, and also has the largest number (1496) of megalithic burials (Deo 1985). The burial customs of the megalithic builders from khairwada are diverse. In addition to the standard type of stone circle with cairn filling (Plate 1), another variety is evident where the stone circle is filled with loose pebbles without any cementing material. This type of stone circle, named *Khairwada type* (Plate 2), has so far not been reported from any of the 72 megalithic sites of the vidarbha region. Interestingly, from this type of stone circle there is no evidence of the typical Black-and-Red ware of the megalithic culture.

* Department of Archaeology, Deccan College, Pune 411 006

Instead, the pottery from these burials appears to be closer in fabric to that of the Early Historic period which suggests a later date to this type of burial. The two types of burials occur intermixed in the area and are not isolated. During the course of excavations five stone circles were exposed, of which two belong to the Khairwada type and the rest of standard type.

Raipur — (Long. 78° 58', Lat. 21° 4.3') is situated 18 km west of Nagpur on the left bank of the river Wurma, a tributary of Wardha which in its turn belongs to the Godavari system. At the site 223 megalithic stone circles are identified which are grouped in four localities. Four megaliths were excavated. One of the megaliths has a cist at its centre while a smaller circular chamber of large boulders was discovered in another stone circle (Plate 3). Both cist and chamber within stone circle are nen types of megalithic construction, not known so far in the Nagpur region. It is, however, surprising to note that both the cist and the chamber were devoid of any mortal remains. In both the cases, the dead was buried outside the central structure, near the periphery of the outer stone circle. Among other notable discoveries are the jaw bones of a young horse alongwith its ornaments and iron bit, painted Black-and-Red ware and painted Black-on-Red ware.

Methodology

Preservation is extremely poor in all the three skeletal series and no bone is complete. Sex determination is impossible and age determination is possible only vaguely since it is based

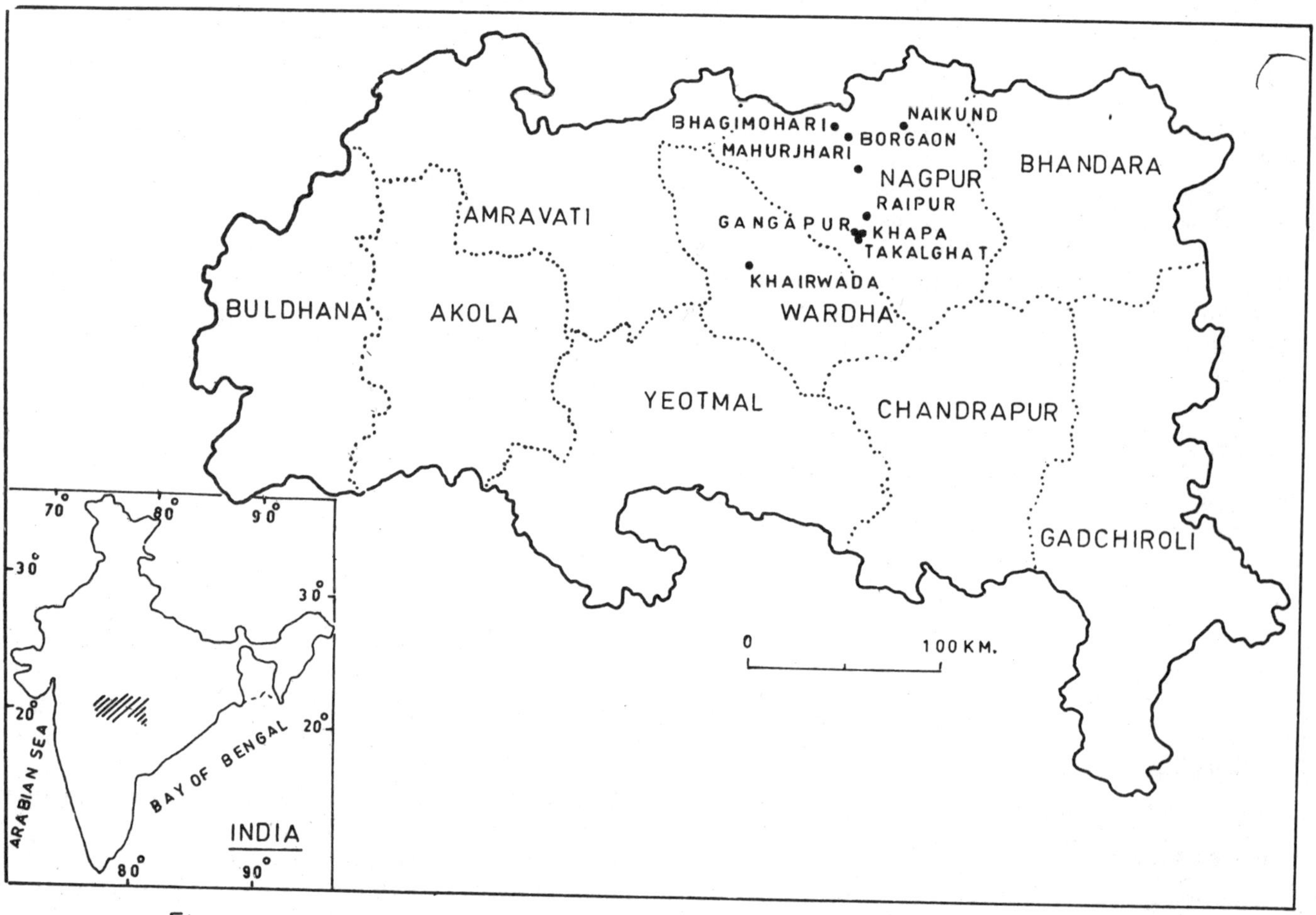

Figure 1. DISTRIBUTION OF EXCAVATED MEGALITHIC SITES IN VIDARBHA

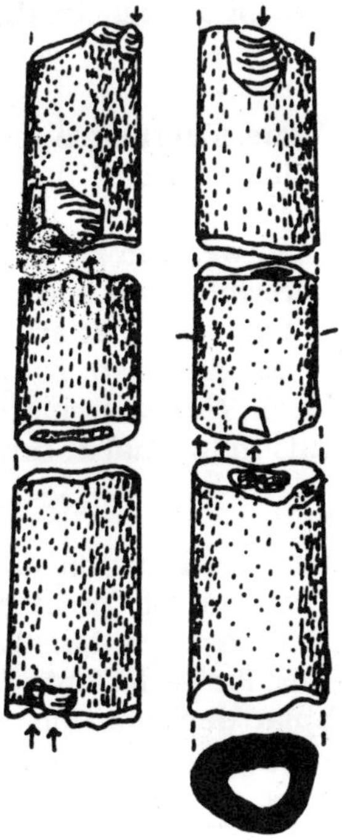

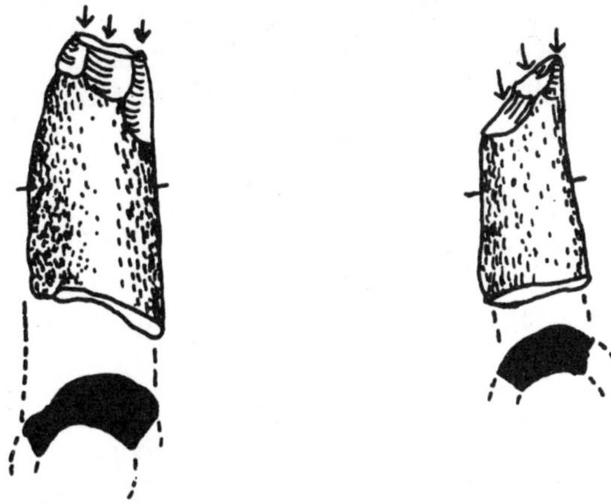

Figure 3. CUT-MARKS : Megalith 1, Locality II, Khairwada

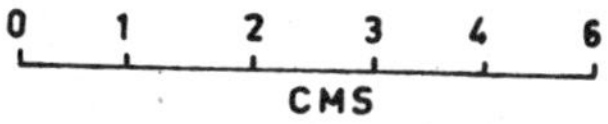

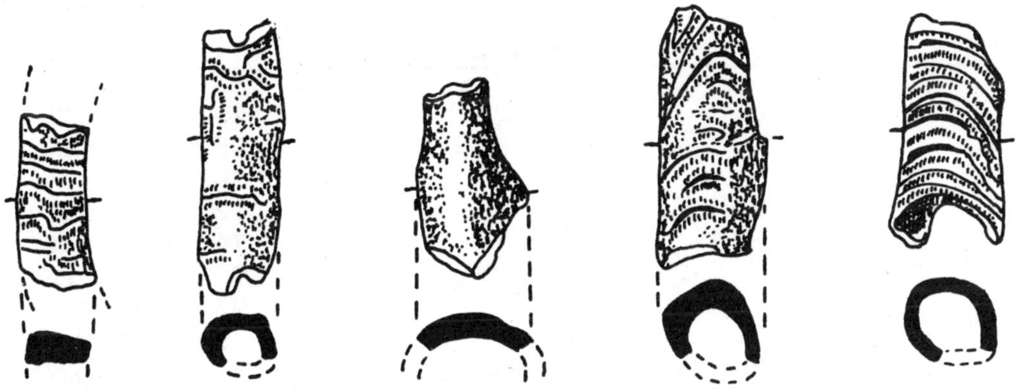

Figure 4. FIRE EXPOSURE MARKS: Megalith 1, Locality III, Khairwada

on the size and appearance of the bones. In some cases wear pattern on dentition provides a clue to assign 'adult' status to the individual. Well preserved dentition enables observation on calcification progress, following Hunt and Glesler (1959) and Schour and Massler (1940), to give more precise age estimate for the Borgaon specimen. Long bone diaphyseal diameters are measured following the techniques recommended by Martin and Saller (1957). Morphological variations of deciduous and permanent dental crowns are observed employing the standardized classificatory categories (Dahlberg 1949, 1963; Hanihara 1963, 1966, 1968; Hanihara and Minamidate 1965; Harris and Bailit 1980; Hellman 1928; Scott 1977, 1980; Turner 1970) Following Moorrees (1957) dental crown dimensions are recorded which include maximum crown length or mesio-distal diameter (MD) and maximum crown breadth or buccal-lingual diameter (BL). Same method of measurement is employed in the determination of deciduous and permanent dental crown dimensions. MAX-CAL electronic digital caliper with an accuracy upto 0.01 mm is used for taking dental measurements. According to the methods prescribed by Wolpoff (1971) computation of dental indices is attempted, which include crown area [MD x BL], crown index [MD/BL x 100] and crown module [(MD + BL)/2]. The diagnosis of skeletal pathology is based on Brothwell (1971).

Preservation and skeletal inventory for each individual is described below. Note on possible morphometric observations is added at appropriate places.

Borgaon

Of the excavated burial Nos. 3, 7, 29, 35 and 36, only two, viz., megaliths 3 and 7 had human skeletal remains in the form of isolated teeth. Most of the material that has been reported here is from megalith 7, the dental elements from megalith 3 being very fragmentary and beyond reconstruction except a single tooth.

Megalith 3

The isolated and identifiable tooth from this megalith is maxillary second molar, M^2—, the mesial (3) surface of which is incomplete. The incompleteness and wear on its occlusal surface precludes side derermination and precise metric observation. The hypocone pattern of this tooth may tentatively be classified as grade 2 (4-, Dahlberg standard). The wear pattern suggests adult status of this individual at time of death.

Megalith 7

The dental elements from this burial are better preserved. It consists of nineteen teeth, 4 deciduous and 15 permanent. Maxillary dentition includes Ldm^1— $RLPm^3$— $RLPm^4$— RLM^1— and RLM^2—. Mandibular dentition includes Rdm_1—, $RLdm_2$—, R⎺c, $RLPm_3$—, LPm_4—, RLM_1— and

Table 1.
Dental Crown Dimensions and Indices: Borgaon. Meg 7.

Tooth	Side	Crown Dimensions		Crown Indices		
		MD	**BL**	**CA**	**CI**	**CM**
Maxilla						
dml	L	7.3	9.2	67.16	79.35	8.25
Pm3	R	7.1	9.3	66.03	76.34	8.20
	L	7.0	9.2	64.40	76.09	8.10
Pm4	R	6.8	9.4	63.92	72.34	8.10
	L	6.9	9.3	64.17	74.19	8.10
M1	R	10.6	11.6	122.98	91.38	11.10
	L	10.7	11.6	124.12	92.24	11.15
M2	R	9.4	11.8	110.92	79.66	10.60
	L	9.5	11.7	111.15	81.20	10.60
Mandible	R	9.1	7.6	69.16	119.74	8.35
dm1	R	9.8	8.3	81.34	118.07	9.05
dm2	L	10.0	8.5	85.00	117.65	9.25
C	R	7.3	(8.2)	59.86	89.02	7.75
Pm3	R	7.0	8.0	56.00	87.50	7.50
	L	7.1	8.1	57.51	87.65	7.60
Pm4	L	7.4	(8.2)	60.68	90.24	7.80
M1	R	11.5	10.9	125.35	105.50	11.20
	L	11.6	10.8	125.28	107.41	11.20
M2	R	11.1	10.4	115.44	106.73	10.75

Note : Estimates are bracketed.

RM_2—. A few dental chips probably represent maxillary canine. The dental crowns are completely calcified in all thc cases and roots in various stages of development. The deciduous elements exhibit considerable wear. The deciduous first molar, Ldm¹—, is worn but exhibit clearly grade 3 (3m2) cusp development. Permanent RLM¹— and RLM²— show grade 3 and grade 2 of hypocone variation, respectively (grade 4 and 4—, according to Dahlberg standard). No carabelli, metaconule, protoconule, paramolar or any other variation is observed on the maxillary molars. Mandibular deciduous first molar, Rdm_1— is worn out. The $RLdm_5$—, however, exhibit 4 cusps. The RLM_1— show Y-5 pattern with trace of C-6, entoconulid (grade 1). RM_2 — also exhibits Y-5 *Dryopithecus* pattern on its occlusal surface.

The deciduous molars, upper as well as lower, show some degree of tartar accumulation. No other pathology is evident.

The odontometric data are given in table 1.

Since the dental elements are recovered isolated age estimation has to be only on the basis of calcification sequence.

The deciduous molars, first and second, appear to be functional at time of death. The dm1 loss is generally between 9 and 11 years, while dm2 is functional till 10 to 12 years. This, alongwith the wear on occlusal surface, suggests age around 10 years at time of death.

All the permanent teeth have completely calcified crowns. The second molar is the last to attain this status in the given series, the third molar germ being missing. The M2 calcification process starts at around 3 years and completes by 8 years, thereby suggesting an age above 8 years for this individual. The roots of these teeth are either not well preserved or not completely calcified. The M1 root calcification is complete by 10 years and this individual appears to have attained this status. For premolars the root development is half complete. On the basis of the above data it may be suggested that individual was around 10 at time of death.

Khairwada

Of the five stone circles excavated, three were from the locality I, and one each from locality II and III. The megalith 3 from locality I and megalith 1 from locality III belongs to the 'Khairwada type', while the rest are of standard type. All the burials had human skeletal remains though very fragmentary.

Megalith 1, Locality I

This burial contains osseous remains of an adult. The preservation is good but bone is fragementary. The skeletal remains described below are lifted from a pit within the stone circle at a depth of 2.5 meters.

The cranial bones are extremely fragmentary. The identifiable elements are two occipital medium-sized fragments preserving a portion of lambdoid border and petrous region of right side. Four other fragments remain unidentified. Left maxillary fragement is preserved which retains the crypts of central and lateral incisor and medial side of canine crypt. Superiorly the body exhibits a part of lower nasal border, the anterior nasal spine is broken. The lower jaw is also preserved for the left side from symphyseal region to the region of LPm_3. The crypts are preserved but damaged heavily from both labial and lingual sides, mostly post mortem deterioration. The inferior border is better preserved. The dental elements are missing.

No morphological or metric observations can be made on cranial preservation. The robustness of mandibular piece is to be recorded. The frament is considerably thick, (13.5 mm at LI_1— region and 16.0 mm at LC region).

The thoracic skeleton ribs or vertebra shoulder and pelvic girdle and right and left humeri are missing. Three long bone chips which do not carry and distinguishing anatomical landmark may very tentatively (?) be identified as a distal humerus. Right and left ulna are represented by the distal ends, both retain well preserved styloid process alongwith the head and shaft measuring about 1 cm in length. Proximal ends are missing for either sides thouth about 4 cm long mid-shaft segment of right ulna is preserved. Left radius is missing; however, right side bone is represented by its head and 5 cm long mid-shift segment. The bone is quite thick, maximum bone thickness, inner-outer table, measuring 4.5 mm for ulna and 4.2 mm for radius. For right ulnar mid-shaft anterior-posterior and lateral diameters are 14.8 mm and 11.8 mm, respectively. The right radius is 14.3 mm in lateral and 11.0 mm in anterior posterior diameter.

The skeleton of hand is very poorly represented only carpal bones are fairly complete. The length and breadth measurements for the preserved carpal bones are as follows:—

Bone	Length	Breadth	Breadth-length indes
Capitate	23.7mm	14.1 mm	59.49
Navicular	18.5mm	26.0 mm	71.15

Lower limb skeleton is partially represented. The left femur is the best preserved element where approximately two-fifths of the shaft, distal to the region of lesser trochanter is present. The spiral line is almost comlete and the glutial line is traceable to its three quarters of length. Linea aspera poreserved measures 73.7 mm in length. Maximum bone thickness (inner-outer table) is 9.4 mm, while in the region of lesser trochanter (on spiral line) this measurement is 11.5 mm. On linea aspera bone thickness is 12.0 mm. Mid-shaft diameter is 27.5 mm anterio-posteriorly and 28.2 mm laterally.

Right patella is almost completely preserved, slight damage has occurred to the medial articular facet area and nonarticular inferior side in posterior view. It measures 40.9 mm in length (height), 39.1 mm in breadth and 19.5 mm in thickness. Breadth-length index is 95.6. The left side sesamoid bone is missing.

Both the shin bones, tibiae, are missing. Distal end of both fibulae are retained. Left fibula is represented by its distal end with 3 cm of shaft; the lateral malleolus process and the malleolar process and 2 cm of its shaft but the region of malleolar fossa is well preserved. The right side bone preserves lataral malleolar process and 2 cm of its shaft but the rigion of malleolar fossa is damaged postmortem . Mid-shaft segment, measuring 4.5 cm. is also present from left fibula, the anterior-posterior and lateral diameter is 15.0 mm and 12.5 mm, respectively.

The skeleton of left foot is better preserved than the right. Third cuneiform and cuboid are present from left side and are undamaged. First cuneiform for either side is present, but both broken breadth-wise permitting only the length measurement. Right cuboid (?) is represented by a broken piece. Metric data on the tarsal bones are given below:

Bone	Side	Length	Breadth	Breadth Length index
Third cuneiform	L	24.1 mm	22.2 mm	92.12
Cuboid	L	35.2 mm	25.5 mm	72.44
First cuneiform	L	37.2 mm	—	—
First cuneiform	R	37.1 mm	—	—

Second, third and fourth metatarsal from right side are present but all broken distally, the damage is apparently post-mortem. From the left metatarsal set only bone preserved is the third metatarsal whose distal end is broken. Four phalanges are present; all of them belong to the first (proximal) row. First and fourth is complete and undamaged. Second and third ones are complete proximally but damaged distally. For the phalangeal bones side discrimination has not been attempted. In length measurement first palanx is 33.0 mm while the fourth is 26.3 mm.

Beside the identifiable elements described above there are a few long bone chips that are very fragmentary, as a result, reconstruction or identification is not possible. The miscellaneous bone collection, however, do not include any bone from the thoracic cage or girdles. It is observed that some of the long bones have very sharp cut-marks (Fig. 2). The evidence of flake scars alongwith the cut-marks possibly indicate an intentional human activity on the bone. Such evidence leads one to conclude that this is a fractional or secondary burial.

On the basis of the size of the long bones it appears that this individual had attained an adult status at time of death. For want of any dental or cranial data no precise age estimation is possible. The nature of mandibular or maxillary crypts suggest that the corresponding dentition was in function at the time of death.

The robustness of femoral shaft suggests maleness.

Megalith 2, Locality I

Skeletal remains of the individual buried here are recovered from the SW quadrant of this megalithic stone circle at the depth of 65 cm. The individual is represented only by two small sized neurocranial fragment and an isolated tooth.The neurocranial fragments are of extremely small size, possibly from the parietal region.

The complete and well preserved tooth is maxillary right third molar, RM^3. It measures 9.56 mm in mesio-distal diameter and 10.55 mm in buccolingual diameter. The crown height is 5.73 mm. The computation of crown indices gives the value of 100.56 for crown area, 90.62 for crown index and 10.05 for crown module. Morphologically the tooth exhibits grade 4 (Dahlberg standard) or grade 2 (Lukacs standard) of hypocone size development. Metaconule of grade 1 has been observed. No other unusual features are evident. The tooth exhibits slight tartar accumulation. For the molar tooth the process of root calcification appears to have completed prior to the death of this individual. This, alongwith the wear on the occlusal surface, suggests an age of above 25 years at time of death.

Megalith 3, Locality I

A few human bone fragments are collected from SE quadrant of this stone circle. It is represented only by fifteen small-size chips of bone. All the fragments remain unidentifiable as no anatomically distinguishing landmarks are evident.

Pathologically, the elements preserved exhibit an evidence of exposure to fire in flesh-on condition. The fragment show characteristic warping, whitening and cracking. The nature of fissuring and distortion is comparable with the evidence on the specimen Megalith 1, Locality III, which is described on the following pages.

Megalith 1, Locality II

The individual buried here is represented by a small collection of bones recovered from the SW quadrant of this circle at the depth of 70 cm. The nature of preservation is good, in the sense, weathering is minimum.

The cranial collection includes 28 small-size fragments from the neurocranial vault which do not carry any anatomically distinguishing mark. The only dental element present is isolated maxillary first permanent molar from left side, LM^1—, which is completely worn out. The mesio-distal diameter is 10.8 mm and buccolingual diameter is 11.9 mm. The values of crown area crown index and crown module are 128.52, 90.76 and 11.35, respectively. The tooth shows slight amount of tartar accumulation.

The post-cranial collection includes numerous small-sized unidentifiable fragments The femora are represented but side determination is not possible. Mid-shaft piece, about 6 cm long, of left ulna is the only identifiable element. The lateral diameter for this bone is 11.7 mm while the anterio-posterior diameter is 13.1 mm. One phalanx is preserved which too is damaged distally, but perhaps represent the first proximal for right (?) foot. The wear pattern on the molar tooth suggests an adult status of this individual.

As noted earlier, this appears to be fractional and secondary burial as is the case for burial 1 in locality. I. This fact is further confirmed following the evidence of cutmarks on most of the large, and, medium-sized fragments of long bone (Fig. 3). This may be taken as intentional human activity.

Megalith 1, Locality III

The skeletal remains of the individual buried here are recovered from two quadrants of this circle, viz. NE and SW, at various levels ranging from 85 cm to 2.4 meters. Apparently all the skeletal remains belong to the same person; this must remain a flexible statement as being derived after studying condition of preservation for various levels. Moreover, there is no duplication of parts either.

This individual also is represented by numerous small-sized fragments, not in proper articulation or orientation. The condition of bone is extremely fragmentary and all the bones show the characteristic effect of charring which are described in greater detail below.

The cranial bones preserved include the left petrous portion of temporal which is recovered from the SW quadrant. The right petrous portion of comparable size come from the NE quadrant. Six other cranial fragments represent the bones of neurocranial vault, possibly parietal, occipital and temporal region. Reconstruction is not possible for these fragments, nor side identification. No dental or gnathic elements are associated with this burial.

The post-cranial element also do not project better picture. The size of the numerous fragments present is extremely small, about 1.5 cm. each, the largest being 4.2 cm in length. Overall weight of the remains is 542 gms. This type of preservation precludes any reconstruction or morphometric observation. However, pathologically this specimen is of great importance. As noted earlier, appears to be a fractional or secondary burial. The other two individuals in this skeletal series exhibit cut-marks on pereserved bones. Here cut-marks cannot be judged, but the pieces invariably show the evidence of exposure to fire in flesh-on condition (fig 3, Plate 4). Most of the bones show fissuring, distoration, twisting and warping. Some of the fragments even show 'clean' breaks as described by Brothwell (1971, pp 18, plate 1) which could be easily mistaken for battle injuries.

Raipur

Of the four megaliths excavated two circles had human skeletal evidence. Both these stone circles belong to the locality iv. While megalith 1 contained osseous remains of atleast two individuals, only one individual is represented in megalith 3. Burial pit from the NW quadrant of megalith 1 contained one individual. NE quadrant of the same megalith yielded osseous remains of second individual. Individual from the NW quadrant is described as Specimen 1 and the one from the NE quadrant is called Specimen 2.

Specimen 1, Megalith 1, Locality IV

Skeletal remains belonging to this specimen were collected at a depth of 70 cm. The body was lying in an extended position in NE-SW orientation, the head towards north. The individual is represented by a few cranial and post-cranial elements; the parts preserved are extremely fragmentary. Observations suggest that the right side is better preserved than the left. Right humerus, right and left ulnae and radii, left femur, right and left tibiae and a left fibular fragment are represented. No bone of thoracic cage is present. No bone is complete enough for morphometric assessment. Three permanent molar teeth, all mandibular, are present. The RM_1—is completely worn out and its buccal half is broken postmortem. The RM_2—exhibit + 4 type of cusp and groove pattern and measures 10.06 mm in MD diameter and 9.32 mm in BL diameter. The computed values of CA, CI and CM are 93.76, 107.36 and 9.69, respectively. The $R(?)M_3$— crown is nearing completion. No trace of root formation is evident.

A raw stature estimate gives a figure of 5 feet 5 inches for this individual. Owing to the incompleteness of this specimen no comment on sex determination is possible. The incompleteness of M_3— crown suggests an age of less than 16 years at time of death.

Some of the long bones exhibit sharp cut-marks; however, these cuts may not convincingly be taken as intentional human activity, rather may be interpreted as breaks due to pressure of filling material of the burial pit.

Specimen 2, Megalith 1, Locality IV

Osseous remains of a second individual are recovered from the NE quadrant. The remains are scattered at three locations; a few neurocranial fragments and a maxillary molar, RM^1_, is collected from a position near the NS section (named in the text as "A" position) while a major skeletal collection, which include a few skull fragments and post-cranial elements in proper anatomical orientation, come from the EW section of this quadrant (named 'C' position). A few post-cranial pieces were also collected in between these two locations (named as 'B' position). Whether the remains, collected from three different positions, approx. 4 to 5 feet away from each other within the same quadrant, represent a single individual is a question which cannot be answered with certainty.

The individual buried in 'A' position, in east-west orientation, is better represented. Though fragmentary, most of the bone of this skeleton are present. The cranial elements include fragments of parietal, frontal and temporal (?). Incompleteness of the parts preserved precludes reconstruction. A mandibular fargment from the symphyseal region to the region of $RPm—_3$ is present.

Dentition is rather well represented and include the following : maxillary: $RLI—^1$, RLI^2—, RLC_, RPm^3—, RLm^1—, Rm^2—, and RLM^3—, mandibular: RLI^1—, $RLPm^3$-, RPm^1—, RLM_2—, and RM_3—. The maxillary central incisors exhibit double lingual ridges (grade 2). Distal marginal ridge is prominent on the maxillary canines. RLM^1— are severely worn exposing extensive secondary dentine. Features on these teeth cannot be evaluated. RLM^3—have grade 1 hypocone. RI_1— is damaged medially, only BL diameter is measurable. The cusp and groove pettern is of + 4 type in all mandibular molars. The odontometric data are presented in table 2.

Dental pathology

The molar teeth exhibit severe wear exposing dentine patches. Most of the teeth have heavy tartar accumulation. Other pathology evident is a enamel hypoplastic lesions in the from of a pit on the labial surface of RI²—. Such defects in the enamel formation are often associated with a wide variety of diseases, such as exanthematous fever or hypoparathyroidism and nutritional deficiencies, especially vitamin-D deficiency. While ecological factors are invloved, enamel hypoplasia are a relatively valid indicator of infant-childhood stress (Goodman et.al. 1984).

The girdles and the skeleton of the thoracic cage is altogether missing. No bone of the right hand is present. Fragments of the left humerus, radius and ulna are present. No carpal bone are preserved but two metacarpal elements from the left side are collected. Skeleton of the lower extremity is more complete and well preserved but for the metabones which are misssing.

No comment on sex determination is possbble. On the basis of the 3rd molar evidence an adult status may be granted to this individual.

Towards the distal end of the reconstructed femoral shaft sharp cut-marks are observed (Fig. 5). The cut-marks are not deep. The posterior edge alongwith the linea aspera exhibits sharp cuts with an evidence of chipped bone. It is not be possible to ass ess the injury as a possible cause of death. It may be recalled that the cutmarks on

Table 2.
Dental Crown Dimensions and Indices: Raipuri Specimen 2, Megalith 1.

Trade	Side	Crown Dimensions		Crown Indices		
		MD	BL	CA	CI	CM
Maxilla						
II	R	8.5	6.4	54.40	132.81	7.45
	L	8.6	6.5	55.90	132.31	7.55
12	R	6.2	5.9	36.58	105.08	6.05
	L	6.1	5.9	35.99	103.39	6.00
C	R	6.8	6.8	46.24	100.00	6.80
	L	6.7	6.8	45.56	98.53	6.75
Pm³	R	5.5	8.2	45.10	67.07	6.85
MI	R	*	*	——	——	——
	L	*	*	——	——	——
M2	R	9.5	10.2	69.90	93.14	9.85
M3	R	8.2.	9.9	81.18	82-83	9.00
	L	8.1	9.9	80.19	80.82	9.000
Mandible						
II	R	*	5.2	——	——	——
	L	4.1	5.3	23.85	84.91	4.90
Pm3	R	6.2	7.0	43.40	85.71	6.60
	L	6.2	6.9	42.78	89.86	6.55
Pm4	R	5.9	8.1	47.79	72.84	7.00
M1	R	10.2	9.5	96.90	107.37	9.85
	L	(10.3)	9.6	98.88	107.29	9.95
M2	R	*	9.1	——	——	——
	L	10.4	9.1	94.64	14.29	9.75
M3	R	9.7	8.9	86.33	108.99	9.30

Note : Estimates are bracketed.
* denotes damaged surface. Tooth is unmeasurable.

the khairwada specimen suggest a secondary nature of the burial. Same interpretation may not be applicable in this case. this essentially a primary burial for the reason that the bones were found in correct anatomical orientation. However, it is difficult to explain the absence of the bones of the thoracic cage and especially the metabones.

The skeletal inventory from the position 'B' include numerous small-sized unidentifiable bone chips. Collection from position 'C' comprises of a few small-sized neurocranial fragments and a maxillary molar tooth (RM^1— ?). Hypocone of grade 1 is seen on the occlusal surface. The MD and BL dimensions are 8.7 mm and 9.6 mm, giving the values of CA, C1 and CM as 83.52, 90.63 and 9.15, respectively.

The size and appearance of the preserved elements from A, B, and C position suggests a single individual.

Megalith 3, Locality IV

Extremely fragmentary and weathered post-cranial bone chips are collected from this stone circle. only identifiable fragments are the mid-shaft of right ulna, radius and humerus(?). No morphometric observation is possible. Any unusual pathological lesion is not evident. The preserved bone suggests an adult Status of this individual at time of death.

Conclusions

Preservation of the skeletal elements is poor for all the three sites. As a result, specific comment on the body composition of these people is difficult. Though there is limited scope for comparison, some of the megalithic sites in this region, esp. Mahurjhari, have yielded ample human skeletal data. In view of the different burial practices, the comparisons amongst these skletal series would have projected an interesting picture. The post-cranial elements from Khairwada and Raipur apparently suggest robust and stouter population.

From the megaliths of vidarbha no infant burials have been reported so far. The youngest individual is in the range of 12 to 15 years from Mahurjhari Kennedy and Burrow, in press). In this context the Borgaon individual (megalith 7) becomes the youngest one, aged around 10 years fromthemegalithic culture of this region.

The skeletal data from Khairwada provide clear evidence for fractional or secondary mode of burials. Of the five individuals described none is fully represented. Two individuals exhibit cut-marks while the other two have evidence of charring. One individual from Raipur also exhibit cut-marks on the long bone. It may be noted that the two stone circles with loose pebble filling from Khairwada yielded skeletal evidence for charring. However, this may not necessarily be indicative of an intentionally evolved method of the dispol of the dead. It is quite likely that like other megalithic populations these groups too had hunting and gathering subsistence pattern. Death occured at distant place while searching food, the osseous remains collected by the fellow-men and ceremonially buried later, this could be one possible explanation. It may be noted, however, that Qamar (1983 pp. 109) interprets the stone circles at Dumlotti, a megalithic site near Karachi city, as burials of secondary nature on the basis of evidence of calcined bones; he says after death the body was burnt somewhere else and subsequently the available bones, salvaged from the flames of fire, were intered in these graves'. In this context it may be mentioned that at Maski (dist. Raichur, A.P.), in five burials with megalithic affiliation, traces of ash were found on the pit floor over which human body was placed. The use of ash in this case is interpretated as a preservative for the skeletal remains (Thapar 1957).

Acknowledgements

I am grateful to Prof. S.B. Deo and Dr. A.P. Jamkhedkar for the invitation to study the skeletal remains and allowing to publish it. Thanks are also due to Prof. K.A.R. Kennedy, Drs. J.R. Lukacs, P.K. Thomas and P.S. Joshi for their help in various ways.

References

Angel J.L. and C.S. Coon 1954

La Cotte de St. Brelade II: Present Status. *Man* London. 54:53-55.

Brothwell D.R. 1971

Digging up Bones. London : British Museum. 1-196.

Dahlberg A.A. 1949

The dentition of American Indians. In W.S. Laughlin (ed) *Physical Anthropology of the American Indians*. New York: Viking Fund. 138-76.

Dahlberg A.A. 1963.

Analysis of the American dentition. In D.R. Brothwell (ed) *Denal Anthropology*. London: Pergamon Press. 149-77.

Deo S.B. 1985

The Megaliths: their culture, ecology, economy and technology. In S.B. Deo and K. Padayya (ed) *Recent Advances in Indian Archaeology*. Pune: Deccan College Research Institute. 89-99.

Goodman A.H., D.L. Martin, G.L. Armelagos and G. Clark 1984 Indications of stress from bones and teeth. In M.N. Cohen and G.L. Armelagos (ed) *Paleopathology at the Origins of. Agriculture*. Orlando, Florida : Academic Press 13-49.

Hanihara K. 1963

Crown characters of the deciduous dentition of Japanese-American hybrids. In D.R. Brothwell (ed) *Dental Anthropology*. London : Pergamon Press . 105-24.

Hanihara K. 1966

Mongoloid dental complex in the deciduous dentition *Anth. Soc.*. 74:61-72.

Hanihara K. 1968

Morphological pattern of the deciduous dentition in Japanese-American hybrids. *J. Anth. Soc.*. 76(3) : 114-21.

Hanihara K. and T. Minamidate 1965

Tuburculum accessorium mediale internum in human deciduous second molars. *J. Anth. Soc.* 73 : 9 -19.

Harris E.F. and H. Bailit 1980

The metaconule: a morphological and familial analysis of a molar cusp in humans. *Am.J. Phy. Anth.* 53: 349-58.

Heliman M. 1928

Racial characters in human dentition. *Am. Phil. Soc. Proc.* 67:157-74.

Hunt E.E. and E. Gleiser 1959

The estimation of age and sex of preadolescent children from their bones and teeth. *Am. J. Phy. Anth.* 13:479-87.

Kennedy K.A.R. and C. Burrow (In press)

An osteological analysis of human skeletal remains from Iron Age Mahurjhari. In S.B. Deo and A.P. Jamkhedkar (ed) *Further Excavations at Mahurjhari.* Bombay: State Deptt. of archaeology.

Lukacs J.R. 1981.

Dental pathology and nutritional patterns of South Asian Megalith builders: the evidence from Iron Age Mahurjhari. *Am. Phil. Soc. Proc.* 125 (3): 220-37

Lukacs J.R. (In press)

Dental anthropology of human skeletal remains from Iron Age Mahurjhari. In S.B. Deo and A.P. Jamkhedkar (ed) *Further Excavations at Mahurjhari.* Bombay: State Deptt. of Archaeology.

Lukacs, J.R., K.A.R. Kennedy and C. Burrow 1982

Note on human skeletal specimen from Naikund. In S.B. Deo and A.P. Jamkhedkar (ed) *Naikund Excavations* (1978-80). Bombay: State Deptt. of archaeology.

Martin R. and K. Saller 1957

Lehrbuch der Anthropologie. Band I. Stuttgart: Gustav fisher Verlog 1-661.

Moorrees C.F.A. 1957

The Aleut Dentition: A Correlative Study of Dental Characteristics in Eskimoid People. Cambridge, Mass: Harward University Press.

Possehl G.L. 1988.

Radiocarbon dates from South Asia. *Man and Environment* XII: 169-96.

Qamar M.S. 1983

Excavation of Megalithic burials at Dumlotti, Dist. Karachi. *J. Central Asia.* VI: 2:97-110.

Rao V.V. 1970

Skeletal remains from Takalghat and Khapa excavations. In S.B. Deo (ed) *Excavations at Takalghat and Khapa* (1968-69). Nagpur: Nagpur University. 60-77.

Rao V.V. 1973

Skeletal remains from Mahurjhari. In S.B. Deo (ed) *Mahurjhari Excavations (1970-72).* Nagpur: Nagpur University. 63-76.

Schour I. and M. Massler 1940

Studies in tooth development: the growth pattern in human teeth. *J. Am. Dent. Ass.* 27: 1778-93, 1918-31.

Scott G.R. 1977

Classification, sex dimorphism, association and population variation of the canine distal accessory ridge. *Human Biology.* 49:453-69.

Scott G.R. 1980

Population variation in Carabelli's trait. *Human Biology.* 52.(1) :63-78.

Thapar B.K. 1957

Maski 1954: A Chalcolithic site of the Southern Deccan. *Ancient India.* 13:4-142.

Turner C.G. II 1970

New classification of non-metric dental variations. *Am. J. Phy. Anth.* 33:144-45.

Wolpoff M.H. 1971

Metric trends in hominid dental evolution. Case western Studies in Anthropology 2:244.

AN ATTEMPT TOWARDS THE INTERPRETATION OF ROCK PAINTINGS AT KETHAVARAM, KURNOOL DISTRICT, ANDHRA PRADESH

N. Chandra Mouli*

Rock art occupies a place of great importance in the reconstruction of the socio-economic, magico-religious, and other aspects of the life prehistoric man. This is particularly so in the Indian context, where no substantial portable art objects have been discovered so far (Kumar & Narvare, 1984, Sali, 1985, Sonawane, 1985). Since the beginning of rock-art research in India progress has been made in recognizing the spatial and temporal zones of the rock paintings, alongwith reconstructing, to a certain extent, the settlement and subsistance patterns of the prehistoric people (Mathpal, 1976, 1984b & 1985, Misra *et. al* 1977, wakankar and Brooks, 1976, Neumeyer, 1978).

This paper attempts to study the rock paintings at Kethavaram to understand the possible meaning of the various themes depicted there.

The Site

Kethavaram (78°11'N and 16° 46' E) is a small hamlet, 16 kilometres to the South-East of Kurnool town close to the village Gargeyapuram which is on the Kurnool-Nandikotkur highway (map 1). The site proper is located about 1-1/2 Km. east of the village where several flat topped limestone hillocks having caves and rock shelters are noticed. The rock shelters have paintings on their walls and ceilings. Alongwith them, stone age artifacts ranging from Middle Palaeolithic upto Mesolithic and early historic material remains in the form of bricks are noticed in various localities of the (site map 2).

Theme of the Rock Paintings

Of the 11 rock shelters 10 have rock paintings in a fairly good state of preservation. The subject matter of the rock paintings revolves mostly around animals like deer, stag, antelope, hyaena, rabbit and reptiles like lizard and a frog. On one occasion a bird is depicted. Among the animals, the concentration is on deer species. On as many as 25 occasions deer species are depicted. Besides, they are the best among the animal depictions. The animals are depicted in several ways—single animals standing, jumping climbing etc., in pairs facing each other in a fighting mood, involved in sexual activity, the adult ones followed by the young, one chasing the other. Some deer figures are interesting as they are drawn in X-ray style, (Figs I, II & III). On two occasions the deer figures, drawn in outline, are shown with an additional horizontal line running across its body from it's mouth upto the legs (Fig II: 9, 10) One peculiar figure, which looks like a frog, has been done in bichrome (Fig.IV.6) while another deer shown pregnant (Fig. II.4).

In the frequency of depiction next comes the human beings. Adults and children are drawn in various postures. Children are, however, crudely depicted (Fig III:2). The adults - all men - are shown in various postures: standing, sitting, kneeling, moving forward with upraised hands, throwing at or carrying some load. But they lack realism (Fig. IV:1-7, 9) The next in order of frequency are the geometric line drawings. Most of them are symmetrically drawn with designs like square, rectangle, horizontal lines, lozenges etc. (Figs. III: 4,5,6 & 9) Another important feature of the paintings is the occurrence of handprints and drawings (Fig. IV: 2).

All the figures described above are done in red colour. In addition to these, there are some more paintings like inscriptions, symbols like swastika, eternal knot, vishnu pada etc. (Fig. III: 10,11 & 12) also done in red colour. But they occur only in one rock shelter.

In one rock shelter (No:6) paintings occur in black colour. The theme of these paintings revolve around the depiction of human beings. In almost all the cases they are drawn in sticklike fashion, the head shown with a diamond. Dear figures are also depicted, but they are crudely drawn (Fig. IV: 6,10,12,13 & 14; II: 5).

In short, the subject matter of the rock paintings at kethavaram include animals-both

* School of History, Culture, and Archaeology, Telugu University, Srisailam - 518 101.

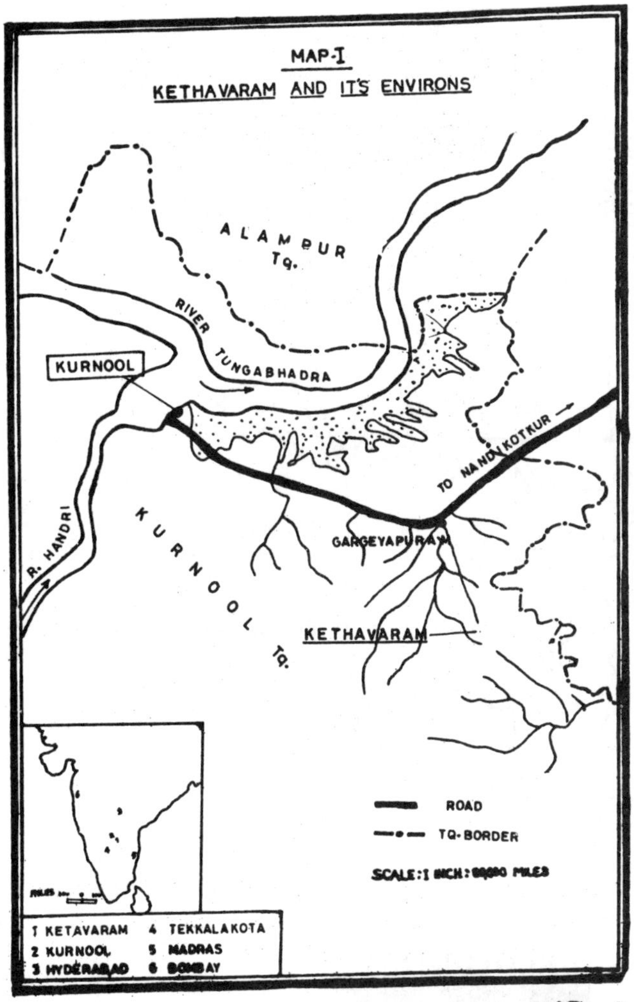

herbivores and carnivores-human figures, hand prints and drawings, geometric line drawings, inscriptions, and symbols like Swastika, eternal knot etc.

At Kethavaram there are several phases of painting activity. To separate these phases, a relative chronological sequence (Table I) is constructed on the basis of the superimpositions, themes, colour schemes and state of preservation of the paintings, which revealed 4 phases of painting activity here.

On the basis of the available material evidence, the earlier two phases of the painting activity, are ascribed to the mesolithic times (Chandra Mouli, 1986 & 1987). The dating of the black paintings of the third phase is problematic as its occurrence is limited to a single rock shelter. However, on the basis of the themes depicted they may be ascribed to chaloclithic or iron age period. The inscriptions of the historical paintings may be dated on palaeographical grounds to c.4th-5th Century A.D. Thus, the four painting phases are dated in ascending order, to Mesolithic times (Phases 1 & 2) Chalcolithic or iron age (?) (Phase: 3) and Historical times (Phase:4).

Interpretation

Now a discussion will be taken up, of the theme of the rock paintings at Kethavaram, to see the

MAP : 2

KETHAVARAM : THE SITE

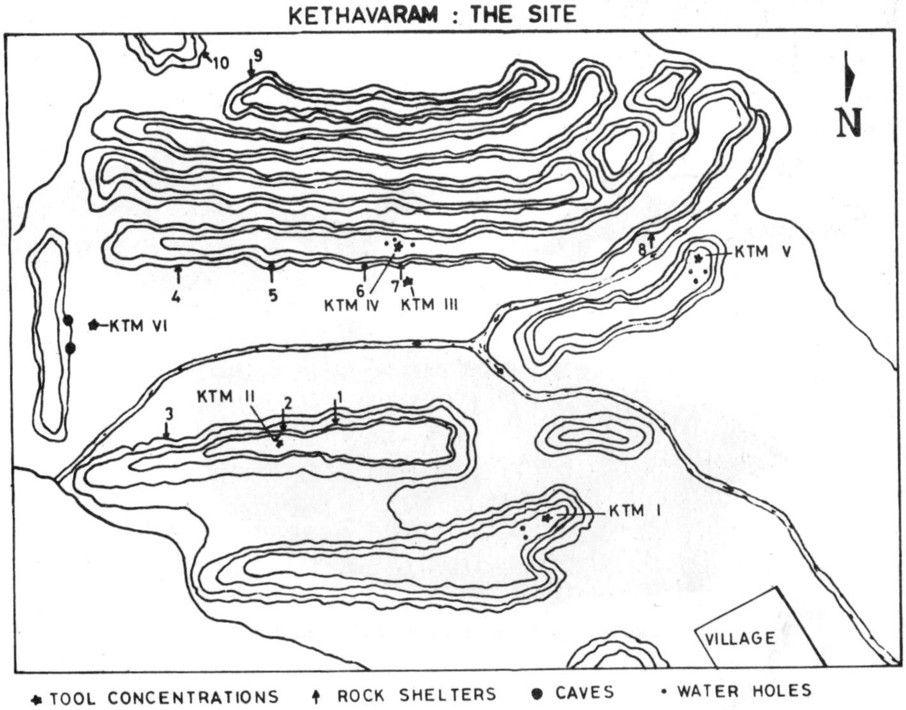

Fig. 1. Rock Paintings at Kethavaram

Fig. 2. Rock Paintings at Kethavaram

possible underlying motives that prompted their authors to paint the rock shelters.

Animal Depictions

The animal depictions here are mostly drawn in pairs and sometimes in isolation. At the first sight, the impression one gets is that the animal figures here are drawn in their natural setting and they were nothing but products of some aesthetic impulse of the mesolithic man as no hunting scenes or injured animals are depicted. But a close observation of these isolated or juxtapcsed animals, probably goes to disprove the above observation. As described above the depiction of some animals is peculiar. Sometimes they are drawn in outline and occasisonally contain an additional horizontal line across the body from the mouth upto the legs (Fig. II: 9,10, Fig. III: 3).

Some animals are drawn in X-Ray style, displaying the inner organs schematically (Fig.IV:6). On one occasion a deer is beautifully shown as, probably, a pregnant (Fig. II-4) . On some occasions, the animal groups appear to indicate their being in natural setting, chasing each other (Fig.I:3), facing each other in a fighting

Table - 1
Relative Chronology of the Rock Paintings

PHASES I	THEME II	STYLE III	SUPER IMPOSITION IV	COLOUR(S) V	ROCK SHELTER(S) VI
4	Painted Inscriptions in Southern Brahmi alphabet and some religious symbols. (Fig.IV: 5,9, 11 & 12)	Thick line and flat wash	6	Red	No.7
3.	Human figures, carts, wheels a metal tipped lance, crudely drawn deer figures, a fish and a chess board pattern (Fig. III: 8,10,11, 13 & 14)	Human figures are in thin outline in stick like fashion, the head in diamond shaped form.	Superimposes in one instance a faint and undiscernible red figure (not illustrated)	Black	No.6
2	Animal figures of deer species human figures, hand prints & drawings, geometric line drawings, a rabbit, a bird, a lizard and a bichrome drawing of a frog like figure (Fig.II:1 to 4,6 to 13, Fig. III: 1 to 7, 9 & 12, fig: IV 1 to 4, 6 to 10.)	Figures are mostly in thin outline and some in flat wash	Superimposes the faint figure of preceding phase in the rock shelters 2,7,9 & 10.	Red & Yellow	All 10 rock shelters
1.	Big animal figures in red colour and some very faint figures in some rock shelters, traces of the faint figures are, however, noticed in all the 10 rock shelters. Few in number. (Fig.I:1 & 4).	Flat wash and thick outline		Red	Rock shetlers 2,7,9 & 10.

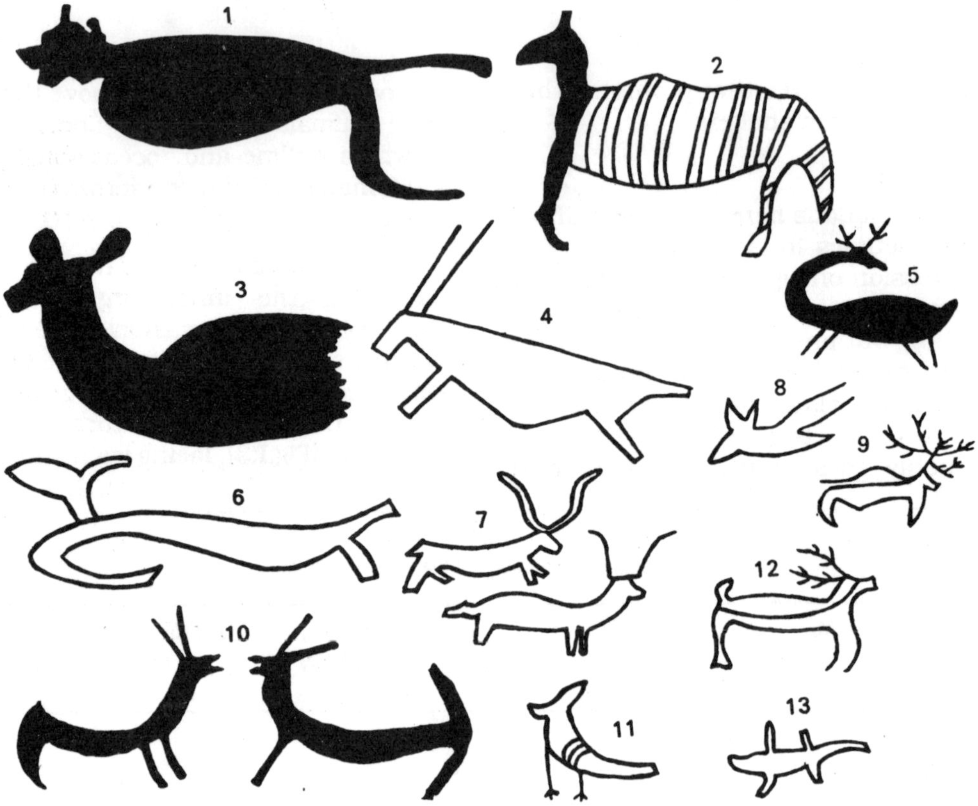

Fig. 3. Rock Painings at Kethavaram

Fig. 4. Rock Paintings at Kethavaram

mood (Fig II: 11) or involved in sexual activity (Fig.II:7).

To cite an analogy, in the Southern San rock-art of Africa superimposing or juxtapositioning of animals or objects suggest that the paintings were associated with a ritual (Williams, 1982: 430). In the European context, such horizontal line is considered to be the 'life line' of the animal. The occurrence of such animal figures in the paintings of Bhimbetka rock shelter complex have been interpreted as the depictions of wind pipe, heart and lungs (Neumeyer, 1978:22). The occurrence of similar deer figures in the kethavaram rock paintings may be interpreted in the same way. However, because of the lesser number of such depictions it cannot be emphasised. An X-ray style depicting the internal organs of animals with anatomical accuracy is rare. Frequently these patterns seem to symbolize some mythological quality with which the depicted animal is endowed (Neumeyer, 1978:14). But it is very difficult to distinguish between the anatomical depiction and mere decorative patterns in the X-ray style of depiction. It is possible that in such paintings the symbolism could have gradually been replaced by convention, when the artist could not have left the space, formed by the outlines of the animal body, undecorated. Similar X-ray style drawings are wide spread in the Art of the Primitive people of Northern Eurasia. Their belief is that by drawing the vital organs of the animals, it could be possible to capture their souls, which will have reincarnation. The X-ray style is a manifestation of these ideas which are basic form to shamanism and the early hunter culture and it is found solely in the area inhabited by hunters (Lommel, 1966:44). The X-ray style depictions of deer figures might be having similar mythical or cultic belief systems behind them. This proposition can particularly be made for the bichrome drawings. The figure which looks like a frog is done in X-ray style. The inner part is filled with yellow colour while the outlines and the inner organs are done in thin lines of red colour. This is the only one of its kind in the Kethavaram rock paintings done in bichrome. In Australian rock art, frogs symolise rain

Hand Prints

Another significant theme in the Kethavaram rock paintings is the hand prints and drawings. They occur in 3 rock shelters (Nos.2,7 & 8). In one rock shelter (No.7) they occur at one place superimposed one over the other (all are positive hand prints). Five such hand prints could be made out from this Jumble. The hand drawing consisting of 6 fingers occur in rock shelter 2.

The occurrence of hand prints in rock art can be traced back to the Upper palaeolithic times. Regarding the meaning of these hand prints and drawings there are several theories. Some say that they could be the result of unintentional and casual acts of the prehistoric man. Others hint at the ritual significance of the hand prints as part of the initiation ritual. Still, some others point out that they could be the signatures of the artist or done just for simple amusement (Bhattacharya, 1978:92, Mathpal, 1981:14). In Kethavaram, the specific location of hand prints, superimposed one over the other may rule out the proposition that they could be due to unintentional working. Regarding the contention that they could be signatures of the artist, needs some consideration here. In the art of Australian Aborgines, the artists make their hand prints, as a signature, after painting the animal (Levine, 1968:720). In the Dordogne region of France the hand prints showing mutilated fingers is taken to indicate the ceremony of mourning. Another Idea, behind the superpositioning of the hand prints one over the other, could be to derive the magical power of the painting (Williams, 1982: 430). If the theory that the superpositioning of animal figures was to gain the magical power of the previous figure upto the latter one is to be accepted as probable, then such a praposition could be made in the case of hand prints also (Huyghe, 1962:76).

Geometric Line Drawings

These geometric forms of drawings are the most intriguing among the rock paintings. Really nothing can even be guessed regarding their meaning. it was, however, said that such geometric forms of signs which appear highly abstract and schematic, may possibly have been naturalistic in origin also (Sieveking, 1979:8). They were also described as schematic representations of Masculine and Feminine elements, and as of naturalistic depictions of huts, traps or weapons (Sieveking, 1979:47, Wakankar, 1987:585).

At Kethavaram, these geometric line drawings occur in every rock shelter. The ones in rock shelters, 7, 9 and 10 are interesting. They are diamond shaped vertical line patterns or linga patterns or simple horizontal lines drawn one over the other (Fig.III: 4,5,6 & 9). What they actually mean to the mesolithic man can never be known. The diamond shaped forms were said to be the result of the earliest attempts of prehistoric man towards schematization or obstraction (Huyghe, 1962: 18).

The dome shaped patterns may represent the huts or enclosed rock shelters. The simple horizontal lines, may be said to represent the schematic rendering of the streamlets that become alive during the rainy days here.

Human Depictions

Human depictions occupy the majority of the rock paintings of the Mesolithic phase. The majority of human depictions are shown in groups and it is here the 'narrative' nature of the Mesolithic rock paintings, becomes apparent. But the naturalism with which the animal figures are endowed, is lacking in the depiction of human figures. Most of the Mesolithic human figures are drawn in a crude fashion. (Mathpal, 1981:11, Neumeyer, 1978:13). All the human depictions at Kethavaram are shown as involved in various activities (Fig. IV: 1-7 and 9), either walking, kneeling, throwing at etc.

Acknowledgement

I am extremely thankful to Prof. M.L.K. Murty, School of History, Culture & Achaeology, Telugu University, Srisailam, for his valuable suggestions in the preparation of this paper.

References

Bhattacharya, D.K. 1978.
The Emergence of Culture in Europe. Delhi: B.R. Publishing Corporation.

Chandra Mouli, N. 1986
A study of Microlithic Culture and Rock Paintings at Kethavaram, Kurnool District. Unpublished M.Phil dissertation, University of Hyderabad, Hyderabad.

____________, 1987.
"An Analytical study of rock paintings at Kethavaram, Kurnool District, A.P." in *proceedings of the Andhra Pradesh History Congress. XII session at Nagaram, Guntur District.*

Huyghe, Rene, (Ed) 1962
Larousse Encyclopaedia of Prehistoric Art. London: Hamlyn.

Kumar, G.R. & G. Narvare, 1984.
"Ostrich egg shells and early rock paintings in India", in *Rock art of India: Painting and Engraving.* PP:118-125 (Ed.) K.K. Chakravarty, Delhi: Arnold Heinemann.

Levine, M.H. 1968
"Prehistoric Art and Ideology". In *Readings in Anthropology.* Vol. II: 708-724, New York: Thomas, Y. Cromwell Company.

Lommel, A. 1966.
Prehistoric & Primitive Man. London: Paul Hamlyn.

Mathpal, Y. 1976.
Rock Paintings of India: an ornithographical interpretation. *Bulletin of Deccan College Research Institute: 34(3-4): 83-89.*

____________, 1981.
Prehistoric Art of India *The eastern Anthropoligist* 31(1): 1-26

____________, 1984[a]
Prehistoric Rock Paintings of Central India. New Delhi: Abhinav.

____________, 1984[b]
"How to date a Rock Painting" in *Rock art of India* (Ed) K.K. Chakravarty, PP: 57-60, New Delhi: Arnold-Heinemann.

____________, 1985
"The Hunter-gatherer way of life Depicted in the mesolithic rock paintings of Central India" in *Recent Advances in Indo-Pacific Prehistory* (Ed) V.N. Misra & Peter Bellwood, New Delhi: Oxford & IBH Publishing Company.

Misra, V.N., Y. Mathpal and M. Nagar, 1977.
Bhimbetka: Prehistoric Man and His Art in Central India. Exhibition souvenir. Poona: Deccan College.

Neumeyer, Erwin, 1978.
Prehistoric Indian Rock Paintings. New Delhi: Oxford University Press.

Sali, S.A. 1985 "The Upper Palaeolithic Culture at Patne, District Jalgaon, Maharashtra, in *Recent Advances in Indo Pacific Prehistory,* (Ed.) V.N. Misra and Peter Bellwood, PP:137-146, New Delhi: Oxford & IBH Publishing Company.

Sieveking, A. 1979.
The Cave Artists. London: Thames & Hudson.

Sonawane,V.H. 1984
"An important evidence to date paintings of mesolithic period" in *Rock art of India* (Ed) K.K. Chakravarty PP: 61-63, Delhi: Arnold Heinemann.

Wakankar, V.S., 1987
"Rock art of India" in *History and Archaeology* (A Ghosh Commemoration volume) (Ed) B.M. Pande & B.D. Chattopadhyaya PP: 583-96, Delhi: Agam Kala Prakasham.

____________ & R.R. Brooks, 1976. *Stone Age Painting in India.* Bombay: B.R. Taraporewala & Sons.

Williams, Lewis J.D. 1982.
The Economic & Social context of Southern San Rock Art. *Current Anthropology* 23 (4) 429-449.

Puratattva No. 18; 1987-88

PROTOHISTORIC INVESTIGATIONS IN THE CENTRAL PENNAR BASIN, CUDDAPAH DISTRICT, ANDHRA PRADESH

P.C.Venkata Subbaiah*

As part of his doctoral dissertation concerning protohistoric sites in the Central Pennar basin covering the Cuddapah district of Andhra Pradesh, the writer has conducted two seasons of field-work in the area (1986-87). This work has brought to light many Neolithic, Iron Age Megalithic and Early Historical sites. The present note gives a brief account of these sites.

Cuddapah district forms the Central part of the Pennar basin in the Rayalaseema region of Andhra Pradesh and lies between 13° 43' and 15° 14' North Lat. and between 77° 55' and 79° 29' East Long. It has an extent of over 15,000 km² and is bounded by the districts of Kurnool, Chittoor, Anantapur and Nellore on the north, south, west and east, respectively. The district falls into three natural divisions as follows: (a) the western plains of black soil belt comprising the taluks of Jammalamadugu, Pulivendla, Proddatur. Cuddapah and Kamalapuram; (b) a well-defined valley in the eastern part of the district covering the taluks of Badvel, Sidhout and Rajampet; and (c) the southern plateau covering the Rayachoti taluk.

Geologically, the area is occupied by rock formations belonging to the Archaean, Cuddapah and Kurnool systems consisting of Schists, granites, dolerites, shales, quartzites, dolomites and limestones. It is drained by the river Pennar and its tributaries. The vegetation is of the dry deciduous and tropical thorn types and the climate is semi-arid with a precipitation of about 680 mm per annum.

Neolithic Site

I.K.Sarma's (1967) previous explorations in the area have brought to light three Neolithic sites, black-on-red pottery being the most important feature associated with these sites. Sarma has ascribed these sites to an early phase of the Southern Neolithic culture and even considered the painted pottery tradition as parental to the type-ware of the Malwa Culture.

The present surveys have made known 32 sites of this culture. These are located within the revenue limits of the following villages: Akkempeta, Balijapalli, Boditippenapadu, Chapadu, Chinnamudiyam, Dannawada, Gadeguduru, Gudemcheruvu, Idamadaka, Inagaluru, Jangalpalli, Kambaladinne, Koduru, Kottagundavaripalli, Kottapalli, Koraguntapalli, Madhavapuram, Mylavaram, Nidivelagala, Paluru, Ramireddipalli, Sambaturu,Tippaluru, Tondaladinne, Ulimella, Upparapalli, Vaddirala, Veparala, Veduduru and Vellala. Almost all of these sites are single culture sites and are confined to the black soil belt mentioned above. All have a riverine locational context; four sites lie on the Pennar and the rest on its feeders such as the Kunderu and the Mogamareru.

All are habitation sites; so far no ashmounds have been noticed in this area. Owing to agricultural activities no mound formations are preserved any longer. The habitation debris is found scattered in cultivated lands. It measures from 50cm to one and a half metres in depth and from 0.5 hectares to 1.5 hectares in extent.

A trial excavation was conducted at Peddamudiyam and a trench measuring 3x3 metres was dug up to a depth of 55cm The strata exposed in this trench are as under:

Layer 1: Humus (disturbed due to cultivation). It is 15cm thick

Layer 2: This layer comprises very loose ashy earth and has given evidence of four post-holes in semi-circular fashion probably of a circular hut. It is 30 cm thick.

Layer 3: This layer consists of dark brown earth below which was found black sticky soil. It is 10cm thick.

The antiquities from all layers comprise pecked and ground stone artefacts, microliths, pottery of different fabrics, charcoal and animal bones.

Department of Archaeology, Deccan College, Poona - 6

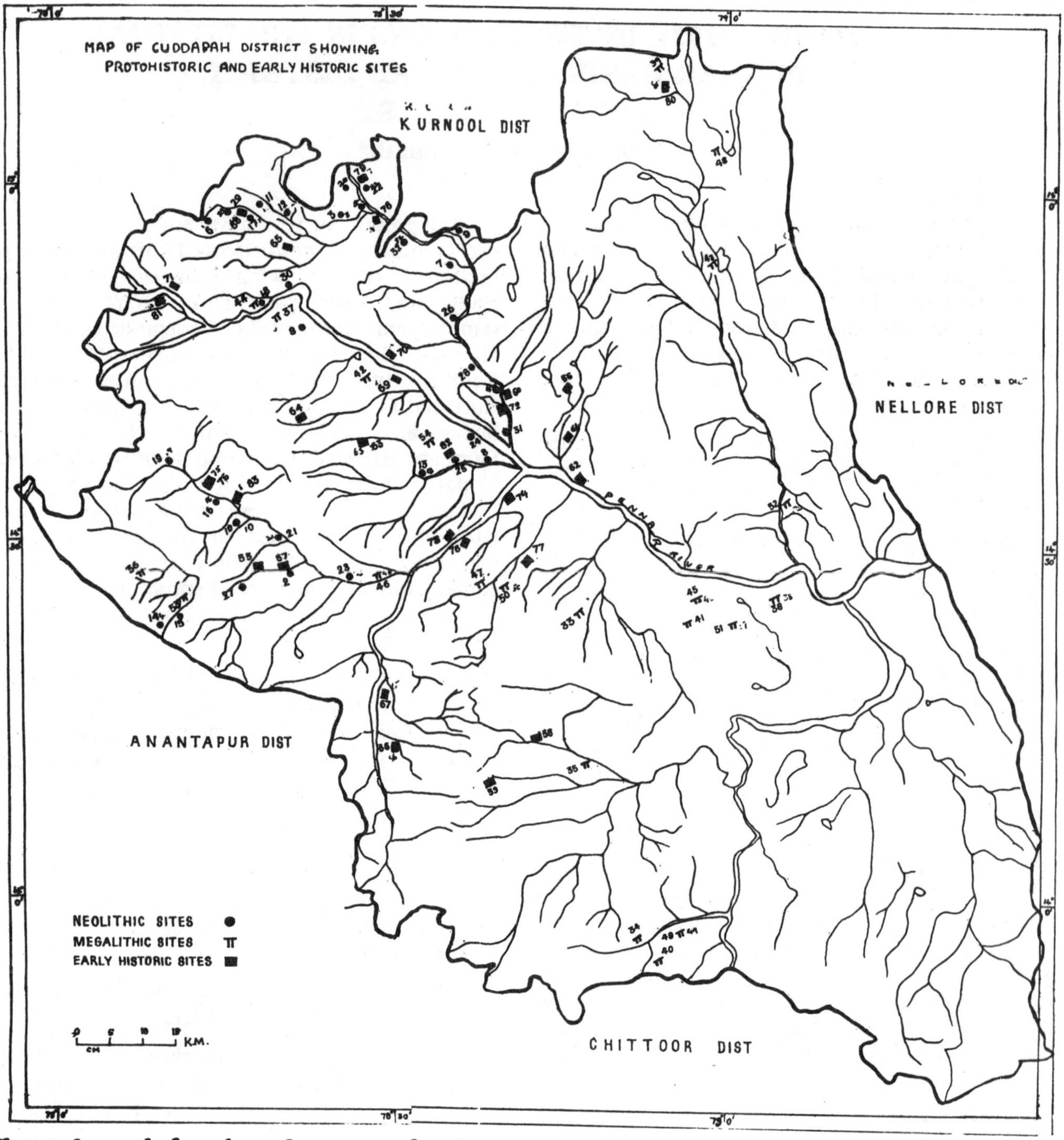

Charcoal sample from layer 3 was sent for C-14 dating to the Birbal Sahni Institute of Palaeobotany, Lucknow. The following date run on this sample on the basis of the 5570± 30 half life value has been announced: BS-758 3060± 120 years B.P. (1060 B.C.). This date goes to strengthen the assignment of the Neolithic sites of this region to the late phase of the Southern Neolithic culture.

The cultural material from the sites consists of pottery of various fabrics, assemblages of the Pecked and ground and short blade industries, animal bones and miscellaneous objects (beads, bone tools, dabbers, lids etc.)

The ceramic industry mainly consists of the red and the grey wares, with the buff, black and tan varieties forming the minor wares. The decorated pottery is of three kinds; painted, incised and combed. The whole mass of pottery is hand-made; the lack of straition marks and the uneven thickness of walls imply the use of turn-table, and beater-and-anvil techniques. That this pottery was baked at a high temperature is revealed by the absence of any blackness in the core.

The black-on-red ware is identical with the A·3 pottery of Piklihal (Allchin 1960:56) and accounts for forty percent of the ceramic industry. The designs comprise simple linear bands (horizontal and vertical), criss-cross lines, etc. The second major category is the grey ware with both coarse and fine fabrics. The common shapes represented in the present assemblages are high-necked jars, bowls of various size, channel-spouted bowls, bowls with six lips, storage jars, lotas and goblets. Perforated pottery is represented both in red and grey wares. It is confined to bowls perforated at the base.

The following specimens are illustrated (Fig.1, Nos.1-9)

1. Fragment of a globular pot with out-turned rim; outer surface of the rim is painted with a criss-cross pattern sandwiched between a horizontal band and salnting lines.
2. Fragment of a small globular pot with slightly out-turned rim; painted with short vertical strokes on the inner side of the rim and a criss-cross pattern on the outer surface.
3. Fragment of a high-necked jar with a slightly out-turned rim; painted with short vertical strokes on the inner side of the rim and two horizontal bands on the outer surface of the neck.
4. Fragment of a deep bowl with a featureless rim and incurved sides; outer part of the rim is painted with two horizontal bands below which are two divergent series of slanting lines.
5. Fragment of a globular pot with out-turned rim and concave neck (Burnished grey ware).
6. Fragment of a bowl with sloping inward sides and a featureless rim; painted with two horizontal bands on the rim and probably a leaf-pattern below it.
7. Fragment of a convex-sided bowl; painted with vertical strokes on the inner surface of the rim. The outer surface of the rim is painted with two horizontal bands and a number of vertical lines below them.
8. Fragment of a storage pot with out-turned rim and concave neck (Burnished grey ware).
9. Fragment of a channel-spouted bowl; the outer surface of the channel is painted with three horizontal bands and a number of vertical lines suspended below them at regular intervals.

The artefacts of the pecked and ground tool industry are fashioned on a wide range of rocks. The edge tools are invariably made of dolerite (Fig. 2, Nos. 10 and 16) and the non-edge tools are made of rocks such as granite, diorite and sandstone. Most of these raw materials are locally available in the form of hills or veins intruding into them. Flaking, pecking, grinding and overall polishing are the basic manufacturing techniques employed in the industry. The present collection comprises axes, adzes, hammerstones, anvils, slingstones, querns, rubberstones and flake-blades.

The blade-tool assemblages are based on the working of chert, and are characterized by the production of tools on blades struck off from fluted cores. The types include scrapers, backed blades, notched blades, simple blades, etc. (Fig.2, Nos. 12 to 14). A few bone points and a chisel (Fig.2, No.11) three disc beads of steatite (Fig.2, No.15) and ivory are also included in the collection.

The animal bones found along with the cultural material have been studied by Dr.G.L.Badam, Deccan College. The species identified include the domestic cattle *(Bos indicus)*, Buffalo *(Bubalus bubalis)*, sheep *(Ovis aries)*, goat *(Capra hircus aegagrus)* and fowl *(Gallus sp.)* and wild animals such as blackbuck *(Antelope cervicapra)*, chital *(Axis axis)* and Sambar *(Cervus unicolor)*. Cattle bones outnumber those of other animals, thereby proving that cattle pastoralism was the main component of the Neolithic economy and was supplemented by other means including hunting and gathering.

Megalithic Sites

Megalithic monuments were discovered at 22 places, and some of these are habitation sites too. The following list gives the names of sites and the type(s) of monuments found there.

(A) Stone Circles Balijapalli Balired-digaripalli, Dappalli, Ganga-peruru, Koduru, Mylavaram, Sankha-varam, Timmasamud-ram and Yerraballa.

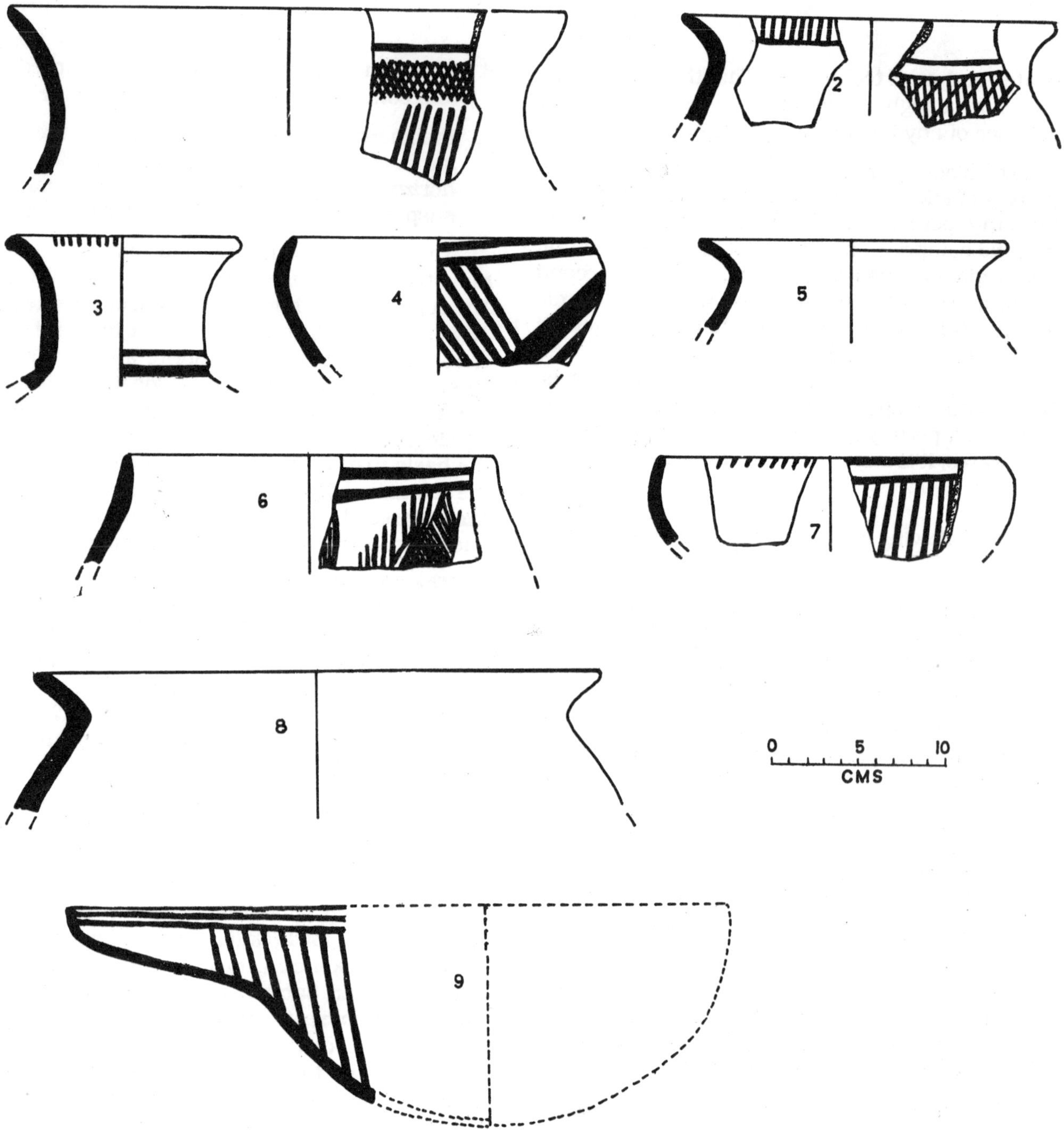

Fig. 2 : Pottery from Pennar basin.

(B) Cairn Circles Balireddigaripalli, Gangayapalli, Jourkulapalli, Kanyathirtham and Nekanapuram.

(C) Dolmenoid Cists Chinnakudala, Kanyathirtham Palagiri, Vontimitta and Yerraballa.

(D) Chamber tombs Gundlapalli, Palagiri, Yerra balla, and Yerraguntla.

Habitation-cum-burial sites occur at Akkireddipalli, Balijapalli, Balireddigaripalli, Gangaperuru, Mylavalam, Pendlimarri, vellaturu and Yamaturu. The habitation debris covers from 0.8 hectares to 1.6 hectares in extent and from 1.5 to 3 metres in depth. The cultural material from these sites comprises pottery (black polished ware, black-and-red ware, red ware and red polished ware), iron slags and animal bones.

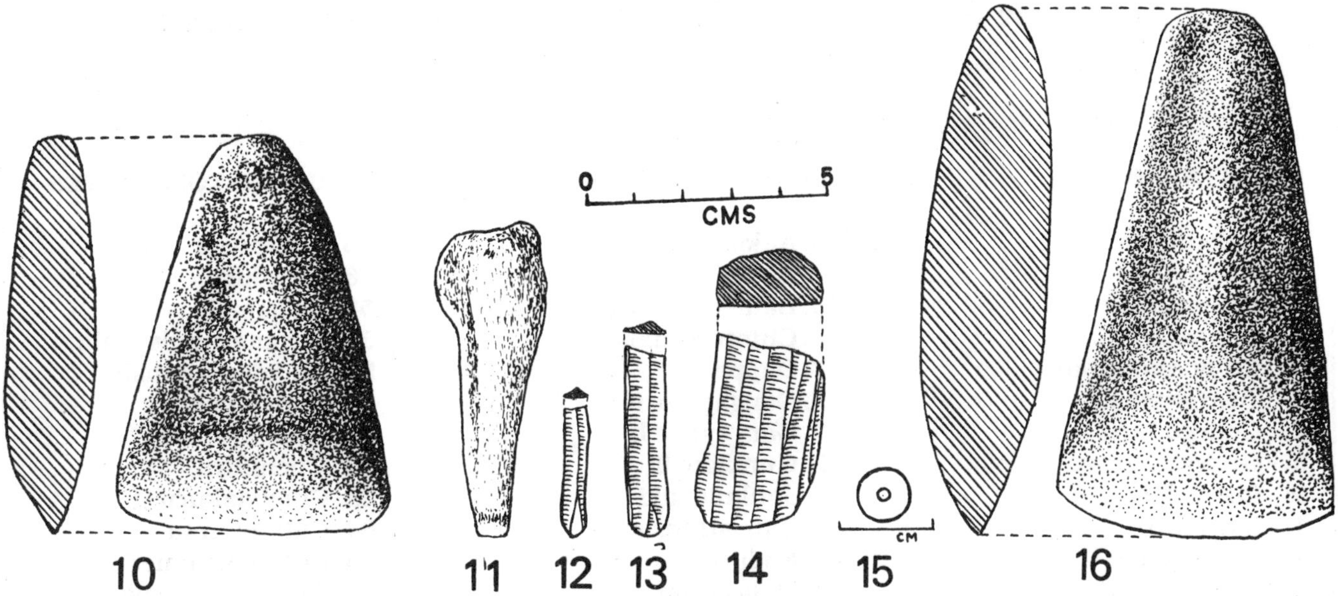

Fig. 2A : 10. adze, Bone chisel, 12-13. Chert blades, 14. Fluted core, 15. Stealite bead.

Bruce Foote (1916:106-107) reported the occurrence of red polished, red painted, black polished and painted wares represented by shapes like bowls, *lotas*, Chatties, globular pots, etc. at vellaturu. At Sankhavaram, a ramshaped terracotta sarcophagus (oblong in shape with six feet) was accidentally discovered in 1935 during the construction of the local church. It contained uncalcined human skeletal remains and pottery, black polished, black-and-red and rouletted wares along with an iron spearhead and fragments of a knife or sickle. Recently, at Mylavaram, a Megalithic stone circle excavated by the Department of Archaeology, Government of Andhra Pradesh, revealed a sarcophagus containing red and black polished wares along with ash.

Early Historical Sites

Early historical sites were discovered by the author at the following places: Achhavelli, Annaluru, Balijapalli, Bayanavandlapalli, Budidaguntapalli, Budidapalli, Buddayaguntapalli, Buddayapalli, Chennuru, Chilamakuru, Chintakunta,Chinnakommerla, Devaragut-tapalli, Gandikovuru, Gollapalli, Illuru, Kottapeta, Koppulu, Kuchupapa, Letapalli, Lebaka, Lomada, Machanuru, Moyillakalava, Nemalladinne, Peddamudiyam, Ramapuram, Tallaproddaturu, Tippaluru and Tonduru. The cultural debris varies from two to six metres in depth and from 1.2 to 3.2 hectares in extent. Pottery belonging to red ware, polished red ware, black-and-red ware and grey wares was found.

With a view to obtaining analogies and parallels that may provide insights into the lifeways of the Neolithic culture of the area, especially in respect of ecological adaptations and the reconstruction of settlement-subsistance patterns, ethnographic investigations have been initiated among the local Kuruba community.

Despite modern influences and acculturation, the Kuruba mode of life still represents a good example of human adaptations in a semi-arid environmental setting and as such supplies a good parallel to the Neolithic culture of the region. Considerable data have already been collected about the location of their settlements, economic organization and related aspects. This work will be pursued further in future field investigations.

The author has planned further intensive surveys, which are expected to bring forth additidonal data bearing upon the protohistoric phase in this part of South India.

List of Protohistoric and Early Historic Sites in Cuddapah District, Andhra Pradesh

NEOLITHIC SITES

1. Akkempeta
2. Balijapalli
3. Boditippenapadu
4. Chapadu
5. Chinnamudiyam
6. Dannawada
7. Gadeguduru
8. Gudemcheruvu
9. Idamadaka
10. Inagaluru
11. Jangalapalli
12. Kambaladinne
13. Koduru
14. Kottagundavaripalli
15. Kottapalli
16. Koraguntapalli
17. Madhavapuram
18. Mylavaram
19. Nidivelagala
20. Paluru
21. Paluru
22. Peddamudiyam
23. Ramireddipalli
24. Sambaturu
25. Tippaluru
26. tondaladinne
27. Ulimella
28. Upparapalli
29. Vaddirala
30. Veparala
31. Veduduru
32. Vellala

MEGALITHIC SITES

33. Akkireddipalli
34. Balijappali
35. Balireddigaripalli
36. Chinnakudala
37 Dappalli
38. Gangaperuru
39. Gangayapalli
40. Gundlapalli
41. Joukulapalli
42. Kanyathirtham
43. Koduru
44. Mylavaram
45. Nekanapuram
46. Palagiri
47. Pendlimarri
48. Sankhavaram
49. Timmasamudram
50. Vellaturu
51. Vontimitta
52. Yamaturu
53. Yerraballa
54. Yerraguntla

EARLY HISTORIC SITES

55. Achhavelli
56. Annaluru
57. Balijapalli
58. Bayanavandlappalli
59. Budidaguntapalli
60. Budidapalli
61. Buddayapalli
62. Chennuru
63. Chilamakuru
64. Chintakunta
65. Chinnakommerla
66. Devaraguttapalli
67. Gandikovuru
68. Golapalli
69. Illuru
70. Kottapeta
71. Koppulu
72. Kuchupapa
73. Letapalli
74. Lebaka
75. Lomada
76. Machanuru
77. Moyillakalava
78. Nemalladinne
79. Peddamudiyam
80. Ramapuram
81. Tallaproddatur
82. Tippaluru
83. Tonduru

Acknowledgement

I am grateful to my research supervisor, Dr. K. Paddayya for many valuable suggestions. I am thankful to Dr. G.L. Badam for the identification of the faunal remains.

References

Allchin, F.R. 1960,
Piklihal Excavations, Andhra Pradesh Government Archaeological Series No.1. Hyderabad.

Allchin, F.R. 1962
Painted Pottery from Patpadu, Andhra Pradesh. *Antiquity* 36: 221-224.

Foote R.B., 1916
The Foote Collection of Indian Prehistoric and Protohistoric Antiquities: Notes on Their Ages and Distribution, Madras Government, Museum, Madras

Gururaja Rao, B.K., 1972
Megalithic Culture in South India. University of Mysore, Mysore.

Sarma, I.K. 1967
Painted Pottery from Pusalapadu, Andhra Pradesh and further Explorations in the Cuddapah and Kurnool Districts, *Indica*, 4(2): 75-94.

Sarma, I.K. 1967-68
Patapadu Revisited: A New Painted Pottery culture of South East India, *Puratattva 1:* 68-83:

Subramanyam, B.R.and David Raju (Not dated) The Black Painted Red ware of Kurnool District. Andhra Pradesh, *Journal of Archaeology in Andhra Pradesh 1.* 57-62

Puratattva no. 18 ; 1987-88

NUMISMATICS AND ARCHAEOLOGY+

Parmeshwari Lal Gupta*

It gives me great pleasure to welcome you all heartily on this occasion on behalf of the Indian Institute of Research in Numismatic Studies, a Maheshwari Foundation, and on my own behalf.

This is the second International Colloquium that is being organised by the Institute. The first one on 'NUMISMATICS AND HISTORY' coincided with the Institute's inauguration. The topic of the present colloquim is 'NUMISMATICS AND ARCHAEOLOGY."

It needs hardly any say that both numismatics and archaeology have developed into scientific disciplines in their own rights. Archaeology reveals the material cuture, hidden under the earth; and coins constitute a most tangible element of it. For archaeologists coins are an important tool which helps them in defining the chronology of an historical culture. For numismatists, archaeology helps define the context. Both the disciplines have a sort of symbiotic relationship. Their interdependence is of vital importance for the proper understanding of the History of our past.

The relationship between archaeologists and numismatists and their interdependence is an accomplished fact in most of the countries of the world. But it is unfortunate that the same is not true in the case of South Asian countries, including India. The fraternity between the disciplines is not as much developed as it ought to be. Numismatics in our country is cirumscribed within those coins that come to the numismatists' hands casually and haphazardly. His studies and researches are confined mostly to the observations on the two faces of the coins. Coins discovered in excavations, with any definite context, rarely come to their hands. On the other hand, archaeologists posses the true environmental and contextual information, being in direct contact with the coins that they discover during excavations. But they seldom realize that the coins form unique class of their discoveries and are of potential interest to them. They do not use them in their excavation reports to the desired extent. They can make the best use of such finds once they realise the need of co-operation with numismatists and the utility of their expertise.

The urgent necessity of co-operation between the archaeologists and the numismatists is for unravelling the history of our very early period. Here both, the numismatists and the archaeologists, are in the dark; both need the help of each other. While the numismatists have something to say to meet the needs of the archaeologists; the archaeologists themselves are not properly attentive to them. What the numismatists expect from the archaeologists, the latter are unable to provide for the present.

In the last few decades our archaeologists have become dependent on their finds of pot-shreds for dating and the chronology of the site that they excavate. This method has probably a parallel with the archaeology of western countries where potteries do not have any long survival nor do they have any wide diffusion. They might be a useful apparatus for the archaeologist there for their purpose. But they may not necessarily be useful elsewhere, as is the case with our own country. Here the excavation, carried out at the ancient sites disclose that our potteries are in no way localised to any particular area nor are they short-lived. For instance, the NBP ware, according to our archaeologists' own admission, was current for at least five hundred years from 600 to 200 B.C. Besides this longevity, this pottery also had a wide expansion. It has been discovered at all the sites right from the Punjab in the west to Bengal in the east; and thus it was spread almost all over Northern India. Any pottery with such a long survival and wide diffusion can be used for any kind of precise dating is unthinkable. Yet our archeologists have reposed their confidence in them. They speak of pottery-culture-periods lasting several centuries and do not provide any

+ Welcome address to the Second International Colloquium organized by I.I.R.N.S., Nasik

* Indian Institute of Research in Numismatics studies, Anjaneri, Nasik

lasting several centuries and do not provide any firm basis for dating the objects of short survivals that they find; often arriving at misleading conclusions.

I do not by saying so, mean to minimise the value of pottery, I only plead that our archaeologists should also realise that coins are amongst the few artifacts which bear quite a short span of life and normally carry with them some evidence, often very specific, of their dates. Furthermore, they are usually the products of some authority, which can well be determined. As such, these are more useful to the archaeologists, than the pottery. With the help of the coins, they can precisely determine the date for each of the layers and the associated finds in their excavations.

Permit me to illustrate the confusing situation as it exists today. Sometime back while I was looking for the stratigraphical contexts of the Silver punchmarked coins in the archaeological excavations, I could find only broadly bracketed periods covering a long span of several centuries viz.

1.	Rupar	Circa	600 to 200 B.C.
2.	Hastinapur	"	600 to 200 B.C.
3.	Purana Quila (Delhi)	"	600 to 100 B.C.
4.	Ujjain	"	600 to 100 B.C.
5.	Tripuri	"	400 to 300 B.C.
6.	Maheshwar	"	400 to 100 B.C.
7.	Bahal	"	300 to 100 A.D.

From this broad-based date, one may say that the punchmarked coins were current between 600 B.C. to 100 A.D. for a period of atleast 700 years. One may also deduce that this coinage was current in the north-western part of the country from 600 B.C.; they spread to central part about a century latter in 500 B.C. and still late in 400 B.C. to the west; and similar was their survivals. But one cannot make out anything from the reports of the excavator and know if coins are of silver or of copper; and if they are of silver, are all of them of one and the same type or if they form any varieties. These pieces of information are vital tu know for the purpose of any kind of dating.

The studies of punchmarked coins by numismatists, reveal that the silver punchmarked coins may clearly be divided into two categories one an earlier coins that was local in nature and the other an imperial one. The local coins were the issues of those *janapadas* and the *mahajanapads* that existed in the various parts of the country prior to the rise of the Magadhan Empire of the Nandas and the Mauryas, and antidate 400BC. The imperial coins were issued by the rulers of the Nandas and the Mauryan dynasties and are found scattered all over the country. The coins of the latter category are known to be of no less than 600 varieties; and they may be placed into six or seven groups, which might be chronological and/or territorial. These assessments of the numismatists can not be verified, substantiated or refuted unless the archaeologists provide them with the precise data about their loci in their trenches and their stratigraphical chronology with the exact identity of the types and varieties of their finds. Such information would not only help the numismatists but also the archaeologists themselves. They would then be able to pin point, within their cultural frame of sequence, the date for the objects they have found; and provide a better and clear picture of the culture and expose the political history.

Lacking in the proper identification of the uninscribed coins, particularly the punchmarked ones archaeologists are themselves confused. Their confusion may well be noticed almost in all the excavation reports. It may invariably be noticed that the coins, that are described in the reports, for instance, the finds of layer I within the period bracketed from 600B.C., would imply that they were the earliest known coins found there but are described in the chapter relating to coin-finds as Mauryan. Here the confusion lies in the fact that the coins, according to stratification, would never be, not only Mauryan but also pre-Mauryan or pre-Nanda. They would only be of the very beginning of the Magadhan imperialism. If the archaeologists try to know and identify the types and varieties of their coin finds and visualise them in their stratigraphical contexts, they would themselves realise their own confusion. Since they are unable to do so, they keep themselves confused and make others confused. To bring out the historical picture from the archaeological excavations, it is essential that this kind of confusion be avoided; and this is possible only when they would realise the necessity to seek the cooperation of numismatists for the proper interpretation of their finds.

Then there is no attempt on the part of

archaeologists themselves to coordinate the results of the excavations at different sites within the same area; as such the coins of the same type or varieties found at different sites, often are not placed in one and the same dating horizon. If the coins are properly studied, they would enable to synchronise the layers, not only of the different trenches of the same site but also different sites with nominal variance of only a few decades in relation to the condition of the coins. If such studies are taken up by the archaeologists, which they only can do, a most coherent historical picture would emerge out of their efforts.

Another point that needs the attention of our archaeologists is the nature of their coin-finds, which is normally not realised. The coins found in the excavations may be distinguished in several categories; of them the main and the important ones are only three;(1) hoards,(2) votive caches and (3) site-finds. Each of them has its own meanings and their interpretation would not be one and the same. The primary need for the excavators is to recognise properly the true nature of their finds and then to interpret them accordingly, which is rarely done for the present.

The find of the coin-hoards in the excavations is rare. But when they are found, they are found kept in some repository buried under the floor or somewhere else in a living room. The coins would not be much affected by the environment and their appearance would have suffered only to the extent of their currency. Such hoards served in those old days as cash boxes. The coins were taken out frequently to meet the domestic needs and added when there was any surplus. As such the content pattern would not be the same as of those hoards that were concealed far off from habitations in fields, forests or other places for safety and included the coins that were then current and were placed only once in the container. The two kinds of hoards would not carry the same meanings. This has to be kept in mind by the excavators for their proper evaluation.

The votive caches are those deposits, that are placed in the foundations of the buildings at the very beginning of their construction. In them the coins would not necessarily be exclusive. This kind of specific deposits needs extra care when dating the building or its associate layers. In no way the coins were placed in such caches being current once or contemporary. They might well be there only to represent the metal specie. So, they may not indicate in any way the precise date of their construction; utmost it may be inferred from them that the construction would have taken place at some later time than the date of the coin-issue. They would, however, be useful to know the purpose of the edifice, whether secular or religious and probably also the religion or sect to which they belonged, on the basis of their other contents.

Most of the coins that excavators come across during their digs, are site-finds and stray. These coins are those that had either lost details due to circulation and were deliberately discarded being unfit for currency or the accidental or casual losses. In both cases, these coins are those that were then in currency and were more or less contemporary to the layers, where they are found. Only these coins are of prime importance for archaeologists to ascertain the date of the layers where they are found; and on its basis, they may also be able to assess the periods of the layers above and below it. For this purpose they would first need the identification of the coins and would like to have as much information as possible. Here is the need of the help of the numismatist. And the the numismatist has to face a great responsibility. If he cannot identify the coins, the coins are useless; if he misidentifies the coins, dreadful results might occur.

The coins that the excavators find in the excavations are, in most cases, of low class metal viz. nominally pure copper, tin-bronze, sometimes of brass, billion and of lead. There are extreme chances to get any silver or gold coin. The coins, found in the excavations are mostly corroded due to their burial environments, which vary in degree not only with the environment but also with the composition of the metal. The corrosion sometimes distorts the coins, and the details fo the surface are lost.

It is only the legibility of the coins that helps the numismatist to identify such coins. It is important for the numismatist's expertise to assess the legibility correctly. Most of the coins that the excavators come across, are unidentifiable to them and they invariably discard them. Such coins, no matter how long you look at it, or how well it is conserved, will not be legible to the archaeologists or any one else. But for the numismatists, there is a threshold of legibility, which is peculiar not only to every coin but to every kind of coin. For example, some coins have such characteristic details of design, fabric of execution that the numismatist can identify them conveniently, even when very little is visible. There are others, which are not necessarily easy in themselves; but the numismatist has only to see a tiny bit of inscription of a characteristic profile to identify it correctly with certainty. There are other coins, which have a low threshold; one had to see a lot on them to be able to identify them in any signfiicant manner. There are many coins, where the determination of one side is enough for the nusmatist to identify and describe it correctly. This is what I mean by the threshold of legibility for the coins, the kind of expertise required to be able to exploit each coin to the full. And this is not in anyway easy to acquire. It is developed only by experience.

Here I would hasten to add that to avail of the maximum legibility of the coins, which is the prime requirements of the numismatist's expertise, is possible only when an experienced technician, who may be called conservator, is available to strip off the corrosion to reveal the residual matter without any loss. This man should know precisely what constitutes the maximum legibility from the numismatist's point of view for the purpose of identification But manore awefully lacking in our country. As a matter of fact, this necessity has not yet been properly realised by our archaeologists; but it should be realised now. I do not mean to say that they do not employ any person for cleaning their coins. The one whom they employ might be highly qualified acadimically, but generally does not understand the needs. He very often plunges the coins into a bath of acids; and when the coins survive, they are bright, shining but indistinct and often crumbling into several pieces. This is nothing but the destruction of evidence.

I have mentioned so far what the archaeologists are lacking for the purpose of numismatics and how the numismatics can be useful to them in their discipline. But in no way do I mean to exalt numismatics and minimise the contributions of archaeology to our knowledge. There are many occassions where numismatists are helpless in themselves and need the help of archaeologists. For long it was believed that the rulers of the Satavahana dynasty immediately followed the Mauryas in the Deccan in about the second century B.C. It is only the spades of the archaeologists that brought to light the fact that a number of small principalities had cropped up after the fall of the Mauryas and before the rise of the Satavhanas, much later in about the first century B.C. In this case, the numismatists knew earlier the coins of many of these new rulers; but in the absence of any proper information, they believed those coins as belonging only to the Satavahanas. There are instances, where the numismatists are still looking forward for the help from archaeology, they have disovered from the coins the names of a large number of rulers who ruled at Kausambi, Mathura, Ahichchhatra, Ayodhya and a few other places, after the Mauryas, But they are unable to give them any chronology by themselves. They badly need the help of Archaeologists, which so far is not available.

While welcoming you, these are a few random thoughts that, as a numismaist, I have in my mind on this occasiosn and which I have expressed to you. They are not the only ones. There are many more such areas, where numismatists and archaeologists, both may supplement and complement each other's efforts. I very much hope that all of them would find your kind consideration on this occasion; and the outcome of the Colloquium would convince us of the necessity of close co-operation between the archaeologists and the numismatists. The archaeologists would ward off their indifferent towards numismatics and would infuse an awareness in them of what they can do for numismatics and tell what numismatists can do for them; what their mutual philosophies are and how both of them fit in each others investigations.

With this hope, I extend to you a hearty welcome to this Institute again.

Puratattva No. 18 ; 1987-88

A NOTE ON PINDIBANDHA-AN ANCIENT DANCE FORM

Anupa Pande*

Classical Indian Dance has hitherto generally been discussed under the two aspects of *Tandava*[1] and *Lasya*[2]. However, there is a distinct third form viz., *Pindibandha* mentioned in the *Natyasastra* of the sage Bharata. The present paper proposes to discuss its nature.

The origin of the *Pindibandha* dance form has been described thus in the *Natyasastra*. While Lord Siva and his consort Parvati were dancing, the formation of *pindis* was observed by the troupes of Siva viz., Nandi, Bhadramukha etc. and they created the *Pindibandhas* with their distinct characteristics.[3] Abhinavagupta, the foremost commentator of the *Natyasastra*, explains *Pindibandha* as being created by the simultaneous combination of *asukumara* (vigorous) and *sukumara* (gentle) i.e., *tandava* and *lasya nrttas* (dances) respectively.

The term *Pindibandha* is explained in the text as *pindinam bandha* i.e. formation of *Pindis*. The fundamental question, therefore, is, what is this *pindi* ? *Pindis* are said to represent well marked emblems (weapons, vehicles, flags, etc.) of the various gods.[5] Bharata clearly says that these *pindis* are named either after the gods themselves or their emblems. He has enumerated the *pindis* of the different gods.[6]

Abhinavagupta states that *pindibandha* is a complex formation using three elements viz. *adhara*, *anga* and *prayoga*.[7] The term *adhara* would mean basis, i.e. the basis of representation itself. This representation of the emblems of the different deities was apparently done within a framework of cosmic symbolism. Thus, it was limited not only to the emblems, but perhaps also accompanied with the representation of cosmic dimensions of space and time. The emblems served to symbolise the deities, and cosmic space and time imparted a befitting context to them.[8] The latter are, therefore, known as *adhara* or basic constituents and are ten in number. These are as follows—The seven worlds, and time with its three divisions of past, present and future. The medium of representation consists of the seven limbs or *angas* which are enumerated thus—two hands, two feet, two eyes and the head. *Prayoga* or rendering is the third constituents and is of four types. It could be executed by one or many dances, either uniformly or in a diversity of ways.[9]

Now, coming to the point of the rendering itself, the question that arises is, how were these *pindis* to be actually exhibited in dance? This is answered by Abhinavagupta. Each god had his *pindi* which was to be formed by making the body take the shape of that *karana*[10] or *angahara*[11] that was able, by its name or form to symbolise (by representing the emblem or cosmic symbolism) the deity concerned.[12] For example, the *pindi* of lord *Vishnu* is Tarksya i.e. Garuda. Hence, this is to be shown by forming the *garuda-plutaka karana*. The *pindi* of *Jahnavi* or *Ganga* is *dhara*, so that is to be displayed by the *gangavatarana karana*. The *sarpa* or *snake pindi* is indicated by the *Nagasarpita Karana*. The showing of the body like a trident symbolizes the *pindi* of Siva. Similarly *Sikhipindi* is said to be indicated by *Mayuralalita karana*. *Karanas* like *Visnukranta*, *cakramandala*, etc. indicate the *pindis* of Vishnu. The *Nisumbhita karana* is said to please Siva and the *talapuspaputa karana* is for appeasing Parvati[13]

Four styles of rendering the *Pindibandha* dance have been described in the *Natyasastra*, viz. *Pindi Srnkhalika Latabandha*, *Bhedyaka*[14]. Bharata says, that from the term *pinda* is derived *pindibandha*, *srnkhala* betokens a *gulma* or *cluster*, the Latabandha suggests a net or *jala*-formation and bhedyaka is with dance.[15] Kapila Vatsyayana has connected the *gulma* with the *pindi*. Since *gulma* means a cluster, she has taken the first to denote a collective dance where closed cluster would be made by the dancers.[16] One may, however, venture to suggest that a close perusal of the verse in the NS makes it apparent that gulma is connected not with the *pindi* style, but with *srnkhala*. Abhinavagupta's commentary, too, makes it clear that from *pindi* is derived *pindibandha*, and *gulma* or cluster is connected

* C/o Prof. G.C. Pande, 11, Balrampur House, Allahabad 211 002

with *smkhala*. He also says that the *Pindi, Smkhalika, Latabandha* and *Bhedyaka* were executed by one, two, three, four dances respectively.[17] Then, again, it may be argued that during the *purvaranga* or the staging of the preliminaries of a play, the Pindi style was danced with the *Kanistha asarita*,[18] and we also know that only one dancer performed this first *asarita*.[19]. How would a cluster formation be possible with one single dancer?

According to M.M. Ghose[20] and Kapila Vatsyayana[21] the *smkhala* was a chain formation. This can be readily accepted. It makes it easy to understand how the *smkhala* (a chain formation) perhaps formed a circle, and such concentric circles would give the appearance of a closed cluster. *Latabandha* is the form where the dancers put their arms around each other[22]. Bharata says that it had a *jala* or net formation, perhaps the dancers, with arms round each other stood in such a position in horizontal rows bisected by vertical rows, giving the impression of a net. *Bhedyaka* is the form where the group formation is broken up and dancers perform individual movements.[23]

Abhinavaguptȧ has described *sajatiya* (homogeneous) and *vijatiya* (heterogeneous) dancing of *pindibandha*. Of the four modes of rendering (*prayoga*), the first two executed by one or many dancers, are clear. The latter two, *sama* (uniform) and *visama* (multiform) modes can be connected with the *sajatiya* and *vijatiya pindibandhas*. Where the different dancers display generically conencted *pindis* (e.g. where they show different *pindis* of the same deity), that would be *sajatiya pindibandha*. Where they exhibit heterogeneous forms of *pindis* (*pindis* relating to different deities) that would be *vijatiya pindibandha*. This distinction is to be seen in the *smkhala* and *latabandha* styles.[24]

In the *purvaranga* of a play the *Tandava* along with the *pindibandha* dance forms, was executed.[25] After the placement of the orchestra, commence the *Asaritas*[26] and the *upohana*[27] is rendered, Stringed instruments like *vina* and percussion instruments are played. The first dancer enters, assuming a proper pose *(sthana)*, performs the *recakas* (i.e. rotatory movements of waist, hand, and feet) and offering flowers to the gods pay obeisance to them. The basic idea is, that initially she is to dance the *paryastaka* (i.e. a sequence of ten *karanas*). This has been described as one of the *angaharas*. Percussion instruments are to be played while she performed the *paryastaka*, and the *vina* was played in a fast tempo. Thus she danced till the conclusison of the first *Asarita*, and with the commencing of the second *Asarita* and upohana entered the second dancer. The first dancer now performs the *pindibandha*, while the second of the newcomer, the *paryastaka*[28]. With the commencing of the third *asarita* and *upohana*, enters the third dancer dancing the *paryastaka*, while the first two now perform the *pindibandha*. The same procedure is repeated with the entrance of the fourth dancer during the fourth *asarita*, and now three dancers execute the *pindibandha*. When the fourth dancer, too, has executed the *paryastaka*, then all four perform the *pindibandha*, and make their final exit from the stage.[29] Thus, four dancers enter with the four *asaritas*. They enter one by one, perform the *paryastaka*, and on the entrance of the others execute the *pindibandhas* and finally all leave the stage together.

In his commentary, Abhinavagupta mentions a number of *uparupakas*. These compositions are not dramas in the strict sense of the word, but have more of dance and song. Abhinava terms them as *nottatmaka prabandhas, te prabandhah nrttatamakah na natyatmaka natakadi-vilaksanah*[30]. In fact, Abhinava is the first person to mention such compositions, which were later terms *uparupakas*. He enumerates a number of them. The last two mentioned are *Hallisaka* and *Rasaka*, which refer to the *pindibadha* style of dancing. The *Rasaka*, which refer to the *pindibandha* style of dancing. The *Rasaka* has been described by him as containing many *nartakis* or dancers-sixty-four pairs are mentioned and containing both *uddhata (vigorous)* and *anuddhata* (gentle), elements.[31] In fact, Bhoja in his *Srngara-Prakasa* says that *Rasaka* is a group of dance by the *nartakis* executing the patterns of the *pindis*. He speaks of sixteen, eighteen or twelve *nartakis* in such raskas.[32] Similarly, the *Natyaraska*, also called *carcari*, the last *uparupaka* mentioned by Bhoja, also has the *pindibandhas* constructed with *latas, bhedyaks* and *gulmas*[33] This dance, to be performed in spring time is a pure dance of the *pindi, bhedyaka* and other group movements and patterns. Initially a pair of *nartakis* enter, strew flowers, dance and exit. Then two others enter; and thus groups are formed which execute the *gulma*, *smkhala* etc. There are percussion isntruments, accompanied by recital of rhythmic syllables, beating of sticks and sogns. Some details of *tala* are also given by Bhoja. The whole performance is to conclude with a *mangala sloka*, which says that *Rasaka* full of *pindi, smkhala* etc. and danced to the accomdpaniment of various instruments, was originated by the *devas* or gods when they danced in joy on getting *amrta* (nectar) in the churning of the milky ocean.

Saradatanaya takes *Rasaka* as being three-fold, viz. *Dandarasaka, Mandalarasaka* and *Natyarasaka*. The *Karpuamanjari* of Rajase khara describes the *dandarasaka* as being performed by numerous *nartakis* wheeling round and forming wonderful patterns[34] In the Sanskrit-Tamil text called the *Suddhanandaprakasa*, the pattern of *pindibandha* are said to be formed with hexagonal and octagonal designs: *"Satkonairastakonaisca pindibandhairmano-haraih"*

The *Hallisaka* has been described as the form where there were several *nayikas* and one *nayaka* and the women danced in circles.[35] We may conclude that *Pindibandha* has two aspects corresponding to the two-fold derivation of the word itself. On the one hand, *pindibandh* a means the constitution of a *pindi* or divide emblem, and stood for a special ritualistic dance used for worship, especially in the worship of goods in the *purvaranga*. It abounded in cosmic symbolism. On the other hand, *pindibandha* means the formation of a pinda or *"lumping"* of the dancers together in a cluster. In this sense, *pindibandha* was a group dance, derived from folk origins[36]. This aspect became clearer in the *uparupakas*, like the *Rasaka* and *Hallisaka*. Thus, one aspect of *pindibandha* constituted its earlier and original phase within the tradition of major drama[37]. The other aspect, dominated in the popular or folk dance dramas.

Notes :

1. In the *Natyasatra*, the *Tandava* is described as the dance taught to sage Bharata by Tandu at the orders of Bord siva. *NS' (B.H.U. ed. 1971, Vol. I, ch. 4)*.
2. The *Lasya* from of dance is said to be created by the goddess Parvati. *NS', 4, 256.*
3. *Pindibandhan stato drstva Nandibhadramukha ganah Cakruste name pindinam bandhamasam salakasanam"*. *NS'*, 4, 257.

   A later work, the *Srangaraprakasa* of Bhoja says that Brahma is the author of the *Pindibandhas — "pindyadya bramhanoingajah" Raghavan SR. Pra.* Vol. II, pp. 425-26.
4. *"dvayoh prayoktrtaya sukumarasukumaranrttayoh samakalaprayogena pindibandhanispattim sucayati — Nandibhadramukha gana iti". AB on NS'*, 4, 257.
5. *Evamanyasvapi tatha devatasu yathakramam dhvajabhutah prayoktavyah pindibandhah sucinhitah, NS'*, 4, 263.

   Kumbha described *pindibandha* as having the form of *pinda* and rendered by the imitation of the form of one's chosen deity. *Sa Cestadevatarupanukaranena smrto budhaih the Tasya Cehanukarena Vidheya cavipascita Pindikarena vijeyah Pindibandhastada punah. Kumbha* as quoted in *Bharatakosa*, p. 886.
6. N.S.', 4, 258-62.
7. *"Tatraite pindibandha adharangaprayogasadhaka-tamabhedabahuprakaram bhidyante." AB*(B.H.U.ed, Vol. I) p. 401. .
8. *".....adhare Svaupusyake ca Vividhami srstim Samasutrayan trailokyasthapatistvameva bhagavanvisv-akrtirjrmbhasi"*. Quoted in op. Cef., p. 402.
9. *"Tatra desah kala iti adharadvyabhedatsapta lokah trayah kala ityadharabhedah dasa. Hastau padau aksini sira ityangabheda api saptetl saptadasa. Ekoneko va prayokta. So pi samaprayogo Visamaprayogo veti caturdhakaranena. Sampadyate angaharena veti purvani caturbih pascat saptadasena ca gunanadastadhika-catuhsatyadhikam dvisahasram paramesvarah pindibandhah." AB*, I, p. 401.
10. *Karana* is a sequence of dance movements culminating in a pose.
11. *Angahara* is a sequence of *Karanas*.
12. *"Pindi adharangadisamgatah Taya badhyate buddhau preaves yate tanubhavena sakalaya va vyomadirupayeti pindibandha akrtivisesah ....Akaro badhyate sampadyate punaranenetl pindibandhah karanangaharadih. Ibid*, p. 403. cf. *Tandavalaksanam*, App. F.
13. *....talapuspaputa-Karanena karmavisesasucakena Bhagavatyah paritosanam Sampadyatte. "Tilake ca karah Sthapyah' ityabhinayena Bhagavatah paritosah, 'Nikuttitau yada hastau' ityanena trisula-krtirya kayasampattih. Garudaplutakena tarksyakara-gatisucanam. Gangavatarena dharapindi. Nagapasarpitena bhogipindi. 'Prasaryotksipya ca karau' ityangaharena akariyabhasmatrisulasivalingadipindi-nispattih."* ibid, p. 405.

    "pindibandhagrahanena sikhipindaprabhrtyupaya-mayuralalitadikaranasamgrahah, ...Yatha Visnu-krantasya Cakramandalasya Ca Vaisnavakridasuca-kasya Sah." ibid. p. 406.
14. *"pindinam vidhayascaiva catvarah Samprakirtitah Pindi Srnkhalika caiva Latabandho 'the Bhedyakah." NS'* 4, 292.
15. *pindibandhastu pindatavat gulmah Srnkhalika bhavet Jalopanaddha ca lata sanrtto bhedyaskah Smrtah." NS'*4, 293.
16. Vatsyayana.K. *Classical Indian Dance in Literature and the Arts*, pp. 33-4.
17. *"Tatra visesantararhaitam hrdyamekaprayojyam*

pindibandharupamityekah prakarovisesanamadhye-avirahatsamanyasabdenoktah. Tadaha-pindibandhah pindibandhadvitiyaprakarah Sajatiyo va ekanalavabaddhakamalayugalavat, vijatiyo va hamsavadanparigrhitanalanalinavat, gulmah Srnkhal-ikasabdavacyah. Nartakitrayaprayojyastu tato 'pi vaicitryasahisnutavajjalavadivicitratam gacchatpur-vatsajatiyavijatiyatma latabandhah. Nartakicatus-tayaprayojyastu..jnato bhedyakah" AB *Vol. I pp. 462-3.*

"They are done by one or more *nartakis*....That done by one is a simple *Pindi.* The pattern executed by two looks like two lotuses on a stalk, or a swan holding by its beak a lotus stalk with the lotus. This *pindi* by two is called a *gulma srnkhalika,* the pattern formed by three is *jala,* by four *latabandha."* Raghavan V., *Bhoja's Srngara-Prakasa,* p. 588.

18. *"Pindibandhah kanisthe tu Srnkhala tu layantare Madhyame ca latabandhah juesthe caivatha bhedyakak." NS'* 4, 294. For meaning of *asarita* See fn 26.

19. *Eka tu prathamam yojya dve dvitiyam tathaiva ca Tisro vastu, trtiyam tu catasrastu caturthakam." NS'* 4, 291.

20. "Of these the *gulma* is a general collective dance, the *srnkhala* is the dance in which partners hold one another's hands, the *lata* is the dance of two putting their arms around each other, and *bhedyaka* is the dance of each one separately away from the group". Ghosh, M.M. (tr) *Natyasastra,* p. 71.

21. Vatsyayana. *K. Classical Indian Dance in literature* and the Arts. p. 34.

22. **l.c.**

23. **l.c.**

24. For *sajatiya and* Vijatiya *pindibandhas* see Footnote 34.

25. *NS'* 4, 276.94

26. *asaritam gitam,* kavi, Ram Krishna, *Bharatakosa,*p. 64 *Asarita* is a kind of music in many parts and with a fixed and elaborate **tala** or beat structure for each part. Its parts *mukha, pratimukha, deha* and *samharana* were compared with *udgitha, Prastara, Pratihara* and *Nidhana* respectively of *saman* singing and some compare a further *asarita* component, the *sirsaka* with the *Samic* part called *upadrava.* l.c.

Four *asaritas* with different *tala*—structures have been described in the connection of *pindibandha....NS* 31, 77. The connection of *pindibandha* with *Asarita* is mentioned elsewhere too.

"Prayogastu yada tvesam pindibandhairvikalpyate pratyekam hyangavinyasastada tesam prthakaprthak. NS' (GOS' ed) 31, 77).

These are in order the *Kanistha, Layantara, Madhyama & Jyestha* respectively. These were distinguished by the number of beats they required.

27. *Upohana* was rendered in the first few initial *kalas* or beats of the *mukha* part of the *Asarita. NA'* (Gaekwad oriental series ed.) 31, 79.

28. *"Prayujya gitavadye tu niskramennartaki tatah anenaiva vidhanena pravisantyaparah prthak." NS'* 4, 283.

"Anyascanukramenatha pindim badhnanti yah striyah. tavatparyastakah karyo yavatpindi na badhyate." NS' 4, 284. Abhinava explains that *niskrama* here does not mean that the dancer will totally leave the stage, but simply that she will follow another.

"Sa niskramedapasaret, Na tu

29. *"Tatha hi — ekam tu prathamamityatra pratha-masaritamabhinayati. Tato Dvitiya dvitiya-saritam. Tatsamakalamtu prathama kevalmangaharam karotiti. Evam trticyasritarthamabhinayati. Tada dve angaharam prayunjate. Caturthi caturthasaritabhinayam yada karoti tisr 'ongaharam ranjayanti Anye tvabhinayaprayoge pi sahitatamahuh." AB NS'* 4, 294.

30. *AB* (B.H.U. ed.) Vol I, pp. 435—37.

31. *Anekanartakiyojyam citratalalayanvitam acatus-sasthiyugaladrasakam masmoddhatam." ibid.* p. 437.

It may be noted that *pindibandha* arose out of *sukumara* and *asukumara nrttas.*

32. *"Sodasadvadas 'astau va yasminnrtyanti nayikahpindi-bandhadivinyasaih rasakam tadudahrtam." Bhoja, Srngara-Prakasa,* Vol. II. pp. 425.

33. *"Latakyhabhedyakaih gulmaih nanapravratta—pradarsakaih patrairekatva—sanyuktam pindi-bandham tukarayeta." ibid.,* p. 427.

34. *"Paribhramantyah vicitrabandhaih imadvisahsan-artakyah khelanti dandarasah." Karpuramanjari* 4, 10.

35. *"Mandalena tu yannrttam hallisakamiti smrtam Ekastatra tu neta Syadgopastrinam yatha harih." AB* (BH-U), Vol. I. p. 437.

36. It should be remembered that folk culture while full of creativity is not *pre se* standardised. While standard forms are created out of it, in itself the folk tradition varies continuously. The relationship of the dialects to the standard language,illustrates the relationship of folk forms to classical forms in arts.

37. The use of *pindibandha* in the *purvaranga* appears to have become obscure by the time of Abhinava, although he clearly knew the practice. It is possible that it hadfallen out of use in the dramatic tradition but continued in the folk tradition. This is suggested by the following lines—

"Nanu sarvo 'yam pindibandhaprakara ihopahogi vana Vetyasankyaha .... na Cayam pindibandhaprakaro laksye vicchinnah. Kevalamrttrna—Kaksayoh patitamahausadhivadanavasthitairabhyudhartum na sakyate savadhanataya tu sakyata eveti natralasyam srayitavyam. Anyatha katham prayogamahuh. AB on *NS'* 4, 295.

Puratattva No.18; 1987-88

CREDIT AND MORTGAGE DOCUMENTS IN THE LEKHAPADDHATI.

Pushpa Prasad*

The well known Gujarat collection of documents, *Lekhapaddhati*[1] contains many documents relating to the credit and mortgage system. Most of the documents are dated V.S. 1288/1251A.D; one is dated V.S. 1332/1275 A.D. and yet another V.S. 1533/1476 A.D. A.K. Majumdar and Lallanji Gopal have treated them quite rightly as giving evidence on conditions of credit in pre-Sultanate Gujarat.[2] An annotated, literal translation of some of the deeds is being presented here for the first time.

One group of documents gives the texts of bills [3] and shows how they were issued and honoured. According to one document dated Samvat year 1533 a son of *rajaputra* was to be paid 124 *drammas* when the royal bill *rajahundika* matured. The period of payment was 15 days. For any delay beyond that time, beginning with the 16th day, the holder was to be paid one *dramma* and one pice *(Kala)*.

The larger part of our documents relate to direct loans and mortgages. Loans were given on personal security of a surety known as *Vyavaharapatra* and *hastaksharani*[4]. Loans contracted without any security were recorded in the *Sanmukhahastaksharani*[5]. Another document, called *Sva hastaksharani*, is more important from the point of view of inheritance. it records that the receipt for 500 drammas was being given by a son to his father. The son states that he had taken this amount from his father in order to start a money lending business and this money has been paid out from his share in the ancestral property. The son agrees that at the time of a division of his father's property at subsequent date, he would receive 500 *drammas* less. There is a provision for a surety and witness.

Loans were taken against the mortgaged objects recorded in *adhaukrta vastunamupari grahitadravya patra Vidhi, Asvaddanaka grahaddanaka patra, Ksetraddanakapatra and Adhipatra* being the names of deeds for mortgaging horses, houses and fields respectively. *Vrddihipalabhogapatra* recorded on usufructuary mortgage. The money borrowed by mortgaging the product of land or other property was recorded in *Valitpatra Vidhi*. The *Grahadulipatram* recorded the mortgage of a house which was lost to the debtor if he did not pay the money within the time limit [7]. Another document records the loan of food-grains to be repaid together with interest in kind such deed being called *Vriddhidhanya sharani*[8].

In all the documents the creditor is known as *dhanika*[9] *Vyavaharaka and Sreshti*[10] who invests his money for the sake of profit. The term *Wevehar* is the Gujarati form of *Vyavaharaka* [11]. The literal meaning of this term is businessmen, trader and merchant.[12]. Here it is used in the sense of the money-lender and merchant as one of the document, records, that the son of a merchant borrowed money for the business of money lending.

The creditors, debtors and sureties are shown in these documents as belonging to Shrimali, Pragavate, Vayada, Oswal and Gurjar castes, These are sub-divisions of the Bania or Vaisya community.[13] The names of the sub-divisions are often derived from the places of origin came to be appended with their castes. the Shrimalis take their name from the town of Shrimal, which is now called Bhinmal, in Marwar.[14] Tod writes "these towns are on the high road to Cutch and Gujarat, which has given them from the most remote times a commercial celebity....... very wealthy mahajans or merchants used to reside here but insecurity both within and without has much injured these cities, the first of which has its name Mal from its wealth"[15] The legend of their origin is that the goddess Lakshmi created from a flower garland 90,000 families, to act as servants to the 90,000 Shrimali Brahmans and these were the ancestors of Shrimali Banias.[16] According to Nando Lal Dey Bhinmal was the capital of the Gurjjaras from about the 6th to 9th century A.D.[17] Commissariat suggests that it remained the capital upto 13th century.[18]

The name of Oswal is derived from the town Osi in Marwar.[19]

Department of History, Aligarh Muslim University, Aligarh 202 001

The loans were made and repaid in coins called *drammas*. Three type of *drammas* are mentioned: *Visalapriya* or *Visvamalla dramma; paraupatha* or *paraupathaka dramma;*[20] *and Dvivallaka drammas.*[21] The *Visalapriya drammas* are probably to be ascribed to king Visaladeva of the Vaghela dynasty.

All these coins were uttered at the mint of Shrimala, the earlier name of Bhinmal.[22] According to Dalal, however, the name does not refer to the town Shrimal or Bhinmal, but to the fact that it was under the charge of goldsmiths, who belonged to the Shrimali caste.[23]

From these documents it appears that the practice of taking sureties for loans was general. Some of the document refer to *Adhipalakas*, *Bhattaputra Kutumbikas* (the cultivators) and merchants who are appointed as a sureties. The deeds are often said to be written in the presence of *Pancakula*[24]. It seems that for realising the money, one had to approach the royal officers. The responsibility of the sureties for the payment of money was held to be equal to that of the debtor himself.

All the documents recorded the rate of interest as 2% per month. Al-Beruni also refers to this rate as the permissible rate of interest.[25]

The translations of the documents follow:

A. **Raja - hundika** (Royal Drafts/Bills)

Hail ! *Mahamandalesvara ranaka* so-and-so instructs officer so-and-so of his *mandala* in the following manner. The order is like this: You should pay 3000 *dr.* in words three thousand ***drammas,*** out of these *dr.*, first collected and to be sent to the royal treasury, to *rajaputra* so-and-so. Likewise you should pay to eight foot soldiers belonging to him (i.e. *rajaputra)* who have come here, 8 dr., perday towards undressed provisions until the account is clear. Samvat year (802) Jyestha Sudi 15, Thursday, signature of Sri. Instructions (have been given to) the messenger.

IIB

Hail! *Mahamandalesvar Ranaka* so-and-so instructs certain officer as follows. The order is like this. You should pay 3000 *dr.* in words three thousand *drammas*, out of these *dr.*, first collected and due to be sent to the royal treasury, to Paramara *rajaputra*. Like-wise you should pay to the eight foot-soldiers belonging to him, who have come here, 8 *drammas* per day towards undressed provisions until the account is clear. Samvat year 1288 Vaisakh/Sudi 15, Monday. The instructions have been given personally to the messenger.

IIIB

By the order of king, on the word of so-and -so of such-and such territory, a bill of exchange is issued to so-and-so in the name of so-and-so as follows. You should pay to *rajaputra* so-and-so son of so-and-so *dr.* 124 in words, one hundred and twenty four *drammas* when the bill (*hundika*) becomes due (*phalit-pade)* according to the usage of the bill. The period (of payment) is 15 days. For each day beyond the limit, you should pay 1 *dramma* 2 ka[26] (i.e. 1-3/16 dr.) Samvat year 1533. Jyestha Sudi 8, Tuesday. Signed.

Vyavahara - patra (Debt Deed)

In the Samvat year 1332 Asvina Sudi 10 Sunday today here at Anahillapatana, during the victorious and auspicious reign of Shri Sarangadeva, who is adorned with the line of kings, Parameshvara, Paramabhattaraka, who obtained valour in consequence of a boon given by the husband of Uma, who harassed enemies, he is indeed an incarnation of Narayana lying on the deep waters, i.e. Vishnu, who is an (it were) a sun, able to open the buds of the lotus field of Chaulukya race, and by the grace of Shri Laksmikanta, i.e. Vishnu, has become a new self chosen husband of royal fortune, he is like a terrible forest conflagration of the time of universal destruction in order to burn down the forest of plant (Kandali)-like enemies. He is the only one, able to tear a part of temples of the host of elephants in the army of the king of South or Dakshina; who is new Chakravarti, while his obedient and loyal servant Mahamatya Shri Dharnidhara holds the office of Shri Karana etc. and conducts the entire business of the royal seal; in these circumstances, while Maharajakula Shri Dharavarsha, is immensely prosperous in Chandravati Karana, which is being enjoyed by him as a consequence of the king's grant of benefice *(prasad)*, and while *Mahantaka* Vijayasimha of Pathaka so-and-so acts as an officer incharge of Dravya Mudra (?) This deed of debt is written in the presence of the *Panchakula*, including Chandisimha who was appointed (by Dharavarsha), in the following manner. Ganapati son of Sahu

Jayac´andra of Oswal caste and resident of Prahladanapura borrowed; for legitimate purposes, from Vyasalakshmidhara 5,000 *drammas*, in words fifty thousand *drammas* (in) old *drammas* issued by *Visvamalla* (?) which were uttered at the mint of Shrimala, thrice tested, and which are still current in the gold market as merchant's money *(Shresthartha)* in one instalment. The monthly interest on these *drammas* is two *drammas* percent per month and interest percent will be accumulated. These *drammas* without the layer of mud; without dispute, quarrel and anxiety, within 24 hours (of the demand) renoucing all claims to it, should be returned all at once with accumulated interest of *drammas* to the satisfaction of Vyasalakshmidhara. For giving (assuring the payment) these *drammas* with interest, for preventing all controversy and harassment Padamsimha, son of Sahu Jagasimha of the Oswal caste *(jati)* and the merchant *(vanij)* Vikramasimha, son of merchant Dharna of Shrimala caste, both residing at the same place are made surities for mental and inner satisfaction of Vyasalakshmidhara. When one is approached the other is supposed to be approached. If one is available and the second is not responding to the summons then the person who is available should take the responsibility of the deed of debt or promissary note, just like the debtor to the money-lender. In this sense the agreement of the debtor and of the sureties is recorded by their signatures/given by their own hands and to the best of their knowledge and judgement. Mahantaka Shri Pala wrote this deed at the request of both the parties. Omission or addition of letters should always be treated as legal/should be condoned.

II B

In the Samvat Year 1288 Vaishakha Sudi 15 Monday today, here at Anahillapataka, during the auspicious and victorious reign of Shri Bhimdeva, who was adorned with the line of kings, Maharajadhiraja, Parameshvara, Paramabhattaraka, who obtained valour in consequence of boon given by the husband of Uma, who had harassed the host of enemies and the seventh *Chakravartin* who by the grace of the husband of Paravati has become the self-chosen husband of royal fortune, a modern (version of) Siddharaja, terrible to the enmey kings, while his loyal servant Mahamataya so-and-so holds the office of Shri Karana and conducts the entire business of the (royal) seal *(Samsta Mudra Vayapren paripanthayti)*; while here in the pathaka such and such *mahantaka* Vijayasimha acts as the officer incharge of *dua Mudra (?)*, in these circumstances in Balua village situated in the Dandahiyapathaka, which is being enjoyed by *rajaputra* Chaturbhuja, having received it from the king as a benefice (prasad), this debt deed is being written in the knowledge of the *Panchakula*, consisting of the *Vahaka* (an official), *rajaputra* Ajayasimha who was appointed by him (*rajaputra* Chaturbhuja), *Mahantaka* Jajala son of *Mahantaka* Yashacandra, and others thus.

The creditor known by the name, 'Shresthi son-and-so, son of Shresthi so-and-so resident of this place employed his money for profit. This (is) his signature, creditor by name. The resident of this very place the cultivator so-and-so, son of cultivator so-and-so, out of genuine need or for legitimate purpose, received 210 *paraupatha drammas* in cash, in words two hundred ten *dr.*, which were uttered at the mint of Shrimala, thrice tested and meant for commercial transactions, and the money, to be paid as interest on these *drammas*, is 2 *drammas* percent per month. These *drammas* should be paid annually in the month of Karttika along with interest, without layers of mud, *(Matta-skandha)*[27] renouncing all claim to it *(Niryogakshema)*, all at once *(Yekmushtya)* within eight *pahars (Asta praharika)* (a day-and night). In order to execute the above mentioned conditions, in order to ensure the payment of the *drammas* and in accordance with the common practice of borrowers, the cultivator so-and-so has been appointed surety and cultivator so-and-so the second surety. Here signature, here witnesses.

Kshetraddanaka (Deed of a mortgage of Field)

In the Samvat year 1228 Vaishakha Sudi 15 Thursday, today, as usual mentioned the dynastic lineage, a deed of mortgage of field is being written in the following manner; That the creditor *(dhanika)* is known by the name merchant *(Vyavaharaka)* Chahada, resident of Shri Pattan, belonged to Shrimalla caste *(jati)* invested his own money for profit. This (is) his signature, debtor *(dharnika)* known by the name. The cultivator *(kutumbika)* Mokhala,, resident of Sankhari village for legitimate purpose, borrowed from merchant Chahada 500 *drammas* in words five hundred *drammas*, old *drammas* issued by Visvamallapriya[29] which were uttered at the mint of Shrimalla, thrice tested and which are still current in transaction. Against these *drammas* and for the inner satisfaction of creditor, own field has been given for mortagaged, a field, which is acquired by the ancestors, is being enjoyed even now, along with nine types of treasurers, *(Navanidhanasahita)*[30] and together with various gardens and rows of trees, with four boundaries and for the enjoyment of usufruct *(Vridhi phalabhogacharena)*. The creditor, after giving the whole (sums of) *drammas* for this field, should be paid (?) on *Akshayatratiya* of every year (or the loan is to be repaid on *Akshayatratiya* day). The income of the field should be enjoyed by the creditor/merchant. On the fourth day (when the date is already over) the debtor will not get his field (*Kshetra*) liberated by ready money tied in a piece of cloth. In order to execute the above mentioned conditions, to prevent this order from the harassment of all the other (?),........... two sureties so-and-so are appointed, and they will see that the conditions laid down in the document should be maintained. When one is approached the others are supposed to have been approached and when all are approached, each would be supposed to be approached. For observing the terms of the written deed if one is available then one should not in reply point to other. In this context, three witnesses along with inhabitants put their signatures for all persons concerned assembled at one place and put their signatures along with three witnesses.

Adhau-krita-vastunam-Uparigrhita dravya patra vidhi. (The Model of a Document for Money taken against mortagaged objects)

In the Samvat year 1288 Vaishakha Sudi 15 Thursday, today, at Shri Pattan, here after mentioning the proper line of the kings a deed of mortagaged objects upon which the *drammas* are borrowed, is being written in the following manner: That *Pattadhara* Malaka of Sankhari village mortgaged with merchant Chahada, a resident of Pragavaṭa caste. After mortgaging, 8 female buffaloes, 16 bullocks 50 cows and 2 *phiks* (bulls?) received 2404/in words two thousand four hundred and four, old Visavamallapriya *drammas*, which were uttered at the mint of Shrimalla, thrice tested, and which are still current in transaction. The monthly interest is two *drammas* per cent. These *drammas* should be paid at the time of Dipavali of each year, without dispute and grumbling within eight *pahars* (day and night), at once by the debtor, even if the creditor *(Vayavaharka)* had gone to another place. If the merchant is not present in the village then the debtor, if it is a joint family, should pay the whole *drammas* to his brother or to his son, and the money must be broguht to the house. In case either creditor or debtor, of these one of them has died or is destroyed and sometime, unfortunately or carelessly, a bad pretext occured, then their sons and grandsons should pay the *drammas* according the deed. On the said day if the debtor fails to pay all the money together with interest to the creditor then the arrears should be made up by selling the appropriate quantity of mortgage objects like vegetables in the market in the presence of the debtor and sureties, and should realise the money. However, if the mortgaged objects mentioned in the need after sale are not sufficient to pay the interest together with other expenses, then the surety should borrow money with interest from the other creditor or by selling things of his own house and should pay the interest to the creditor. The debtor and sureties should not report any dispute to the royal court. In case of caste-controvesy *(jativivad)*, or dispute, even all the expenses should be borne by the debtor as a defeated party. However, if a part of the mortgaged object get damaged or destroyed by an act of the gods or natural calamity, such as fire, theft and excessive rain, then the guaranter and debtor would still be liable to pay the principal and other expensès to the creditor and (he became) free from the burden. The creditor is not concerned with the loss of the mortgaged objects and (any) quarrel-some talk. Now if the creditor is ever under the necessity of obtaining money due to some work occurred in his own house, then the creditor, accompanied by the *Bhattaputra*,[31] will approach the sureties and obtain them the principal (*mulya*) together with interest. In this connection expenses on account of the process involving the *Bhattaputras* should be borne entirely by the debtor and sureties. For maintaining the above mentioned provisions, for giving the interest along with principal and expenses, to confirm the provisions or terms recorded in the deed, for observing the security of the mortgaged objects the sureties are to be considered as debtor and also maintained along with the creditor. If there are many sureties available then one of the sureties is approached, all will be supposed to have been approached, and when all are approached, each would be supposed to have been approached and each single person should make out all the payment to the creditor. There is no difference between the surety and debtor. When one is approahced, he in reply should not point to the others, and the creditor should obtain the terms, amount and interest with expenses same as mentioned in the deed that of debtor.[32] The sureties should tell themselves in their mind that they are debtors. For this purpose having given up all the complaints and ful-filling the *Adhipalakas* are enjoyed to effect the payment of the loan with interest to the creditor on the strength of the present deed. For this purpose provisions are made for naming four *Adhipalas*, resident of a certain village and belonging to such-and-such caste. They gave their signatures by hand and debtor also gave his own signature by hand. And neighbourers of certain caste and five persons known by name are witnesses. Parthijayat wrote this deed at the request of both the parties. Omissions of additions of letters should always be treated as legal/should be condoned.

Valita-Patra-Vidhi (A Particular kind of Mortgage Deed)[33]

1A

In the Samvat year 1288 Vaishakh Sudi 15 Thursday, today, hereafter mentioning the proper line of the king, a deed of mortgage of the produce of land, is being written in the following manner. Thus the creditor is known by name, resident of a certain village belonging to a certain caste, invests his own money for profit. Here is the signature of the debtor known by the name. Here the resident of this very place as mentioned earlier so-and-so, due to his own need; received 300/in words three hundred *drammas* which were uttered at the mint of Shrimalla, thrice tested and still current in transactions. In furture every year, these *drammas* after adding the interest would amount to double and become 600 *drammas*. In the context of these *drammas*, for the inner satisfaction of the creditor, 50 trees of mangoes of a certain garden have been mortgaged. From the price of these mangoes of the trees the creditor should record 100 *drammas* at the back of the deed. After completing six years, one's own accord the mango (trees) will be free from the bond of the creditor. After six years the creditor will have no connection with mango trees, but upto the point the mango-trees will exclusively belong to the creditor. For executing above mentioned deed, for giving the mangoes, in order to prevent all type of harassment of other family members, heirs, and members connected with other creditors, two sureties are appointed, (and) two *Rakshapalas*, of such-and-such are (also) appointed for the inner-satisfaction of the creditor. When one is approached all are supposed to have been approached. If one signature of the creditor is available then he should not in reply point to the other, and should observe all the conditions of the deed. In this sense, debtor and sureties gave their signatures by their own hand, written in the knowledge of 5 witnesses and neighbourers.

Vrddhi-phalabhoga-patram (Usufractuary Mortgage Deed)

In the Samvat year 1288 Vaishakha Sudi 15 Monday, here at Anahillapattaka, after mentioning the proper line of the kings, today, at Balau village a deed of usufructuary mortgage is being written in the following manner. The creditor is known by the name............ A certain villager, a resident of this very place due to need, borrowed in cash 100 Shri *paurapath drammas*/ in word 100 *drammas*, which were uttered at the mint of Shrimalla thrice tested and still current in transactions. In connection with these *drammas*, and for the satisfaction of the creditor, a house, facing to the east, with a good threshold, double storied with an open space surrounded by four boundaries mortgaged for the enjoyment of usufruct *(Vriddhiphalabhoga)*. There is no rent of the house, no interest upon *drammas*. This is the principle of enjoying the interest on a deposit. The damaged and collapsed (condition) of the house and repairing expenses, all should be added in the deed in the presence of the debtor. When the house is being vacated, the expenses of repairing the house should be obtained by the creditor. (As to) this house, only after paying the entire amount with expenses on *Akshayatratiya* then only the debtor will get release this house. The boundaries of this house are as follows.... For performing the above mentioned terms and conditions, for paying the *drammas* with expenses, sureties are appointed; the cultivator so-and-so, and the second surety so-and-so. Here is the signature, here is the witnessess.

Grhaddanaka-patra-vidhi (A Deed of Mortgage of a House)

In the Samvat year 1288 Vaishakha Sudi 15 Monday, today after mentioning the proper line of the kings, at Chandravati, a deed of mortgage of a house is being written in the presence of *Panchakula* and *raula* (ravata) Dharavarsha in the following manner. The creditor is known by the name, resident of certain village, belonging to such-and-such caste, son of so-and-so-, invests his own money for profit. Here is the signature of the debtor, known by the name. The resident of this very place of Vayada caste, Suraka son of merchant Kura, due to his own need received 400/ four hundred Shri Visavamallapriya *drammas*, which were uttered at the mint of Shrimalla, thrice tested, and still current in transactions, from the creditor. In the context of these *drammas* and for the mental satisfaction of the creditor, his own house, with four boundaries mentioned below, and for the enjoyment of usufruct, has been given for mortgage; the house which was acquired by the ancestors, is being still enjoyed, with an open space, four sides surrounded by the verandah, with a first room of the house and kitchen, covered with tiles, well founded, double storeid and facing the east. There is no rent of the house, no interest upon *drammas*. It is for usufructuary enjoyment. The boundaries of the house are in this manner. In the east the boundary line is upto the verandah of temple, in the south, limit is *Nivapata*[34] of Deva's house, in the west the limit is the wall of compound of royal palace, and in the north up to the high way, or royal way. With these four boundaries my own house which was acquired by my ancestors mortgaged for five years from today for the mental satisfaction of the creditor. If any sort of expenses are claimed on this house by the sons, relatives, heirs and the government, then all should be borne by the debtor. Now at any time when the creditor falls into strained circumstances (and is) in the need of money, then he can forcibly collect the *drammas* from the debtor. Or else, this very bond, he can mortgage to any other creditor with the consent of the debtor and receive the money. If the house, is damaged due to natural calamities, fire, excessive rain, burnt, collapses, or is damaged, then the debtor after investing his own money should repair the house in the same manner and should give to the creditor. In case the debtor is unable to do so then the creditor in the knowledge of the debtor should repair the house in the same way on the original foundation. The money invested on wood, tile, mason, and day labour should be entered on the back of the bond with interest, in the presence of the debtor. The creditor should not construct the granary with in the house or a store house for gram and salt. If any sort of damage occured in the house due to their disturbances then the creditor, after investing his own money, should repair the house and the creditor should enjoy this house at own's sweet will upto the time limit mentioned in the deed. After the time limit, every year at the time of Dipavali, paid the whole expenses along with original amount and got the house released. On the next day of Dipavali the debtor will not get released (his house) by ready money tied in a piece of cloth. For observing the above mentioned conditions, for paying the original amount with expenses collectively, in order to prevent all types of harassment from the sons, relative, heirs of the family and other family, are appointed *Adhipala* as a surety and two certain persons of such-and-such caste, sons of so-and-so, and the creditor should also observed the terms and conditions of the deed same as the debtor. If one surety is available to the creditor he should not reply "go to the other surety". He should fulfill all the conditions and stipulations as if he is the debtor himself. In this context debtor and *Adhipala* gave their signatures by their own hand in the presence of the five witnesses and neighbours. Parthijayat wrote this deed with the consent of both the parties. Omissions or additions of the letters should be treated as legal/should be condoned.

Asvaddanaka-patra (A Deed of Mortgage of Horse.)

After mentioning the proper line of the kings, in the Samvat year 1288, Vaishakha Sudi 15, Monday, here at Patan, a deed of mortgage of horses is being written in the following manner. The creditor is known by the name. Here the resident of this very place Hedau [35] Nagaden due to his own need received 800/ eight hundred old and Visamallapriya *drammas* which were uttered at the mint of Shrimalla, thrice tested and still current in transaction. For the mental satisfaction of the creditor Asadhira, Hedau Nagaden has tied his own horses, one Hirau and other one Shri Khandau, at the door of Asadhira. For both the horses, tied at the door, grass for eating, a place for shed, medicine, physician, and a guard, and all (other) expenses should be met out by the debtor. If the debtor does not bear the daily expenses according the deed then the creditor will provide for the (debtor's) horses, prickly shurbs in place of shed, a gravel in place of grass, and urine in place of water. In observing these conditions in this context the debtor should not create any obstacle to the creditor. If the debtor at such time does not accomplish the expenses according to the deed, then after one day, the creditor for every day's expenses required one and half *dramma* for each item; medicine and physician, all should be written at the back of this deed. The security and welfare of both the horses should be maintained by the creditor honestly same as the debtor. These two tied horses at the door should be used for roaming /riding upon the earth, upto the sea shore either by the creditor for his own purpose or by his servants. If at any time due to the excessive riding, vomiting and blood these two horses die, or run away.......... if death is caused by drawing the ropes round the hind legs of horses, die out of frightened, drowned in the water, due by a stake, die due to disease, killed by the tiger, loin and other wild animals of the caves, die due to the invasion of enemy; while entering the house of the debtor's enemy to be killed, die due to the hurt of the edge of pin, or some enemy cut of tongue and killed, unable to walk due to wound developed in the feet, die due to fire, excessive water, air and bite of snake, die some time due to another natural calamity, then Hedau Nagaden (will) replace the previous died horses: of the same breed, same colour or any two of the same age, and tied at door of creditor Asadhira. For these two horses, Hedau Nagaden, from this day in the course of two month, may be liberated after paying the money with interest and expenses, at one time without quarrel and dispute, excluding the reduplication, to the creditor. If on the said day in the course of two months, the debtor, after paying the money with interest and expenses, is unable to release these two horses from the creditor according to the deed, then the creditor, in the knowledge of the debtor, after bringing these two horses in the market sell them on the current prices like vegetables, sugar and *badari* fruit. Even after selling the two horses, if the amount of money lent along with expenses can not be recovered in full, then the creditor should realise the money by selling any other objects from the house of the debtor or of any two sureties. And the debtor should not make any quarrel with the creditor in relation to higher and lesser prices of the sale horses in present and future. For executing the above mentioned terms and conditions of the deed, are appointed two sureties, Puna son of the merchant Jagsi of Shrimala caste and Khokhaka son of merchant Mokha of Gurjar caste, both sureties should observe the terms and conditions of written deed same as debtor. If one signature is available to the creditor, to maintain the term and conditions of the deed then the other should not reply. The creditor should observe the terms and conditions of the deed like debtor. In this sense debtor and surety gave their signatures by own hand.

Adhi-patram (Mortgage Deed)

In the Samvat year 1288, Vaishakha Sudi 15 Monday, today, at Shri Pattan after mentioning the dynastic list, a deed of mortgage is being written like this. The creditor is known by name. The resident of this very place the creditor Khemako invests his own money for profit. Here is the signature of debtor, known by the name. The resident of this very place merchant *(Vanija)* Punaka, for the sake of his own need, received 200 two hundred *dvivallakya*[36] Shri Visalpriya *drammas*, uttered at the mint of Shrimalla, thrice tested and still current in the market. The monthly interest is two *drammas* percent. Now for paying these *drammas* and the inner satisfaction of the creditor the merchant Punaka mortgaged (a house) facing to the east with a good threshold, double storied, well founded, covered with titles, with an open space on all sides, with a court-yard, with four boundaries as mentioned. The four boundaries of the house are in the following manner. In the east the boundary is the merchant Jagasi's house, in south the boundary is the merchant Chahad's compound wall, in the west up to the high way; in the north the boundary is the varandah of Deva Shri Adinath temple. Now his own house with four boundaries has been mortgaged to the creditor. This house would be liberated on *Akshyatratiya* after paying the amount with interest, free from the layers of earth, at one time according to the terms of the deed without any quarrel to the creditor. If the debtor is unable to get the house release on *Akshyatratiya*, then, each year beyond, should release the house after paying the extra money to the creditor. In case the house is damaged due to the calamities owing to the acts of the king and god, or burnts, collapses or damage then the debtor and sureties should repair this house in the same way and should give to the creditor. According the deed the creditor should enjoy this house permanently as long as (till the sun and moon endure) till the debtor would not pay the amount with interest (to the creditor). In the sense, for maintaining the terms of this deed two sureties are appointed; Puna son of Jagasi of Oswal caste, Chahada son of Nagarbahada. If one signature is available then the other should not reply, and sureties should observe the terms and conditions of the deed same as debtor. In this context debtor and sureties both have signed by their own hand. Parthijayat wrote this mortgage deed with five witnesses as mentioned and (this should be treated as legal.

Notes :

1. *Lekhapaddhati (LP)* edited by Dalal and Srigondekar, *Gaekwad Oriental Series*, (Baroda 1925) XIX, pp.10-11, 19-20, 33-42, 56.
2. A.K. Majumdar, *Chaulukyas of Gujarat*, (Bombay 1956), pp.275-82; Lallan Ji Gopal, *Economics Life of Northern India* (Delhi, 1965), pp. 162-70.
3. *Hundika*, mod. *Hundi* (R.N. Saletore, *Encyclopaedia of Indian Culture*, II (Delhi, 1982), p. 550). The term *hundika* for a bill of exchange does not seem to have been attested prior to Kalhan's *Rajatrangani*, V,266, 275, 302, which was composed between 1148 and 1150 A.D. but S.R. Sharma recently reviewed a Bakhshali Manuscript edited by Takao Hayashi. Here certain rules as *hundikasamyanayana* are mentioned. The editor has assigned this manuscript tentatively to the seventh century A.D. (*Aligarh Journal of Oriental Studies*, III, No.2, pp. 156-158). Several examples of hundika are mentioned in *Lokaprakash of Kshamendra* (*The Kashmir Series of Texts and Studies*, No. LXXV, ed. by J.Z. Shastri (Srinagar 1947), Ch.II. pp.13-18.
4. *L.P.* p. 55 Translation of this document is not given here.
5. *Ibid.*
6. *L.P*. p. 56 (Not translated here).
7. *L.P*. p. 38.
8. *Ibid. p. 21.*
9. The term *dhanika* occurs frequently in the Manusmriti and other Smriti literature. (*The Sacred Books of the East*, edited by Max Muller, XXV, Chapter VIII, 47, 51, 176, 177. Reference to *dhanika* in the sense of creditor are found in the Jaunpur brick inscription and Kasrak Copper Plate Inscription of 13th Century. *Journal of U.P. Historical Society, XVIII (Lucknow, 1945), Pt. II, pp. 196-201 : Annual Report of Indian Epigraphy; 1962-63 List No. A-51, A-52.*
10. The term *Shreshti* means, a banker, merchant or the foreman of a guild. D.C. Sircar, *Indian Apigraphical Glossary*, (Delhi 1966) p. 317.
11. B.N. Mehta and B.B. Mehta, *The Modern Gujarati English Dictionary* (Baroda, 1925).
12. Wilson, *Glossary of Judicial and Revenue Terms* (Delhi 1968), p. 552.
13. B.N.S. Yadava, *Society and Culture in Northern India* (Allahabad, 1973), p.38.
14. R.V. Russell and Rai Bahadur Hira Lal, *The Tribes and Castes of the Central Province of India*, II (Delhi 1975), pp. 160-161.New this town is situated in Jaswantpura in Jodhpur district about 105 miles south-west of Jodhpur city. *The Imperial Gazetteer of India*, VIII, p. 111. An earliest evidence of Bhinmal is available in Hiuen-Tsiang's account. Beal transliterates this name as Balmer or Barmer (*Buddhist Records of the Western World*, II, (Reprint Delhi, 1969), pp. 269-70.
15. James Tod, *Annals and Antiquities of Rajasthan*, III, 1269 fn. 3. Since *mal* is a Persian word, the popular etymology must be wrong.
16. *Bombay Gazetteer*, I, Pt. p.99.
17. *The Geographical Dictionary of Ancient And Medieval India*, Calcutta, 1899, pp. 192, 224.
18. *Bombay Gazetteer*, I, Pt. I, pp. 2-5. MS Commissariat, *A History of Gujarat*, I, pp. XXXVIII-XXXIX.
19. James Tod, *Annals and Antiquities of Rajasthan*, II, p.127.
20. Dalal takes *paraupatha* to represent a proper name. (L.P., p.114). The adjective *Shrestha* and *Jirna* refer to the good and old conditions of the dramma; while the word *Shrimat* does not suggest that *paraupath* is a proper name as it is used before the name of a city also. Alexander Kyd Nairne suggests that *paruttha drammas* are to be equated with Parthian *drammas*. *Bombay Gazetteer* I, Plt. II, p.21). But V.S. Agarwal is of the opinion that they were the same as Byillamalla or Srimaliya *drammas*. (*Journal of Numismatic Society of India*, XVII, Plt. II (Bombay 1955, p. 75).
21. *Dvivallkya drammas* are also recorded in *Khartaragaccha brhad gurvavali*, (*Journal of Numismatic Society of India, XXII*, (Varanasi, 1960), p. 197. For detail see Lallanji Gopal, *The Economic Life of Northern India*, (Delhi 1959), p. 203; D. Sharma, *Early Chauhan Dynasties* (Delhi 1959), p. 303.
22. Ksemakriti in his commentry on *Brhatkalpa Bhasya* refers to the *drammas of Bhillamala* (J.N.S.I, XIV, Pt.I (Bombay, 1952), p. 109. D. Sharma. *Early Chauhan Dynasty, p. 302.*
23. *L.P.*, p. 109.
24. *Panchakula* means an assembly of five members. A.K. Majumdar suggests that the Panchakula were normally associated with *Mahamatyas, dandanayaka* and others, and that it was obligatory to receive the assent of the *Panchakula* before issuing deeds (*Chaulukyas of Gujarat*, pp. 246-42).
25. *Alberuni's India*, translated by E.C. Sachaw (Delhi, 1983), II p. 150.
26. *Ka* is an abbreviation of *Kala*. Lit. a small part of any thing. (Apte, *Sanskrit English Dictionary*, S.V.) The editor says that it may be sixteenth part of a *dramma* (*L.P.* p. 103).
27. *Sami* if we understand it to be annual, then payment is only of interest each year. The *mattaskandha vivirjitaha* should be amended as *mahaskandha vivirjita* which may mean minus the big part, i.e. capital. Then *savyajaka* would make no sense. Other possibility is that the money should be returned whenever it is done at the end of Karttika.
28. Dalal translates the term 'Kshetra' in sense of a house which is incorrect. Here it is used for land *L.P.* p.116.
29. *Visalapriya drammas* were current in the areas which recognised the overlordship of Chaulukyas and may be presumed to have issued by Vaghela ruler Visaldeva (1244-1262 A.D.). A.K. Majumdar, *Chaulukyas of Gujarat*, p.269.
30. According to D.C. Sircar this term may be explained as 'new taxes imposed for the first time, probably a fresh assessment of taxes. *Indian Epigraphical Glossary*, p.214. See also A.K. Majumdar, *Chaulukyas of Gujarat*, p. 249.

31. *Bhatta* is a title of respect, usually used in addressing princess and learned Brahmans. Here the term has used to mean soldiers (cf. *rajaputra*). A.K. Majumdar, *Chaulukyas of Gujarat*, p. 230; D.C. Sircar, *Indian Epigraphical Glossary. p. 52.*

32. Instead of *dhanikvat* read as *dharinkavat.*

33. *Vult-Dan* is the Gujarati form of *Valitapatra lit.* 'the money borrwed by mortgaging the produce of land or other property or any fund pledged to repay the amount of loan'. H.H. Wilson, *A Glossary of Judicial And Revenue Terms* , (Delhi 1968), p.540.

34. *Nivapata*, 'the falling of the rain water from the eaves' (D.C. Sircar, *Epigraphical Glossary*, p.220).

35. *Hedau* is a title for those who wonders along with a herd of cattle for selling. D.C. Sircar, *Epigraphical Glossary*, p.128.

36. According to D.C. Sircar in these coins there is a mixture of two *Vals (6 ratis)* of base metal. *Epigraphical Glossary*, pp. 105, 361.

Puratattva No.18; 1987-88

MAHAMRITYUNJAYA IN ART

A. Gurumurthi*

Mrityunjaya means 'conquering Death', 'victory over Death'. Lord S'iva is called 'the conqueror of Death'. Mrityunjaya is an epithet of S'iva and the name of one among the group Ekadasa Rudras[1]. Rudra was produced from the crown of Brahma or Vishnu and he was divided into eleven minor forms of Rudra which are given differently in *Amsumadbhedagama, Visvakarma silpa* and *Rupamandana.* But Mrityunjaya appears as the sixth Rudra only in the list of names of Ekadasa rudras enumerated in *Rupamandana.*[2]

The Mahamrityunjaya *Mantra* of Rudra Tryambaka has power over life and death[3]. In *Siva Purana* and *Brahmanda Purana*, the Mahamrityunjaya *mantra* is described as a highly potential *vedic mantra*[4]. Siva once taught Mrityunjaya *mantra* to a black bird to protect itself and its species from the aggressions of stronger species[5].

Puranas and other literary works give several exploits of Siva with the theme of Siva's victory over Death. Once Sukra taught Dadhica about the *Vedic mantra*, Mahamrityunjaya. He describes this *mantra* as the most excellent of all and if meditation is conducted in the presence of Siva there is no fear of death from any where. Accordingly, Dadhica performed penance repeating the *mantra*. Siva delighted at this appeared before him and gave three bons viz., adamantine bones, impossibility of being killed and absence of distress. Thus, Dadhica was able to defeat Ksuva,a devotee of Visnu. Visnu, who came to help his devotee, was unable to hurt Dadhica in any way[6].

In another incident, thanks to the cuse of Daksa, the moon was on the decay. On the advice of Brahma, the gods and sages took the moon to Prabhasa (Kathiawar—Somanath) to propitiate Siva according to Mrityunjaya rites. The moon, by repeating the Mrityunjaya *mantra* and by meditating on Mrityunjaya, pleased Siva and inturn the moon was saved from complete decay. Siva bleassed and told him that the digit of moon would decline day by day in one fortnight and increase steadily in another[6A].

The story of sage Sveta reveals that how the god of Death was subdued by Siva. Sveta's span of life was short and nearing its end. Hence, he worshipped the great Lord with devotion. Then the god of Death approached the sage to take him to his world since 'Sveta's span of life has come to an end. Siva manifested before the sage and subdued the Lord of Death. Thus, Siva is described as the conqueror of the god of Death[7]. This story of Sveta is merely an imitation of the better known Markandeya story.

The more popularly known story of ´´Siva as the subduer of Mrityu (´Kala´or Yama) is associated with ´Markandeya. The rishi Mrikandu was blessed with a son whose life was limited to sixteen years. He was called ´Markandeya. As an young boy, Márkand´éya was greatly devoted to the worshipp of S´iva. As he grew up, his parents were very grief stricken as their son approached the end of his appointed time on earth. When the news aof his short life reached his ears, Markandeya was unperturbed and spent all his time worshipping S´iva at all important places of pilgrimage. The day of his death came and the boy sat before the *S´ivalinga* in deep meditation. The servants of the god of Death, himself came to fetch his life. At this M´árkand´éya crying for help embraced the *linga* before him. Yama threw his noose in a loop and it went and circled round the *linga* also. At this juncture, Siva pleased at the boy, rose from the *linga* in great anger and administered a kick on the chest of Yama, which almost killed the lord of Death and thus saved the boy. After that at the request of the **d´evas,** Siva gave life to Yama again and blessed M arkandeya to be of sixteen years for ever. Thus, S´iva became Mrityunjaya and Kalakala[8]. The story of M´arkand´éya or

* School of History, Culture and Archaeology, Telugu University, Sri Sailam, Andhra Pradesh.

K'alarimurti formed a favourite theme in art.

Another important episode by which S'iva became Mah'ámrityunjaya is the swallowing of Kálakúta by Síva. The churning of Ksír started by *dévas* and *asuras* for *amrita*, 'the elixir of immortality'. Vásuki, the snake, was as the churning rod. When the churning became very intense, a burning mass of posion, the terribleKálkúta, emerged out of the Milk-ocean. On the emergence of the deadly poison the *asures* and the *devas* got frightened. On the whole it appeared as though the entire world would be reduced to ashes. At the request of Brahmá and in order to protect everyone, Lord Síva put all the Kálakúta into his mouth. Frightened at it Párvatí held 'Siva's throat by her hands so that the poison did not enter his stomach. At the same time Mahá Visnu covered with his hands Síva's throat by her hands so that the poison was not siptted out. Kálakuta, thus prevented from going down into the stomach or being vomited from Síva's throat, got itself digested in the throat giving it a blue colour. Thus, Síva became Nílakantha[9]. Although the terrible Kalakúta seemed to burn down the whole world, it did not harm Maháde'va, who held it in his throat and where the enter of purity is situated. Hence, Síva is recognised as the liberator from death and destruction. As Mrityun'jaya, he reabsorbed into himself its deadly darkness, the destruction of phenomenal existence[10].

By consuming Kálakúta, Síva saved the world and he himself survived by consuming that **deadly** poison. Hence, Síva is Mahámrityunjaya. **But the** burning heat emanating from the Kálakúta was so great that Síva was obliged to take bath himself by pouring water over his head to cool down his body. This version agrees with the description of the form of Mahámrityu'njaya given in *Síva Purána*.

The description of the form of Mahamrityunjaya is found in S'iva Purana and Rupamandana. In S'iva Pur'ana it is stated that the three-eyed lord, *Mahámrityun'jaya* should accompanied by *Párvati.* He should be pouring water on his head from two vessels held in his lotus-like hands; by means of other pair of hands, he should be holding two water vessels filled with water; he should have placed two hands with a pot full of water on the lap; and he should be holding as usually the *rudráksa* garland and a deer in the other two hands. His body should be rendered cool and wet by the nectar exuding from the moon worn on the head[11].

In *Ru'pamandana*, Mrityun'jaya, the sixth Rudra, is described as follows. Mrityun'jaya should wear a garland of skulls on his head, clad in garments made of tigers skin, and carrying in two out of three of his right hands the *trisula* and the *akshama'la*, and the *Kamandalu* while the remaining right hand and the left hand should be kept in the *yo'ga-mudra* pose[12].

According to another version Mrityun'jaya has the characteristic *mudras-dhya'na* and *j'nána* and his attributes are *ajina* , *mundama'la, aksamála, kamandalu, Kapála, mriga, pa'sa B and Btri'sula*[13].

The story of Márkande'ya or Kálárimu'rti formed a favourite theme of the painter or the sculptor of different periods since ancient times in Deccan and South India. But Mahámrityun'jaya as described in *Síva Purána* is noticed on the architrave of the Pápanásés'vara temple within the *mukhamandapa* of the famous vírabhadrasvámi temple at Lépa'kshi in Anantapur district, Andhra Predesh. A painting illustrating the same god, defaced to a large extednt, is found on the ceiling of the southern wing of the pillared corridor running outside and abutting the *Mukhamandapa* of the same temple. The third exaple is noticed on one of the pillars of the interior part of the southern entrance *mandapa* of the Sangame svara temple at Animala in Cuddapah district, Andhra Predesh.

In the painting of Lépa'kshi, Mrityun'jaya is shown seated in *padmasana*. Though defaced, the figures of Mrityun'jaya and two sages standing on either side are very attractive in colours. The deity is bedecked with *jatámakuta*, tiger's skin and other ornaments. Out of his six hands, the upper two hands are raised above the level of his head and pouring water on himself with two pots. Two of his hands, raised upto the level of his shoulders, are also shown holding two pots filled with water. The lower two hands hold a pot and rest in the centre of his lap. Another interesting figure of Mrityun'jaya is found sculptured on the architrave above the *dvára* of the *antarála* of the Pa'panásés'vara shrin. In this the two *rishis* noted in the painting are absent. Here the god is shoen sitting in *padmásana* posture and adorned with *jatámakuta, vaj nópavitá* and other ornaments. The deity has six hands. The two upper hands holding two water on himself. The lower two hands are holding a single pot full of water and resting on his lap. The middle two hands raised upto the level of his shoulders are shown holding two water pots.

The third example is of a fine variety noticed and indentified by the author himself for the first time in the Sangamé´swara temple at Animala (Fig. 1). The Sangame´s´vara temple is surrounded by a *prákára* with four gateways in the four cardinal directions. Except the southern gateway all the other three have *gôpura-dvåras.* The southern entrance has a *mandapa-dva´ra.* The image of Mrityun´jaya is sculptured on a pillar of the southern entrance *mandapa* facing the inner courtyard. In depicting the image of Maha´mrityun´jaya, the sculptor has shown all his mastery over the theme. This sculpture deviates from the earlier examples of Le´pa´kshi in certain respects. Like a full blown lotus, here Maha´mrityun´jay is represented with all the minute details. The sculptor is also successful in depicting the god as a handsome person. The deity is shown seated in *padmásana* on a pedestal having the mouldings like *jugati, padma, gula, padma* and *patta.* Mrityun´jaya has eight hands. The upper two hands, raised above the head and holding two water pots, are in the action of pouring water on himself. The next two lower hands are holding the usual attributes of Siva, ie.. *parasú* and *mriga* in the right and left hands respectively. The third pair of hands are holding two pots full of water at the shoulders level. The lower or the fourth pair of hands clasped together are holding a single pot full of water and resting in the centre of the lap. The three eyed lord is adorned with *Jatamakuta, chakra* and *makhara kundalas, manikantha, yajnopavita, keyuras,* armlets, bracelets, *unarabandha* and *purnorukha.* The eyes of the lord are kept wide open. Just below the god on the pedestal and in the rectangular aperture, the figure of Nadi, the *vahana* of Lord Siva, is found sculptured.

The sculpture and painting of Mrityunjaya on the architrave of the Papanasesvara shrine and on the ceiling of the southern wing of the pillared corridor respectively in Virabhadravami temple at *Lepakshi were first noticed by* S. Gopalkrishnamurti. But he was not definite about the identification of these two figures as Mahamrityunjaya [14]. Dr. V. Kameswara Rao, in his book, *The Lepakshi Temple,* gave a description of the figure of Mrityunjaya found in the paintings on the ceiling of the southern corridor. He further stated that an identical image of Mrityunjaya was found on a pillar of the *mukhamandapa* of the Virabhadra temple [15].

The figures of Mahamrityunjaya found in the Virabhadrasvami temple at Lepakshi were identified as Abhishekamurti form of Siva by Dr. C. Poorna chand[16]. While giving the location of one sculpture he stated that the sculpture of Siva (Mrityunjaya) was found carved on the centre of the door-way lintel of the Devi shrine located adjacent to the *sabhamandapa* of the Virabhadra svami temple. He noticed another sculpture of the same description on a pillar in the *mukhamandapa* of the same temple. From these studies one has to presume that there were altogether three identical sculptures and one painting of Mahamrityunjaya in the Virabhadrasvami temple at Lepakshi. But to the astonishment of the present author, only two figures of Mrityunjaya, one in painting and the other, a sculpture, were noticed in the Virabhadrasvami temple[17]. C. Poornachand further observed: "The scultpure under our consideration has been styled by some as Mrityunjaya. As the deity is shown in the act of self-bathing, it would be more appropriate to call it Abhishekamurti. Neither the puranas nor agamas nor silpa texts could give mythological background or the iconographical features of the image under our study......"18. The identification of Mrityunjaya form of Siva as Abhishekamurti is much against the description found in the texts. The second point of the above statement is very drastic and made without going into the details of mythological background and the iconographical features of the image. Apart from the efforts of the present author, T.A. Gopinatha Rao, long before, in his monumental work *Elements of Hindu Iconography.* gave some mythological and iconographical details of Mrityunjaya which are referred earlier.

The *murti* of Mahamrityunjaya noticed in the above examples is a unique aspect of Siva and not found elsewhere. the mythological background of Mahamrityunjaya as illustrated in the beginning gives the meaning of the word Mahamrityunjaya and also the instances in which Siva won over the god of Death or death itself. It further needs an indepth study to identify the exact mythological background for this action of Lord Siva taking batch himself. The figure of Mrityunjaya sculptured on the architrave of the antarala of the Papanasesvara shrine seems to be an indicative of the presiding deity of this shrine as Mahamrityunjaya, the liberator from death, destruction and sin. In all these three examples Siva is not associated by the figure of Parvati much against the description found in Siva Purana. The two examples of Mrityunjaya at Lepakshi have six arms each where as the third example of Animala has eight arms. The image of Mahamrityunjaya noticed in the Sangamesvara temple at Animala agrees mostly with the description given in Siva Purana except with regard to the atribute of one hand which holds *parasu* instead of rosary and the absence of the figure of Devi. The wide opened and bulging eyes of this image reminds us the ferocious forms of Siva like, Bhairava and Virabhadra. Siva, who at the request of Brahma consumed the deadly poison, might have assumed this angry looks at the very sight of Kalakuta. The three examples of Mahamrityunjaya under our consideration are very rare and beautiful examples in Indian art. The antiquity of these examples may be traced back to the Vijayanagara times, i.e., 15th-16th centuries A.D. as both the temples are also dated to the same period and ascribed to the Vijayanagara style of art and architecture. Moreover these temples are located in the adjoining districts - Anantapur and Cuddapah. Hence, it may be assumed that all the three figures were depicted by a common school of sculpture influenced by a common tradition.

References

1. Gosta Liebert, *Iconographic Dictionary of the Indian Religions*, Leiden, E.J. Brill, 1976, p. 181.
2. T.A. Gopinatha Rao, *Elements of Hindu Iconography*, Delhi, 1971, 11.2 pp. 386-87.
3. Vishva Bandhu, ed., *Rigveda*, Part V (Mandalas VII-VIII), Vishvesvaranand Vedic Research Institute, Hoshiarpur, 1964, 7.59. 12;, H.H. Wilson, tr., *Rig-veda Samhita*, Vol. \ V (The fifth Ashtaka), New Delhi, 1977, 7.59.12, pp. 132-133: Albrecht Weber, ed., *Vajasaneyi-Samhita*, Varanasi, 1972, 3.60.
4. J. L. Shastri, ed., *The Siva Purana*, Motilal Banarsidass, Delhi, 1977. I. 38.30-31; Ganesh Vasudeo Tagare, tr., *The Brahmanda Purana*, Motilal Banarsidass, Delhi, 1977, IV. 36. 19 .
5. T.A. Gopinatha Rao, *O.P. cit.*, p. 409.
6. J.L. Shastri, ed., *The Siva purana, op. cit.*, I. 38.1-44.

6A. *Ibid.*, 111. 14.35-45.

7. J.L. Shastri, ed., *The Linga Purana*, Motialal Banarasidass, Delhi, 1973, I. 30.
8. T.A. Gopinatha Rao, *Op. cit.*, II. 1, pp. 158-61.
9. Jamna Das Akhtar, ed., *The Matsyapuranam*, Oriental Publishers, Delhi -6, 1972, 249. 23-82, 250.1-61 Ganesh Vasudevo Tagore, tr., *The Bhagavata Purana*, Motilal Bana-rsidass, Delhi, 1976, III. 7.5-45; Vishnu S. Sukthankar, ed., *The Mahabharata*, Poona, 1933, I.16. 6-38.

   Motilal Banarasidass, Delhi, 1976, III. 7.5-45;

   Vishnu S. Sukthankar, ed., *The Mahabharata*, Poona, 1933, I.16. 6-38.
10. Stella Kramrisch, *The presence of Siva*, Delhi 1981, p. 147.
11. J.L. Shastri, ed., *The Siva Purana, op. cit.*, I. 38.34.
12. T.A. Gopinatha Rao, *Op. cit.*, II. 2, p. 391.
13. Gosta Liebert, *Op. cit.*, p. 181.
14. S. Gopalakrishnamurti, *The Art of Lepakshi*, Hyderabad, (n.d.) Pl. II pp. 3-4; About the sculpture the author observes: A friend of mine said that he is Mrutyunjaya. How could this one enjoying Varuna's right be Mrutyunjaya ? Where is Yama, the god of death and where is Markandeya ?"
15. V. Kameswara Rao, *The Lepakshi Temple*, Tirupati, 1982 p. 64.
16. C. Poornachand, The Virabhadraswami Temple at Lepakshi, Studies in Vijayanagara Architecture, Art, Iconography and paintings" unpublished Ph. D. thesis, S.V. University, Tirupati, 1984, pp. 235-236.
17. The present author visited and studied the Sangamesvara temple at Animala and the Virabhadrasvami temple at Lepakshi in the years 1979 and 1987 respectively.
18. c. Poornachand, *Op. cit*, p. 236.

Puratattva No.18; 1987-88

SCULPTURAL ART IN PAYAR TEMPLE

Bansilal Malla*

Payar is located about 10 Km. south-east of Avantipura in Anantanaga district in Kashmir. It is said that the name Payar has been shortened form of ancient Parvatipura, which is however, not firmly established on logical ground. Cunningham and Vigne, however, took the name of the village as 'Payech' a derivative of Payachchhagrama, representing the present Payar. The modern site of Payar has a very simple old small size temple belonging to 11th century A.D. The temple seem to was dedicated to Siva (fig 1). It enshrines a linga. The other Saivite elements include bulls on the capitals of the pilasters and the figure of Lakulisa (fig.3) on the entrance doorway.[1] The temple above the basement is constructed of ten stones and consists of a single square chamber, 8 feet along each side intenally and a rectangular doorway on each side. The doorways are surmounted by trefoil arches which are enclosed by pediments. The pediments which are resting on the pilasters are surmounted by capitals bearing pairs of geese with long faliate tails. The pilasters from which the trefoiled arch springs are crowned by recumbent bull capitals. The roof which is pyramidal is divided into two sections by an ornamental band. The blank sides of the upper pyramid are relieved by gabled niches which are the replicas of the doorways, the only difference being that the trefoil of the latter is replaced by a semicircular top, and the tympanum is filled by a flower ornament[2]. The total height of the temple from the base is 21 feet. "In the interior the walls are plain, but the roof is hollowed out into a hemispherical dome of which the centre is decorated by an expanded lotus flower. The lower edge of the dome is ornamented by three straight edged fillets and by a beaded circle. The spandrels are filled by single undraped winged figures (of rather spirited execution), who with outstreatched arms and legs appear to be supporting the roof...... They are probably Yakshas. The dome itself rests upon the cornice, which is formed of six plain straight line mouldings.[3] This eleventh century temple built up by the side of a river, is also found to be relieved with the figures of Bhairava (fig 2), six armed Nataraja Siva with musicians (fig.4) and the figure of Mahesvara (fig. 5). The association of some such Saivite figures with a religious establishment was found in the cave of Elephanta, in the Kailasanath temple at Ellora and even in certain murals of central Asia.[4]

Kashmir has been a great centre of saiva religion and philosophy. It is, therefore, quite natural that under the tremendous impact of saivism and due to the keen interests of many kings in medieval Kashmir, a large number of saivite images were made either for the installation in the sanctum of Siva temples or relieved on the outer walls of the Saivite temples. There is a terrific rendering of a four handed Bhairava (fig. 2) on the south pediment of Siva temple at Payar in which the badly eroded figure of Bhairava is shown in *alidhasana* and to his left a tiny figure of a female (?) shown terrified by the approach of the Bhairava. Payar also yielded an image of Lakulisa, an incarnation of Siva (fig. 3). Lakulisa is shown seated cross legged on a high stool like the image of Mahesvara (fig.5). As per the iconographical prescription, the ascetic teacher (fig.3) carries a staff (Lakuta) in his left hand while by his eroded right hand he is seen instructing his two disciples who flank him on either side. Like the figure of Lakulisa, the figure of six armed Nataraja (fig.4) is also conceived within a shallow niche. The attributes in his hands are very difficult to discern because these are badly eroded and mutilated. The figure of two musicians are depicted on either side of Siva, playing musical instruments. On the northern side of Siva temple at Payar there is an eroded image of Mahesvara (fig.5) whose all the three faces are damaged. This image is flanked by two eroded figures on either side. The hands of this three headed Siva are also damaged.[4] *Trisula* however, is seen clearly in one of his left hands.

Artistically speaking, in these sculptures, the energy of each god is shown concentrated near the central part of the body and from there in the case of Nataraja (fig. 4) and Bhairava (fig. 2) the power defused in different parts of the limbs. In the figure

* Bharat Kala Bhawan, Banaras Hindu University, Varanasi - 221 005

of Nataraja, one finds a rhythemic movement, a compromise of balance and cadence. The Bhairava on the other hand is shown in alidhasana. It is conceived with a monumental stride. The image of Lakulisa (fig.3) is shown seated in cross legged posture and shown explainting something to the disciples nearby. While Nataraja (fig. 4) and Bhairava (fig. 2) are depicted in action, Lakulisa (fig. 3) and Mahesvara (fig. 5) are presented in repose. But even in these, the concentration of power in the centre part of the body is clearly evident. All these images appear to have received certain amount of inspiration from the Rashtrakuta sculptures of Ellora and Elephanta. A reference may be made in this connection to a terrific form of Siva (fig. 2) carved in grey limestone that was enshrined within a shallow horse-shoe shaped niche. The lone witness of this terrific form of Siva Bhairava is a female who appears to have become alarmingly terrorised. Such an image with similar frenzied movement has also been noticed on a panel in the Kailasa temple at Ellora, where Siva is shown taking a great stride for the killing of the elephant demon Gajasura.[5] The compositional and psychological resemblances of these sculptures persuade one to form an opinion that sculptures of Siva temple at Payar were somehow or other familiar to the Ellora relief sculptures. Incidentally, it may be mentioned here that at a certain stage of history, Kashmiri rulers befriended the Rashtrakuta rulers in their march against the king of Kanauj.[6] The Bhairava image of our issue clearly evince the impact of Rashtrakuta mannerism over the art of Kashmir.

PLAN AND ELEVATION OF SIVA TEMPLE AT PAYAR

ELEVATION

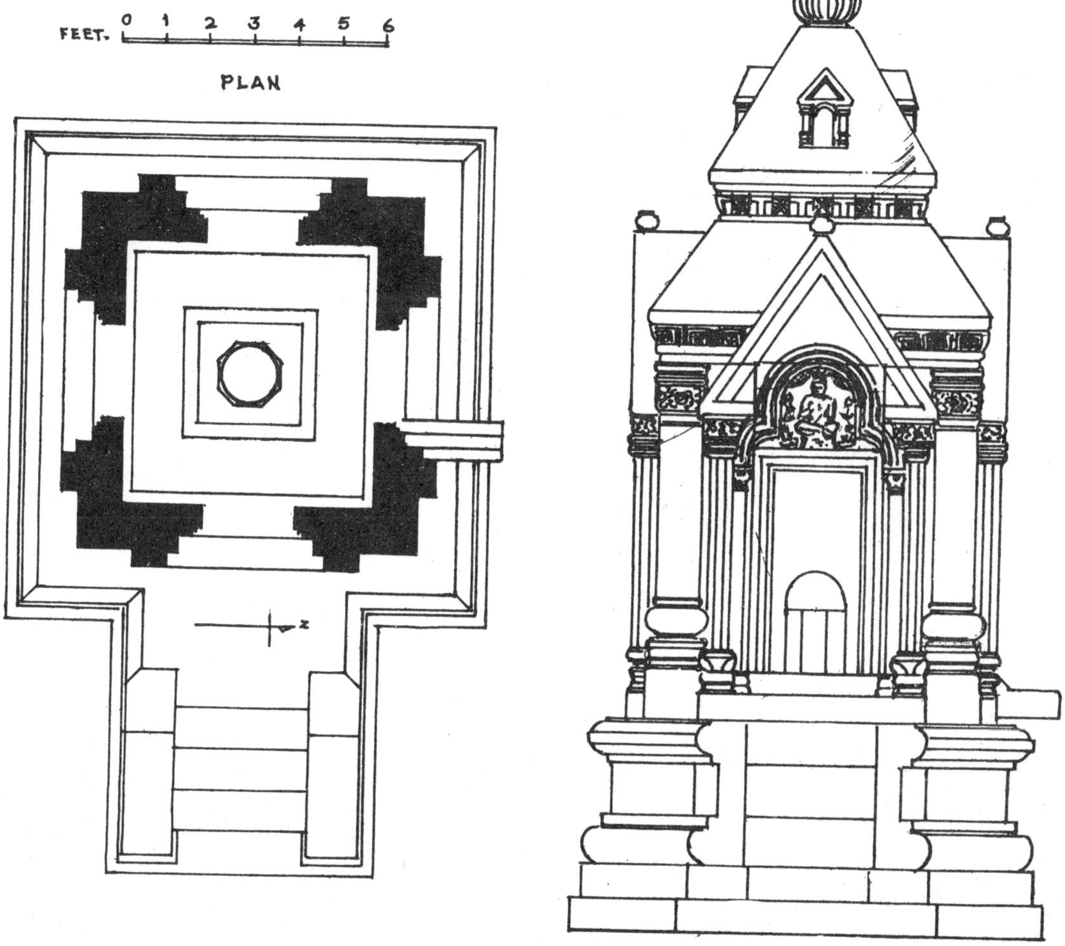

References

1. Gen. Cunningham identified this temple with Narendrasvami founded by Narendraditya, whose reign he places between the years 483 and 490 A.D., adding that the payar temple is one of Siva and that Svami is a name of Siva. Now, we know that this is not the case, the term Svami being applied exclusively to the names of Vishnu temples. But a stronger evidence against the identification proposed by him is afforded by the style of construction of the temple, which is very similar to that of the temple of Puranadhisthana. See Sahni, D. R., 'Pre-Muhammadan monuments of Kashmir', *Archaeological Survey of India (Annual Report)*, 1915-16, p.76

2. Kak, R.C. *Ancient Monuments of Kashmir*, London, 1933, p.127.

3. Ibid., pp. 127 - 28. c.f. Cunningham, A. 'Ariayan style of Architecture', *Asiatic Society of Bengal*, Vol.17 (2), p.256.

4. Sivaramamurti, C., *The Art of India*, New York, 1977, p. 455. For detailed discussion see Kak, R.C., op.cit., London, 1933, pp. 126-28.

5. See Gangoly, O.C., *The Art of Rashtrakutas*, Bombay, 1958, pl.20.

6. Goetz, H., "A Masterpiece of Mediaeval Kashmiri Metal Art", *Journal of Asiatic Society Letters*, Vol. XIX, 1953, p.54.

IRON AT AHAR: A COMMENT

Makkhan Lal*

The antiquity of iron in India (and other parts of the World) is deservedly a subject of interest among archaeologists. That so far it is datable only from the context in which it is found and not directly by any scientific method of absolute dating, must temper our interest with caution.

When H.D. Sankalia and his colleagues excavated Ahar, they pronounced Period I as Chalcolithic, in spite of the fact that ten pieces of iron were found in strata that also contained Period II material (the mixture being assigned to a hypothetical Period IC). One did not rely need Sankalia's explanation given in a subsequent review (Sankalia, 1979) that **"there were deep pits"** and **" a great chance for contamination, the later objects getting mixed up with the earlier".** He stated this in a comment on M.D.N. Sahi's paper "Iron at Ahar" (Sahi, 1978); but the statement was overlooked by both Dilip Chakrabarti (1984: 83) and F.R. and B. Allchin (1982: 325-26, 345), who accepted Sahi's arguments despite the fact that, at the very least, this would attribute to Sankalia and his colleagues a monumental carelessness which was surely not borne out by their methods of work.

It seems necessary, therefore, to look at the celebrated report on Ahar once again, and see how far there is any justification for tracing iron back to the middle of the second millennium B.C. on the basis of the excavator's finds there.

In the 1961-62 excavations at Ahar 79 iron objects were found. Of these 36 were slag pieces. Of the remaining 43 seventeen were corroded and unidentifiable. Twentyfive objects have been illustrated in the Report. Of these, ten objects are said to have come from the layers belonging to the Period IC. The trenches from which these iron objects came were -- X, C, D, L, E and H, and it is the location of these trenches that are of principal significance in elucidating the present question. The mound of Ahar is very high, its elevation at the centre being 50 ft. As we go towards the periphery it slopes: Trench X is located at the highest point while all others are located on the slopes (Fig. 1; Fig. C in Sankalia *et al.* 1969). The slope can be seen in (Fig.2; fig.D in Sankalia *et.al.* 1969). The trenches C, D, E and L are 20 to 25 ft. below trench X. Furthermore, in all these trenches there is no deposit above the layer from which pieces of iron were found. (See chart; fig. B in Sankalia *et.al.* 1969). These pieces were found just below the humus. Thus there is all the probability of external material getting deposited there since the settlement of later period from which it could come is higher up in the mound, having been found in trench X. In fact, it would not be surprising if the entire IC material is really redeposited mixed material of Period I and Period II. It is because of this mixing the stratigraphical gap between Period I (the Chalcolithic phase) and Period II (the NBPW phase) got lost. After discussing the mixed material in the Period IC the excavators observe: ***"Thus there is a long chronological gap between Period I and II which, however, is not attested by stratigraphical evidence. It appears that at the end of Period I, the site was deserted for reasons not known. However, it does not seem to have been characterised by a thick mantle of vegetation, which would have left a layer of black soil as at Nevasa. The occupants of Period IIa came to settle directly on the debris of Period I, and disturbed the horizons of Ic which is attested by numerous and extensive pits."*** (Sankalia *et.al.* 1969: 6).

From the above observation of excavators it is very clear that the material of Period Ic comes from the disturbed layers and can offer no acceptable evidence for the presence of iron in Period I.

If it were not condescending for one to say so, far from Prof. Sankalia and his colleagues being ignorant of stratigraphic and chronological principles, it is so much to their credit that they did not fall into the trap of sensationalism and made no claims that they had practically found the origin of iron in India. Perhaps, there is something here for all of us to learn from.

* Department of History, Aligarh Muslim University, Aligarh-202001

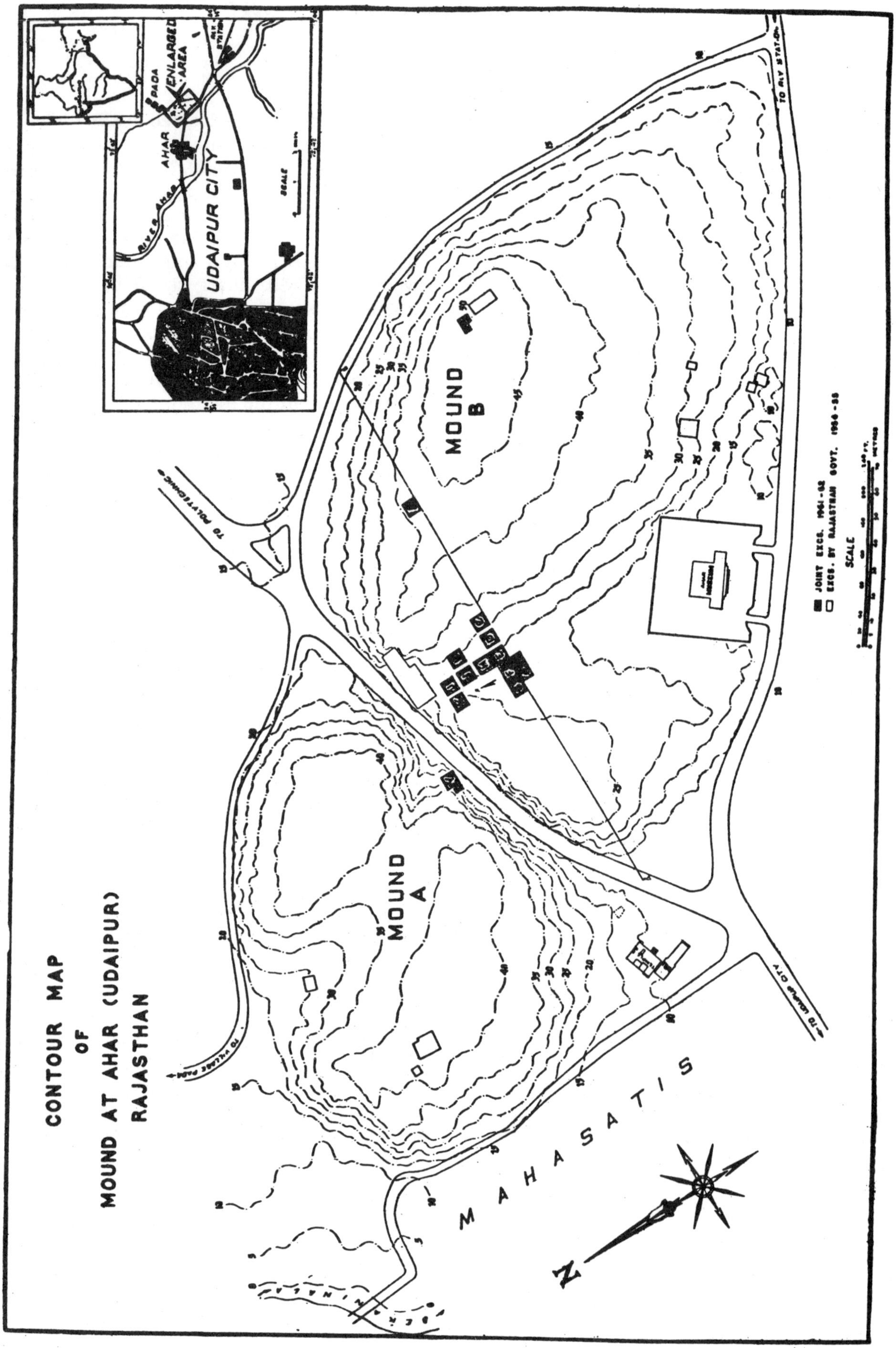

FIG. 1: Contour Map of Mound at Ahar

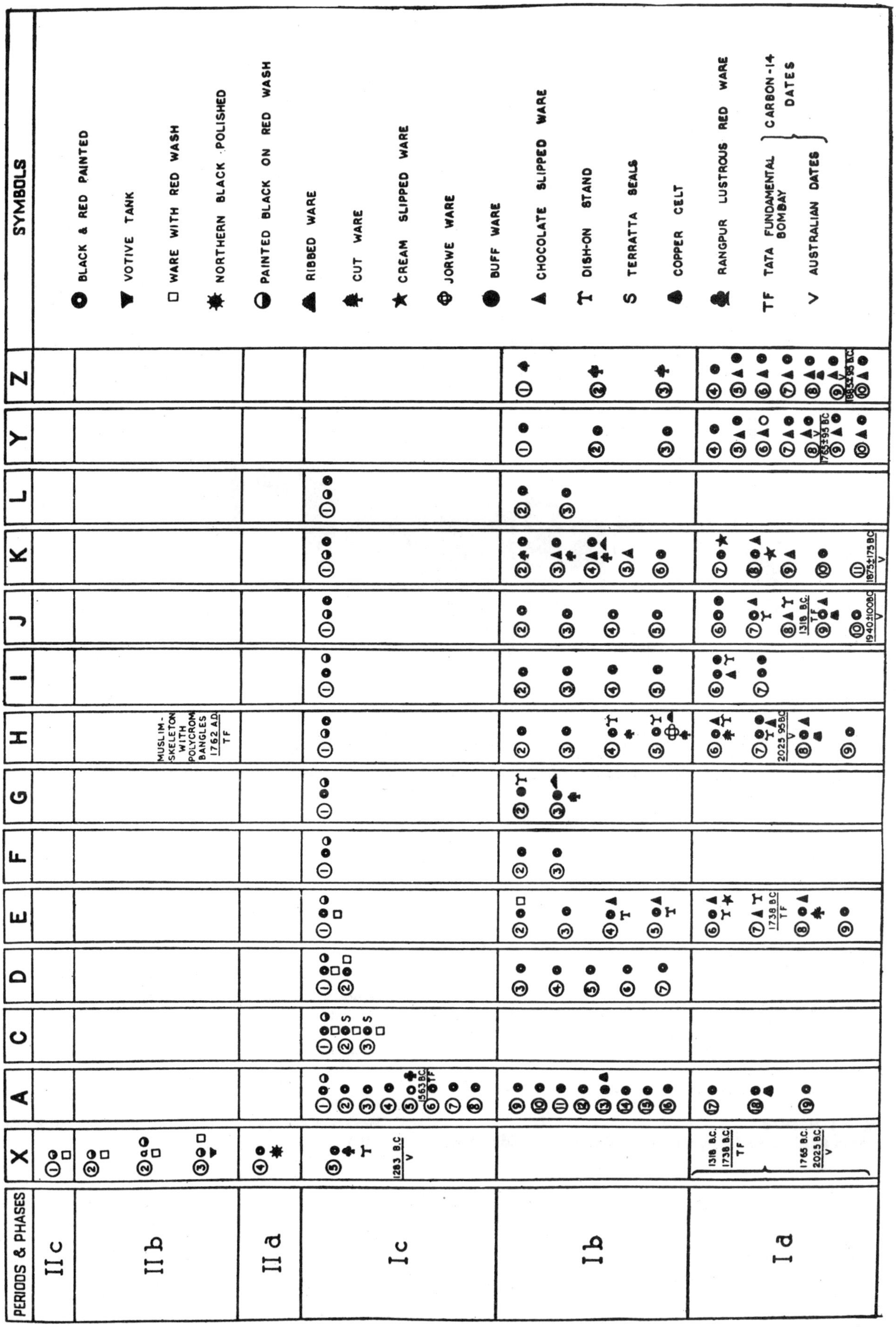

Concordance and Correlation of Layers.

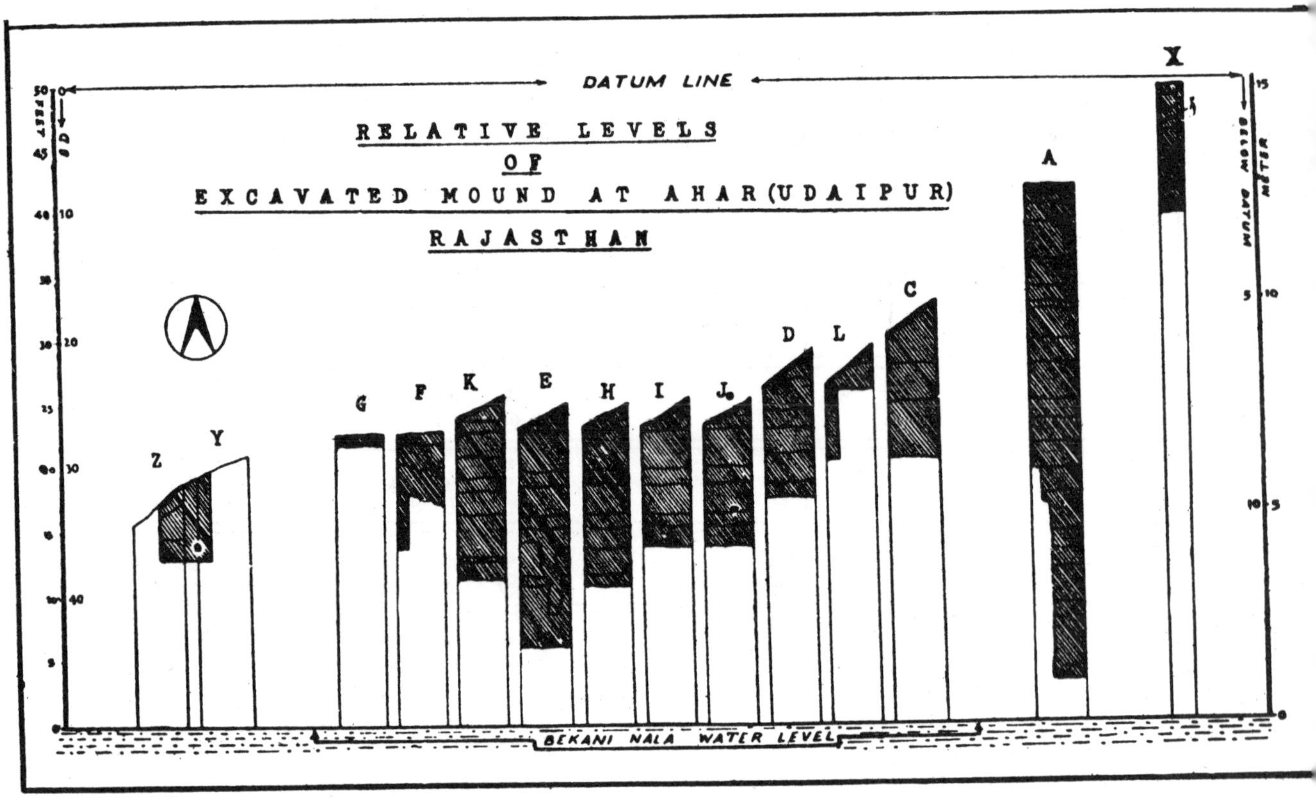

FIG. 2.: Plan of the trenches and their relative levels

References

Allchin, B and F.R. 1982
Rise of Civilization in India and Pakistan Cambridge: Cambridge University Press.

Chakrabarti, D.K. 1984:
Study of Iron Age in India. *Puratattva* No.13-14: 81-85.

Sahi, M.D.N. 1978.
Iron at Ahar. In *Essays in Indian Protohistory*. Eds. D.P. Agrawal and D.K. Chakrabarti, pp. 365-68. New Delhi; BR Publishing Co.

Sankalia, H.D., S.B. Deo and Z.D. Ansari. 1969.
Excavations at Ahar, Poona; Deccan College.

Sankalia, H.D. 1979
Review of Essays in Indian Protohistory *Commerce* August 1979; pp. 1-2

INDIAN ARCHAEOLOGY, A REVIEW: GUIDE TO EXCAVATED SITES 1953-54 THROUGH 1984-85

Prepared by
Gregory L. Possehl*

INTRODUCTION

This Guide was developed as a personal research tool and no attempt has been made to treat individual site entries in an even-handed way. There is a distinct bias in favour of prehistoric sites.

In most instances the terminology used in the Guide summaries of the excavation reports has not been changed from the original. This means that some of them, especially the older ones, will appear to be somewhat archaic. It is also fair to note that the summaries in *Indian Archaeology, A Review* itself are generally very short and the most preliminary sort of reports. They are certainly not the final word on an excavation reports under "Exploration" titles. These are not systematically handled by the Guide.

Entries in the Guide have been listed in alphabetical order by site, including State and District. There have been some changes in political boundaries, and terminology, since 1953. This document has reproduced the information found in the original report. Joseph Schwartzberg's *A Historical Atlas of India* may be consulted to clarify some of these administrative shifts and changes.

Several individuals have assisted me in assembling and editing this document. They are in the order of their participation: Nancy Pinto Orton, Stephen Carmen and Elizabeth Reistroffer.

The following abbreviations have been adopted:

IAR	*Indian Archaeology, A Review*
NBP	Northern Black Polished Ware
OCP	Ocher Colored Pottery
PGW	Painted Grey Ware
RPW	Red Polished Ware

THE GUIDE

1. Adamgarh Cave 1960-61. pp. 12-14, 16.
   Madhya Pradesh, District Hoshangabad. Rock shelters, Lower, Middle, Upper Palaeolithic, microliths, paintings, domesticated animals. Section drawings.

2. Adiyamankottai 1980-81. p. 65.
   Tamil Nadu, District Dharmapuri. Period I, 100 B.C. 200 A.D., black, bright red slipped, black and red wares, iron, Megalithic level. Period II, 200 to 900 A.D., coarse red ware, black and black and wares. Period III, 900 to 1800 A.D., coarse red ware.

   Adiyamankottai 1981-82. pp. 62-63.
   Tamil Nadu, District Dharmapuri. Period I, 100 B.C. to 300 A.D., Russett-coated Ware, black and red ware, iron. Period II, 300 to 1000 A.D. Period III, after 1000 A.D.

3. Adkot 1957-58. pp. 20-23.
   Gujrat, District Madhya Saurashtra, Harappan pottery. Beaker, dish on stand. Pottery drawings. In an Exploration Report.

4. Agiripalli 1976-77. p. 5.
   Andhra Pradesh, District Krishna. Megaliths, burials, black and red ware, red slipped ware, pale red ware.

5. Agroha 1978-79 pp. 68-69.
   Haryana, District Hissar. Saka-Kushan to early Gupta times, Red ware, copper and iron objects, structures.

   Agroha 1979-80. p. 31.
   Haryana, District Hissar. Period I, 3rd/4th to 2nd century B.C., NBP, red ware, and grey ware, iron and copper objects. Period II, 1st century B.C. to 1st century A.D., red ware, structures, iron and copper objects, copper coins, clay seal bearing inscription. Period

The University Museum, Department of South Asia Regional Studies, University of Pennsylvania

III, 2nd to 6th century A.D., red ware painted in black, dull and bright red ware with stamped designs, structures, clay seal with legend. Period IV, 7th to 12th century A.D., red ware. Period V, 12th to 13th century A.D., red ware. Period V, 12th to 13th century A.D., glazed and dull red wares.

Agroha 1980-81. pp. 15-16.
Haryana, District Hissar. Gupta temple.

6. Ahar 1954-55. pp. 14-15.
Rajasthan, District Udaipur. Trial excavation in 1952 by the Rajasthan Archaeological Department. White painted black and red ware associated with a red ware. Long cultural sequence. Thought that Ahar type black and red ware came from Central India.

Ahar 1955-56. p. 11.
Rajasthan, District Udaipur. Excavations by the Government of Rajasthan.

Ahar 1961-62. pp. 43-44
Rajasthan, District Udaipur. White painted black and red ware, Lustrous Red Ware, Jorwe Ware, NBP, copper implements, Kushans, Brahmi script.

7 Ahichchhatra 1963-64. pp. 43-44.
Uttar Pradesh, District Bareilly. PGW, NBP, plain red ware, fine brownish-red ware, fine red ware with black slip, plain grey ware, thick grey ware, Kushan sprinkler, stamped ware, coins of Kushans, Panchalas, Achyu, 4th century A.D.

Ahichchhatra 1964-65. pp. 39-42.
Uttar Pradesh, District Bareilly. OCP, PGW, NBP, Kushan, Gupta, copper coins of Achyu. Site plan and pottery illustration.

8. Alagarai
Tamil Nadu, District Tiruchchirappalli. Painted black and red, plain black and red, Russet-coated painted ware, black polished ware, inscribed sherds similar to Arikamedu, red ware, slipped red ware. Medieval.

9. Alamgirpur 1958-59. pp. 50-55.
Uttar Pradesh, District Meerut. Harappan site. Section and pottery drawings.

10. Allahpur 1970-71. pp. 40-41.
Uttar Pradesh, District Meerut. PGW.

11. Amahata 1980-81. pp. 37-38.
Madhya Pradesh, District Rewa. Megaliths, black and red ware.

12. Amaravati 1958-59. p. 5.
Andhra Pradesh, District Guntur. Stupa site with three periods: Period I, Mauryan, NBP. Period II, Ist and 2nd centuries B.C., NBP. Period III, Satavahanas.

Amaravati 1973-74. pp. 3-5.
Andhra Pradesh, District Guntur. Stupa site. Adds Period IV and V. Section drawing.

Amaravati 1974-75. p. 2
Andhra Pradesh, District Guntur. Stupa site.

13. Ambari 1968-69. pp. 3-4.
Assam, District Kamrup. Sculptures, 12th to 14th centuries A.D. Salvage archaeology on a building site.

Ambari 1970-71. p. 4.
Assam, District Kamrup. 1st century to 10th century A.D.

14. Ambkheri 1963-64. p. 56.
Uttar Pradesh, District Saharanpur. OCP, washed grey ware, degenerate Harappan link to PGW.

15. Amirthamangalam 1954-55. pp. 20-22.
Tamil Nadu, District Chingleput. Urn field. Drawing of a grave.

16. Amra 1955-56. p.7
Gujarat, District Halar. Tests at Lakhabaval, Amra and Somnath. Period I, Harappan with black and red ware. Period II, RPW. Period III, Medieval.

17. Anagwadi 1964-65. p. 30.
Karnataka, District Bijapur. Lower Palaeolithic.

18. Anand Bhawan Campus 1973-74. p. 26.
Uttar Pradesh, District Allahabad. Medieval site.

19. Anhilwad Patan 1978-79. p. 68.
Gujarat, District Mahasena. Fortification wall, red, black glazed, Celadon wares, Chinese porcelain. 11th to 12th century A.D.

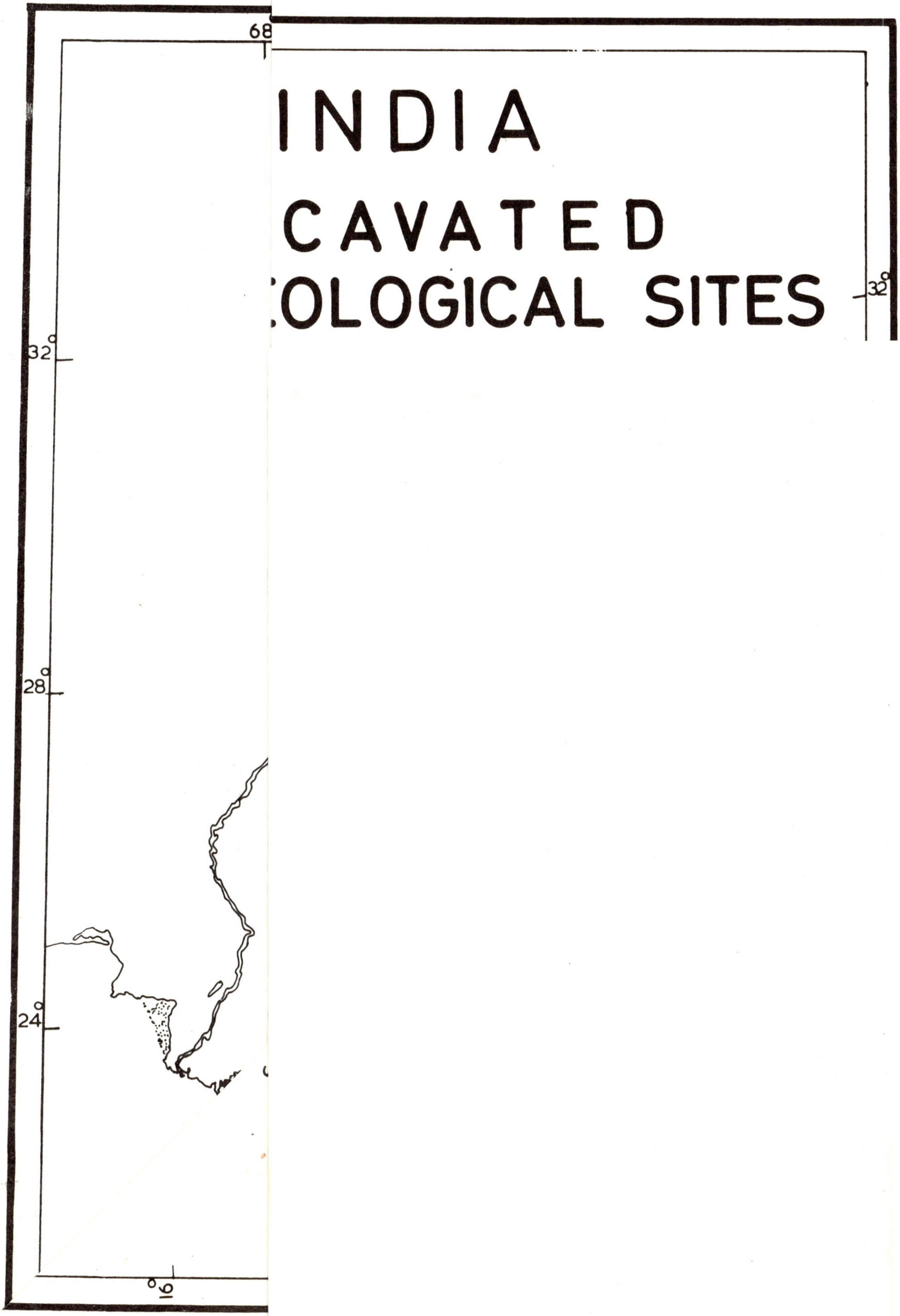

INDIA
CAVATED
OLOGICAL SITES
68
32°
32°
28°
24°

querns and pestles.

Antichak 1979-80. pp. 12-13.
Bihar, District Bhagalpur. Excavation in front of the Main Gate reveals 103 votive stupas. Probe of the Jangalisthan mound reveals a rampart with salients, possibly built in the 14th century following the destruction of the monastery. Excavation of Malkapur reveals votive stupas.

Antichak 1981-82. p. 10.
Bihar, District Bhagalpur. Work on the main gate of the Mahavihara and clearing in the Mahavihara itself. Stupa excavation, proto-Devanagari inscription.

21. Apegaon 1976-77. p. 39.
Maharashtra, District Aurangabad. Malwa, Jorwe Ware, Ramatirtha Ware (red painted blackish-brown slipped ware), microliths.

22. Aphsad 1973-74. pp. 10-11.
Bihar, District Nawadah. NBP, Gupta temple.

Aphsad 1977-78. pp. 16-17.
Bihar, District Nawadah. Vishnu temple, red ware.

Aphsad 1978-79. p. 67.
Bihar, District Nawadah. Vishnu temple, red ware, terra-cotta, stone and glass beads, iron objects, bronze bangles.

Aphsad 1979-80. p. 14.
Bihar, District Nawadah. Vishnu temple of Late Gupta times. Bangles of glass and bronze, iron.

Aphsad 1980-81. p. 9.
Bihar, District Nawadah. NBP, Vishnu temple.

Aphsad 1981-82. p. 12.
Bihar, District Nawadah. Exposure of the lowermost *pradaksinapatha* of a five-tiered Vishnu Temple. NBP.

Aphsad 1982-83. pp. 25-26.
Bihar, District Nawadah. Spelled Apsadh in the report. Investigation of the *pradaksinapatha*. Stone figures of Surya and Vishnu.

Aphsad 1983-84. p. 14.
Bihar, District Nawadah. One trench on southern side of the mound. Exposed the lower-most tier of a brick temple. NBP.

23. Appukallu 1976-77. pp. 47-48.
Tamil Nadu, District North Arcot. Megaliths, Early Historical black ware with lustrous polish, black and red ware, iron slag, ground stone, Neolithic celt, slipped red ware, coarse red ware, fine black ware, Rouletted Ware.

Appukallu 1979-80. p. 70.
Tamil Nadu, District North Arcot. Megalithic, Early Historical and early and late Medieval levels, floor levels with post holes, terra-cotta, shell and iron objects.

Apsad
See Aphsad.
Apsadh
See Aphsad.

24. Arni 1978-79. pp. 71-72.
Maharashtra, District Yavatmal. Megalithic, Mauryan and Satavahana levels, painted tan, black and red, micaceous red, RPW, NBP, Rouletted Ware, kaolin ware, copper and lead coins, terra-cotta sealings, iron slag.

Arni 1984-85. pp. 55-56.
Maharashtra, District Yavatmal. Continuation of earlier work identifies a Post-Satavahana Period. List of antiquities.

25. Ashtabhuja 1956-57. p. 29.
Uttar Pradesh, District Mirzapur. 9th century sculpture.

26. Asurgarh 1972-73. p. 27.
Orissa, District Kalahandi. 3rd century B.C. to 5th century A.D. Hoard of coins.

27. Atranjikhera 1962-63. pp. 34-36.
Uttar Pradesh, District Etah. Red slipped ware, PGW, plain grey ware, black and red ware, black slipped ware, red wares, NBP, red ware of medium fabric (early Christian era), Sunga, early Medieval ? Pottery illustration.

Atranjikhera 1963-64. pp. 45-49.
Uttar Pradesh, District Etah. PGW, OCP, black and red ware, black slipped ware, grey ware, red slipped ware, plain red ware, black and red ware, microliths.

Atranjikhera 1964-65. pp. 20-22.
Uttar Pradesh, District Etah. OCP, PGW, NBP.

Atranjikhera 1965-66. pp. 44-47.
Uttar Pradesh, District Etah. OCP, PGW, NBP, black and red ware.

Atranjikhera 1967-68. pp. 45-46.
Uttar Pradesh, District Etah. PGW, NBP, OCP, Kushan-Sunga, Gupta.

Atranjikhera 1968-69. pp. 37-38.
Uttar Pradesh, District Etah, PGW, NBP, flood.

Atranjikhera 1979-80. pp. 75-76.
Uttar Pradesh, District Etah. Post-NBP Period structures, glazed and Celadon ware, iron. Jain temple.

28. Attirambakkam 1964-65. pp. 20-22.
Tamil Nadu, District Chingleput. Early and Late Stone Age, microliths. Section drawing.

29. Atud-Khas 1984-85. pp. 44-45.
Madhya Pradesh, District East Nimar.
Period V Medieval
Period IV Early Medieval
Period III Early Historical, Buddish image
Period II Chalcolithic, not described in detail.
Period I Pre-Chalcolithic, blades, incised, unpainted pottery.

30. Auroville 1984-85. p. 77.
Tamil Nadu, District South Arcot. Excavation of two Megalithic burials.

31. Autha 1964-65. pp. 33-34.
Harayana, District Gurgaon. PGW, NBP, plain red ware, black slipped ware, black and red ware, iron.

32. Awra 1959-60. pp. 24-25.
Madhya Pradesh, District Mandasor. NBP, Punch marked coins, glazed pottery, Chalcolithic, red ware with black painting, white painted black ware, coarse black ware, black burnished ware, painted black and red wares, Satavahana coins, burnished red slipped ware, coarse red ware.

33. Ayodhya 1969-70. pp. 40-41.
Uttar Pradesh, District Faizabad. NBP, Early Historic.

Ayodhya 1976-77. pp. 52-53.
Uttar Pradesh, District Faizabad. NBP, late PGW, Rouletted Ware, Early Historic.

Ayodhya 1979-80. pp. 76-77.
Uttar Pradesh, District Faizabad. NBP, terra-cotta figurines, weights, Sunga, Kushan, Gupta levels.

Baghor
See Bhaghor.

34. Bagor 1967-68. pp. 41-42.
Rajasthan, District Bhilwara. Microliths, pottery with dull brown slip, brick red ware.

Bagor 1968-69. pp. 26-28.
Rajasthan, District Bhilwara. Microliths, early animal domestication.

Bagor 1969-70. pp. 32-34.
Rajasthan, District Bhilwara. Microliths, early animal domestication, copper.

35. Bahal 1956-57. pp. 17-18.
Maharashtra, District East Khandesh. Chalcolithic, Jorwe, Pre-Jorwe, Blotchy Grey Ware.

36. Baharia 1966-67. pp. 43-44
Uttar Pradesh, District Shahjahanpur. OCP, NBP, painted red ware, pale red ware similar to Atranjikhera, Saka-Parthian and Gupta, copper hoard.

37. Baharia 1959-60. pp. 34-37.
Maharashtra, District West Khandesh (Dhule). Tapti Valley. Chalcolithic. Black, purple or chocolate over red or brownish ware, red ware, burnished black ware, black and grey ware (similar to early Ahar), microliths, red ware, coarse grey ware, black painted red ware, associated with NBP. Pottery Illustrated. See Sawalda also.

38. Bairat 1962-63. p. 31.
Rajasthan, District Jaipur. PGW, NBP, Medieval, Iron.

39. Bakraur 1973-74. pp. 9-10.
Bihar, District Gaya Buddhist site.

40. Balirajgarh 1962-63. pp. 3-4.
Bihar, District Darbhanga. NBP. Site plan.

Balirajgarh 1972-73. p. 7.
Bihar, District Darbhanga. Fortified NBP plan.

Balirajgarh 1974-75. 9-10.
Bihar, District Darbhanga. Sunga, red ware, NBP, grey ware.

41. Ballal Dhipi 1982-83. p. 105.
West Bengal, District Nadia. Site associated with the Senas of Bengal. Exposure of structure. Stuccos like those from Rajbadidanga and dated to 9th-10th centuries A.D.

Ballal Dhipi 1983-84. pp. 94-95.
West Bengal, District Nadia. Excavation at an exposed structure believed to be a *pancharata* temple. List of copper objects found on an exposed floor. Sculpture dated to the 10th/12th centuries A.D.; the period of the building.

Ballal Dhipi 1984-85. p. 99.
West Bengal, District Nadia. Continued excavation of a brick temple.

42. Balu 1978-79. p. 69.
Haryana, District Jind. Late Siswal ceramics, Mature Harappan ceramics, non-Harappan ceramics. Harappan structures, terra-cotta objects, copper objects.

Balu 1979-80. pp. 31-32.
Haryana, District Jind. Harappan structure, terra-cotta and copper objects.

Balu 1983-84. pp. 28-29.
Haryana, District Jind. Pre-Harappan, Harappan and Late Harappan occupations are all discontinuous. Harappan fortification. Late Harappan kilns, ovens and structures. List of Harappan antiquities including copper arrow heads, triangular terra-cotta cakes and steatite.

Balu 1984-85. pp. 20, 22.
Haryana, District Jind. Investigation of the Harappan fortification wall.

43. Banahalli 1973-74. p. 17.
Karnataka, District Kolar. Neolithic, burnished grey ware. Refers to "pure neolithic occupation," presumably no copper. Microliths. Megalithic ?

Banahalli 1983-84. pp. 42-46.
Karnataka, District Kolar. Also known as "Mound originally covered an area of approximately 500 meters rising to a height of 6.5 meters. Four periods: I, Neolithic; II Neolithic/Megalithic: III, Megalithic; IV, Early Historic. Period I has large quantities of charred bone, some with cut marks. Early phase has black on red pottery, earliest occurrence in the region. Later pottery in this phase was a thick buff red ware comparable to the early pottery from Nagarjunakonda and Daikalmalai. Period II has both Neolithic and Megalithic pottery with iron nails and a copper spoon. Period III is purely Megalithic. Period IV is Early Historic Andhra with Russetcoated Painted Ware. Section drawing.

44. Banamilia-Bahera 1962-63. pp. 38-39.
Uttar Pradesh, District Mirzapur. Megaliths, dull red ware sometimes with red slip, over fired red ware, black slipped ware, black and red ware, microliths.

45. Banavasi 1970-71. pp. 28-29.
Karnataka, District North Kanara. Historic site. Temple, chaitya, 7th century A.D. Plan of the chaitya.

46. Bankadagarh 1979-80. p. 60.
Orissa, District Puri. Post-Gupta temple

Bankadagarh 1980-81. p. 45.
Orissa, District Puri. Post-Gupta temple. Sculpture. Sailodbhava Dynasty, 6th to 7th century A.D.

47. Banawali 1983-84. pp. 24-29.
Haryana, District Hissar. Period I, Pre-Indus levels with two phases of architecture. Fortified settlement oblique to the cardinal directions. Period II, "Indus Culture" with stratigraphic and cultural continuity from Period I. Continuation of Period I ceramics side by side with Mature Harappan. Model of a clay plow. Black stone with human figures carved on it. Defensive wall with moat and gate complex. Radial or semi-radial street pattern. Cart wheels, both solid and spoked. Sealings, gold, lapis, etched carnelian, clay crucible. Period III, Post Indus. Stratigraphic discontinuity. Main habitation outside the east wall of Period II. Ceramics of Bara, Sanghol IB and Mitathal IIB. Some small finds. Site plan.

48. Banki 1982-83. p. 57.
Madhya Pradesh, District Sidhi. Mesolithic

site with lunates, scrapers, points, triangles and trapezoids. Tools like Bhaghor II and Medhauli I, both in the vicinity.

49. Bara 1954-55. pp. 9-10.
Haryana, District Ambala. Harappan wares, PGW, Kushans. Section drawing. See also Salaura.

50. Baragaon 1956-57. p. 29.
Uttar Pradesh, District Sitapur. Note only mentions an excavation.

51. Baragaon 1963-64. pp. 56-57
Uttar Pradesh, District Saharanpur. OCP, Harappan Ware, Indus goblet.

52. Barudih 1963-64. p. 9.
Bihar, District Singhbhum. Stone axes and adzes, celts, grey ware, orangebrown ware, black ware. Refer to Exploration in District Singhbhum, IAR 1962-63: 6-7.

53. Batesvara 1975-76. pp. 42-43.
Uttar Pradesh, District Agra. Black and red ware, PGW, black slipped ware, pale red slipped ware, red ware, NBP, thick grey ware, dull red ware, RPW with sprinklers, coins, C-14 date.

54. Battalavallam 1968-69. p. 1.
Andhra Pradesh, District Chittoor. Palaeolithic.

55. Bavikonda 1983-84. p. 7.
Andhra Pradesh, District Vishakhapatnam. Buddhist settlement with four stupas, four *chaityas*, and a monastic complex with a 24 celled vihara. Brahmi inscription of 4th century A.D.

56. Belgal 1980-81. p. 26.
Karnataka, District Bellary. Neolithic and Early Historical levels, burnished grey and black and red pottery, polished tools.

57. Besnagar 1963-64. pp. 16-17.
Madhya Pradesh, District Vidisha. Black and red ware, black slipped ware, plain red ware, iron, NBP, kaolin ware, Sunga, sprinklers, red slipped ware, Naga-Kushan, Gupta, stamped ware, black painted red ware, punch marked coins.

Besnagar 1964-65. pp. 19-20.
Madhya Pradesh, District Vidisha. Chalcolithic, black painted red ware, black and red ware, microliths, grey ware, PGW, NBP, punch marked and Kshatrapa coins, Maurya, Sunga, Gupta, Heliodoros pillar.

Besnagar 1975-76. pp. 30-31.
Madhya Pradesh, District Vidisha. Chalcolithic, PGW, NBP, Mauryan, black slipped ware, black and red ware, red ware, coins, Sunga, Naga-Kushan, sprinklers, Kshatrapa-Gupta.

Besnagar 1976-77. pp. 33-34.
Madhya Pradesh, District Vidisha. Punch marked coins, NBP, iron, Buddha, microliths, Chalcolithic, black on red ware, white painted black and red ware, fine grey ware, red ware, pale brown ware, PGW, Sunga-Satavahana, Naga-Kushan, Kshatrapa-Gupta, Medieval.

58. Bhadahawan Hillock 1963-64. pp. 57-58.
Uttar Pradesh, District Varanasi. Megaliths. See Kakoria and Hathinia-Pahar also.

59. Bhagi Mahari 1982-83. pp. 61-62.
Maharashtra, District Nagpur. Same as Bhagimahari. Site has more than 70 stone circles and a large habitation area. It also appears to be the northern-most megalithic site in Nagpur District. Floors with lime plaster. Circular structures 3.25 and 3.8 meters in diameter surrounded by post holes. Semicircular hearths. Horse, cattle, sheep, goats pig bones with many from birds. Black and Red Ware, Micaceous Red Ware, black burnished ware, and black on red ware as at Naikund, Khairwada and Takalghat. Iron tools listed. Three stone circles excavated. Menhir. Unique constructions within the Megaliths are described.

Bhagimohari 1983-84. pp. 57-58.
Maharashtra, District Nagpur. Megalithic circles and habitation. Rectilinear house ca. 5 by 2.5 meters. Lime plastered floor; horse shoe shapped hearth; post holes on

periphery. Food grains: rice, wheat, barley, lentil, pea. Note of bird bones and bone tools.

60. Bhaghor 1979-80. pp. 49-50.
Madhya Pradesh, District Sidhi. Upper Palaeolithic, Mesolithic levels, tools, microliths. Rendered "Baghor" in publications by G.R. Sharma and J. Desmond Clark.

Bhaghor 1981-82. pp. 41-43.
Madhya Pradesh, District Sidhi. Bhaghor I, Upper Palaeolithic. Bhaghor II, Mesolithic, microliths. Bhaghor III, evidence for the earliest small blade industry in the Son Valley and probably the earliest of the three sites.

Bhaghor IV 1982-83. p. 57.
Madhya Pradesh, District Sidhi. Investigation of the relationship between Bhaghor I and Bhaghor IV.

61. Bhagwanpura 1975-76. pp. 16-17.
Haryana, District Kurukshetra. "Late" Harappan, transition to PGW.

62. Bhainsaur 1962-63. pp. 37-38.
Uttar Pradesh, District Mirzapur. Microliths, OCP, iron, rock shelter.

63. Bharat Mandir 1982-83. p. 96.
Uttar Pradesh, District Dehra Dun. Period IA, crude NBP, unpainted grey ware. 2nd century A.D. to 1st century A.D. Period IB, Sunga/Kushan. Period II, 8th century A.D.

64. Bharatpur 1971-72. p. 50.
West Bengal, District Burdwan. Stupa and monastery.

Bharatpur 1972-73. pp. 36-37.
West Bengal, District Burdwan. Stupa and Monastery. Chalcolithic pottery like Mahisdal and Pandu Rajar Dhibi. Early Iron Age.

Bharatpur 1973-74. pp. 32-33.
West Bengal, District Burdwan. Period I, Neolithic/Chalcolithic, pottery like Birbhanpur, Mahisadal (sic), and Pandu Rajar Dhibi, copper, celts, etc. Period II, Iron Age, NBP near the top. Period III, Gupta. Period IV, stupa of 8th to 9th century A.D.

Bharatpur 1974-75. p. 51.
West Bengal. District Burdwan. Neolithic/Chalcolithic. Overlap of Periods I and II with the introduction of iron. NBP.

Bhardvaja Ashram.
See Bhardwaj Ashram.

65. Bhardwaj Ashram 1978-79. p. 56.
Uttar Pradesh, District Allahabad. Black slipped, grey, red wares, NBP.

Bhardwaj Ashram 1982-83, p. 90.
Uttar Pradesh, District Allahabad. Part of the "Ramayana Project." Gupta Period materials in addition to NBP and black slipped ware. Reference to a report in 1981-82 was not confirmed.

66. Bhatinda Fort 1954-55. p. 26.
Punjab, District Fort begun in Medieval times.

67. Bhattiprolu 1969-70. p. 1.
Andhra Pradesh, District Guntur. Stupa, RPW.

68. Bhimbetka 1971-72. pp. 30-31.
Madhya Pradesh, District Raisen. Palaeolithic, microliths, painted rock shelters.

Bhimbetka 1972-73. pp. 18-19.
Madhya Pradesh, District Raisen. Palaeolithic, painted rock shelters.

Bhimbetka 1974-75. pp. 24-28.
Madhya Pradesh, District Raisen. Upper Palaeolithic and Mesolithic, microliths, grey ware, red ware. Lower Palaeolithic, Acheulian tools. Middle Palaeolithic. Drawings of stone tools and rock paintings.

Bhimbetka 1975-76. pp. 23-24.
Madhya Pradesh, District Raisen. Acheulian, Middle Palaeolithic, Mesolithic.

Bhimbetka 1976-77. pp.29-30.
Madhya Pradesh, District Raisen. Paintings, microliths, plain red ware and grey ware of historical period and Early Historical, red ware, ground stone, human burials, Mesolithic.

Bhimbetka 1981-82. pp. 35-36.
Madhya Pradesh, District Raisen. Painted rock shelters. Microliths.

69. Bhinmal 1953-54. p. 12.
Rajasthan, District Jodhpur. Capital of the Gujaras in Medieval times.

70. Bhitari 1968-69. pp. 38-39.
Uttar Pradesh, District Ghazipur. Brick temple, Gupta.

Bhitari 1969-70. p. 41.
Uttar Pradesh, District Ghazipur. Gupta temple.

Bhitari 1971-72. p. 47.
Uttar Pradesh, District Ghazipur. Exposed the remaining plan of the Gupta temple.

71. Bhojasala 1972-73. p. 14.
Madhya Pradesh, District Dhar. Medieval.

72. Bhokardan 1972-73. pp. 20-21.
Madhya Pradesh, District Aurangabad. RPW, Satavahana.

Bhokardan 1973-74. p 20.
Madhya Pradesh, District Aurangabad. Satavahana to post-Kshatrapa.

73. Bilawali 1962-63. p. 10.
Madhya Pradesh, District Dewas. Black and red ware, red slipped ware, vesiculated ware (similar to Ujjain I), punch marked coins. Stones with Mauryan polish. Early Medieval.

74. Billa Surgam 1970-71. pp. 2-3.
Andhra Pradesh, District Kurnool. Palaeolithic cave complex. Microliths, fluted cores.

75. Birbhanpur 1953-54. p. 6.
West Bengal, District Burdwan. Microlithic site. Mesolithic.

Birbhanpur 1956-57. p. 15.
West Bengal, District Burdwan. Microlithic site. Mesolithic. Section drawing.

76. Birdpur 1976-77. pp. 49-50.
Uttar Pradesh, District Basti. Buddhist.

Bodh Gaya
See Taradih.

77. Boregaon 1980-81. p. 40.
Maharashtra, District Nagpur. Forty-eight stone circles. Five megaliths excavated. Black and red ware, copper lid with peacock handle, other copper objects, iron objects, 300 etched and plain agate beads, gold, horse skeleton.

78. Broach 1959-60. p. 19.
Gujarat, District Broach. Black and red ware, NBP, bead industry, RPW, red ware, grey ware. Early Historical, Kshatrapa coins, Medieval.

79. Budhitittu 1968-69. p.24
Karnataka, District Mysore. Neolithic/ Megalithic overlap, pottery head rests.

80. Budidapaddu 1979-80. p. 8.
Andhra Pradesh, District Mahbubnagar. Megalithic burials, black and red ware, early and late Medieval levels.

81. Budigepally 1976-77. pp. 3-4.
Andhra Pradesh, District Karimnagar. Neolithic. Megaliths, rock shelters, burnished grey ware and dull red ware, microliths, black and red ware.

82. Burogoan 1965-66. pp. 52-53.
Uttar Pradesh, District Jhansi. 10th century temple, plain red ware.

83. Burzahom 1960-61. p. 11.
Jammu and Kashmir, District Srinagar. Neolithic "pit dwellers," mat-impressed grey ware, burnished red ware, polished stone axes, black burnished ware (not NBP), red ware. Megalithic. Early Historical.

Burzahom 1961-62. pp. 17-21.
Jammu and Kashmir, District Srinagar. Neolithic, Early Historic, Megalithic. Crude ware, burnished black ware, red ware, slipped ware, polished axes.

Burzahom 1962-63. pp. 9-10.
Jammu and Kashmir, District Srinagar.

Neolithic. Animal and human burials from phases II and III.

Burzahom 1964-65. p. 13.
Jammu and Kashmir, District Srinagar. Neolithic, black painted red ware, engraved hunting scene on stone slab.

Burzahom 1965-66. p. 19.
Jammu and Kashmir, District Srinagar. Phase I and II excavation. Inscribed slab of Phase II photographed.

Burzahom 1966-67. pp. 16-17.
Jammu and Kashmir, District Srinagar Megalithic, Neolithic.

Burzahom 1968-69. p. 10.
Jammu and Kashmir, District Srinagar. Historic, Megalithic, Neolithic.

Burzahom 1971-72. p. 24.
Jammu and Kashmir, District Srinagar Neolithic.

Burzahom 1973-74. p. 15.
Jammu and Kashmir, District Srinagar. Neolithic.

84. Buxar 1963-64. pp. 8-9.
Bihar, District Shahabad. Red ware, black ware, grey ware, NBP, sprinkler, Kushan, Medieval ware.

Buxar 1965-66. p 11.
Bihar, District Shahabad. NBP, black ware, grey ware, red ware, iron, sprinkler, Kushan, Medieval glazed ware.

85. Calingapatnam 1977-78. p. 14.
Andhra Pradesh, District Srikakulam. Stupa on the seashore. Red ware, black and red ware, brown or chocolate slipped ware, Rouletted Ware.

Calingapatnam 1978-79. p. 66.
Andhra Pradesh, District Srikakulam. Stupa, black and red, pale red, red polished knobbed and Rouletted Wares. Period I, Pre-Stupa Levels, 300 B.C.. to 100 A.D. Period II, Main Stupa, 100 to 200 A.D. Period III, Later Additions, 200 to 400 A.D.

Calingapatnam 1979-80. p. 11.
Andhra Pradesh, District Srikakulam. Stupa.

86. Chagatur 1977-78. pp. 11-12.
Andhra Pradesh, District Mahbubnagar. RPW, red ware, black ware, red and black ware, dull red ware, sprinklers, Lower Palaeolithic tools, Megaliths, black polished ware, burnished grey and black wares, microliths, brownish grey ware, painted black on red ware.

Chagatur 1978-79. p. 64.
Andhra Pradesh, District Mahbubnagar. Structures, cist burials.

87. Champa 1969-70. p 2.
Bihar, District Bhagalpur. NBP.

Champa 1970-71. pp. 4-5.
Bihar, District Bhagalpur. NBP.

Champa 1971-72. p. 5
Bihar, District Bhagalpur. NBP and mixed levels.

Champa 1972-73. pp. 6-7.
Bihar, District Bhagalpur. NBP Kushan, Gupta.

Champa 1974-75. pp. 8-9.
Bihar, District Bhagalpur. Coarse black and red ware, (similar to Chalcolithic Chirand), NBP, Gupta, jewelry manufacturing center.

Champa 1975-76. p. 7.
Bihar, District Bhagalpur. NBP, Kushan, Gupta, Pala.

Champa 1976-77. pp. 11-12.
Bihar, District Bhagalpur. Coarse black and red ware, red ware, NBP, coarse grey ware, Medieval Period.

Champa 1982-83. pp. 15-16.
Bihar, District Bhagalpur. Excavation of Pre-NBP Phase. Period I, coarse black and red ware, black ware, red ware. Period II, Sunga style figurines, iron. Period III, Post-NBP, Kushan and Gupta style objects.

88. Champaner 1970-71. pp. 15.
Gujarat, District Panch Mahals. 15th century Islamic fort and city.

Champaner 1971-72. p. 21.
Gujarat, District Panch Mahals. 15th century Islamic fort and city.

Champaner 1972-73. pp. 11-12.
Gujarat, District Panch Mahals. 15th century Islamic fort and city.

Champaner 1974-75. pp. 14-15.
Gujarat, District Panch Mahals. Chinese porcelain, Celadon Ware. Islamic fort and city.

Champaner 1975-76. pp. 14-15.
Gujarat, District Panch Mahals. Medieval Islamic city and citadel. Excavation of shops.

89. Chandahadih 1977-78. p. 15.
Bihar, District Muzzaffarpur. NBP, red ware, grey ware.

90. Chandavaram 1972-73. p. 3.
Andhra Pradesh, District Prakasam. Buddhist site.

Chandavaram 1973-74. p. 7.
Andhra Pradesh, District Prakasam. Buddhist, Rouletted Ware, dull red ware, black ware, lead coins.

Chandavaram 1974-75. pp. 6-7.
Andhra Pradesh, District Prakasam. Stupa, Rouletted Ware.

Chandavaram 1975-76. pp. 3-4.
Andhra Pradesh, District Prakasam. Stupa, Monastery, Satavahana coins.

Chandavaram 1976-77. pp. 3-4.
Andhra Pradesh, District Prakasam. Monastery complexes, black and red ware, red ware, black ware, red slipped ware, black slipped ware, grey ware, Rouletted Ware, coin.

91. Chandigarh 1970-71. pp. 7-8.
Chandigarh. Harappan.

92. Chandoli 1960-61. pp. 26-27.
Maharashtra, District Poona. Chalcolithic, Jorwe Ware, red painted grey ware, plain grey ware, coarse red ware, Malwa Ware, cream slipped ware and black and red ware. Urn burials (children), microliths, copper mid-ribbed dagger, querns, polished celt.

93. Chandraketugarh 1956-57. pp. 29-30.
West Bengal, District 24 Parganas. Pre-Mauryan and Gupta site. Pottery illustrations.

Chandraketugarh 1957-58. pp. 51-53.
West Bengal, District 24 Parganas. Temple site. Pottery illustrations for Periods I through IV.

Chandraketugarh 1958-59. pp. 55-56.
West Bengal, District 24 Parganas. Confirmation of massive structure seen in 1957-58 as a Gupta temple. Three broad periods. Period I, evidence for bamboo structures with tiled roofs, a few terra-cottas with Kunshana-like characteristics. Period II, Gupta. Period III, poorly represented.

Chandraketugarh 1959-60. pp. 50-52.
West Bengal, District 24 Parganas. Mauryan, NBP, black and red ware, Sunga, Gupta, Kushan, cast copper coins, Rouletted Ware. Pottery illustrations.

Chandraketugarh 1960-61. pp. 39-40.
West Bengal, District 24 Parganas. Cast copper coins, NBP, black ware, red ware, grey ware, Rouletted Ware, Gupta, Sunga Brahmi sealings. Pottery illustration.

Chandraketugarh 1961-62. pp. 62-63.
West Bengal, District 24 Parganas. Coarse painted grey ware, NBP, terra-cotta chariot, black over red ware, cast copper coins, Rouletted Ware, early Gupta, late Gupta.

Chandraketugarh 1962-63. pp. 46-47.
West Bengal, District 24 Parganas. "Ship type" Punch marked coins, NBP, thick grey ware, Rouletted Ware, Gupta Period.

Chandraketugarh 1963-64. pp. 63-65.
West Bengal, District 24 Parganas. NBP, plain grey ware, dark grey ware, punch

marked coins, cast copper coins, Rouletted Ware, stamped grey ware, red slipped stamped ware, Gupta Period. Black slipped ware. Two sites excavated: Khana-Mihirir-Dhipi, and Itkhola.

Chandraketugarh 1964-65. pp. 52-53.
West Bengal, District 24 Parganas. Fort of 1st century B.C. to 1st century A.D., 8th century A.D. temple

Chandraketugarh 1965-66. pp. 59-60.
West Bengal, District 24 Parganas. Gupta, NBP, punch marked coins, Sunga, Kushan, ceramics associated with Rouletted Ware.

Chandraketugarh 1966-67. p. 48.
West Bengal, District 24 Parganas. NBP, "ship type" punch-marked coins, Rouletted Ware, Mauryan, Kushan, Sunga, Gupta.

94. Chandravalli 1977-78. pp. 27-29.
Karnataka, District Chitradurga. Neolithic, Megalithic, rock shelters, Russetcoated painted ware, Satavahana coins, Early Historical amphora. Section drawing.

95. Chaubis-Khamba Gate 1964-65. p. 18.
Madhya Pradesh, District Ujjain. Remains of a temple dated to ca. 1100 A.D., partly utilized for the construction of a small mosque of the 15th century.

96. Chechar-Kutubpur 1977-78. pp. 17-18.
Bihar, District Vaishali. Pre-NBP slipped red wares, black and red ware with burnished surfaces, grey ware, similar to Neolithic at Chirand, NBP, Kushan, Gupta.

97. Cheraman-Parambu 1968-69. p. 10.
Kerala, District Trichur. 13th to 16th centuries A.D.

98. Chidu-Chimri 1972-73. p. 3.
Arunachal Pradesh, Dibang Subdivision. Medieval.

99. Chinnamarur 1978-79. p. 64-65.
A ndhra Pradesh, District Mahbubnagar. Neolithic, Chalcolithic, pale grey ware, burnished grey and black wares, pottery kilns, microlithic tools, burials.

Chinnamarur 1979-80. p. 8.
Andhra Pradesh, District Mahbubnagar. Black on red ware, burnished grey ware, black and red ware, black and red ware, polished stone celts, structures, burials, Chalcolithic, Megalithic levels.

100. Chirand 1962-63. p. 6.
Bihar, District Saran. White painted black and red ware, Neolithic celt, microliths, iron, NBP, grey ware, black ware, Buddhist monastery, Kushan.

Chirand 1963-64. pp. 6-8.
Bihar, District Saran. White painted black and red ware, microliths, plain black ware, painted black ware, steel grey ware, red wares, NBP, sprinkler, monasteries, Kushan coins. Pottery illustration.

Chirand 1964-65. pp. 6-7.
Bihar, District Saran. Microliths, Neolithic celt, Chalcolithic, NBP, punch marked coins, cast copper coins, monastery.

Chirand 1968-69. pp. 5-6.
Bihar, District Saran. Chalcolithic, NBP, Kushan, later.

Chirand 1969-70. pp. 3-4.
Bihar, District Saran. Chalcolithic.

Chirand 1970-71. pp. 6-7.
Bihar, District Saran. Chalcolithic.

Chirand 1971-72. pp. 6-7.
Bihar, District Saran. Chalcolithic.

Chirand 1972-73. pp. 7-8.
Bihar, District Saran. Chalcolithic.

Chirand 1980-81. pp. 9-10.
Bihar, District Saran. Excavation in the lower level yielded polished celts, iron, and other objects. NBP.

Chirand 1981-82. pp. 13-14.
Bihar, District Saran. Period IA and B, Neolithic. Period II, Chalcolithic. Period III, NBP, iron. Period IV, NBP, rammed brick floor. Period V, red ware of the early Christian era.

101. Chirki

See Chirki Nala.

Chirki Nala 1966-67. p. 22.

Maharashtra, District Ahmadnagar. Lower Palaeolithic site. Tools may be *in situ.*

Chirki Nala 1967-68. pp. 31-32.

Maharashtra, District Ahmadnagar.

Acheulian site, Early and Middle Stone Age tools.

Chirki Nala 1968-69. pp. 13-14.

Maharashtra, District Ahmadnagar. Lower palaeolithic.

Chirki Nala 1969-70. pp. 17-18.

Maharashtra, District Ahmadnagar. Lower Palaeolithic.

102. Chitor Fort 1958-59. p. 46.

Rajasthan, District Chitorgarh. Historic fort.

103. Chopani Mando 1966-67. p. 38.

Uttar Pradesh, District Allahabad. Microliths, incised light pink and drab pottery.

Chopani Mando 1977-78. pp. 51-52.

Uttar Pradesh, District Allahabad. Late Upper Palaeolithic.

Chopani Mando 1978-79. pp. 56-57.

Uttar Pradesh, District Allahabad. Microliths, ocherous red ware, stone tools.

Chopani Mando 1982-83. pp. 90-91.

Uttar Pradesh, District Allahabad. Investigation of the last phase of occupation. Floors, post holes, microliths, handmade pottery.

104. Cranganore 1969-70. pp. 13-15.

Kerala, District Trichur. 10th century temple.

105. Cudiyam 1963-64. p. 19.

Tamil Nadu, District Chingleput. Late Acheulian, Post-Acheulian and Middle Palaeolithic tools.

106. Dadheri 1976-77. pp. 43-44.

Punjab, District Ludhiana. PGW, "Late" Harappan.

107. Daimabad 1958-59. pp. 15-18.

Maharashtra, District Ahmadnagar. Chalcolithic. Report on the Deshpande excavation. Artifact illustrations.

Daimabad 1974-75. pp. 29-31.

Maharashtra, District Ahmadnagar. Report on the four bronzes with photographs. Period I< Neolithic. Period II, Malwa. Period III, Jorwe, Malwa, Lustrous Red Ware. "Late" Harappan. Urn burials. Furances in Malwa and Malwa/Jorwe overlap. Indus signs painted on Jorwe pottery. List of small finds.

Daimabad 1975-76. pp.. 31-34.

Maharashtra, District Ahmadnagar. Chalcolithic, Jorwe Ware, Savalda Ware, "Late" Harappan, urn burials. Domestic wheat, rice, barley, safflower, jowar, ragi, gram, peas and lentils. Microliths, ground stone.

Daimabad 1976-77. pp. 33-38.

Maharashtra, District Ahmadnagar. Savalda ware, burnished grey ware, thick coarse red ware, black burnished ware, Harappan (?) red ware slipped and black painted, rebbed bichrome ware similar to Harappan sites in Gujarat and Rajasthan, Harappan script, microliths, buff ware cream ware with slip and black designs, white painted grey ware, black painted Malwa Ware, Jorwe Ware.

Daimabad 1977-78. pp. 34-37.
Maharashtra, District Ahmadnagar. Savalda Ware, "Late" Harappan, Buff and Cream Ware, Malwa Ware, Jorwe Ware.

Daimabad 1978-79. pp. 46-52.
Maharashtra, District Ahmadnagar. Late Harappan, Malwa, Buff and Cream Ware, Jorwe, and Savalda cultures. Pot burials, residential structures, terra-cotta objects. Illustration of pottery and a terra-cotta cylinder seal.

108. Damdama 1982-83. pp. 99-100.
Uttar Pradesh, District Pratapgarh. Mesolithic habitation site with human burials. Hard living surfaces, charred animal bone. Cattle, sheep, goat, pig, stage, deer. Blades, bladelets, triangle, trapeze, microburin. Bone arrow points. No mention of crescents or lunate. Querns, mullers. Two burials.

Damdama 1983-84. pp. 90-92.
Uttar Pradesh, District Pratapgarh. Also called "Warikalan." Excavation of a mesolithic *cum* burial site. Nine graves (8 single; 1 male/female); all adults. Skeletons resemble Sarai Nahar Rai and Mahadaha. Millet-like seeds. Lunates, trapezes, triangles, blacked elements, etc. Bone arrow head and pendants. Stone quern, mullers and other ground stone tools. Bones of cattle, sheep/goat, ass, deer, stag, tortoise and bird, some charred.

109. Danwada 1978-79 pp. pp-70-71.
Madhya Pradesh, District Ujjain. Ahar and Malwa Wares, Pre-Mauryan and Mauryan levels, blacks and red ware, NBP, Sunga-Kushan, Gupta, Paramara levels.

Dangwada 1979-80. pp. 54-55.
Madhya Pradesh, District Ujjain. Ahar and Malwa Chalcolithic cultures, plain and painted black and red ware, painted back on red, incised grey and Lustrous Red Wares, microlithic tools, urn burials, structural remains, storage storage jars with charred grains. Pre-Mauryan, Mauryan. Sunga-Kushan, Kshatrapa-Gupta, Paramara levels.

Dangwada 1982-83. pp. 59-61.
Madhya Pradesh, District Ujjain. Nine periods : IX: Muslim coins and glazed ware. VIII : Pratihar, Paramar pottery. VII: Painted red ware, Buddha figurine. VI: Kshatrapa coins, no black and red ware. V: Black and red ware, copper coins, Ujjaini coins, Siva temple. IV a: Black and red ware, grey ware early NBP copper coin. IV b: Black and red ware, late NBP. IVc: Malwa with Pre-Mauryan ceramics. IIId: Malwa with rectangular houses. III e: Malwa Suparma and Sun symbol; apsidal temple. III f: Malwa, temple ?, bulls. II a: Ahar ceramics, no Kayatha Wares. IIb: Malwa dominates, but Ahar ceramics as well. Ia: Pure Kayatha. Ib: Kayatha with black and red ware.

110. Daojali-Hading 1962-63. p. 3.
Assam, District of Mikir and North Cachar Hills. Neolithic site, coarse ill fired pottery, ground stone, eastern Neolithic.

Daojali-Hading 1963-64. pp. 4-5.
Assam, District of Mikir and North Cachar Hills. Neolithic jhum cultivators.

111. Daulatabad 1980-81. pp. 39-40.
Maharashtra, District Aurangabad. Excavation of a citadel of the 15th century A.D.

Daulatabad 1981-82. pp. 48-49.
Maharashtra, District Aurangabad. Excavation of the house complex near the Delhi Gate. Many iron arrow heads, Celedon Ware with Chinese characters.

Daulatabad 1984-85. p. 51.
Maharashtra, District Aurangabad. Four house complexes exposed in a residential area near the Bharatmata temple. Garden plot also exposed. List of antiquities.

112. Daulatpur 1968-69. pp. 8-9.
Haryana, District Karnal. Harappan, NBP, PGW, misc.

113. Daulatpur 1976-77. p. 19.
Haryana, District Kurukshetra. Harappan, thick red ware with incised designs and black paint, PGW, coarse grey ware, black slipped ware, iron, Early Historical, coins.

Daulatpur 1977-78. p. 23.
Haryana, District Kurukshetra. PGW, Late Harappan, Early Historical.

114. Daulatpur 1984-85, pp. 86-88.
Uttar Pradesh, District Bulandshahr. OCP camp on the Kali Nadi. Post holes and hearths in rectangular and round huts. No architecture save for stratified floors. List of antiquities. Pottery drawing.

115. Deopani-Than 1962-63. p. 3.
Assam, District of Mirkar and North Cachar Hills. Vishnu image.

116. Desalpur 1963-64. pp. 10-12.
Gujarat, District Kutch. Harappan script on seals, Mature Harappan, "Late" Harappan, Vasai Ware (Early Historical-Rang Mahal), thin grey ware with bluish-green paint, coarse grey ware with bluish or reddish brown pigment (links with Lothal A II and Somnath I B), cream slipped bichrome ware, plain black and red ware, grey painted black and red ware (similar to Ahar I), handled saucepan, red slipped with black painting, cream slipped with black painting.

117. Devasthan 1984-85. p. 8.
Assam, District Nowgong. Brick Siva temple excavation. No date given.

118. Devnimori 1959-60. pp. 19-21.
Gujarat, District Sabarkantha. Stupa and monastery, Late Gandhara (Indo-Afghan) Period ca. 400-600 A.D., Kshatrapa coins, Maitraka coins, RPW, kaolin ware.

Devnimori 1960-61. pp. 9-11.
Gujarat, District Sabarkantha. RPW, Kshatrapa coins, black burnished ware, stupa, Brahmi characters, embossed ware similar to Rang Mahal and Sirkap Mound at Taxila, microliths.

Devnimori 1961-62. pp. 12-13.
Gujarat, Distric Sabarkantha. Stupa, RPW, Kshatrapa coins, Maitraka coins, Sassanian coins.

Devnimori 1962-63. p. 8.
Gujarat, District Sabarkantha. Stupa, Kshatrapa coins, Buddha images.

119. Dhanora 1956-57. p. 35.
Madhya Pradesh, District Durg. Megaliths.

120. Dharanikota 1962-63. pp. 1-2.
Andhra Pradesh, District Guntur. Site on the right bank of the Krishna River. Phases I (ca. 200 B.C.) and II with Megalithic black and red ware and an embankment *cum* wharf. Wharf improved in Phase III, associated with Rouletted Ware. Phases IV and V, no datable material. Phase VI, Satavahana coins, inscribed sherd of ca. 4th century A.D. Phase VII, Post-Ikshvaku period.

Dharanikota 1963-64. pp. 2-4.
Andhra Pradesh, District Guntur. Rouletted Ware, NBP, all black ware, red wares, Megalithic, black and red ware, wharf. Section drawing.

Dharanikota 1964-65. pp. 2-3.
Andhra Pradesh, District Guntur. Black and red ware, Megalithic, Rouletted Ware, black ware, red ware, grey ware, Satavahana coins, amphora.

121. Dhatva 1967-68. pp. 19-20.
Gujarat, District Surat. Chalcolithic, microliths, RPW, black and red ware, amphora.

122. Dhauli 1962-63. p. 17.
Orissa, District Puri. 7th century temple.

123. Dholavira 1984-85. pp. 14-17.
Gujarat, District Kutch. Not an excavation report, but a good description of this large, Mature Harappan site with standing architecture. Site area is 400,000 square meters, or 40 hectares.

124. Dhulikatta 1974-75. p. 3.
Andhra Pradesh, District Karimnagar. Satavahana, black and red ware, dark red ware, red ware, coins, microliths.

Dhulikatta 1975-76. pp. 2-3.
Andhra Pradesh, District Karimnagar. Satavahana, stupa, black polished ware, red ware, figure of a Roman (?), kaolin, coins of Gautamiputra.

Dhulikatta 1976-77. pp. 4-5.
Andhra Pradesh, District Karimnagar. Stupa, red ware, brown ware, tan ware, dull black and red ware, Brahmi inscription, Satavahana coin, pale red ware, red slipped ware, Roman coin in silver with bust of Emperor Agustus.

125. Didwana/Marwar Balia 1980-81. pp. 57-63.
Rajasthan, District Nagaur On pp. 59-60 report of an excavation in this vicinity. Information on the ancient environmental history of the Rajasthan desert. Schematic section drawing. Map of sites. See Singi Talav Quarry and Indola-Ki-Dhani.

Didwana 1981-82. pp. 56-58.
Rajasthan, District Nagaur. Excavation of a Palaeolithic site. Litho Unit II has Upper Palaeolithic tools. Litho Unit III has Middle Palaeolithic tools. Small cordiform handaxe from Litho Unit II. Litho Units I and II dated to 16,000 to 30,000 B.P. by TL and C-14. Material comes from a dune. Diagram of the Litho Units and associations.

Didwana 1982-83. pp. 68-69.
Rajasthan, District Nagaur. Horizontal exposure of a site with Late Middle Palaeolithic or Early Upper Palaeolithic tools.

Didwana 1983-84. pp. 72-74.
Rajasthan, District Nagaur. Detailed report. Acheulian tools at Singi-Talav. Late Acheulian/Early Middle Palaeolithic tools in excavated context. "Neotectonics and climate changes of the Neogence and Quaternary can explain the morpho-dynamic history of this part of the Thar Desert." Rich mesolithic site 8 km south of Bikaner. Acheulian sites in the semi-arid parts of the Thar. Middle Palaeolithic sites extend into the arid desert. Mesolithic sites of the Early Holocene are abundant in the entire Thar. Thar had a sub-humid climate in the late Tertiary/Early Pleistocene.

126. Dihar 1983-84. pp. 92-93.
West Bengal, District Bankura. Period I is Chalcolithic. Beaten earth floors with nodules and lime. Black and Red Ware, pale red ware, black slipped ware, grey ware, buff ware. Many antler tools and bone implements. "Microliths." Copper and antimony rods. Period II is Early Historic, Sunga/Kushan ?

Dihar 1984-85. pp. 92-95.
West Bengal, District Bankura.
Period I Early Historic
Period II Chalcolithic with black and red ware. No architecture, but floors.

127. Dongalasani 1977-78. p. 1
Andhra Pradesh, District Cuddapah. Brick temple of the ca. 10th century.

128. Dongarkada 1970-71. pp. 23-24.
Maharashtra, District Parbhani. Suspected

habitation site of the Middle Palaeolithic. Fire.

129. Dupadu 1976-77. p. 3.
Andhra Pradesh, District Guntur. Buddhist stupa, Brahmi inscription.

130. Dwarka 1962-63. p. 7.
Gujarat, District Jamnagar. RPW, Roman amphorae, Carbon-14 date of late layer (1630±90 A.D.). Deccan College excavation.

Dwarka 1979-80. p. 25-29.
Gujarat, District Jamnagar. Temple, Lustrous Red Ware and "Late" Harappan ware. Pottery illustrations. Table of successive habitation and stages of temple construction.

131. Eran 1960-61. pp. 17-18.
Madhya Pradesh, District Sagar. Period I, Chalcolithic, microliths, black and red ware, thick grey ware, black on red ware (Malwa fabric), plain thin grey ware, light red painted thick grey ware, copper. Period II, iron, coarse red ware, NBP sherd, punch marked coin, cast copper coin, Mauryan Brahmi script. Period III, RPW, coins of Naga, Indo-Sassanian and Ramagupta, seal of Kshatrapa ruler, iron. Period IV, coins of Bhopal and Gwalior states.

Eran 1961-62. pp. 24-25.
Madhya Pradesh, District Sagar. Chalcolithic pottery, microliths, black and red ware, thick grey ware, thin plain grey ware, black painted red ware, white painted black and red ware, painted red ware, NBP, punch marked and tribal coins, RPW in layers with punch marked coins, Naga coins, Kshatrapa coins, Ramagupta coins and Indo-Sassanian coins. Early Gupta.

Eran 1962-63. pp. 11-12.
Madhya Pradesh, District Sagar. Chalcolithic pottery, microliths, black painted red ware, white painted black and red ware, grey ware painted in black, copper, iron, red ware, RPW, Western Kshatrapa, Naga coins, Late Medieval.

Eran 1963-64. pp. 15-16.
Madhya Pradesh, District Sagar. Chalcolithic, white painted black and red ware, white black painted red ware, grey ware, deep red shiny slip ware, channel spout, black painted red ware, Neolithic celt. NBP, iron, plain black and red ware, microlithic, punch marked coins, stamped red ware, RPW, Kshatrapa and Naga coins, Gupta Period, Medieval glazed ware.

Eran 1964-65. pp. 16-18.
Madhya Pradesh, District Sagar. Chalcolithic, Neolithic, microliths, black and red ware, coin moulds of Kshatrapas, protohistoric to historic transition.

132. Fatehpur Sikri 1976-77. pp. 48-49.
Uttar Pradesh, District Agra. General investigation of the site.

Fatehpur Sikri 1977-78. p. 51.
Uttar Pradesh, District Agra. Continuation of 1976-77.

Fatehpur Sikri 1978-79. pp. 53-56.
Uttar Pradesh, District Agra. Extensive report on major excavations.

Fatehpur Sikri 1979-80. pp. 71-72.
Uttar Pradesh, District Agra. Excavation of houses, *hammam*, shops, wall, mint.

Fatehpur Sikri 1980-81. pp. 66-67.
Uttar Pradesh, District Agra. Excavation between the Diwan-i -Am and the Agra Gate. Shopping complex and *hammam*.

Fatehpur Sikri 1981-82. pp. 63-66.
Uttar Pradesh, District Agra. Excavation in the vicinity of the Mint, Delhi Gate, Diwan--i-Am and in the "Taksal" area. Evidence suggests that the was built after the reign of Akbar. Plan of the Mint area.

Fatehpur Sikri 1982-83. pp. 89-90.
Uttar Pradesh, District Agra. Investigation of the *ibadat khana* and *Shabistan-e-Iqbal*. Trenches in the vicinity of the Chandrapole brick structures.

Fatehpur Sikri 1983-84. pp. 81-82.
Uttar Pradesh, District Agra. R.C. Gaur project. Excavation at six places: near the *Badshahi* Gate; *Ibadat Khana*; the southern part of the Turkish hammam; a quadrangle of the *Diwan-i-Am*; leopard cell and horse stable; and *Ghoda Mahal*. Discovery of a Christian chapel built by Akbar.

Fatehpur Sikri 1983-84. pp. 83-84.
Uttar Pradesh, District Agra. Exposure of structures in the area between the Treasury Building and the Diwan-i-Am.

Fatehpur Sikri 1984-85. pp. 80-83.
Uttar Pradesh, District Agra. Work in five areas: 1) The Church, 2) Zoo, 3) Abdur-Rahim Khan-i-Khanan's Palace, 4) the Stable near Hauz-i-shirin and 5) the *Samosa Mahal* area.

Fatehpur Sikri 1984-85. pp. 83-84.
Uttar Pradesh, District Agra. Continued excavation in the vicinity of the Treasury in areas FPS I and II.

133. Gandluru 1982-83. pp. 1-2.
Andhra Pradesh, District Guntur. Three Neolithic phases: Phase I, 4 dwelling pits, post holes, ground stone axe, cattle bones with butchering marks. Phase II, oval and apsidal houses, copper wire and axe, steatite disk beads, pot burial, clay lined hearths in floors. Phase III, rectangular house, some with mud brick walls. Pottery from preceding phase continues with the addition of Megalithic Black and Red Ware; no iron.

Gandluru 1983-84. pp. 1-2.
Andhra Pradesh, District Guntur. Excavation in an area called Gandluru III. Neolithic occupation. Phase I has pit dwellings, 12 excavated. Child burial in a pot. Phase II has house floors surrounded by post holes. Rock-cut pit. Most bones are cattle.

134. Ganeshwar 1981-82. pp. 61-62.
Rajasthan, District Sikar. Three periods of OCP and microliths, many copper tools. Earlier find of 58 flat axes and 2 barbed arrow heads. More copper this season. Microliths, lunates, triangles and trapezes. Incised OCP like Jodhpura.

Ganeshwar 1983-84. pp. 71-72.
Rajasthan, District Sikar. House floors and platforms with post holes, storage facilities. Microliths include lunates, trapezes, triangles, backed pieces and blades. List of abundant copper implements. Pottery includes white painted decoration as in the Sothi material and a characteristic red slipped painted ware.

135. Gangaikondacholapuram 1979-80. p. 71.
Tamil Nadu, District Tiruchirappalli. Excavation of a mound called "Maligaimedu," probably a palace complex of the Cholas.

Gangaikondacholapuram 1983-84. pp. 80-81.
Tamil Nadu, District Tiruchirappalli. Brick structure of the Cholas. Historical references cited to this place and other architectural details. Large quantity of iron.

136. Gangapur 1968-69.p. 17.
Maharashtra, District Nagpur. Megaliths. See Khapa as well.

137. Ganwaripur 1968-69. p. 17.
Maharashtra, District Nagpur. Megaliths. See Khapa as well.

138. Ganwaria 1974-75. pp. 39-41
Uttar Pradesh, District Basti. Site near Piprahwa. Two massive buildings with multiple rooms. Period I, begins ca. 8th century B.C., grey ware. Period II, deluxe NBP. Period III, Post-NBP wares, Kushan Period. See Piprahwa as well. Ancient Kapilavastu.

Ganwaria 1975-76. pp. 47-50.
Uttar Pradesh, District Basti. Black polished ware, fine grey ware, red ware, NBP, black painted red ware, Buddha image, Sunga-Kushan, monastery, stupa.

Ganwaria 1976-77. pp. 50-52.
Uttar Pradesh, District Basti. Grey ware, black polished ware, red ware, NBP, Brahmi inscription, Kushan, coin hoards, Sunga, Stupa. See Piprahwa as well.

139. Gauhati 1974-75. p.7
Assam, District Gauhati. Boat.

140. Gazulbanda 1970-71. pp. 3-4
Andhra Pradesh, District Nalgonda. Stupa.

141. Ghagharia 1979-80. pp. 50-52
Madhya Pradesh, District Sidhi. Mesolithic rock shelter, paintings, microlithic tools, red ware, brownish grey and corded and burnished red wares, Lower and Middle Palaeolithic tools. Table of layers.

142. Ghantasala 1984-85. pp. 5-6
Andhra Pradesh, District Krishna. Excavation of a Buddhist site of three periods:
Period III : Post —Ikshvaku.
Period II : Ikshvaku.
Period I : Satavahana.

143. Ghod Valley 1981-82. p.50
Maharashtra, District Pune. Excavation of Pleistocene deposits opposite the Chalcolithic site of Inamgaon. Finds include Middle and Upper Palaeolithic tools, Leptobos, Bos/Bubalus, Hippopotamus, cervids and equids. See also Inamgaon 1980-81, pp. 42-43.

144. Ghumali 1968-69. p.8
Gujarat, District Jamnagar. Late Medieval site.

145. Ghuram 1976-77. pp. 44-45
Punjab, District Patiala. Grey ware, micaceous grey ware, red ware, NBP, black slipped ware, PGW, stamped ware, late Harappan, Audumbra coins (2nd to 1st century B.C.), Brahmi inscription.

146. Gilaulikhera 1981-82. pp. 33-34.
Madhya Pradesh, District Morena. Period IA, B and C, Prothohistoric. IA has grey ware, black and red ware, red ware and black ware. IB pottery predominantly grey ware. some similarities to Malwa ceramics. IC continuity of IB with the introduction of PGW (?) and NBP. Iron in Period I as is a chocolate slipped ware akin to Kayatha Ware. Period II, Maurya-Sunga. Period III, Kushan. Period IV, Gupta. Period V, Post-Gupta.

Gilaulikhera 1983-84 pp. 51-52
Madhya Pradesh, District Morena. Period IA, Protohistoric with black and red ware, red ware, grey ware, black ware. Period IB, dominated by grey ware with black and red ware. Fine red ware shapes close to Malwa Ware. Period IC has PGW, NBP and iron. Period II is Maurya/Sunga. Period III, Kushan. Period IV, Gupta. Period V, Post-Gupta.

147. Gilund 1959-60. pp. 41-46.
Rajasthan, District Udaipur. Chalcolithic,

microliths, painted black and red ware, plain and painted black ware, burnished grey ware, red ware, black on cream ware, black on red ware, polychrome ware (black, bright red and white paint on red), copper. Post-Chalcolithic, Sunga and Kushan bowls in red ware, sprinkler in red slipped ware, kaolin ware, grey ware. Pottery illustrations.

148. Gingee Fort 1973-74. p. 25.
Tamil Nadu, District South Arcot. Historic site.

149. Golconda 1970-71. p.1.
Andhra Pradesh, District Hyderabad. Mosque of the Qutab Shahi Period, 1618-89. Ming porcelains.

Golconda 1971-72. pp. 1-2.
Andhra Pradesh, District Hyderabad. Mosque of the Qutab Shahi Period, 1618-89.

Golconda 1972-73. pp. 1-2.
Andhra Pradesh, District Hyderabad. Qutab Sahahi Period tombs.

Golconda 1973-74. p.5.
Andhra Pradesh, District Hyderabad. 17th Century Islamic site.

Golconda 1974-75. pp. 2-3.
Andhra Pradesh. District Hyderabad. 17th Century Islamic site.

150. Gollathagudi 1958-59. p.11
Andhra Pradesh, District Mahbubnagar. 9th and 10th Century temple site.

Gollathagudi 1970-71. p.3
Andhra Pradesh, District Mahbubnagar. Temple site.

Gollathagudi 1971-72. p.3.
Andhra Pradesh, District Mahbubnagar. Temple site.

Gollathagudi 1972-73. pp. 2-3
Andhra Pradesh, District Mahbubnagar. 9th-10th century.

Gollathagudi 1973-74. p.6.
Andhra Pradesh, District Mahbubnagar. Jain Site. Brick temples.

Gollathagudi 1974-75. p.6
Andhra Pradesh, District Mahbubnagar. Buddhist remains.

151. Goraj 1982-83. p. 31
Gujarat, District Vadodara. Excavation behind a Siva temple. Brick foundations. Micaceous Red Ware, red slipped wares. Dated to 3rd to 5th centuries based on stylistic similarities to Devnimori and Kayavarohan.

Goraj 1983-84. pp. 23-24.
Gujarat, District vadodara. Continued excavation of a brick temple. Images of Parvati and Vishnu in late levels. Dated to 2nd/3rd century A.D. to 14th/15th century A.D.

Goraj 1984-85. pp. 19-20.
Gujarat, District Vadodara. Continued excavation of the temple.

152. Gorkal 1977-78. p. 30.
Karnataka, District Raichur. Three Neolithic ash mounds in the vicinity of Gorkal in Manvi Taluk. Three infant urn burials. Burnished grey ware, burnished black ware, cream wares, plain hand made grey, red and buff wares. Microliths. In an Exploration and Excavation Report for Raichur District.

153. Goswamikhanda 1963-64. pp. 60-61.
West Bengal, District Burdwan. Fossil wood scraper from lowest level. Platform and historical material, possibly of ca. 10th century A.D.

154. Gudimallam 1973-74. pp. 1-2.
Andhra Pradesh, District Chittoor. Early Historic temple.

155. Gudiyam 1962-63. p. 12.
Tamil Nadu, District Chingleput. Rock Shelter, Burkitt's series II tools, post-Acheulian, microliths.
Gudiyam 1963-64. p. 19.
Tamil Nadu, District Chingleput, Cave site. Middle Palaeolithic.

156. Gufkral 1981-82. pp. 19-25.
Jammu and Kashmir, District Pulwama. Long report. Period IA, Aceramic Neolithic. List of plants and animals. Period IB, Neolithic. Period IC, Neolithic Period II, Megalithic. Period III, limited excavation, iron, rice, list of animals. Pottery illustrations, sectiond rawings.

Guntrumurthy See Gutturmalai.

157. Guttur 1982-83. p. 71.
Tamil Nadu, district Dharampuri. With report on Gutturmalai. Ash mound.

158. Gutturmalai 1982-83. pp. 71-72
Tamil Nadu, District Dharampuri. Noted as the site of guntrumurthy in the report. Period III, Late Medieval to modern. Period II, Early Historic and Early Medieval. Period I, Megalithic, 300 B.C. to 200 A.D..

159. Halingali 1965-66. p. 34.
Karnataka, District Bijapur. Megalithic red ware, Chalcolithic - Neolithic grey ware.

160. Hallur 1964-65. pp. 31-32.
Karnataka, District Dharwar. Lower Neolithic, upper Neolithic with Chalcolithic, Megalithic. Coarse brown and black ware, pale grey ware, burnished black ware with red ochre paint, ground stone, black painted red ware, copper, blade industry, black and red ware with white paint. Early iron.

Hallur 1976-77. p. 25.
Karnataka, District Dharwar. Confirmation of sequence. Chalcolithic child burials in single, double and triple urns. Grains. Gold ornaments.

161. Hampi 1975-76. pp. 20-21.
Karnataka, District Bellary. Vijayanagara. Structures. Chinese porcelain.

Hampi 1976-77. p. 25.
Karnataka, District Bellary. Vijayanagara. China ware, coarse black, red and grey wares.

Hampi 1978-79. pp. 43-45.
Karnataka, District Bellary. Vijayanagara. China ware bearing Chinese script, copper coins, iron objects, a ring of gold.

Hampi 1979-80. p. 33.
Karnataka, District Bellary. Vijayanagara. China ware, black and plain red wares, copper coins, structures.

Hampi 1980-81. pp. 26-28.
Karnataka, District Bellary. Vijayanagara. Plan of the King's Audience Hall.

Hampi 1981-82. pp. 25-26.
Karnataka, District Bellary. Vijayanagara. Excavation between the King's Audience Hall, the Mahanavami-dibba and the Mint Area.

Hampi 1982-83. pp. 32-33.
Karanataka, District Bellary. Report on the Government of Karnataka work. Excavation in the Nobleman's area and the Royal residential area. Exposure of so-called Nobleman's Palace I and Nobleman's Palace 2. Clearing of the temple of Nagareshware and the Krishna temple on the road from Hazara Rama temple to the Talari-ghat.

Hampi 1982-83. pp. 33-35.
Karnataka, District Bellary. Report on the

work of the Archaeological Survey. Excavation to teh south of the King's Audience Hall to investigate the structural complex there as well as to trace the plan of the citadel complex.

Hampi 1983-84. pp. 35-37.
Karnataka, District Bellary. M.S. Nagaraj Rao's excavation. Work at the "Nobleman's Palace." sites number 1 through 4. Exposure of a toilet.

Hampi 1983-84. pp. 37-39.
Karnataka, District Bellary. Mid-Southern Circle project resumes excavation of the King's Audience Hall and traces a complete plan of the so-called "Citadel." Description of architecture, tanks, list of small finds and pottery.

Hampi 1984-85. pp. 25-28.
Karnataka, District Bellary. Excavation in the Royal Enclosure and in the vicinity of the King's Audience Hall. Description of three new structures, a unique steeped tank and an aqueduct. List of antiquities.

Hampi 1984-85. pp. 28-29.
Karnataka, District Bellary. Karnataka State excavations of four major buildings, called "Nobelman's Palaces."

162. Haraipur 1964-65. p. 46.
West Bengal, District Birbhum. Plain and painted black and red ware, red slipped grey ware.

163. Harwan 1973-74. pp. 15-16.
Jammu and Kashmir, District Srinagar. Buddhist site.

164. Hashmatpet 1970-71. pp. 1-2.
Andhra Pradesh, District Hyderabad. Megaliths.

165. Hathinia-Pahar 1963-64. p. 57.
Uttar Pradesh, District Varanasi. Megaliths, microliths, black and red ware, pottery types comparable to Chalcolithic. See Kakoria and Bhadahawan Hillock as well.

166. Hathkhamba 1970-71. p. 27.
Maharashtra, District Ratnagiri, Microliths.

Hathkhamba 1972-73. p. 25
Maharashtra, District Ratnagiri, Microlithic cave site.

167. Hazurnagar 1983-84. p. 5
Andhra Pradesh, District Nalgonda. Excavation of a cist grave with swastika plan. Fragmentary skeletal remains. Faceted carnelian bead. Black and red ware.

168. Hemmige 1963-64. pp. 26-27.
Karnataka, District Mysore, Middle Stone Age tools, ground stone, rough red ware, slipped red ware, Russet-coated Painted Ware, Chalcolithic handmade burnished wares in black, red and brown, some with red painting.

169. Hoysalesware Temple Telex 1984-85. p. 31.
Karnataka, District Hassan. Work at a Hoysala dynasty temple with an inscription mentioning Vishnvadrhana and Narasimha I. Dated to 11th and 12th Century.

170. Hulas 1978-79. pp. 60-61.
Uttar Pradesh, District Saharanpur. Harappan and non-Harappan wares, PGW, plain grey, black and red, black slipped, red wares, NBP. Sunga-Kushan and Gupta levels, terra-cotta objects, structures.

Hulas 1979-80. p. 82.
Uttar Pradesh, District Saharanpur. Period I, Harappan, structures, terra-cotta figures, painted pottery, Period II, PGW. Period III, NBP, grey and red wares.

Hulas 1980-81. pp. 73-76.
Uttar Pradesh, District Saharanpur. Period I, Harappan mud platform and note of antiquities. Period II, PGW, iron slag and antiquities. Period II, PGW, iron slag and fragments of cruicible. Period IV, massive burnt brick structure, 7 copper coins. Illustration of PGW.

Hulas 1981-82. pp. 72-74.
Uttar Pradesh, District Saharanpur. Period I, Harappan, pits, strucrtures, platform small furnaces, burnt brick. Period II, PGW. Period III, NBP. Period IV, Kushan. Period. V, ivory scale marked by circles. Illustration of Harappan pottery.

Hulas 1982-83. pp. 100-103.
Uttar Pradesh, District Saharanpur. Investigation of three phases of Harappan occupation. Covers 2000 square meters. 43 structures. Rectangular and brick strucrtures. Circular structures, Furnaces. Chula. In Harappan context : rice, wheat, barley, horse gram, green gram, black gram, peas, and ragi of finger millet. Non-Harappan pottery in lowest levels. Copper fish hooks, chisels, needles, spiral rings, etc. Also occupations of PGW, and Kushan.

171. Hulaskhera 1978-79. pp. 74-75.
Uttar Pradesh, District Lucknow., 6th century B.C. to 5th Century A.D., NBP, black and red ware, red ware, silver punch marked coins, Kushan coins, potter's stamp.

Hulaskhera 1979-80. p. 77.
Uttar Pradesh, District Lucknow.
Kushan and Gupta levels, structures.

Hulaskhera 1980-81. p. 71.
Uttar Pradesh, District Lucknow. Gateway, Kushan road, coins and other antiquities.

Hulaskhera 1981-82. pp. 71-72.
Uttar Pradesh, District Lucknow. Excavation of Kushan period road and the Gupta citadel. Coins. List of small finds.

Hulaskhera 1982-83. pp. 98-99.
Uttar Pradesh, District Lucknow. Excavation of Kushan/Gupta site. Exposure of a fortification. Kushan structure, copper coins. Small finds listed.

Hulsskhera 1983-84. pp. 88-89.
Uttar Pradesh, District Lucknow. Excavation of Kushan/Gupta site. Excavation of the fortification and gate. . Kushan houses and road described. Kushan coins and small finds listed.

172. Hullikallu 1978-79. p. 62-63.
Andhra Pradesh, District Anantapur. Neolithic, Chalcolithic and Megalithic levels, black Neolithic, Chalcolithic and Megalithic levels, black and red ware, unburnbished grey or black, burnished grey wares, burials, polished stone tools, ash mounds.

173. Hunsgi 1974-75. pp. 19-20.
Karnataka, District Gulbarga.
Acheulian tools.

Hunsgi 1975-76. p. 22.
Karnataka, District Gulbarga. Lower Palaeolithic.

Hunsgi 1977-78. p. 22.
Karnataka, District Gulbarga. Acheulian, Mesolithic.

174. Hunur 1968-69. pp. 20-21.
Karnataka, District Belgam. Megalithic.

175. Inamgaon 1968-69. pp. 18-20.
Maharashtra, District Pune. Period I, Malwa, rectangular houses, *jowar*, blade tools.

Period II, Jorwe, 21 houses, some round, some rectangular, copper fish hook, human and animal figurines, bead making area, urn burials for children, adult inhumation.

Inamgaon 1969-70. pp. 25-27.
Maharashtra, District Pune. Excavation of Late Jorwe Levels. House with a conical roof, chula, storage bins, blade tools, copper implements (fish hook, pan, poker) burials. Large house. Pottery illustrations.

Inamgaon 1970-71. pp. 25-26.
Maharashtra, District Pune. period I, Malwa, twin urn burial, rectangular houses. Period II, Early Jorwe, 8 rectangular houses, twin urn burial, extended burials, No specific mention of Period III, Late Jorwe, copper bangles. Figurine of a "Mother Goddess" and a bull in a clay box from Early Jorwe house.

Inamgaon 1972-73. p. 24.
Maharashtra, District Pune. Period I, Malwa. Large rectangular house with hearth, in situ grinding stone and storage bin. Divided into two rooms. Circular house near by. Period II A : Early Jorwe potter's kiln. Period II b, Late Jorwe. Copper ore, storage jars.

Inamgaon 1974-75. pp. 32-36
Maharashtra, District Pune. Period II, Early Jorwe house complex. Discussion of burials. Drawing of human cranium. Table of burials. List of mammals from the excavation Hippopotamus from the river.

Inamgaon 1977-78. pp. 40-41.
Maharashtra, District Pune. Excavation of Jorwe levels. Investigation of houses, description of storage silo, chula, burials. Copper and paste beads, polished stone tools.

Inamgaon 1978-79. pp. 52-53.
Maharashtra, District Pune. Investigation of transition from Malwa Period I to Jorwe Period II, gradual transition. Pit silos, mud platforms for storage bins, small pottery kiln, storage jar, burials, copper, stone objects.

Inamgaon 1979-80. pp. 58-59.
Maharashtra, District Pune. Malwa Period investigation. Description of site preparation, houses, features in houses, Child burials but no adults. Tools and beads of copper, bone points, male and female figurines. Barley, millets, pea, lentil, hunting, fishing, sheep/goat, cattle, buffalo.

Inamgaon 1980-81. p. 41.
Maharashtra, District Pune. Work on Period III, Late Jorwe. Grains of barley, lentil, peas, hyacinth bean, etc. extended burial, manufacturing site for microlithic blades, urn burials, barbed copper arrowhead comparable to Harappan types and other antiquities.

Inamgaon 1980-81. pp. 41-42.
Maharashtra, District Pune. Late Pleistocene deposits on River Ghod just opposite the Chalcolithic site of Inamgaon. Middle and Upper Palaeolithic tools. List of fossil fauna. See also Ghod Valley.

Inamgaon 1981-82. pp. 50-51.
Maharashtra, District Pune. Period II (Early Jorwe) house excavated with teen age human buried in a four-legged urn. Crocodile figurine, antler pick. Period III (Late Jorwe) houses are both circular and rectangular. One is roughly triangular in plan. Burial with spherical copper beads, sea shells (?). Floors of Period III houses less well made than earlier floors. Crocodile bones. Less grain and more sheep/goat bones in Period III suggests a shift to pastoralism.

Inamgaon 1982-83. pp. 62-63.
Maharashtra, District Pune. Excavation of 5 Late Jorwe houses, 4 rectangular and squarish. Adult and child burials. Aerial survey evidence for ditch and irrigation canal.

176. Indari 1980-81 p.72.
Uttar Pradesh, District Mirzapur. Neolithic. Cord impressed ware, rustricated ware, burnished red ware, burnished black ware. Microliths. Hut plans, floors and post holes, wattle and daub impression.

Indo-ki-Dhani
See Indola-Ki-Dhani.

177. Indola-ki-Dhani 1980-81.pp. 57-63
Rajasthan, District Nagaur. Report on Palaeolithic and palaeoenvironmental work near Didwana. Schematic section and map of sites. See singi Talav Quarry and Didwana/Marwar Balia.

178. Indragarh 1958-59 p.28
Madhya Pradesh, District Mandasor, Temple Site.

179. Jaderua 1971-72 pp.29-30
Madhya Pradesh, District Gwalior. Period I, mid-1st millennium B.C. PGW. Period IIA, mid-4th to 2nd Century B.C. NBP, metal tools, iron slag.Period IIB, 1st century B.C. to 2nd century A.D., Naga Coins, Sunga Style figurines. Period III, 9th and 10th centuries A.D., pottery. Mughal coin from the village.

180. Jaḍigenahalli 1956-57, pp. 34-35
Karnataka, District Bangalore. Megaliths.

181. Jagatgram 1953-54, pp.10-11
Uttar Pradesh, District Dehra Dun. Horse sacrifice site of 3rd Century a.D. Transitional Brahmi inscriptions. King Silavarman is Post-Kushan and Pre-Gupta.

182. Jaḥanpanah 1964-65 pp.7-8
Delhi. Muhammad bin Tughluk Fort, 1324-51, A.D. See also Qila Rai Pithora.

183. Jajmau 1956-57 p.29
Uttar Pradesh, District Kanpur. NBP
Jajmau 1957-58 p. 49.
Uttar Pradesh, District Kanpur. NBP, iron, ivory bangles, dice, terra-cotta figurines.
Jajmau 1968-69. pp 39-40
Uttar Pradesh, District Kanpur Trial excavation noted in an Exploration Report. NBP

Jajmau 1973-74 p.31.
Uttar Pradesh, District Kanpur. PGW, NBP, highway cut, copper coins.

Jajmau 1974-75 p.48
Uttar Pradesh, District Kanpur. Kushans, Medieval Period.

Jajmau 1975-76 pp.52-53
Uttar Pradesh, District Kanpur.NBP, red ware, red slipped ware, Brahmi inscriptions, Mauryan, Kushan.

Jajmau 1976-77 p.54
Uttar Pradesh, District Kanpur NBP, sprinklers, stamped red ware.

184. Jakhera 1974-75. pp.43-45
Uttar Pradesh, District Etah. Period I comparable to Period II at Atranjikhera (16 km downstream) based on pottery. Period II, PGW, Period III, NBP.

Jakhera 1975-76 pp. 50-51
Uttar Pradesh, District Etah. Period I, black and red ware, red wares, part of a floor, hearth. Period IIA, painted red ware, figurines. Period IIB, PGW, wattle and daub houses, iron tools and weapons listed, copper, antimony., terra-cotta small finds. Period III, NBP, iron objects, manufacture of bone points, terra-cotta small finds. Channel or moat.

185. Jalukbar 1967-68. p.8
Assam, District Kamrup. Boat-shaped object of burnt clay containing storage jars.

186. Jaugada 1956-57.pp 30-31
Orissa, District Ganjam. Period I, Iron, black and red ware, dull red ware, beads from many materials listed, unfinished beads. Period II, Puri-Kushan coins, rampart, ditch, fortification.

187. Jiwangarh 1972-73 p.33.
Uttar Pradesh, Distrtict Dhera Dun. Bricks with Brahmi inscriptions. Medieval platform.

188. Jodhpura 1972-73. pp.29-30
Rajasthan, District Jaipur. Period I, OCP, copper. Period II, plain black and red ware with similarities to that at Noh. Period III. PGW. Period IV. NBP. Period V, Sunga/ Kushan pottery.

189. Jokha 1966-67.p.10
Gujarat, District Surat. Microliths, Neolithic celt, Late Harappan, Malwa, Jorwe, red ware, black ware, Early Historical and Medieval pottery.

190. Jonnawada 1976-77. p.9
Andhra Pradesh, District Nellore. Megalithic burials, black and red ware, black ware, red ware.

191. Junapani 1961-62. pp.32-34
Maharashtra, District Nagpur. Megalithic cairn circles, black and red ware, all black ware, plain red wares, micaceous grit ware, black paint on a hole mouth spouted red ware.

192. Kadambapur 1974-75. pp. 3-4
Andhra Pradesh, District Karimnagar. Megalithic site, red ware, black ware, dull red ware, black and red ware.

193. Kakoria 1962-63 pp. 39-41
Uttar Pradesh, District Varanasi. Megaliths, microliths, ill fired red ware, black and red ware, all black ware.

Kakoria 1963-64. pp.57-58
Uttar Pradesh, District Varanasi. Megaliths. See Hathinia-Pahar and Bhadahawan Hillock as well.

194. Kalibangan 1960-61 pp. 31-32.
Rajasthan, District Ganganagar. Harappan, Painted pottery, black over unslipped dull red (similar to early Kot Diji), steatite seals, Harappan script, etched carnelian, copper.

Kalibangan 1961-62. pp.39-44
Rajasthan, District Ganganagar. Pre-Harappan, Harappan. Drawings of Pre-Harappan pottery motifs and some shapes. Discussion of architecture when Harappans arrived.' Description of large Harappan building.

Kalibangan 1962-63 pp.20-31
Rajasthan, District Ganganagar. Pre-Harappan, Harappan. Discussion and drawings of pottery, fabrics A to F. Discussion of architecture and fortification. Claim for grid town plan. Note on small finds.

Kalibangan 1963-64 pp.30-39
Rajasthan, District Ganganagar. Pre-Harappan, Harappan, Carbon 14 dates noted but not given here. Two brick sizes in Harappan. Grid town plan. Harappan small finds listed. Four pages of pottery from burials.

Kalibangan 1964-65. pp.35-39
Rajasthan, District Ganganagar. Pre-Harappan, Harappan. Discussion of fortifications and burials. Drawing of burial.

Kalibangan 1965-66 pp.38-41
Rajasthan, District Ganganagar. Pre-Harappan fortification and other architecture.

Kalibangan 1966-67. pp.31-33
Rajasthan, District Ganganagar. Pre-Harappan, Harappan.

Kalibangan 1967-68. pp.42-45
Rajasthan, District Ganganagar. Pre-Harappan, Harappan. Site plan.

Kalibangan 1968-69. pp. 28-32
Rajasthan, District Ganganagar. Pre-Harappan. Harappan. Pre-Harappan plowed field, second site plan, Harappan small finds, burial types, grave goods.

195. Kallerimala 1978-79 p.73
Tamil Nadu, District North Arcot. Black and red ware, grey ware, urn burial, single polished stone axe.

196. Kalyadi 1976-77. p. 26
Karnataka, District Hassan. Copper mine.

197. Kamauli 1963-64 p.58
Uttar Pradesh, District Varanasi. Part of the Rajghat Project. Period I, Protohistoric red ware, chert blade. Period II, Late

Medieval.

198. Kambarmedu 1982-83, pp. 72, 89.
Tamil Nadu, District Thajavur. Late Megalithic site with "neolithic remnants." Medieval occupation with Chola coins.

Kambarmedu 1983-84. pp. 78-80.
Tamil Nadu, District Thanjavur. Excavation of a Megalithic site with Neolithic elements like red painted grey ware and polished axe. Magalithic black and red ware.

199. Kampil 1975-76. pp 51-52
Uttar Pradesh, District Farrukhabad. PGW, fine grey ware, black slipped ware, black and red ware.

200. Kanauj 1955-56 pp.19-20
Uttar Pradesh, District Farrukhabad. Period I, 1000 B.C. and later, PGW sherd with a mass of red and black slipped ware. Period II, 600 to 200 B.C., NBP and associated wares. Period III red ware, Kushan to Early Medieval. Period IV, Late Medieval.

201. Kanchipuram 1962-63 p.12.
Tamil Nadu, District Chingleput. Megalithic black and red ware, red ware, black slipped ware Rouletted Ware, bright red slipped ware, amphorae, Satavahana coins in stratigraphy, Pallava lead coins, Medieval.

Kanchipuram 1969-70 pp. 34-35
Tamil Nadu, District Chingleput. Fine black and red ware (ca. 3rd century B.C.) Rouletted Ware, through 16th century A.D.

Kanchipuram 1970-71 pp. 32-33.
Tamil Nadu, District Chingleput. Buddhist, Rouletted Ware, etc.

Kanchipuram 1971-72. pp. 42-43
Tamil Nadu, District Chingleput. Stupa-like structure. Rouletted and Arretine Wares. Brahmi graffiti, Satavahana coins.

Kanchipuram 1972-73 p.30
Tamil Nadu, District Chingleput. Investigation of a stupa-like structure. Rouletted Ware in period IB.

Kanchipuram 1974-75 pp. 37-38
Tamil Nadu, District Chingleput. Period IA, Russet-coated Painted Ware. Period IB, black and red ware, brown slipped ware, Arretine and Rouletted Ware dated to 100 B.C. to 300 A.D. Period II, ceramics and small finds dated to 300 to 800 A.D. Period III, ceramics and small finds dated to 800 to 1500 A.D.

Kanchipuram 1975-76 p.39
Tamil Nadu, District Chingleput. Periods I, II and Medieval. Excavation in Little Kanchipuram.

202. Kandhar 1983-84 pp. 58-59
Maharashtra, District Nanded, Excavation of a stone structure of human shape, 23 meters long surrounded by pavement located in a cultivated area. Historical information indicates that this may be a 'temple' of Ksetrapala, protector of the fields.

203. Kanewal 1977-78 p.21
Gujarat, District Kheda Harappan, Mesolithic, microliths, plain and painted red ware, course red ware, buff ware, Lustrous Red Ware similar to Lothal B and Rangpur IIC and III, Harappan script.

204. Kanheri 1969-70 pp. 21-22
Maharashtra, District Bombay. RPW, 3rd-4th to 10th Century A.D.

205. Kankarbagh 1970-71 p.6
Bihar, District Patna. NBP.

206. Kannanur 1983-84 p.81
Tamil Nadu, District Tiruchirappalli, Excavation near Samayapuram undertaken to expose a water channel so as to understand its construction.

207. Kaothe 1984-85 pp. 52-53
Maharashtra, District Dhulia. Excavation at a "Late Harappan" site with Gujarati type Harappan ceramics associated with Savalda and Kayatha Ware. Pit houses, chulas. Charred seeds of *Bajra* or Pearl Millet and sesame both reported, it is noted that the site is under cultivation. No

stone or metal tools, but an abundance of bone implements. Four burials. C-14 1920+70 B.C.

208. Karaikadu 1966-67 p.21
Tamil Nadu, District South Arcot.
Red Slipped ware, black and red ware, Rouletted Ware, trading station.

209. Karapakala 1979-80 pp.8-9
Andhra Pradesh, District Mahbubnagar. Period I, handmade coarse red and coarse grey wares. Period II, grey ware of Period I, plus black and red ware, coarse red ware. Megaliths near by, one excavated, copper bell with bone tongue.

210. Karain 1954-55 p.26
Bihar, District Darbhanga. Site of ca 900-1800 A.D.

211. Karnachaura 1979-80 pp.13-14
Bihar, District Monghyr. NBP, black slipped ware, Pala to Post-Muslim occupation, red, black and grey wares.

212. Karvan 1974-75. pp.15-16
Gujarat, District Vadodara. Pre-Gupta, Coins of Kshatrapa and Maitraka.

Karvan 1975-76 p.15.
Gujarat, District Vadodara. RPW, red ware, stamped red ware, coarse black ware, thick grey ware, Kshatrapa coins.

Karvan 1976-77 p.18
Gujarat, District Vadodara. RPW, red ware, greyware, stamped ware, coins.

Karvan 1977-78, pp.22-23
Gujarat, District Vadodara. RPW, black slipped ware, Early Historical.

213. Kaseri 1969-70. p. 43.
Uttar Pradesh, District Merrut. OCP, PGW, historic periods.

214. Kashipur 1965-66. pp. 53-54.
Uttar Pradesh, District Nainital. NBP, PGW, Kushan gold coins, Buddhist.

Kashipur 1970-71. pp. 41-45.
Uttar Pradesh, District Nainital. Medieval site. Plan of the temple.

215. Kasital 1975-76. p. 17.
Haryana, District Karnal. PGW, black and red ware, red ware. Early Historical, Medieval.

216. Kathpalon 1976-77. p. 42.
Punjab, District Jullundur. PGW, "Late" Harappan, Kushan.

217. Katragarh 1975-76. p. 8
Bihar, District Muzaffarpur. NBP, red ware, grey ware, Kushan inscription. Sunga fort, Mauryan, Gupta.

Katragarh 1976-77. pp. 12-13.
Bihar, District Muzaffarpur. NBP, black painted grey ware, grey ware, red ware, black ware, micaceous red ware, sprinklers, stamped ware, Sunga fort, Mauryan, coin of Huvishka, Pala Period.

Katragarh 1977-78, pp. 15-76.
Bihar, District Muzaffarpur. NBP, grey ware, red ware, black ware, micaceous red ware, rusticated red ware, Sunga, Kushan, coins.

Katragarh 1978-79. p. 67.
Bihar, District Muzaffarpur. NBP, rampart excavation, defenses.

Katragarh 1979-80. p. 14.
Bihar, District Muzaffarpur. Kushan and Post-Sunga findings. Brahmi script.

218. Kaundanpur 1961-62. pp. 29-30.
Maharashtra, District Amravati. Megalithic black and red ware, grit tempered ware, etched carnelian beads with designs similar to south Indian, NBP, Russet-coated Painted Ware, punch marked copper coins, Brahmi characters of 1st century A.D., Satavahana coin.

219. Kausambi 1953-54. p. 9.
Uttar Pradesh, District Allahabad. Excavation of the Ghoshitarama monastery. Rampart excavation indicates settlement in the 6th century B.C. NBP.

Kausambi 1954-55. pp. 16-18.

Uttar Pradesh, District Allahabad. Excavation of the Ghoshitarama monastery and rampart. Dates monastery to 2nd century A.D. Three stages of construction to the rampart. Coin molds and sealings with royal names.

Kausambi 1955-56. pp. 20-22.
Uttar Pradesh. District Allahabad. Cointinued excavation of the Ghoshitarama monastery. Report includes a plan of this building. Site occupied from 6th century B.C. to 6th century A.D. in 16 phases. NBP.

Kausambi 1956-57. pp. 28-29.
Uttar Pradesh, District Allahabad. Excavation of rampart and tower. Goshitarama area also worked. NBP.

Kausambi 1957-58. pp. 47-49.
Uttar Pradesh, District Allahabad. Period I. Defenses constructed. NBP. Period II change in plan. NBP. Period III, *purrushamedha* (human sacrifice) and *yena-chiti* (eagle-alter) reported, coins of the Mitra kings, upper limit of NBP. Period IV, a small amount of change in site plan. Period V, site destruction with many antiquities. Dates: Period I ca. 700 B.C. ; II, 500 B.C. ; III, 200 B.C.; IV, 50 B.C.; V, 150 A.D.

Kausambi 1958-59. pp. 46-48.
Uttar Pradesh, District Allahabad. Pre-defense deposits. Excavation reveals phases in rampart and defenses construction. Moat. Iron in Pre-NBP context. "Decadent stage of PGW." Pottery from early levels illustrated.

Kausambi 1959-60. p. 46.
Uttar Pradesh, District Allahabad. Correlation of fortifications with habitation. NBP.

Kausambi 1960-61. pp. 33-35.
Uttar Pradesh, District Allahabad. Stone palace 315 by 150 meters with a tower. The first phase of the palace pre-dates the NBP. Phase two dates to the earliest phase of NBP. Terracotta figurines and other small find. NBP, red ware, Early Historical.

Kausambi 1961-62. pp. 50-52.
Uttar Pradesh, District Allahabad. Exposure of the stone palace. NBP, Some possibly post-Harappan Chalcolithic pottery types: painted black on red surface, incised, grey (painted and plain), red wares.

Kausambi 1962-63. pp. 32-33.
Uttar Pradesh, District Allahabad. Work on the stone palace. Earliest phase there has pottery similar to Navdatoli III, Rangpur IIC and III, black paintings on sherds. NBP.

Kausambi 1963-64. p. 40.
Uttar Pradesh, District Allahabad. Excavation at the stone palace. Rampart on Yamuna side. Ditch fortification. Landing on the Yamuna. NBP, black slipped ware, grey and red wares.

Kausambi 1966-67. pp. 38-39.
Uttar Pradesh, District Allahabad. Excavation of the stone palace to determine the relationship between the building and the tower on the Yamuna. NBP, red ware.

220 Kausa 1965-66. pp. 28-29.
Maharashtra, District Aurangabad. Period II, burials with large, painted pot, Jorwe Ware. Period II, Satavahana (200 B.C. to 100 A.D.), ring wells, copper coins, bullae in imitation of Roamn coins, kaolin figurines. See Paithan as well.

Kaveripattanam
See Kaveripattinam

221. Kaveripattinam 1962-63. p. 13.
Tamil Nadu, District Thanjavur. Megalithic black and red ware, Chola port city, early Medieval deposits.

Kaveripattinam 1963-64. p. 20.
Tamil Nadu, District Thanjavur. Megalithic black and red ware, Rouletted Ware, square copper coin, early Cholaport.

Kaveripattinam 1964-65. pp. 24-25.
Tamil Nadu, District Thanjavur. Megalithic black and red ware, Rouletted Ware, square copper coins of Cholas, Buddhist

remains of the 4th to 5th century A.D.

Keveripattinam 1965-66. pp. 24-25.
Tamil Nadu, District Thanjavur. Continued excavation of the monastic site of Kaveripattinamin Melaiyur. Early Medieval.

Kaveripattinam 1966-67. p. 21.
Tamil Nadu, District Thanjavur. Early to late Medieval Chola coins.

Kaveripattinam 1970-71. p. 35.
Tamil Nadu, District Thanjavur. Temple.

Kaveripattinam 1972-73. pp. 32-33.
Tamil Nadu, District Thanjavur. Buddhist site.

Kaveripattinam 1973-74. p. 25.
Tamil Nadu, District Thanjavur. Medieval stupa.

Kaveripattinam 1977-78. p. 50.
Tamil Nadu, District Thanjavur. Excavation in Pallavaneswaram. Vihara and shrine exposed. Stucco figures.

222. Kayatha 1964-65. pp. 18-19.
Madhya Pradesh, District Ujjain. Chalcolithic, NBP, sturdy ware with dark brown, cream, mauve-purple or dull red slip with painted designs, white painted black and red ware of Ahar fabric, microliths, black painted red ware, cast copper coins, Buddha figure, Sunga, Gupta.

Kayatha 1967-68. pp. 24-25.
Madhya Pradesh, District Ujjain. NBP, chocolate slipped ware with violet paint, red painted buff ware, incised red ware, steatite micro-beads, white painted black and red ware (similar to Banas valley), microliths, carbon 14 (19th century B.C.), black painted red ware,
Malwa, Early Historical red ware.

223. Keesaragutta Hill 1975-76. pp. 1—2.
Hill Andhra Pradesh, District Hyderabad. RPW, brown polished ware, dull red ware, sprinklers, Early Historical fort and temples, coins of the Vishnukundins.

224. Kessaragutta 1976-77. p.3.
Andhra Pradesh, District Hyderabad. Black ware, grey ware, red were, red slipped ware, black slipped ware, Vishnukundin coins.

Keesaragutta 1978-79. pp. 63-64.
Andhra Pradesh, District Hyderabad. Shrines and structures, coins of Visnukundins, iron objects, terra-cotta objects.

Keesaragutta 1980-81. p. 8
Andhra Pradesh, District Hyderabad. Six structures excavated, both ritual and domestic buildings.

225. Kenduli 1964-65. pp. 32-33.
Orissa, District Puri. 8th century temple.

226. Kesarapalli 1961-62. pp. 1-2.
Andhra Pradesh, District Krishna. Period I, Chalcolithic, red ware, black and red ware, grey ware, black slipped. Period II, iron, Megalithic pottery. Period III, Rouletted Ware. Period IV, Ikshvaku lead coin, early Medieval. Drawing of Period I pottery.

227. Khairwada 1981-82. pp. 51-52.
Maharashtra, District Wardha. Megalithic site with 1400 stone circles. First noticed in 1869. Excavation of both the Megaliths and the habitation area. Black and red ware, iron. Layer 4 of the habitation site has a transition from Megalithic to Satavahana. Layer 3 is Late Satavahana. Layer 2 is later material. List of small finds.

228. Khajuraho 1980-81. p. 32.
Madhya Pradesh, District Chhatarpur. Temple site. 1 km east of the western group of temples.

Khajuraho 1981-82. pp. 29-30.
Madhya Pradesh, District Chhatarpur. Excavation of a brick structure complex. Early or Pre-Chandella.

Khajuraho 1982-83. p. 37.
Madhya Pradesh, District Chhatarpur. Excavation to further understand the nature of previously excavated triple shrines with a common *mandapa* and

229. Khalaua 1965-66 pp. 41-42.
Uttar Pradesh, District Agra. PGW, black and red ware, black slipped ware, plain red wares.

230. Khalkatapatna 1984-85. p. 59.
Orissa, District Puri. Medieval mound of 12th-14th century. Chinese ceramics and coins. No structures.

231. Khangkhui 1968-69. p. 20.
Manipur. Palaeolithic rock shelter.

232. Khapa 1967-68. pp. 33-34.
Maharashtra, District Nagpur. Megaliths, black painted red ware, black and red ware, micaceous red ware, iron, copper. See Takalghat also.

Khapa 1968-69. p. 17.
Maharashtra, District Nagpur. Megaliths. See Gangapur as well.

233. Kheradih 1980-81. pp. 69-70.
Uttar Pradesh, District Ballia. Phase I of Period I, NBP and associated wares. Phase II of Period I, ca. 3rd to 2nd century B.C. recalls Rajgahat IC. Iron and other antiquities. Period II, Sunga/Kushan.

Kheradih 1981-82. pp. 67-70.
Uttar Pradesh, District Ballia. Period I, pre-NBP, black and red ware, black slipped ware in PGW shapes, red ware. Period II, NBP, list of small finds. Period III, burntbrick structures. Period IV, no NBP, apparently a KUshan urban settlement. Period I begins in 8th or 9th century B.C. and the settlement extends to the 4th century A.D.

Kheradih 1982-83. pp. 92-94
Uttar Pradesh, District Ballia. Period I, plain and painted varieties of black and red ware, black slipped ware and plain and painted red ware. No iron, but copper present. Period II, NBP, some of it painted. uniscribed coins, punch marked coins. Period III, road surface.

Kheradih 1983-84. pp. 86-87.
Uttar Pradesh, district Ballia. Period I, same pottery, post holes and fragmentary wall. Period II, iron smith's workshop, furnaces, finished tools, slag, carnelian pendant in the shape of a monkey. More work on the roadway described.

234. Khomananta 1982-83. pp. 64-65.
Orissa, District Phulbani. Listed as "Excavation in District Phulbani." Trial excavation at an open air Mesolithic site. Tools were scarce but included triangles, backed blades, retouched blades, crescent and a heavy tool component. Polished stone celts on the surface.

235. Khuntitoli 1965-66. p. 10.
Bihar, District Ranchi. Megalith. See Saradkel also.

236. Koldihawa 1971-72. p. 44.
Uttar Pradesh, District Allahabad. Microliths, rice, possible early food production.

Koldihawa 1973-74. pp. 26-27.
Uttar Pradesh, District Allahabad. Microliths, Neolithic.

Koldihawa 1975-76. pp. 45, 47.
Uttar Pradesh, District Allahabad. Neolithic with cord impressed pottery, red ware, black and red ware, microliths, rice, carbon 14 dates, Chalcolithic with red ware, red slipped ware, black slipped ware, iron age.

237. Kolhua 1976-77. p. 13.
Bihar, District Muzaffarpur. Stupa, Buddhist plaques.

238. Komaranahalli 1980-81. p. 29.
Karnataka, District Chitradurga. Description of the excavation of 4 megaliths near Hallur. White painted conical lids found here and at Hallur where they were in the Chalcolithic/Iron Age overlap, ca. 1000 B.C.

239. Korkai 1968-69. p. 32.
Tamil Nadu, District Tirunelveli. Megaliths, ancient port, The Periplus.

240. Kotia 1963-64. pp. 40-41.
Uttar Pradesh, District Allahabad Megaliths, black and red ware, red ware, dull black ware, grey ware.

241. Kotilingala 1980-81. p.2.
Andhra Pradesh. District Karimnagar. Satavahana brick structures, coins, iron. RPW. Stupa excavation near by.

242. Kotturu 1954-55. pp. 23-24.
Andhra Pradesh, District Visakhapatnam. Buddhist site.

243. Kovalanpottal 1979-80. p. 69.
Tamil Nadu, District Madurai. Urn burials, Megalithic pottery. Neolithic and microlithic tools.

244. Kovalli 1964-65. p. 30-31.
Karnataka, District Bijapur. Middle Palaeolithic and microliths.

245. Kuchai 1961-62. p. 36.
Orissa, District Mayurbhanj. Neolithic, coarse grit tempered red ware, adze, microliths. Artifact and section drawing on page 35.

246. Kundan 1961-62. pp. 72-73.
Nepal, District Taulihawa. Ashokan pillars, temple.

247. Kudavelli 1978-79. pp. 37-42.
Andhra Pradesh, District Mahbubnagar. Period I, 4th to 6th century A.D. red slipped ware, dull red ware, RPW, black and red ware, black polished ware, and kaolin ware. 2 gold coins (Roman and Byzantine), 2 Satavahanana coins, terra-cotta, glass, semiprecious stones, shell, stone and terra-cotta discs, wheels, spindle whorls, shell bangles, iron spearhead, nails, copper rings, antimony rods. Period II, 8th to 16th century A.D., temple, red slipped ware, dull red ware, dull black ware, black ware, black slipped ware, chocolate slipped ware, copper, iron, terra-cotta trinkets. Pottery illustration.

Kudavelli 1982-83. p. 9.
Andhra Pradesh, District Mahbubnagar. Excavation of the Sangamesvara temple. Three phases. Phase I, Red Polished Ware, red slipped ware; Phase II, similar ceramics continue; Phase III, inscribed slab with Chalukyan characters of ca. 6th century A.D. Plan of the temple.

248. Kumrahar 1953-54. pp. 9-10
Bihar, District Patna. Ancient Pataliputra. Four periods. NBP. Sunga and Gupta terra-cottas.

Kumrahar 1954-55. pp. 18-19.
Bihar, District Patna. Mauryan pillared hall.

249. Kunjhun 1981-82. pp. 43-44.
Madhya Pradesh, District Sidhi. Kunjhun noted in IAR 1975-76, pp. 25-27. Kunjhun II has six levels with corded ware, microliths and other tools of high quality. About 100 meters north of Kunjhun II is another area of habitation with the same corded ware, red ware, black and red ware, black ware and gritty ware. Rice and rice husk usped as temper in these ceramics. Pottery like that from Koldihawa and Mahagara. A few sheards of Malwa Ware in the assemblage.

250. Kunnattur 1955-56. p. 23.
Tamil Nadu, District Chingleput. Megaliths.

Kunnattur 1956-57. pp. 31-34.
Tamil Nadu, District Chingleput. Megaliths. Plan of graves, section drawing, pottery illustrated.

Kunnattur 1957-58. pp. 37-38.
Tamil Nadu, District Chingleput. Megaliths.

251. Kupgal 1964-65. pp. 28-29.
Karnataka, district Bellary. Neolithic, Pre-Neolithic.

Kurma See Kuruma

252. Kuruma 1974-75. p. 37.
Orissa, District Puri. Buddhist site near Konarak of ca. 9th to 10th century date. Images of Buddha, Avalokitesvara and Heruka.

Kurma 1975-76. p. 37.
Orissa, District Puri. Buddhist site 8 km southeast of Konarak. Red ware, Images of Buddha, Avalokitesvara and Heruka.

Kuruma 1976-77. p. 40.
Orissa, District Puri. Buddhist.

253. Laharia-Dih 1980-81. p. 72.
Uttar Pradesh, District Mirzapur. Rock shelter I. Upper Levels, wheel made and handmade pottery, microliths. Middle Level, both geometric (triangles) and non-genemetric (lunates and backed bladelets) microlithis tools, handmade and "worn out" pottery. Lower Levels, devoid of pottery and geometric tools, non-geometric microliths present. Rock shelter-II. Upper levels, both geometric and non-geometric microliths, glass bangles, iron slag, wheel made pottery. Lower Level, handmade and wheel made pottery, geometric microliths and bladelets.

254. Lakhabaval 1955-56. p. 7.
Gujarat, District Halar. Tests at Lakhabaval, Amra, Somnath. Period I, Harappan with black and red ware. Period II, RPW. Period III, Medieval.

255. Lakhneswar Dih 1956-57. p. 29.
Uttar Pradesh. District Ballia. NBP, stone and terra-cotta objects.

256. Lal Kot 1957-58. pp. 24-25.
Delhi Late Medieval site, vicinity of Qutab Minar. See also Qila Rai Pithora.

Lal Kot 1958-59. p. 25.
Delhi. Medieval site.

Lal Kot 1960-61. p. 6.
Delhi. Medieval site.

257. Lal Qila 1968-69. pp. 35-37.
Uttar Pradesh, District Bulandshahr. OCP, broken crucible. Pottery illustration.

Lal Qila 1969-70. pp. 38-40.
Uttar Pradesh, District Bulandshahr. OCP. Copper hoard at Kiratapur 3 km. away. TL dates. Discussion of ceramics and small finds. Terracota figurines.

Lal Qila 1971-72. pp. 45-46.
Uttar Pradesh, District Bulandshahr. OCP. Pottery illustration.

258. Lalitpur 1961-62. p. 57.
Uttar Pradesh, District Jhansi Lower Palaeolithic factory site.

Lalitpur 1963-64. pp. 49-51.
Uttar Pradesh, District Jhansi. Lithic sites, microliths.

259. Laljal 1982-83. p. 104.
West Bengal, District Midnapur. Trial excavation of a cave. Layer 1, iron, human bone, coarse brown pottery; layer 2, microliths, broken ring stone.

260. Langhnaj 1953-54. p. 8.
Gujarat, District Mehsana. Microliths, burials.

Langhnaj 1963-64. p. 12.
Gujarat, District Mehsana. Microliths, copper, burials.

261. Lekhahia 1963-64. pp. 51-53.
Uttar Pradesh, District Mirzapur. Rock shelters, microliths, open air sites, burials.

262. Lotapahar 1966-67. p. 7.
Bihar, District Singhbum. Upper Palaeolithic tools, microliths, Lower Palaeolithic tools.

263. Lothal 1954-55. p. 12.
Gujarat, District Ahmedabad. First season report on an Harappan site Note of Rangpur excavations.

Lothal 1955-56. pp. 6-7.
Gujarat, district Ahemdabad. Harappan site. Pre-defence, Defence and Post-defence periods. Platform built after Period I floods. Note on warehouse and list of small finds.

Lothal 1956-57. pp. 15-16.
Gujarat, District Ahmedabad. Harappan site. Six periods noted. List of small finds.

Lothal 1957-58. pp. 11-13.
Gujarat, district Ahmedabad. Harappan site. Note on cemetery. List of small finds.

Lothal 1958-59. pp. 13-15.
Gujarat. District Ahmedabad. Harappan site. Mention of "dockyard." Claim that the town was twice as large as the present mound. Copper smith's workshop, bead

factories. Cemetery with 10 graves, 3 with double burials. Five phases or periods.

Lothal 1959-60. p. 16-18.
Gujarat, district Ahmedabad. Harappan site. Excavation beyond the mound found midden 500 feet to the south. Excavation of inlet and outlet channels to "dockyard." Pottery drawing. Proposed to have been the final season of work.

Lothal 1961-62. pp. 9-10.
Gujarat, District Ahmedabad. Harappan. Micaceous red ware, black and red ware, copper ingot and slag, Persian Gulf seal, Indus seals. Little gap between Lothal A and B.

Lothal 1962-63. p. 7.
Gujarat, District Ahemedabad. Harappan site. Work on dockyard.

264. Machad 1974-75. p. 21.
Kerala, District Trichur. Stone circles and cists. Urn burial covered by huge, granite capstone. Black and red ware, red ware, black ware. Iron, etched beads, etc. See Pazhayannur also.

265. Magha 1980-81. pp. 72.73.
Uttar Pradesh, District Mirzapur. Megalithic burials, red ware, black slipped ware, black and red ware, copper fragments.

266. Mahadaha 1977-78. pp. 58-59.
Uttar Pradesh, District Pratapgarh. Microliths, Mesolithic site with graves.

Mahadaha 1978-79. pp. 59-60.
Uttar Pradesh, District Pratapgarh. Microliths, graves, hearths, butchered animal bones.

267. Mahadeo Piparia 1962-63. p. 11.
Madhya Pradesh, District Narsinghpur. Lower Palaeolithic. In an Exploration Report.

Mahadeo Piparia 1964-65. p. 16.
Madhya Pradesh, District Narsinghpur. Lower and Middle Palaeolithic, microliths.

268. Mahagara 1975-76. pp. 46-48.
Uttar Pradesh. District Allahabad. Microliths, Neolithic celt, corded ware, burnished red ware, burnished black ware. Pottery illustrations.

Mahagara 1977-78. pp. 52-55.
Uttar Pradesh, District Allahabad. Neolithic.

Mahagara 1978-79. p. 57.
Uttar Pradesh, District Allahabad. Neolithic, corded, rusticated and burnished wares.

Mahagara 1982-83. p. 91.
Uttar Pradesh, District Allahabad. Investigation of Gravels III and IV.

269. Maheswar 1953-54. P. 8.
Madhya Pradesh, District Nimar. Three historic periods with NBP in the lowest. Proto-Neolithic. Chalcotithic.

270. Mahisdal 1963-64. pp. 59-60.
West Bengal, District Birbhum. Black and red ware (plain and painted black or white), black painted red ware, red ware, black ware, channel spout, buff ware, grey ware, microliths. Neolithic.

271. Mahtab Bagh 1979-80. p. 72, 74.
Uttar Pradesh, District Agra. Investigation of the suspected site of Shah Jahan's tomb foundations across the Yamuna River from the Taj Mahal. Expopsure of a tank with decoration similar to that at Babur's garden at at Dholpur. No evidence for Shah Jahan's large tomb.

272. Mahurjhari 1970-71. pp. 24-25.
Maharashtra, District Nagpur. Megaliths. Pottery illustrations.

Mahurjhari 1971-72. pp. 33-35.
Maharashtra, District Nagpur. Megaliths,

Mahurjhari 1978-79. p. 71.
Maharashtra, District Nagpur. Megaliths black and red ware with graffiti, micaceous red ware, dull red ware, iron objects, copper objects.

Mehurzari See Mahurjhari

273. Mainahai 1963-64. pp. 41-42.
Uttar Pradesh, District Allahabad. Gupta and Mauryan sculptures.

274. Makhdum Sabib's Mosque
1973-74. pp. 11-12. Delhi. 1300-1517 A.D.

275. Malaiyamputtu 1970-71. pp. 34-35.
Tamil Nadu, District North Arcot. Temple over site with post-megalithic material.

276. Malari 1982-83. p. 95.
Uttar Pradesh, district Chamoli. Burials in caves dug in limestone. Located 4000 meters above MSL near Joshimath. Horse skeleton, iron and bone arrow heads. Called "protohistoric," painted ceramics, two pots illustrated in photographs. Tentatively dated to ca. 1000 B.C.

277. Malhar 1974-7. pp. 21-22.
Madhya Pradesh, District Bilaspur. Black and red ware, red ware, thin ware with black polished interior and red and black exterior, punch marked coin, red slipped ware with incised, late Gupta inscriptions, late Buddhist.

Malhar 1975-76. p. 23.
Madhya Pradesh, district Bilaspur. Period I, ca. 4th century B.C. to 2nd century A.D., black and red ware. Period II, ca. 3rd to 6th century A.D., black and red ware with associated ceramics, Brahmi inscription. Period III, ca. 7th to 9th century A.D., Buddhist temple complex. Period IV, ca. 9th to 13th century A.d., red and coarse wares.

Malhar 1977-78. pp. 30-31.
Madhya Pradesh, District Bilaspur. Satavahana.

278. Malinithan 1972-73. p. 3.
Arunachal Pradesh, District Siang. Temple site. Images of Surya, Aruna and Ganesa.

279. Mallappadi 1977-78. p. 50.
Tamil Nadu, district Dharmapuri. Megalithic site, rock shelter, Neolithic, Early Historical with Russet-coated Painted Ware.

280. Malvan 1969-70. pp. 7-9.
Gujarat, District Surat. Harappan. Rangpur IIB-C site. Pottery and artifact illustrations.

281. Manda 1976-77. pp. 19-23.
Jammu and Kashmir, District Jammu. Pre-Harappan red ware, Harappan red ware, both plain and painted, rusticated ware, grey ware, Harappan script, thick burnished grey ware, Early Historical pottery, Kushan pottery, both stamped and incised. Pottery illustration and graph of the frequency of the different wares.

282. Mandhal 1975-76. p. 36.
Maharashtra, District Nagpur. RPW, red ware, copper plate, black and red ware, black painted red ware, black slipped ware, sprinklers in red slipped ware, Satavahana, Gupta-Vakataka period.

Mandhal 1976-77. pp. 39-40.
Maharashtra, District Nagpur. Megaliths. Vakataka Period (4th-5th century A.D.), temples.

283. Maner 1984-85. pp. 11-12
Bihar, District Patna. Period III Pala Period II NBP, Period I Chalcolithic with black and red ware.

284. Manjih 1983-84. pp. 15-16.
Bihar, district Saran. Site also known as Manjih-ka-Tila. Period I on virgin soil. Black and red ware, black ware and associated red ware, no iron, no date. Period II, NBP; three subperiods, some indication of changes in NBP, brick structures, bone tools, inscribed sealings, list of small finds. Period III(?) figurnies, inscribed sealing of 2/3rd century A.D. Period IV, reoccupation after abandonment, no date.

Manjih 1984-85. pp. 12-13.
Bihar, District Saran. Excavation of all three periods. Exposure of a road in late NBP times (Period II). Period III associated with Saka/Kushanas.

285. Manoti 1959-60. p. 25.
Madhya Pradesh, District Mandasor. Black and red ware (similar to Ahar), red ware with black paint (similar to Maheswar and Lothal), coarse black ware, Early Historical.

286. Manwa 1962-63. p. 39.
Uttar Pradesh, District Sitapur. NBP to Medieval sequence. See Nazirabad also. Could be the same site as Manwan.

287. Manwan 1968-70. p. 44.
Uttar Pradesh, District Sitapur. NBP, Sunga, Kushan, Gupta.
Manwan-dih 1968-69. pp. 39-40
Uttar Pradesh, District Sitapur. Early Historical material. Trial excavation in an Exploration Report. Could be the same as Manwan.

288. Maragoda 1983-84. pp. 61-63.
Orissa, District Kalahandi. Trenching of the three sites: Ranimahal, Trisul mound and Mahal mound. Mahal mound has a double storeyed building which is described. Trisul has a three tiered mound with brick temple, monastery; both described. A large hall was found at the Ranimahal. Some dates, all medieval.

289. Martand 1969-70. p. 13.
Jammu and Kashmir, district Kashmir South. Excavations found floor levels below the present temple supporting the belief expressed in the *Rajatarangini* (12th century) that the temple at Martand was built on the ruins of an earlier one.

290. Masaon 1964-65. pp. 42-43.
Uttar Pradesh, District Ghazipur. Plain coarse red ware, grey ware, black and red ware, NBP, black slipped ware, red ware, punch marked coins, microliths, Sunga, Kushan coins, Gupta, red slipped ware.

Masaon 1965-66. pp. 49-52.
Uttar Pradesh, District Ghazipur. NBP, black slipped ware, fine grey ware, slipped grey ware with black painting, black and red ware, red ware, punch marked coins, Sunga, Kushan coins.

Masaon 1967-68. pp. 46-47.
Uttar Pradesh, District Ghazipur. Black slipped ware, fine grey ware, coarse red ware, slipped red ware, black and red ware, microliths, NBP, punch marked coins, Sunga, Kushan, Gupta.

Masaon 1970-71. pp. 38-39.
Uttar Pradesh, District Ghazipur. Pre-NBP through 6th century A.D.

291. Maski 1953-54. pp. 8-9.
Karnataka, District Raichur. Ashokan rock edict. Period I, Chalcolithic, copper, microliths. Period II, Megalithic, black and red ware, iron, burials. Period III, Satavahana coins, Russet-colored Pottery.

292. Mathura 1954-55. pp. 15-16.
Uttar Pradesh, district Mathura. PGW and NBP at the Katra Mound.

Mathura 1973-74. pp. 31-32.
Uttar Pradesh, district Mathura. Katra mound, Dhulkot, NBP, Kushan.

Mathura 1974-75. pp. 48-50.
Uttar Pradesh, District Mathura. Dulkot has 2 phases of fortification in different Periods. Period I, ca. 3rd century B.C. wall constructred, NBP, Mauryan, copper punch marked coin. Period II, ca. 1st century B.C. fortification apparently not used or maintained. Period III, Saka/ Kushan times, fortifications revived.
General dates: Period I, ca. 4th to 3rd century B.C. NBP, house floors, etc., Period II, 2nd to 1st century B.C. NBP, Sungas. Period III, 1st to 3rd century A.D. Saka/ Kushans. Period IV, 4th to 5th century A.D. At Kankali-Tila, site of a Jain stupa, a tank complex of Period III was exposed.

Mathura 1975-76. pp. 53-55.
Uttar Pradesh, district Mathura. PGW, red ware, black polished ware, black and red ware, grey ware, NBP, punch marked coin, stamped and spouted red ware, amphora, Kushan coins. Pottery drawing.

Mathura 1976-77. pp. 54-56.
Uttar Pradesh, District Mathura. Plain grey ware, red ware, black slipped grey ware, NBP, Buddha images, coins.

293. Medhauli 1982-83. pp. 57-58.
Madhya Pradesh, District Sidhi. Mesolithic site with sandstone fragments, microliths, mullers, querns and hammer stones.

294. Milinithan 1972-73. p. 3.
Arunachal Pradesh, District Siang. Histyoric site.

295. Mirzapur Mound 1975-76. p. 18.
Haryana, district Kurukshetra. Harappan. Beakers and perforated jars are absent, goblets are rare. Copper chisels, needle, rings and parasu. Beads, faience and small finds. See Raja Karna-ka-Quia.

296. Misimagiri 1975-76. pp. 36-37.
Meghalaya, Garo Hills. Early and Middle Palaeolithic tools. In 200 square meters there were 252 stone tools in mint condition. Tools included handaxes, choppers, scrapers, blade tools, and points.

297. Modhera 1964-65. p. 12.
Gujarat, District Mehsana. Sun temple.

Modhera 1965-66 p.18
Gujarat, District Mehsana, Sun Temple.

298. Modi 1958-59. p. 28.
Madhya Pradesh, District Mandasor. Painted rock shelter, microliths. Drawing of painting in rock shelter.

299. Moradhwaj 1978-79. pp. 73-74.
Uttar Pradesh, district Bijnor. 5th century B.C. to Kushan times, NBP, fine grey ware and red ware, structures, terra-cotta, copper and iron objects.

Moradhwaj 1979-80. p. 75.
Uttar Pradesh, District Bijnor. Kushan temple and sculptures,. copper and iron objects.

Moradhwaj 1980-81. p. 70.
Uttar Pradesh, District Bijnor. Kushan temple, stupa, tablets bearing Buddha image.

Moradhwaj 1982-83. pp. 94-95. Uttar Pradesh, District Bijnor Excavation of Kushan temple complex.

300. Motidharai 1957-58. pp. 20-21.
Gujarat, District Gohilwad. Period I, Harappan. Period II, Lustrous Red Ware. In an Exploration Report.

301. Mottur 1978-79. pp. 72-73.
Tamil Nadu, district North Arcot. Megaliths, black and red ware, all black ware, all red ware, monolithic anthropomorphic figure, copper objects.

302. Motupalli 1973-74. p. 7.
Andhra Pradesh, District Prakasam. Sea port in Chirala Taluk, 10th century and later.

303. Mukhalingam 1961-62. p. 3.
Andhra Pradesh, District Srikakulam. Rouletted Ware, black and red ware, Satavahana coin.

304. Mumma Khan 1953-54. p. 12.
Jammu and Kashmir, District Srinagar. Trial trenches in Srinagar City where Pravarpura, built by the pravarasena in the 6th century. Remains of the Afghan Period. Coin hoard.

305. Munhai 1980-81. pp. 38-39.
Madhya Pradesh, District Rewa. Chalcolithic and Megalithic levels, Megalithic burials, red ware, grey/black ware, black and red ware, black slipped ware, microliths, copper. Iron objects, fragments and slag.

306. Muravkonda 1981-82. pp. 2-3.
Andhra Pradesh, District Kurnool. Middle Palaeolithic site on the Krishna River. Some Acheulian tools. Inferred date of ca. 40,000 for the Middle Palaeolithic.

307. Muttalavadi 1974-75. pp. 20-21.
Karnataka, District Mysore. Period I, Neloithic, burnished grey ware, ground stone axes, fragments of head-rest, date to 1600 B.C. Period II, Megalithic black and red ware. 19th century occupation.

308. Nagal 1961-62. pp. 11-12.
Gujarat, district Broach. One principal occupation in 3 phases, all with black and red ware, none with structures. This is a mound site. Phase 1, bone points, copper rings and beads, silver (coin?), ivory comb. Phase 2, incised grey ware, interesting graffiti on all wares (photographs), animal figurines, large agate bead, ivory combs, querns. Phase 3, etched carnelian beads,

bone points, pestles, copper antimony rods, bangles of shell, ivory and bone, net sinkers, double barbed and tanged arrowhead. No NBP. Uppermost Phase 3 dated to 2nd century B.c. Habitation floors in each phase. Many animal bones. Suggestion that this site fills the gap between the end of the Rangpur sequence and the beginnings of NBP in this region.

309. Nagar 1971-72. pp. 39-40.
Karnataka, district Shimoga. Excavation of a 17th century palace. Plan of the excavations.

310. Nagar 1976-77. p. 42.
Punjab District Jullundur. PGW, "Late" Harappan, Kushan, early Gupta. Brahmi inscriptions, early Medieval.

Nagara 1963-64. pp. 9-10.
Gujarat, district Kaira. Black and red ware, plain red ware, burnished red ware, NBP, punch marked coin, RPW, Roman amphorae, burnished black ware, Medieval glazed ware.

Nagara 1964-65. pp. 11-12
Gujarat, District Kaira. Black and red ware, plain red ware, burnished red ware, NBP.

311. Nagari 1962-63. pp. 19-20.
Rajasthan, District Chitorgarh. Plain red ware, plain grey wear, RPW, kaolin ware, punch marked coins, Kshatrapa coins, Madhyamika coins, tribal coins, Sunga and Gupta styles, associated NBP wares (no NBP sherds).

312. Nagarjunakonda 1954-55. pp. 22-23.
Andhra Pradesh, District Guntur. Opened 7 different sites in the area. Most are viharas and stupas. Short summaries of most excavated areas.

Nagarjunakonda 1955-56. pp. 23-26.
Andhra Pradesh, District Guntur. Project has uncovered 15 monasteries, 8 stupas, a Medieval temple and a *ghat* on the Krishna River. 1955-56 investigated more monasteries, stupas, structures in the place area and a pillared pavilions.

Nagarjunakonda 1956-57. pp. 35-38.
Andhra Pradesh, District Guntur. Palaeolithic sites. Neolithic/Chalcolithic. Neolithic near Nallarallabodu. Megalith. Buddhist structures. Pillared building, fortifications, monasteries. List of small finds.

Nagarjunakonda 1957-58. pp. 5-9.
Andhra Pradesh, district Guntur. Six Neolithic graves. Drawing of one grave and some pottery. Citadel wall on the Krishna, site plan. Southern Zone structures. More Buddhist remains. List of small finds.

Nagarjunakonda 1958-59 pp.5-10
Andhra Pradesh, District Guntur. Microliths, Neolithic, Megalithic burials, burning *ghat*, temple of Ashtabhujasvamin, wide irrigation canal, and a thirty-six pillared *mindapa*. Neolithic pottery drawings. Plan and section of a Megalithic burial. Map of site localities.

Nagarjunakonda 1959-60. pp. 5-10.
Andhra Pradesh, District Guntur. Palaeolithic cleavers, blade-flakes. Microliths. Neolithic. Megalithic. Section drawing of a Palaeolithic site. Excavation of a Neolithic site. Twelve of 18 megaliths excavated, each with short summary of the work. Pit circles. Plan and section of Megalith V.

Nagarjunakonda 1960-61. p.1
Andhra Pradesh, District Guntur. Excavation of Acheulian site with unrolled tools. Note of Middle Palaeolithic.

313. Nagda 1955-56. pp. 11-19.
Madhya Pradesh, dostrict Ujjain. Extensive report. Period I, Chalcolithic, painted red ware, black and cream ware, thick grey ware, copper, microliths. Period II, iron, black and red ware, microliths. Period III, NBP. Schematic section, pottery drawings.

314. Nageswar 1983-84. pp. 18-22.
Gujarat, District Jamnagar. Harappan site on a lake at the western tip of Saurashtra. Working of *Turbinella pyrum and Chicoreus ramosus*. Stone rubble structures. Reserved slip ware, Mature Harappan fabric; no black and red ware or Lustrous Red Ware. Two structural phases, IA and IB

with continuity. List of shell objects, copper. Cattle, goat, sheep, buffalo, nilgai, antelope, spotted deer, sambar and marine fish. Pottery drawings and plan of "fire alter."

315. Nagnoor 1980-81. pp. 2-3.
Andhra Pradesh, District Karimnagar. Temples.

316. Nagra 1979-80. p. 56.
Maharashtra, District Bhandara. Vakataka temple.

Nagra 1980-81. p. 40.
Maharashtra, District Bhandara. Vakataka temple, sprinklers, lamps.

Nagra 1981-82. p. 49.
Maharashtra, District Bhandara. Excavation of a brick temple temple of the Vakataka Period.

317. Naikund 1977-78. p. 39.
Maharashtra, district Nagpur. Megaliths.

Naikund 1979-80. pp. 57-58.
Maharashtra, District Nagpur. Megalithic burials and habitation remains, iron smelting factory area, black and red ware, micaceous red ware, plain red ware, painted black on red ware, burnished black wares.

318. Nakjhar-Khurd 1979-80. p. 52.
Madhya Pradesh, District Sidhi. Middle Palaeolithic industry.

319. Nalanda 1975-76. pp. 8-9.
Bihar, district Nalanda. Excavation of a 7th-8th century Buddhist temple.

Nalanda 1976-77. p. 13.
Bihar, district Nalanda. Buddhist site.

Nalanda 1977-78. p. 16.
Bihar, district Nalanda. Buddhist site.

Nalanda 1978-79. p. 67.
Bihar district Nalanda. Buddha image, shrine, stupa. Listed under Sarai Mound, Nalanda.

Nalanda 1979-80. p. 14.
Bihar, District Nalanda. Excavation of a Buddhist shrine.

Nalanda 1981-82, p. 12.
Bihar, District Nalanda. Excavation at the Sarai Mound. NBP, figurines.

Nalanda 1982-83, p. 25.
Bihar, District Nalanda. Excavation of the Sarai Mound. Exposure of a portion of the periphery wall to the main temple. Votive stupa. Ring well with decorated sections. NBP.

320. Na-nath 1984-85. p. 8.
Assam, District Nowgong. Excavation of a living monastic site. Salvage work. Some sculpture mentioned.

321. Nandalur 1979-80. p.1.
Andhra Pradesh, District Cuddapah. Buddhist Site. Stupas of the 2nd century B.C. to 3rd to 4th century A.D.

322. Nandur 1980-81. pp. 37-38.
Madhya Pradesh, District Raisen. Period IA, 5th to 4th century B.C., black and red ware, black ware. Period IB, 4th to 3rd century B.C., red ware, black and red ware, black slipped ware, cast and punch marked coins. Period II, 2nd century B.C. to 1st century A.D., copper coins, iron objects. period III, 1st to 4th century A.D. Kushan-Ksatrapa inscribed seals. Period IV, 4th to 6th century A.D., grey ware, inscribed seals and sealings. Artifact illustration.

Nandur 1981-82. pp. 36-37.
Madhya Pradesh, District Raisen. Period IA, Pre-Mauryan, 7th to 4th century B.C. Period IB, Mauryan, 4th to 2nd century B.C. Period II, Sunga-Satavahana, 2nd century B.C. to 2nd century A.D. Period III, Kshatrapapa Naga, 2nd to 4th century A.D. Period IV Gupta, 4th to 6th century A.D. Period V, Medieval, 7th century A.D. NBP.

Nandur 1982-83. p.40.
Madhya Pradesh, District Raisen. Excavation to understand the structural deposit of the Gupta-Kshatrapa and its extension. Three periods: I, Muslim; II Early Medieval; III, Gupta.

323. Nanganallur 1973-74. p.24
Tamil Nadu, District Madras. Pallava linga, 9th and 10th century A.D. Temple.

324. Nanur 1963-64. p.60
West Bengal, District Birbhum. Red ware, black painted ware, white painted and plain black and red ware, grey ware (all shapes similar to Mahisdal), proto-historic to historic transition.

325. Narhan 1984-85. pp. 89-90
Uttar Pradesh, District Gorakhpur.Period V Red Ware Period IV Red Ware Period III NBP Period II No Black and Red Ware Period I Black and Red Ware. NBP levels with wheat, barley, rice, kodon millet, black gram, green gram pea, *khesari*, sesame, jujube and anwala. Three C-14 dates for NBP.

326 Navdatoldi 1957-58. pp. 29, 30-33, 35.
Madhya Pradesh, District Nimar. Chalcolithic houses. Drawing of Chalcolithic pottery. List of antiquities. NBP, RPW.

Navdatoli 1958-59. pp. 30-31
Madhya Pradesh, District Nimar. Square and round Chalcolithic houses. Copper sword.

Navdatoli 1970-71. pp. 20-22
Maddhya Pradesh, District West Nimar. Report on J. Armand Lower Palaeolithic excavation near the Navdatoli mound in Durkadi nala. Ca. 1,100 tools from factory site. General stratigraphy for the nala.

327. Nayveli 1965-66. p.24.
Tamil Nadu, district Chingelput. Middle Palaeolithic.

328. Nazirabad 1962-63. p.39.
Uttar Pradesh, District Sitapur. NBP to Medieval sequence. See Manwa also.

329. Nelakondapally 1976-77. p.5
Andhra Pradesh, District Khammam. Stupa, coins of Ikshvaku Period, red ware.

Nelakondapally 1977-78. p.3.
Andhra Pradesh, District Khammam. Ikshvaku coins.

330. Nevasa 1954-55. pp. 5-9.
Maharashtra, District Ahmadnagar. Lower and Middle Palaeolithic. "Nevasian." Chalcolithic, polished axes, crested ridge flakes, ties to Navdatoli. NBP. RPW. Lead coin of Tiberius, Satavahana coins, Indo-Roman. Medieval Period. Bahamani Period. Section derawing. Drawings of artifacts.

Navasa 1955-56. pp.8-11.
Maharashtra, District Ahmadnagar. Period I, Lower Palaeolithic. Period. Period II, Middle Palaeolithic. Period III, Neolithic/ Chalcolithic (Jorwe), with pottery drawings. Adult and child burials. Period IV, Satavahana with pottery drawings. Period V, Indo-Roman.

Nevasa 1959-60. pp. 25-28.
Maharashtra, District Ahmadnagar. Jorwe architecture described. Jorwe pottery described and some drawn. Silk and cotton with Jorwe materials. Note of millet in Chalcolithic. Burials, copper necklace List of small finds Early HIstorical, Indo-Roman, Muslim-Maratha Period VI. Pottery illustration.

Nevasa 1960-61. pp. 19-21.
Maharashtra, District Ahmadnagar. Early and Middle Palaeolithic, Chalcolithic, Muslim-Maratha. Jorwe Ware, child urn burials, copper. Early Historical, black and red ware, Satavahana coins, Indo-Roman Period, RPW, Black and red ware, Rouletted Ware, amphorae.

331. Neyveli 1965-66. p.24.
Madras, District Chingleput. Middle Palaeolithic, See Poondi as well.

332. Noh 1963-64. pp. 28-29.
Rajasthan. District Bharatpur. OCP, black and red ware, grey ware, PGW, black polished ware, red ware, cast copper coins, Buddhist sculpture.

Noh 1964-65. pp. 34-35.
Rajasthan, District Bharatpur. Black and red ware, PGW, NBP, OCP, coarse red ware, black slipped ware, charred rice, copper, cast coins, Kushan pottery.

Noh 1965-66. p.38.
Rajasthan, District Bharatpur. PGW, red ware of Sunga-Kushan.

Noh 1966-67. pp. 30-31.
Rajasthan, District Bharatpur. PGW, NBP, plain grey ware, red ware, iron, cast coins, Sunga-Kushan pottery, channel spouts.

Noh 1968-69. p.26.
Rajasthan, District Bharatpur. OCP, PGW, NBP, Kushan.

Noh 1970-71. pp. 31-32.
Rajasthan, District Bharatpur. Chalcolithic, OCP.

Noh 1971-72. pp. 41-42
Rajasthan, District Bharatpur. OCP, PGW, NBP, Kushan.

333 Oriup 1966-67. pp. 6-7.
Bihar, District Bhagalpur. Stupa, black and red ware with white paint, NBP, microliths, black slipped ware, red ware, fish hooks, grey ware, iron, Neolithic celt. Medieval glazed ware.

334. Pabumath 1977-78. p.21.
Gujarat, District Kutch. "Late" Harappan, painted black on red, reserve slipped wares, beads, animal bones, pot burials.

Pabumath 1978-79. pp. 67-68.
Gujarat, District Kutch. Harappan site. Copper arrowhead, borken seal.

Pabumath 1980-81. p.14.
Gujarat, District Kutch. Harappan site. Red ware with painted designs, inscribed seal with unicorn motif, animal bones.

335 Pachad 1969-70. pp. 23-24.
Maharashtra, District Kolaba. Ceramics, microliths, Lower Palaeolithic.

Pachad 1970-71. pp. 22-23.
Maharashtra, District Kolaba. Microliths.

336. Padrauna 1984–85. p. 88.
Uttar Pradesh, District Deoria. Said to be ancient Pavapuri, associated with Mahavira. Excavations revealed levels later than mid-first millennium B.C.

337. Pagara 1980-81. pp. 32-33.
Madhya Pradesh, District Dhar. Period I, 1st to 3rd century A.D., red ware with slip, black and red and black wares. Period II, 4th to 6th century A.D., black ware. Period III, 7th to 12th century, iron and copper objects, grey ware.

338. Pagidigutta 1978-79. p. 65.
Andhra Pradesh, District Mahbubnagar. Chalcolithic/Megalithic levels, burnished grey ware, black on red ware, black and red ware, Rouletted Ware, iron implements, stone tools, storage jars, hearths, post holes.

339. Paisra 1980-81. p. 9.
Bihar, District Monghyr. Report of good Acheulian tools and workshop in an Exploration Report.

Paisra 1983-84. pp. 13-14.
Bihar, District Monghyr. Excavation of an Acheulian site of 2.5 sq. km. Expansion of excavated area into 5 locatities (A-E). Massive stone alignment in Locality E. Working floors and post-holes in Locality E. Trench B. (15x5 m.) has evidence for a habitation surface. Handaxes, cleavers, scrapers, cores, etc., tools of Upper Acheulian character.

340. Paithan 1965-66. pp. 28-29.
Maharashtra, District Aurangabad. Period I, ca. 300 B.C. to 100 A.D., Satavahana lead coins, glass beads, crystal ear reels, lion capital in bone or ivory, NBP. Period II, ca. 100 to 500 A.D., heavy flood. Period III, ca. 600 to 800 A.D., brick temple conditionally placed with the Rashtrakuta Period. Period IV, ca. 1700 to 1800 A.D., Muslim/Marahta material. See Kausan as well.

341. Paiyampalli 1964-65. pp. 22-23
Tamil Nadu, District North Arcot. Neolithic, Megalithic hand made grey ware, burnished grey ware, Megalithic black and red ware, ground stone axes, red ware, pink ware, Russet-coated Painted Ware.

Paiyampalli 1967-68. pp. 26-30.
Tamil Nadu, District North Arcot. Neolithic, Megalithic, C-14 dates, 1390 ± 200

B.C. and 315 ± 100 B.C. Black and red ware, grey ware, burnished grey ware, pale grey ware, red ware, all black ware, Russet-coated Painted Ware. Pottery illustrations.

342. Palampet 1973-74. p. 8
Andhra Pradesh, District Warangal. Temple site.

343. Palavoy 1966-67. pp. 1-2.
Andhra Pradesh, District Anantapur. Ash mounds, Neolithic site, microliths.

344 Palayarai 1983-84. pp. 79-80.
Tamil Nadu, District Thanjavur. Palayarai was the secondary capital of the Cholas. Red Polished Ware, Medieval finds. No structures of particular note.

345. Pallavamedu 1953-54. p.12.
Tamil Nadu, District Kanchipuram. Tradition links this site, on the outside of Kanchipuram, to the Pallavas. Four phases, earliest has fragmentary ring wells associated with an urn interment. No typical Pallava finds.

Pallavamedu 1970-71. p. 33.
Tamil Nadu, District Chingelput. Pallava site. Period I, red ware of the 6th to 9th centuries A.D. Period II, red ware, black ware, beads of crystal and glass. Period III, glass beads, small *linga*, dated to the end of Pallava rule in the 9th century.

346. Pambarwan 1973-74. p.14.
Jammu and Kashmir, District Jammu. Historic site.

347. Panchoh 1975-76. p. 47.
Uttar Pradesh, District Allahabaa. Corded ware, red ware, celts, microliths.

348. Pandharpur 1967-68. pp. 35-36.
Maharashtra, District Sholapur. Phased I, black grey ware. Phase II, Indo-Islamic Materials. Phase III, Early Maratha Period.

349. Pandu Rajar Dhibi 1961-62. pp. 59-62.
West Bengal, District Burdwan. Painted ware, channel spouted bowls, crude ware, black and red ware, black painted bright red ware, white painted bright red ware, white painted black and red ware, perforated ware, fine black burnished ware with incised decoration, microlithic tool, domestic pig, possible chronological affiliation with Ahar, Gilund and Navdatoli. Pottery illustrations.

Pandu Rajar Dhibi 1962-63 pp. 43-46.
West Bengal, District Burdwan. Black and red ware, grey ware, pale red ware, microliths, channel spouted bowls, painted and plain black and red ware, black painted Lustrous Red Ware, black painted chocolate ware, polished stone axes, black burnished ware with incisions, copper, sprinkler, vases, Early Historic. Pottery illustrations.

Pandu Rajar Dhabi 1963-64. pp. 61-62
West Bengal, District Burdwan. Hand made grey ware, Chalcolithic painted or plain black and red ware, Lustrous Red Ware, channel spouts, red ware with black paint, white painted black and red ware, black burnished ware, microliths, iron slag, Neolithic celts, early historical black polished ware, pale red ware, NBP. Pottery illustration.

Pandu Rajar Dhibi 1964-65. pp. 46-48.
West Bengal, District Burdwan. Report covers all four periods, which confirm earlier findings. Pottery illustration.

Pandu Rajar Dhibi 1984-85. pp. 97-98.
West Bengal, District Burdwan. Period V NBP. Period IV Black on red ware, incised black polished ware and others ca. 600-300 B.C. Period III Black and red ware, black on red ware, and others, copper and iron implements, ca. 900-600 B.C. Period II Black and red ware, black on red ware, and other ceramics. Lapis Lazuli. Iron in upper levels. ca. 1200-900 BC. Period Handmade pale red and grey wars. Fossil wood implement. ca. 1600-1400 B.C.

350. Panduwala 1982-83. p. 99.
Uttar Pradesh, District Garhwal. Short report on the excavation of a Kushan settlement.

351. Panhale kazi 1973-74. p. 22.
Maharashtra, District Ratnagiri. Rock-cut caves of Brahmanical, Buddhist and Jain traditions. Dated to ca. 11th century A.D. Same site as Panhali Kazi and Panhalikazi.

Panhale Kazi 1977-78. pp. 41-42.
Maharashtra, District Ratnagiri. Rock-cut caves.

Panhale Kazi 1979-80. p. 59
Maharashtra, District Ratnagiri. Rock-cut caves.

352. Papanasi 1982-83. pp. 9-13.
Andhra Pradesh, District Mahbubnagar. Excavation at a group of 23 temples dated from ca. 9th to 12th centuries. Site plan and illustration of ceramics and small finds.

353. Parsi-Parlo 1983-84. p. 10.
Arunachal Pradesh. District Lower Subansiri. Trial excavation, stone tools, pot sherds ground axes and the like.

354. Pariar 1978-79. pp. 61-62
Uttar Pradesh, District Unnao. OCP, black slipped ware, black and red ware, PGW, NBP, Sunga-Kushan.

355. Pataliputra 1955-56. pp. 22-23.
Bihar, District Patna. Period I, (ca. 600 to 150 B.C.) NBP, nandi, polished architectural pieces. Period II, (150 B.C. to 100 A.D.) NBP, red ware, grey ware, cast and punch marked coins, Kausambi "lanky bull" coins, list of small finds. Period III, (ca. 100 to 300 A.D.) red ware, grey ware, coins of Huvishka with Greek letters and Roman goddess. Period IV, (ca. 300 to 600 A.) red ware. Period V, (1600 A.D. and later), Islamic coins and ceramics.

356. Patne 1972-73. pp. 21-23.
Maharashra, District Jalgaon. Palaeolithic, microliths. Table of the cultural sequence, Periods I to IIIC.

357. Patpara 1979-80. pp. 52-53.
Madhya Pradesh, District Sidhi. Lower and Middle Palaeolithic. Table of layers.

358. Paunar 1966-67. p. 27.
Maharashtra, District Wardha. Burnished black and red ware, painted black and red ware, micaceous red ware, thick black and red ware of the Early Historical times, iron, RPW, amphora, Satavahana coins, early Medieval and Celadon ware.

359. Pauni 1968-69. pp. 14-16.
Maharashtra, District Bhandara. Stupa. NBP, RPW, Mauryan Brahmi inscriptions.

Pauni 1969-70. pp. 20-21.
Maharashtra, District Bhandara. Stupa, Satavahana coins.

360. Paya 1965-66. p. 35.
North East Frontier Agency, District Lohit, Excavation of the foundations of a Siva temple of the Ahom Period. Not in an Excavation Report.

361. Pazhayannur 1974-75. p. 21.
Kerala, District Trichur. Cist burials, Megalithic black and red ware. See Machad also.

362. Peddabankur 1967-68. p. 2.
Andhra Pradesh, District Karimnagar. Buddhist, black and red ware, RPW, black ware, dull red ware, Russet-coated Painted Ware red ware. black ware.

Peddabankur 1968-69. pp. 1-2.
Andhra Pradesh, District Karimnagar. Megaliths and Satavahana.

Peddabankur 1970-71. p. 2.
Andhra Pradesh, District Karimnagar. Continuation of work on this Megalithic and Satavahana site. Materials of the 3rd century B.C.

Peddabankur 1971-72. pp. 2-3.
Andhra Pradesh, District Karimnagar. Pre-Satavahana and Satavahana.

Peddabankur 1972-73. p. 2.
Andhra Pradesh, District Karimnagar. Pre-Satavahana and Satavahana.

Peddabankur 1974-75. p. 5.
Andhra Pradesh, District Karimnagar. Satavahana coins, black and red ware, black polished ware, dull red ware.

Peddamarrur 1977-78. pp. 12-13.
Andhra Pradesh, District Mahbubnagar. Four Megaliths described. RPW, tan ware, black and red ware, black polished ware, buff ware, Satavahana coarse red ware, black and red ware.

363. Peddavegi 1984-85. pp. 7-8.
Andhra Pradesh, District West Godavari. Excavation of Vengi, a site mentioned by Hiuen-Tsang. Temples and stupas exposed. Intaglio gemstone illustrated.

364. Perur 1970-71. pp. 33-34.
Tamil Nadu, District Coimbatore. Period I, 1st to 3rd centuries A.D., Megalithic black and red ware, red ware, all black ware. Period II, 3rd to 6th centuries A.D., Russet-coated Painted Ware. Period III, 6th to 9th centuries A.D., troughs for the preparation of potassium nitrate.

Phulbani See Khomananta.

365. Piparia 1968-69. pp. 12-13.
Madhya Pradesh, District Satna. Gupta Temple.

366. Pipilya Lorka 1983-84. pp. 52-53.
Madhya Pradesh, District Raisen. Period I has Jorwe and Kayatha type painted designs on pottery. Copper tools, list of small finds. Period II, Early Historic. Period III, Mauryan to Medieval.

367. Piprahwa 1970-71. p. 37.
Uttar Pradesh, District Basti. Ancient Kapilavastu, RPW.

Piprahwa 1971-72. p.45.
Uttar Pradesh, District Basti. Ancient Kapilavastu. Clearance of a stupa, relic casket intack. Monastery-like structure dated by RPW to ca. 2nd or 3rd century A.D.

Piprahwa 1972-73. p. 33.
Uttar Pradesh, district Basti. Ancient Kapilavastu. Brahmi inscriptions of the 1st or 2nd century A.D. Stupa excavation yielded NBP, punch marked Kushan and Ayodhya coins, copper and antimony.

Piprahwa 1873-74. pp. 27-28.
Uttar Pradesh. District Basti. Ancient Kapilavastu.

Piprahwa 1974-75. pp. 39-41.
Uttar Pradesh, district Basti. Confirmation of structures in early phases at Piprahwa. Sealings with legend "Kapilavastu" found. See Ganwaria also.

Piprahwa 1976-77. pp. 50-52.
Uttar Pradesh, district Basti. Grey ware, black polished ware, red ware, NBP, Kushan, Brahmi inscriptions, coin hoards, Sunga, stupa. See Ganwaria also.

368. Pithadia 1957-58. pp. 20-21.
Gujarat, District Madhya Saurashtra. Period I, Harappan with coarse grey ware. Period II, Lustrous Red Ware. In an Exploration Report. Pottery drawing.

369. Pochampad 1963-64. p. 1.
Andhra Pradesh, District Adilabad. Cairn circles, cists, Megalithic black and red ware, black ware, red ware, microliths.

Pochampad 1964-65. p. 1.
Andhra Pradesh, District Adilabad. Megalithic cairns, black and red ware, copper, iron.

Pochampad 1966-67. p. 1.
Andhra Pradesh, District Adilabad. Megalithic burials, hours burials, black and red ware, black ware.

370. Polakonda 1975-76. pp. 5-6.
Andhra Pradesh, District Warangal. Neolithic site, grey ware, dull red ware, Megalithic site, brown ware, black and red ware, black and brown ware, dark brown ware, Saka coin, Satavahana, red ware, black and red ware, bright red ware, Neolithic burnished grey ware and black ware, microliths, ground stone.

Polakonda 1976-77. p. 10.
Andhra Pradesh, District Warangal. Neolithic with ground stone and microliths, burnished grey ware, pale grey ware, blotchy brown (tan) ware, black burnished ware, pale red ware, Megalithic or Early Historical with Black and red ware, burnished brown and black wares, Kakatiya Period.

371. Poluvanpatti 1979-80. pp. 68-69.
Tamil Nadu, District Coimbatore. Temple with inscriptions. 11th century A.D.

372. Poondi 1965-66. p. 24.
Tamil Nadu, District Chingelput. Middle Palaeolithic. See Neyveli as well.

373. Prabhas Patan (Somnath) 1955-56. pp. 7-8.
Gujarat, District Sorath. Listed under "Somnath." Period I, Lustrous Red Ware, of Rangpur II, Lustrous Red Ware, black and red ware. Period III, finely burnished black and red ware with links to South India. Period IV, plain red ware, coarse black and red ware, 2000 Gupta and Valabhi coins.

Prabhas Patan (Somnath) 1956-57. pp. 16-17.
Gujarat, district Sorath. Period IA, "Late" Harappan pottery, segmented faience beads. Period IB "Late" Harappan ceramics with dish on stand, "sauce pan handle" (stud-handeled bowl?), hemispherical bowls Prabhas Ware ties to Ahar ceramics. Period III, 4 subdivisions, black and red ware, NBP?, gritty ware, iron, pully shaped ear stud, ivory hair pins and plaques, rubble pavement. Period IV, no black and red ware but gritty ware of Period III continues, iron, ivory objects, rubble floor. Period V, RPW, human and animal figurines, Kshatrapa and Gupta coins.

Prabhas Patan (Somnath) 1971-72. pp. 12-13.
Gujarat, district Junagadh. Harappan. 4th century B.C. to 6th century A.D., RPW.

Prabhas Patan (Somnath) 1975-76. p. 13.
Gujarat, district Junagadh. Harappan, Prabhas Period. Early Historical Period.

Prabhas Patan (Somnath) 1976-77. pp. 17-18.
Gujarat, District Junagadh. Prabhas Period "public" building. Harappan domesticated cattle, sleep, goat, pig. Hosses in Early Historic.

374. Prahaladpur 1962-63. pp. 40-41.
Uttar Pradesh, District Varanasi. Black and red ware, black slipped ware, dull red ware, microliths, iron, NBP, punch marked coins. Pottery illustrations.

375. Prakash 1954-55. p. 13.
Maharashtra, district West Khandesh. Period I, first millennium B.C., description of ceramics, some small finds. Period II, ca. 5th to 1st century B.C. , NBP. Period III, 1st century B.C. to 4th century A.D. , RPW, sprinkler, shell, copper, antimony. Period IV, 5th century A.D. and later, black ware, red slipped ware, glass and a Ganesha figure.

376. Pune 1984-85. p. 55.
Maharashtra, District Pune. Lower Palaeolithic tools on the Bombay/Pune Road.

377. Purana Qila 1954-55. pp. 13-14.
New Delhi. Period I, PGW. Period II, NBP with baked brick structures. Kushans, rulers of Mathura.

Purana Qila 1969-70. pp. 4-6.
New Delhi. Mauryan structures and small finds. Sunga structures, figurines. Saka-Kushan baked brick structures, small finds. Gupta brick structures. Post-Gupta. Rajput Period structures of re-used bricks, small finds. Sultanate Period. Mughal.

Purana Qila 1970-71. pp. 8-11.
New Delhi. A few PGW sherds, none in good contexts. Plan of Gupta building. Review of all periods, especially Mauryan.

Purana Quila 1971-72. pp. 7-8.
New Delhi. Mughal and Rajput Period materials excavated. Note on Sunga Period.

Purana Quila 1972-73. pp. 8-9.
New Delhi. Mughal Period floors, horse figure, tandoors, *hammam*, ceramics reviewed. Kushan coins.

378. Quila Rai Pithora 1957-58. pp. 24-25.
Delhi. Late Medieval site near the Qutab Minar. See Lal Kot as well.

Qila Rai Pithora 1964-65. pp. 7-8.
Delhi. Excavation in Qutub Minar vicinity. See Jahanpanah as well

379. Raibania 1974-75. p. 36.
Orissa, District. Balasore. Excavation of the Jaya Chandi temple site associated with the Raibania Fort.

380. Raipur 1984-85. pp. 53-55.
Maharashtra, District Nagpur. Excavation of four megaliths with unique features for this area. List of antiquities.

381. Raisen Fort 1976-77. p. 30.
Madhya Pradesh, district Raisen. Excavation at a Medieval fort. Upper phase dated to the 15th century.

382. Raja Karna Ka Qila 1970-71. pp. 15-16.
Haryana, District Karnal. NBP, Early Historic.

Raja Karna Ka Qila 1971-72. pp. 23-24.
Haryana, District Karnal. 5th century B.C. through late Medieval with breaks.

Raja Karna Ka Quila 1972-73. pp. 12-13.
Haryana, district Karnal. Early Historic.

Raja Karna Ka Qila 1974-75. p. 16.
Haryana, district Kurukshetra. "Late" Harappan.

Raja Karna Ka Qila 1975-76. p. 18.
Haryana, district Kurukshetra. "Late" Harappan, grey ware, red ware.

383. Rajahmundry 1979-80. p. 1.
Andhra Pradesh, district East Godavari. 2nd to 4th century A.D. deposit, monastery, stupa, RPW and Arretine wares.

Rajahmundry 1980-81. p. 1.
Andhra Pradesh, District East Godavari. Brick structure, fine porcelains, grey ware, (13th century A.D.)

Rajbadidanga See Rajbadi-Danga.

384. Rajbadi-Danga 1962-63. p. 46.
West Bengal, district Murshidabad. Stupas, Buddhist seals, /Gupta heads, grey ware `painted in black, decorated ware, bottle necked sprinklers, NBP (out of stratigraphic context).

Rajbadi-Danga 1963-64. pp. 62-63.
West Bengal, district Murshidabad. Stupa, C-14 dates, (1200 BP), Gupta, post-Gupta.

Rajbadi-Danga 1964-65. pp. 48-51.
West Bengal, District Murshidabad. Early Christian era, 7th to 8th century A.D., Buddhist, dull red ware, red, orange, brown, chocolate brown, polished ware, sprikler.

Rajbadi-Danga 1966-67. pp. 46-47.
West Bengal, District Murshidabad. Buddhist monastery, sprinklers, polished black ware.

Rajbadi-Danga 1968-69. p. 43.
West Bengal, district Murshidabad. 2nd to 13th century A.D.

Rajbadi-Danga 1971-72. pp. 50-51.
West Bengal, District Murshidabad. Monastery, ca. 3rd to 10th century A.D.

Rajbadi-Danga 1972-73. pp. 37-38.
West Bengal, distict Murshidabad. Historic site.

Rajbadi-Danga 1981-82. p. 75.
West Bengal, District Murshidabad. Limited excavation.

385. Rajghat 1957-58. pp. 50-51.
Uttar Pradesh, District Varanasi. Period I, 6th to 3rd century B.C., NBP, figurines. Period II, 2nd century B.C. to 1st century A.D., NBP, terra-cotta seals, copper coins. Period III, 2nd to 4th century A.D., thick red ware, copper coin. Period IV, 5th to 8th century A.D., red ware, black ware, sprinklers, glazed ware, copper coins, charred human bones in jars. Period V, 9th to 14th century A.D., structures, terra-cottas. Period VI, 14th to 17th century A.D., glazed ware, red ware, Ganesha figurine.

Rajghat 1960-61. pp. 35-39
Uttar Pradesh, District Varanasi. Black slipped coarse black and red ware, ocherous red ware, red ware, red ware, grey ware, NBP, black slipped ware, cast copper coins, stamped spouts and pots. Section and pottery drawings.

Rajghat 1961-62. pp. 57-59.
Uttar Pradesh, District Varanasi. thick grey ware. NBP.

Rajghat 1962-63. pp. 41-42.
Uttar Pradesh, district Varanasi. Black and red ware with white painting, dull red ware, black slipped ware, black and red ware.

Rajghat 1963-64. pp. 58-59.
Uttar Pradesh, District Varanasi. Grey ware, black slipped ware, NBP, coarse red, fine red, black and red wares, white painted red ware, violet painted red ware, rouletted Ware, Gupta coins.

Rajghat 1964-65. pp. 44-45.
Uttar Pradesh, district Varanasi. Iron in earliest levels. NBP in Period IB. In Period II the grey wares of Period I disappear.

Rajghat 1965-66. pp. 54-55.
Uttar Pradesh, district Varanasi. Pre-NBP red ware similar to Chirand, black slipped ware, NBP.

Rajghat 1966-67. p. 44.
Uttar Pradesh, District Varanasi. Massive well of the 4th or 5th century A.D. Structures of 1st century B.C. or 2nd century A.D.

Rajghat 1968-69. p. 41.
Uttar Pradesh, district Varanasi. Disturbed material.

386. Rajgir 1953-54. p. 9.
Bihar, district Patna. Excavation of the Jivakamravana site where Jiva, physician to Bimbisara, is said to have built a monastery for the Buddha. Three phases: I, with red ware but apparently no NBP; II NBP with painted ware; III, red ware.

Rajgir 1954-55. pp. 16-17.
Bihar, district Patna. Renewed work at the Jivakamravana site with a plan. Post-NBP residential building.

Rajgir 1957-58. p. 11.
Bihar, district Patna. Jivakamravana excavation. reservoir probably identified with Sumagadha of Pali literature.

Rajgir 1958-59. p. 13.
Bihar, district Patna. Jivakamravana site excavation. New site plan.

Rajgir 1961-62. pp. 6-8
Bihar, district Patna. Investigation of fortifications. Section drawing.

Rajgir 1962-63. pp. 5-6.
Bihar, District Patna. Investigation of the fortification and rampart. NBP in earliest Period I with 3 meters of earth work. Period II is a mud rampart. Period III is a massive stone fortification. C-14 date (245±150 B.C.).

Rajgir 1974-75. pp. 10-11.
Bihar, district Patna. In period I (2nd to 3rd century B.C.) there are rammed earth floors and a cairn circle with an urn burial, dull red ware, coin, NBP, red ware, deep red slipped red ware. Period II (1st to 2nd century A.D.) red wares, copper coins, etc. Period III (1st century A.D.), diverse burial practices.

387. Ramapuram 1980-81. pp. 3-7.
Andhra Pradesh, district Kurnool. Period IA, microliths, burnished red, grey, black wares, copper. Period IB, burnished grey and brown ware, copper. Period IC, iron, copper, grey and brown ware, black and red ware, megalithic burials, domesticated animals, bone tools. Illustration of sequence with artifacts. microlithic stone tools, graffiti, and copper objects.

Ramapuram 1981-82. pp. 3—8.
Andhra Pradesh, district Kurnool. Megalithic burials and habitation. Opened 120 trenches 10 x 10 meters. Worked down to the top of Period IB. Clustered huts, as many as 72 in one sub-phase, in the habitation area. List of small finds. four megaliths excavated. Black and red ware, list of small finds, iron. Pottery illustrations, plan and section of Megalith I.

Ramapuram 1982-83. pp. 3-6.
Andhra Pradesh, district Kurnool. Continued exposure of occupations A and B. Phase A circular huts 3.3 to 4.35 m in diameter, some with paving, one with infant pot burial. Nothern area has a large

number of finished and unfinished microliths. Copper wire, steatite disk beads. Phase B typology of burials given. Phase C has Chalcolithic Black and Red Ware, black, red, and grey ware plus a grey and brown ware. Some wheel made pottery.

Ramapuram 1983-84. pp. 3-5.
Andhra Pradesh, district Kurnool. Excavation of 11,000 sq. m. revealed 34 circular structures (9.3 to 2.55 m. diameter) and 5 oval houses in Period IA. Grain silos present. In IB silos converted to animal burial pits or filled with rubbish. In IB & C the inhabitants used above ground bins. List of IA small finds, some pottery as in 1982-83. I B1 has 53 circular and 11 oval huts. I B2 has 39 circular and 6 oval huts, 9 burials, list of pottery. IC two sub phases with 10 and 11 houses each. Copper in IC. Microlithic level under IA possibly pre-pottery Neolithic.

388. Rambagh 1976-77. p. 49.
Uttar Pradesh, District Agra. Excavation of drainage system in a garden.

389. Rampur 1981-82. p. 44.
Madhya Pradesh, District Sidhi. Epi-Palaeolithic tools like those from Bhaghor I located on a red brown, sandy clay loam.

390. Rangpur 1953-54, p. 7.
Gujarat, district Jhalawar Microliths, Chalcolithic, Late Chalcolithic, red ware, black and red ware.

Rangpur 1954-55. pp. 11-12.
Gujarat, district Jhalawar. Harappan. Fortification in earliest period. Black and red ware.

391. Rangpuram 1979-80. p. 9.
Andhra Pradesh, district Mahbubnagar. Early Chalukyan temple.

392. Rani-ki-Vav 1964-65. p. 12.
Gujarat, District Mehsana. 11th to 12th century sculptures.

392. Ranihat 1978-79. p. 75.
Uttar Pradesh, District Tehri. Period I, 6th century B.C. to 4th century B.C., red, grey and black polished wares, terra-cotta, copper and iron objects. Period IIa, 4th century B.c. to 2nd century B.C., NBP, red ware, brick structures, oven. Period IIb, 2nd century B.C. to 2nd century A.D. Period II, 6th to 12th century A.D.

394. Ranipur Jharial 1975-76. p. 37.
Orissa, District Bolangir. Buddha image and temple.

395. Ratanppura 1984-85. pp. 17-18; 15-16.
Gujarat, District Mehsana. Excavation of four mounds. I and II have Lustrous red Ware and Ahar type white painted black and red ware in quantity. Mound III has microliths and bone, without pottery. Mound IV, near the river has ashy pits suggested to have been ritual structures. There are no formal buildings at the site, suggesting short term occupation. Stud handled bowls; Lustrous red Ware. Pottery drawings.

396. Ratnagiri 1957-58. pp. 39-41.
Orissa, District Cuttack. Buddhist site.

Ratnagiri 1958-59. pp. 33-36.
Orissa, District Cuttack. Buddhist monastery.

Ratnagiri 1959-60. pp. 38-39.
Orissa, district Cuttack. Buddhist monasteries.

Ratnagiri 1960-61. pp. 28-30.
Orissa, district Cuttack. Monastery, stupas.

397. Raygad 1980-81. p. 43.
Maharashtra, district Raygad. Investigation to determine the presence of the superstructure over the throne platform of Shivaji at the Raygad fort.

398. Rohira 1982-83. pp. 65-66.
Punjab, District Sangrur. Excavations to understand the Harappan and Pre-Harappan occupation as well as the fortification wall. Period IA, red and pink pottery fabrics painted in black, no complete house plans, furnace and gold foil in what may be a gold smith's house, cart wheels, beads of agate, carnelian and steatite. Period IB, "arrival" of the

Harappans with Pre-Harappan pottery continuing in quantity. Fortification wall. Sealings, one seal copper objects. Period IC, Bara occupation. Period II, black slipped pottery copper bell. Period III, Late Kushan. Period IV has knife-edged bowls and associated wares.

399. Rojdi 1957-58. pp. 18-23.
Gujarat, district Madhya Saurashtra. In an Exploration report. Sub-period IA, Harappan pottery, similar to Prabhas IA. IB has pottery like Prabhas IB. Note of a wall of large boulders around the site and a red ware sherd with four Harappan characters inscribed on it. Pottery drawing.

Rojdi 1962-63. p. 8.
Gujarat, District Madhya Saurashtra. Two Phases: A and B. Phase A structures built on a platform. Seven plasterings, first three were burned. this is a purely Harappan level. Phase B Harappan pottery and ties to Lustrous Red Ware and Prabhas. Period II, RPW, Early Historic. Period III, Medieval. Two carbon 14 dates (1970±105 B.C.).

Rojdi 1964-65. p. 12.
Gujarat, district Rajkot. In an Exploration Report a not that 520 microbeads and 8 bicone barrel beads of gold, parts of a necklace, were found below a structure of Period IB.

Rojdi 1982-83. p. 28.
Gujarat, District Rajkot. Short report on renewed excavation. List of pottery fabrics.

Rojdi 1983-84. pp. 19-20.
Gujarat, district Rajkot. Exposure of Harappan materials on the South Extension attributed to Rangpur IIB/C times. Copper/bronze tools, list of small finds, no seals.

Rojdi 1984-85. p. 18.
Gujarat, district Rajkot. Short report on the excavation of this Urban/Post-urban Harappan site in Saurashtra.

400. Runija 1980-81. p. 39.
Madhya Pradesh, district Ujjain. Period IA, Chalcolithic pottery of Ahar type. Period IB, Runija Ware (photographs) and wall with wooden beams in place. Period IIA and B, Early Historical pottery, Iron, etc. Period III, Sunga/Satavahana Period. Period IV, Kushan/Kshatrapas. Period V, Guptas.

401. Rupar 1953-54. p. 6-7.
Haryana, District Ambala. Period I, Harappans. Period II, PGW. Period III NBP. Period IV, Indo-Greeks. Period V, Medieval.

Rupar 1954-55 p.9.
Haryana, District Amabala. Investigation of the Harappan cemetery. disturbed by PGW occupation. Note of pottery and small finds. tank in Period III.

402. Saipai 1970-71. p. 38.
Uttar Pradesh, district Etawah. Excavation following a report of a Copper Hoard being found. Excavation produced OCP and a copper harpoon of Hoard type, in association. Othe small finds noted.

Saipai 1971-72. pp. 46-47.
Uttar Pradesh, District Etawah. OCP, no copper.

403. Salargarh 1975-76. pp. 47, 49-50.
Utar Pradesh, district Basti, Buddha image, Sunga-Kushan stupa, black polished ware, fine grey ware, red ware, NBP, black painted red ware, monastery.

404. Salaura 1954-55. pp. 9-11.
Punjab, District Ambala. Adjacent to Bara, 5 miles from Rupar. PGW, Kushans, Medieval. Section drawing. See Bara as well.

405. Salihundam 1953-54. p. 11-12.
Andhra Pradesh, District Srikakulam. Buddhist site. Stupa, chaitya, 2 apsidal temples, epigraphic evidence identifies the site as "Kattaharama," or "Kattahara arama" of the 2nd century A.D.

406. Sanganakallu 1964-65. pp. 29-30.
Mysore, District Bellary. Microliths, Neolithic, "Polished Axe Culture," pale grey ware, burnished grey ware with ocher painting, black painted red ware. Megalithic black and red ware.

407. Sanghol 1968-69. pp. 25-26.
Punjab, District Ludhiana. Period I, "Late" Harappan, no Mature pottery shapes.

Period II, PGW. Period III, NBP associated wares but no NBP itself. Period IV, Sunga style terracottas. Period V, Kushan and Gupta. Period Vi, Pre-Mughal glazed ware.

Sanghol 1969-70. pp. 31-32.
Punjab, District Ludhiana. "Late" Harappan Period I has some ceramics like Cemetery H. Also some similarities to Early Harappan Kalibangan I. PGW, NBP, RPW, Gupta.

Sanghol 1970-71. pp. 30-31.
Punjab, District Ludhiana. "Late" Harappan, PGW, NBP.

Sanghol 1971-72. pp. 39, 41.
Punjab, District Ludhiana. NBP associated wares, stupa.

Sanghol 1972-73. p.28.
Punjab, District Ludhiana. "Late" Harappan.

Sanghol 1977-78. pp. 43-44.
Punjab, District Ludhiana. "Late" Harappan pottery similar to Bara. PGW Indo-Parthian, Kushan.

Sanghol 1980-81. p.46.
Punjab, District Ludhiana. Period IA, "Late" Harappan (Bara) drawing of tigress and cubs on pottery. Period IB, 6 Bara structural phases. Monastery of later (?) period. "Eye-shaped" beads noted.

Sanghol 1984-85. pp. 62.64.
Punjab District Ludhiana. Continued excavation of the stupa. stucco of the Buddha.

Saradkel 1964-65. p.6
Bihar, District Ranchi. Habitation site. Kushans, coarse red ware, grey ware, black and red ware. See Khuntioli also

409. Sarai-Mohana 1967-68. pp. 48-49.
Uttar Pradesh, District Varanasi. Period I has sub-periods A, B and C. IA has plain and painted black and red ware, black slipped ware, other ceramics similar to Hastinapur II. NBP, red ware similar to Hastinapur III appears in IB. Sub period IC ceramics also like Hastinapur III, but has no black and red ware. Period II is Late Medieval. Drawing of Sub-period IA pottery.

Sarai Mound See Nalanda 1978-79.

410 Sarai Nahar Rai 1969-70. pp. 43-44.
Uttar Pradesh, District Pratapgarh. Microliths, eight extended burials.

Sarai Nahar Rai 1971-72. pp. 48-49.
Uttar Pradesh, District Pratapgarh. Microliths, burials.

Sarai Nahar Rai, 1972-73. p.35.
Uttar Pradesh, District Pratapgarh, Microliths, burials.

411. Sastevadi 1971-72. p. 35.
Maharashtra, District Pune. Chalcolithic on Mula-Mutha River, Jorwe-Rangpur IIC-III (?)

412. Satanikota 1974-75. pp.5-6
Andhra Pradesh, District Kurnool, Satavahana, red ware, black and red ware.

Satanikota 1977-78. pp. 3-11.
Andhra Pradesh, District Kurnool. Satavahana fort. Mesoslithic (?) with microliths, black and red ware, Rouletted Ware, Russet-coated Painted Ware, Kaolin ware, RPW, chocolate slipped ware, red wares both slipped and unslipped. black ware both slipped and unslipped, Brahmi inscription, Neolithic celts, megaliths. Drawings of a coin from Period II, stone tools, pottery, section, and plan.

Satanikota 1978-79. pp. 35-36
Andhra Pradesh, District Kurnool. Rouletted Ware, black and red ware, fortification wall. Map of the fort.

Satanikota 1979-80. pp. 2-6
Andhra Pradesh, District Kurnool. Middle Palaeolithic and microlithic tools. Magalithic burials, black and red,

413. Sawalda 1959-60. pp.34-37.
Maharashtra, District West Khandesh. Chalcolithic. Black, purple or chocolate over red or brownish ware, red ware, burnished grey ware burnished black ware, black and grey ware (similar to early Ahar),

microliths, NBP associated pottery. Pottery illustration. See Bahurupa also.

414. Sejakpur 1965-66. p.18.
Gujarat, District Surendranagar. Excavation of the foundations of the Navalkha temple at Sejakpur.

415. Selbalgiri-2 1967-68. p.8.
Assam, District Garo Hills. Topmost Layer 1 has 6 stone axes, both ground and chipped, one scraper and an abundance of pottery. Layer 2 yielded a core, 4 hammers and several small flakes, plus pottery. Layer 3 had many microliths, both geometric and non geometric, with pottery. Thirteen lunates and 4 trapezes along with a large number of points and some arrow heads were found. Pottery is all plain, hand made, coarse, gritty and grey, grey brown or dull brown in colour. The Exploration Report on p.7, preceding this Excavation Report, notes Lower Palaeolithic at the site (5 handaxes), as well as an abundance of other worked stone and pottery on the surface.

Semathan See Semthan.

416. Semthan 1977-78. p.24.
Jammu and Kashmir District Anantnag. Early Historic red ware.

Semthan 1978-79. pp. 69-70.
Jammu and Kashmir, District Anantnag. NBP, black slipped, plain red ware, grey ware, red ware, copper coins, seal.

Semthan 1980-81. pp. 21-23
Jammu and Kashmir, District Anantnag. Period I, five wares described, including red ware, ocherous ware and burnished as well as plain grey ware. Specimens of wheat, barley and rice were found. Period II, red ware, NBP, cast copper coins. Period III, Indo Greek level. Pottery illustrations for Periods I and II.

417. Shamlaji 1961-62. pp. 13-14.
Gujarat, District Sabarkantha. Kshatrapa, black painted red ware, RPW, stamped ware, Kshatrapa coin, burnished grey ware.

418. Shyamsundar Tila 1984-85. pp. 78-79.
Tripura, District South Tripura. Excavation of a ca. 10th century stupa. List of sculpture and antiquities.

419. Siddarajalingapuram 1979-80. p.6
Andhra Pradesh, District Kurnool. Middle Palaeolithic tools, black and red ware, fine and coarse red wares.

420. Sihawal 1979-80. p.53.
Madhya Pradesh, District Sidhi. Lower and Upper Palaeolithic industry.

421. Singh Bhagwanpur 1980-81. pp. 49-54.
Punjab, District Rupnagar. Period I, 700 to 400 B.C. PGW, plain grey, black slipped, dull red wares, iron slag and objects. Period II, 200 to 300 A.D, red ware, Indo-Greek and Kushan coins, iron objects. Period III, 900 to 1500 A.D., grey and red wares. Pottery illustrations.

422. Singi Talav Quarry 1980-81. pp. 57-63.
Rajasthan, District Nagaur. Investigation of Palaeolithic and palaeoenvironmental history of the area in the vicinity of Didwana. Table of layers. Schematic section and map of sites. See Indola-Ki-Dhani and Didwana/Marwar Balia as well.

Singi-Talav 1981-82. pp. 58-59.
Rajasthan, District Nagaur. Palaeolithic site 2 km. west of Didwana. Same site as Singi Talav Quarry.

Singi-Talav 1982-83. p.69.
Rajasthan, District Nagaur. Excavation confirms a primary occupation in a lake shore, pool environment with Acheulian tools. Percentages of tools types given.

423. Siri Fort 1976-77. p.14.
Delhi. Fort of Ala-ud-Din Khalji, ca. 1303 A.D.

424. Sirpur 1953-54. p.12
Madhya Pradesh, District Raipur. Capital of the Pandava Dynasty. Siva temple, sculpture and architectural fragments.

Sirpur 1954-55. pp. 24-26.
Madhya Pradesh, District Raipur. Temple/ Monastery. Plan of monastery.

Sirpur 1955-56. pp. 26-27.
Madhdya Pradesh, District Raipur. Buddhist.

425. Sisupalgarh 1970-71. p.30
Orissa, District Puri. 2 structural phases to the fortification wall. Phase I, laterite blocks. Phase II, baked brick renovation of the wall, 2 Puri-Kushan coins, Rouletted Ware, iron.

426. Sittanavasal 1975-76. pp. 39-42.
Tamil Nadu, District Pudukottai. Megaliths, black and red ware, red ware, black polished ware, all black ware.

Sittanavasal 1975-76. pp. 39-42.
Tamil Nadu, District Pudukottai. Megaliths, black and red ware, red ware, black polished ware, all black ware, iron.

427. Sohagaura 1961-62 p.56.
Uttar Pradesh, District Gorakhpur. Period I, plain and painted black and red ware, grey ware, plus other wares. Period II, NBP. Period III, no NBP, terra cotta figurines, one with Sunga headdress, coins of Ayodhya, Panchala and Kushans. Period IV, Medieval. Pottery illustrations for Periods I and II.

Sohagaura 1974-75 pp. 46-47.
Uttar Pradesh, District Gorakhpur. Period I, hand made, mat impressed ware. Period II, potters wheel, black slipped and associated wares, 2 C-14 dates. Period III, NBP C-14 date. Period IV, no NBP, coins of Kushans and Ayodhya. Period V, Medieval glazed wares.

Somnath See Prabhas Patan.

Sonepur See Sonpur.

428. Songaon 1964-65. pp. 26-28.
Maharashtra, District Poona. Chalcolithic, Early Historical, Jorwe Ware, burnished grey ware, Malwa Ware, ground stone, urn burials, charred wheat, coarse red ware, grey ware, microliths, black and red ware of early Chritian era, slipped red ware. Pottery illustration.

429. Sonkh 1966-67. pp. 40-43.
Uttar Pradesh, District Mathura. Period I, PGW and associated wares, iron slag, stone balls and other small finds Period II, NBP and other ceramics, Mauryan "Mother Goddess" terra-cotta. Period III, 2nd century B.C., ceramics. Period IV, 2nd century B.C. radio carbon date. Period V, ? Period VI, Kushan relief wall. Period VII, walls, kaolin bowl. Period VIII, a few structures, C-14 date in 1st Century A.D. Period IX, floor, conflagration. Late Kushan/Gupta. Period X, conflagration, abandonment. Period XI, gateway tower and C-14 date in 15th century A.D. Period XII, upper most phase.

Sonkh 1968-69. p.40.
Uttar Pradesh, District Mathura PGW. Mauryan, Kushan and Gupta levels. Kushan structure noted.

Sonkh 1969-70. pp. 42-43. Uttar Pradesh District Mathura. Seven Kushan structures. Jar with 120 copper Kushan coins. Apsidal Kushan structure. Terr-cotta, stone and metal images of Kushan date.

Sonkh 1970-71. pp. 39-40.
Uttar Pradesh, District Mathura. Kushan.

Sonkh 1971-72. pp. 47-48.
Uttar Pradesh, District Mathura. Apsidal temple, Kushan.

Sonkh 1972-73. pp. 33-35.
Uttar Pradesh, District Mathura. PGW through Early Historic. Table of the 37 cultural levels.

430. Sonpur 1956-57 pp. 19-20.
Bihar, District Gaya. Pre-NBP black and red ware, NBP, Early Historical.

Sonpur 1959-60. p.14.
Bihar, District Gaya. Coarse black and red ware, red and black ware, fine black and red ware, copper wire, urn burials, post-cremation burials in Period IA-B (700 B.C.) NBP, steatite weights iron, punch marked coin in Period II. NBP, red ware with sprinklers in Period III (BC/AD). Pottery drawing.

Sonpur 1960-61. pp. 4-5
Bihar, District Gaya. Period IA, black and red ware, black ware, no structures. period IB, finer pottery than in IA, rice. Period II, NBP, black and red ware of Period I continues, white paint on both red and black wares, polished stone axes, iron, post cremation pit burials. Period III NBP, red ware, sprinkler.

Sonpur 1961-62. pp. 4-5.
Bihar, District Gaya. Black and red ware, black ware, red ware, NBP, painted ware, microliths.

Sonpur 1970-71. pp. 5-6
Bihar, District Gaya. Chalcolithic and NBP.

431. South Kanara 1980-81. p.31.
Karnataka. District South Kanara. Mesolithic sites.

432. Sravasti 1958-59 pp. 47-50.
Uttar Pradesh, District Bahraich. NBP through Early Historic. Pottery illustrations.

433. Sringaverpur 1977-78. pp. 54, 56.
Uttar Pradesh, District Allahabad. period I, ca. 8th to 6th century B.C., no PGW, black and red ware, other ceramics. period II, ca. 6th to mid-3rd century B.C., NBP and some PGW in lowest levels. Period III, ca. mid-3rd century B.C. to 3rd century A.D., Gupta. Period IV, 6th to 13th century A.D., Post-Gupta.

Sringaverpur 1978-79. pp. 57-59.
Uttar Pradesh, District Allahabad. Red Ware, black and red ware, black slipped, burnished grey, ochre colored ware (OCP?), PGW, NBP, a large rectangular tank, Maurya, Sunga Kushan, Gupta, Rajput and Medieval occupational debris.

Sringaverpur 1979-80. pp. 73-74.
Uttar Pradesh, District Allahabad. Brick-built tank, terra-cotta figurines. Plan of the tank.

Sringaverpur 1980-81. pp. 67-68.
Uttar Pradesh, District Allahabad. Brick-built tank, terra-cotta figurines and lamps.

Sringaverpur 1981-82. pp. 66-67.
Uttar Pradesh, District Allahabad. Excavation of a tank complex with eight structural phases dating from Kushan times to Medieval times. Medieval residences. Sunga/Kushan figurines, Brahmi script, copper coins, gold plated(?.) silver coins of Govindchandra. List of small finds. Same site as Sringaverpur.

Sringaverpur 1982-83. pp. 91-92.
Uttar Pradesh, District Allahabad. exposure of retaining wall and steps associated with the tank. House complex near the tank. Another house complex follows the abandonment of the tank and dates to ca. 3rd century AD.

Sringaverpur 1983-84. pp. 84-85.
Uttar Pradesh, District Allahabad. Continued exposure of the tank. Circular structure found to the south. terra-cotta sealings with Brahmi script. List of small finds.

Sringaverpur 1984-85, pp. 85-86.
Uttar Pradesh, District Allahabad. Continued excavation of the tank. Excavation in the Late Kushan habitation area.

434. Sugh 1963-64. pp. 27-28.
Haryana District Ambala. NBP, grey ware, PGW, Sunga, Kushan, cast copper coins.

Sugh 1965-66. pp. 35-36.
Haryana, District Ambala. PGW, NBP, punch marked and Indo-Greek coins, cast coins with Mauryan characters, stamped wares, Early Historical pottery.

435. Sunari 1980-81. pp. 55-56.
Rajasthan, District Jhunjunu. PGW, grey ware, black and red, black slipped wares, NBP, iron implements, copper objects, iron furnaces, Sunga-Kushan level.

436. Sunet 1983-84. pp. 67-70.
Punjab, District Ludhiana. Period I, "Late" Harappan. Pottery like Sanghol. No structures or antiquities. Period II, PGW, Bara Ware, black slipped ware, red ware. Period III, black slipped ware, grey ware and red ware of ca. 600-200 B.C. Period IV.

Sunga-Kushana. Period V, Gupta. Period VI, Early Medieval. Section drawing.

437. Surkotada 1970-71. pp. 13-15.
Gujarat, District Kutch. Harappan. Period I, goblet and beaker, fortification wall, list of small finds. Period II, Harappan, Ahar black and red ware, list of small finds. Period III, Harappan, fortification. Citadel and lower town.

Surkotada 1971-72. pp. 13-21.
Gujarat, District Kutch. Change of terminology from Periods I, II and III, to IA, IB and IC. Extensive report on the site with site plan, schematic section drawing, plan of a burial and pottery illustrations.

438. Surpan 1980-81. p.11.
Gujarat, District Bharuch. Temple, kaolin ware and sprinklers of the Early Historic Period.

439. T. Kallupatti 1976-77. pp. 46-47.
Tamil Nadu, District Madurai. Megalithic, burnished grey ware, black and red ware, white painted black and red ware, white painted black ware, Russet-coated White, Painted Ware, coarse red ware, black on red ware, coins.

T. Kallupatti 1979-80. p.69.
Tamil Nadu, District Madurai. Microlithic tools and dull red ware, black and red ware, white painted black ware, Russet-coated White Painted Ware.

440. T. Narasipur 1958-59. p.33
Mysore, District Mysore "T" stands for "Tirumukkudal," where three rivers come together. Period I, Neolithic, burnished grey ware, 2 pots with painted rims with parallels at Bahal, channel spouts, ground stone axes, no microliths, no copper. Period II, Megalithic black and red ware, fragment of an iron dagger, profuse graffiti on pottery. Russet-coated pottery on surface.

T. Narasipur 1959-60. p.38.
Mysore, District Mysore. Neolithic, Period I, burnished grey ware in large quantities, coarse grey thick ware incised. Chalcolithic claimed for middle period, sherd of Jorwe Ware. Period III, Megalithic, polished red ware, black polished ware. Middle Palaeolithic tools from river.

T. Narasipur 1961-62. pp. 35-36.
Mysore, District Mysore. Neolithic burial. Summar of all pottery types.

T. Narasipur 1964-65. p. 32.
Mysore, District mysore. Biconical copper bead found in the upper levels of the Neolithic. Followed by Megalithic.

T. Narasipur See T. Narasipur.

441. Tadakanahalli 1978-79. pp. 44-46.
Karnataka, District Dharwar. Megalithic urn burials, black and red ware (with white painting), other black and red wares, iron implements. Pottery illustrations.

442. Takalghat 1967-68. pp. 33-34.
Karnataka, District Bellary. Megalithic habitation site, black painted red ware, white painted black and red ware, Russet-coated Painted Ware, Megalithic black and red ware. Copper. Graffiti. See Khapa also.

443. Takiaper 1971-72. p.49.
Uttar Pradesh, District Varanasi. Period I, NBP and associated wares, iron. Period II, materials of the early centuries of the Christian Era, stone house complex, Brahmi inscription of 1st or 2nd century A.D.

444. Tamluk 1954-55. pp. 19-20.
west Bengal, District Midnapur. Ancient Tamralipti. Period I, Neolithic. Period II, 2nd and 3rd century B.C., figurines, copper coins, pottery like contemporary wares. Period III, 1st to 2nd century A.D., Rouletted Ware, tank, beads. Period IV, 3rd to 4th century A.D., Kushan and Gupta, not well represented.

Tamluk 1973-74. p. 33
West Bengal, District Midnapur. Period, I, Pre-NBP black and red ware, "lingering Chalcolithic." Period II, NBP. Period III red ware, Sunga Period objects. Period IV, Rouletted Ware, RPW. Overlying material disturbed during Medieval period.

445. Taradih 1981-82. pp. 10-12.
Bihar, District Gaya. Excavation of the Taradih Mound near the Mahabodhi

Temple at Bodh Gaya. period I, red ware dominant, black and red ware, black ware, copper, chalcedony blade, Chalcolithic. Period II, NBP, iron, list of small finds. Period III< Kushans. Period IV, Gupta and late Gupta, images of Buddha and Avalokitesvar. Period V, Pala material, images of Tara and Buddha.

Taradih 1982-83. pp. 16, 25.
Bihar, District Gaya. Excavation of the Taradih mound NE of the Mahabodhi temple at Bodh Gaya. Period I, Chalcolithic, wattle and daub huts, 'neolithic' axe, red ware, Black and Red Ware. Period II, NBP. Period III, Kushan. Period IV, Gupta. Period V, Monastery of the Pala Period.

Taradih 1983-84. pp. 12-13.
Bihar, District Gaya. Period I, Chalcolithic on virgin soil. Wattle and daub houses. Red, black and black and red wares. Period II, iron, black and red ware, red ware. Rice husk impressions. Lime coated, rammed earth house floors. List of small finds. period IIB, NBP, other features appear to continue. Period III Kushan. Period IV, Gupta. Period V, monastery.

Taradih 1984-85. pp. 9-10.
Bihar, District Gaya. Identification of Pre-Chalcolithic levels without metal and akin to Chirand I. Review of Stratigraphy and periodization.

446. Taraghda 1978-79. p.68.
Gujarat, District Rajkot. Harappan. Pottery similar to Prabhas Patan. Copper ring, carnelian beads and weights.

447. Tarsang 1977-78. pp. 21-22.
Gujarat, District Panch Mahals. Painted rock shelter. Three phases. Phase I, apparently weathered rock. Phase II, microliths, lunates, crescents, trapezes, trapezoids, ca. 80,000 pieces of worked stone, no pottery, dentalium shell, Mesolithic. Phase III, antiquities of Early Historic to Medieval times.

448. Tekkalakota 1963-64. pp. 24-25.
Mysore, District Bellary. One of 19 Neolithic settlements south of the village. Period I, Southern Neolithic, bone tools, copper axe, gold ornaments, fractional burials. Period II, Southern Neolithic, copper, black painted red ware, circular houses, extended burials.

449. Tekwada 1956-57. pp. 18-19.
Maharashtra, East Khandesh. Chalcolithic burial site.

450. Tenmalai 1983-84. p.48.
Kerala, District Quilon. Very short report on the excavation of a "Mesolithic rock shelter."

451. Ter 1957-58. pp. 23-24.
Maharashtra, District Osmanabad. 4th Century B.C. to 4th century A.D. occupation. NBP, RPW. Iron, rice, wheat pulses.

Ter 1966-67. pp. 25-26
Maharashtra, District Osmanabad. Period I, Mauryan (ca. 300 to 100 B.C.) ends with a flood. Period II (ca. 100 B.C. to 100 A.D.) most prosperous occupation, several sub-periods, large scale fire. period III, Satavahana (ca. 50 to 200 A.D.) contacts with Rome. Remains of a large house, plan included. Medieval occupation.

Ter 1967-68. p.35.
Maharashtra, District Osmanabad. Excavation of a stupa. Apsidal brick temple with a stupa inside dated by associated coin of Pulumavi. Roman objects.

Ter 1968-69. pp. 17-18.
Maharashtra, District Osmanabad. Stupa, RPW, Roman goods.

Ter 1974-75. p.32.
Maharashtra, District Osmanabad. Phase I, NBP, good black and red ware, no Satavahana coins. Phase II, wooden barricade no NBP. Phase III, black and red ware, a associated wares, kaolin, coins of the Satakarni and subsequent kings of the Satavahanas. Habitation ends ca 3rd century A.D.

452. Terdal 1965-66. p.34.
Karnataka, District Bijapur. Megaliths, black and red ware, plain red ware, microliths, black painted red ware of

Savalda type, white painted grey ware.

453. Thakurani Tila 1984-85. pp. 79-80.
Tripura, District South Tripura. Excavation of a temple with large Surya image of the ca. 13th century.

454. Thapli 1982-83. p. 103.
Uttar Pradesh District Tehri-Garhwal. Single phase PGW site. Terra cotta bird figurine, copper bangles, copper nail parers, terra cotta beads, rice (?), *Bos*, *Sus*, *Equus caballus*.

455. Theur 1969-70. pp. 27-29.
Maharashtra, District Pune. Jorwe with stone rings outlining houses on surface.

456. Tilaura-Kot 1961-62. pp. 73-74.
Nepal, District Taulihawa. NBP, red ware, grey ware, black slipped ware, painted red ware, painted grey ware coins. Sunga, Mauryan, Kushan, Panchala coins.

457. Tildah 1954-55. p.23.
West Bengal District Midnapur. NBP (1 sherd), Gupta site.

458. Tilwara 1967-68. pp. 39-41.
Rajasthan, District Barmer. Microlithic site, house circles on surface, house floors, ground stone, grey ware, red ware with pale red slip. Pottery more sophisticated than Bagor. Iron lumps.

459. Tirukkambuliyur 1961-62. p.28.
Tamil Nadu, District, Tiruchirapalli. Russet-coated Painted Ware, black and red ware, polished black ware, incised or impressed ware, fine red slipped ware, unslipped red ware.

Tirukkambuliuyur 1962-63. p. 14.
Tamil Nadu, District Tiruchirapalli. Russet-coated Painted Ware, Megalithic black and red ware, all black ware, red slipped ware, coarse slipped and unslipped red pottery.

460. Tiruvakkarai 1984-85. pp. 77-78.
Tamil Nadu, District South Arcot. Excavation of Megalithic tombs in a very rich locality.

461. Tripuri 1965-66. pp. 21-22.
Madhya Pradesh, District Jabalpur. Black and red ware, NBP, white slipped ware, fine red ware, coins of Tripuri, satavahana, and Kshatrapas, Kaolin ware, RPW with sprinklers, brass.

Tripuri 1966-67. pp. 17-19.
Madhya Pradesh, District Jabalpur. Chalcolithic, Neolithic, Indo-Sassanian coin, NBP, black and red ware, coarse red ware, whitish slipped ware, fine red ware with shining surface, punch marked oins, cast coins (Tripuri and Satavahana), stamped pottery, kaolin ware, sprinklers, Brahmi inscriptions, Kalachuri Period (5th to 6th century A.D.).

Tripuri 1967-68. pp. 23-24.
Madhya Pradesh, District Jabalpur. Satavahana coins, Bodhi coins, Indo-Sassanian coins, Kalachuri coins, Tripuri coins.

Tripuri 1968-69. pp. 11-12.
Madhya Pradesh, District Jabalpur. Early Historic.

Tripuri 1970-71. p. 20.
Madhya Pradesh, District Jabalpur. Early Historic.

462. Tuljapur Garhi 1984-85. pp. 48-50.
Maharashtra, District Amaravati. Excavation of a two phase Malwa, Jorwe site. Child burial with carnelian beads. Pottery illustrated.

463. Tulsipur 1967-68. pp. 49-50.
Maharashtra, District Pune. Jorwe with stone rings outlining houses on surface.

464. Tumain 1971-72. pp. 27-28.
Madhya Pradesh, District Guna. Ancient Tumbavana. Period I, 5th to 2nd century B.C., NBP, black and red ware, small finds. Period II, 2nd century B.C. to 1st century A.D., NBP, red ware, Brahmi inscription. Period III, 1st to 5th century A.D., RPW. Period IV, 6th to 12th century. Mauryan stupas.

Tumain 1972-73. pp. 15-16.
Madhya Pradesh, District Guna. Gupta

and Pratihara sculpture, pillars. Kushan settlement.

465. Turakapadu 1967-68. p.7.
Andhra Pradesh, District Visakhapatnam. Disturbed Medieval site.

466. Udayagiri 1958-59. pp. 38-40.
Orissa, District Puri. Early Historic site,. Plan of apsidal building.

Udayagiri 1961-62. pp. 36-37.
Orissa, District Puri. Caves, ca. 1st century A.D., punch marked coin, microliths.

Udayagiri 1965-66. p. 35.
Orissa, District Puri. Stupa.

467. Udayapur 1983-84. p. 56.
Madhya Pradesh, District Vidisha. Excavation of a temple dated to ca. 1059 A.D. by an inscription on one of the walls.

468. Udayesvara 1981-82. p.48.
Madhya Pradesh, District Vidisha. Excavation at a temple.

469. Ujjain 1955-56. pp. 19-20.
Madhya Pradesh, District Ujjain. Period I, NBP, black and red ware. Chipped stone tools. List of small finds. Period II, Medieval.

Ujjain 1956-57. pp. 20-28.
Madhya Pradesh, District Ujjain. Extensive report on 4 periods. Site Plan, section drawing, pottery and small finds illustrated.

Ujjain 1957-58. pp. 32, 34, 36.
Madhya Pradesh, District Ujjain. Pre-NBP through Early Historic. Extensive report. Pottery and stone objects illustrated.

Ujjain 1964-65. p. 18.
Madhya Pradesh, District Ujjain. NBP.

470. Ukkirankottai 1970-71. p. 35.
Tamil Nadu, District Tirunelveli. 7th to 10th century A.D.

471. Unchgaon 1956-57. p. 29.
Uttar Pradeshs, District Sitapur. Medieval brick temple.

472. Uppalapadu 1977-78. p.12.
Andhra Pradesh, District Mahbubnagar. Megaliths, black and red ware, red ware, black ware, iron.

Uppalapadu 1978-79. pp. 65-66.
Andhra Pradesh, District Mahbubnagar. Period I, Megalithic black and red ware, chipped stone tools, list of small finds. Period II, Medieval.

473. Uraiyur 1964-65. pp. 25-26.
Tamil Nadu, District tiruchirapalli. Chola capital, Megalithic black and red ware, Russet-coated Painted ware, Rouletted Ware, Arretine ware, red ware, black ware, red slipped ware.

Uraiyur 1965-66. pp. 26-27.
Tamil Nadu, District Tiruchirapalli. Black and red ware, red ware, black ware, Rouletted Ware, red slipped ware, ancient capital of the Cholas, Medieval pottery and Celadon ware.

Uraiyur 1967-68. pp. 30-31.
Tamil Nadu, District Tiruchirapalli. Black and red ware, Russet-coated Painted Ware, Rouletted Ware, Brahmi inscriptions, red slipped ware, coarse red ware.

474. Utnoor 1958-59. p.11.
Andhra Pradesh, District Mahbubnagar. Neolithic, post holes, stockade C-14 date.

Untur See Utnoor.

475. Vadagaon Madhavpur 1971-72. pp. 38-39.
Karnataka, District Belgam. 5th Century B.C. to 3rd century A.D.

Vadagon Madhavpur 1972-73. p. 26.
Karnataka, District Belgam. Megalithic, Pre-Satavahana, Satavahana.

Vadagaon Madhavpur 1973-74, pp. 16-17.
Karnataka, District Belgam. Late Medieval.

Vadagaon Madhavpur 1974-75. p. 17
Karnataka, District Belgam. Satavahana, red ware, black and red ware.

Vadagaon Madhavpur 1975-76. p.19.
Karnataka, District Belgam. Black and red ware, Russet-coated Painted Ware, coins of Kshatrapa and Satavahana.

Vadagaon Madhavpur 1976-77. pp. 21, 24.
Karnataka, District Belgam. Roman coin, Neolithic celts.

Vadagaon Madhavpur 1977-78. pp. 24-25.
Karnataka, District Belgam. Satavahana, RPW, black and red ware, coarse red ware, Satavahana coins, Kshatrapa coins.

476. Vadamadurai 1966-67. pp. 20-21.
Tamil Nadu, District Chingelput. Lower Palaeolithic.

477. Vadapadra 1975-76. p. 16.
Gujarat, District Vadodara. Excavation at the Udayanarayan Temple. Site occupied ca. 7th to 17th century A.D.

478. Vaddamanu 1981-82. p. 1-2.
Andhra Pradesh, District Guntur. Excavation at two sites. Site I earliest structures are two votive stupas. Also a hall with 16 pillars. Site II has stupas and a vihara associated with NBP and punch marked coins of Mauryan date. Brahmi inscription.

Vaddamanu 1982-83. pp.2-3.
Andhra Pradesh, District Guntur. Excavation of an open air gallery in front of a stupa and the exposure of a stairway and revetment. Ikshvaku coins and inscriptions. Sherd reading "Vadhama."

Vaddamanu 1983-84. pp. 2-3.
Andhra Pradesh, District Guntur. Excavation of another stupa. Dated to the ca. 2nd century B.C. on the basis of stylisitic ties to Bharhut. Vishnukundin structures over those of the Ikshvakus.

Vaddamanu 1984-85. pp.3-4
Andhra Pradesh, District Guntur. Work on Period III. Exposure of architecture. NBP recovered from Period I. Period IV Vishnukundin AD500-AD600 Period III Ikshvaku AD250-AD500Period II Satavahana AD100-AD250 Period I Post-Mauryan 200BC-AD100.

479 Vadnagar 1953-54 p.10
Bombay (Gujarat), District Mehsana. Period I, 100 to 200 A.D., crude pottery of type noted at Baroda, Timberva and Amreli. Period II, 200 to 600 A.D. RPW, painted pottery with black designs on bright red slip, also found in Saurashtra. Period III, 600 to 1200 A.D., coarse red slipped ware with black on white background. Last ware also found at Baroda and Timberva.

480. Vaisali 1957-58. pp. 10-11
Bihar, District Muzaffarpur. Investigation of a stupa and tank of this Buddhist site associated with the Lichchavis. Pre-NBP, NBP, Mauryans.

Vaisali 1958-59. p.12
Bihar, District Muzaffarpur. Investigation of the fortifications which sit on NBP deposits. Massive rampart of Sunga, Kushan and Gupta periods.

Vaisali 1959-60. pp. 14-16
Bihar, District Muzaffarpur. Pre-Sunga, red ware and grey ware, Gupta Period, Brahmi legends, cast copper and iron, stupas, NBP.

Vaisali 1960-61. p.6
Bihar, District Muzaffarpur. NBP and associated wares (red.) Kushan, Gupta, Muslim glazed ware, black and red ware, grey ware with black wash paint.

Vaisali 1961-62. pp. 5,7.
Bihar, District Muzaffarpur. NBP, red ware, cast and punch marked coins, stupa, black ware, grey ware, sprinklers.

481. Valabhi 1979-80. p.24.
Gujarat, District Bhavnagar. Harappan buff, perforated, crude and Lustrous Red and black and red wares, Post-Harappan pottery, grey ware, sprinklers.

482. Vamulapadu 1978-79 pp. 35,37.
Andhra Pradesh, District Kurnool. Lower Palaeolithic, tools (discoidal scraper, bifacial chopper on a thick core, sub-triangular flake). Early Historical, a black and red ware, Rouletted Ware.

483. Vasavasamudram 1970-71. p. 33
Tamil Nadu, District Chingelput. Rouletted Ware.

484. Velha Goa 1983 84 pp. 16-17.
Goa, Daman and Diu. Excavation in the vicinity of the Adilshahi Palace Gate Porcelain and celadon wares with more day to day cermaics.

485. Vidisha 1971-72. p. 31
Madhya Pradesh. District Vidisa Temple remains discovered beneath a mosque.

486 Virabhadra 1973-74. pp. 28-30
Uttar Pradesh, District Dehra Dun. 1st century to 6th century A.D.

Virabadhra 1974-75. pp. 41-42.
Uttar Pradesh, District Dehra Dun. Excavation of a temple site active from the early centuries of the Christian era to the 8th century A.D.

Visakhapatnam See Turakapadu.

487. Yelleswaram 1957-58. pp. 9-10.
Andhra Pradesh, District Nalgonda. Salvage work behind a proposed dam. Megaliths, iron furnaces and slag, temples, Buddhist remains.

Yelleswaram 1958-59. p.11.
Andhra Pradesh, District Nalgonda. Temple site, Megalith, stupa.

Yelleswaram 1960-61. p.3.
Andhra Pradesh, District Nalgonda. Stupa, Early Historical pottery, Megalithic burial.

Yelleswaram 1961-62. pp. 2-3.
Andhra Pradesh, District Nalgonda. Cist, urn burials.

Yelleswaram 1962-63. pp. 2-3.
Andhra Pradesh, District Nalgonda. Megaliths, RPW, Roman coin of Septimus Serverus.

Yelleswaram 1963-64. p.4.
Andhra Pradesh, District Nalgonda. Megalithic black and red ware, red ware, all black ware, coins of Visnukundins of about the 4th century A.D.

488. Yesar 1973-74. pp. 21-22
Maharashtra, District Dhule. Palaeolithic, microliths.

489. Zawar 1983-84, p.77
Rajasthan, District Udaipur. Excavation of zink distillation furnaces. Zink mines to - 120 m. Dates for mining and distilling are: 2120±60 B.P. and 1920±50 B.P.

490. Zekhada 1977-78. pp. 20-21.
Gujarat, District Banaskantha. Pottery similar to Harappan at Rangpur, Chalcolithic.

BOOK REVIEWS

Archaecometry of Glass. ed. Dr. H.C. Bhardwaj, Indian Cramic Society, Central Glass & Ceramic Research Institute, Calcutta - 1987. Pp. 110 . Price not mentioned.

Of late, there is a growing realisation in the minds of modern glass technologists that some aspects of glass such as weathering with time, the prudent use of raw materials, recipes for colours etc. can best be understood by the study of ancient glass. This has resulted in the International Congress on Glass held in New Delhi in 1986. The credit goes to Dr. H.C. Bhardwaj for successfully organising the session and also promptly publishing the papers in a book form. While giving a glimpse of the tools possibly used by the ancient glass makers, he has reviewed the archaeometric studies of Indian glass. In his key paper, Robert Brill has emphatically postulated that most of the Early Indian glasses were made indigenously as against the popular belief of the archaeologists that they were imported either from the West or the Near East. His argument is based on the chemical analyses of ancient Indian glasses which often show high alumina contents. Brill has put the Indian glasses into six groups on their alumina contents. Abdurazakov has however classified the Indian glass into sixteen chemical types which reveal that nine of them are indigenous. He observes a close connections between India and Central Asia. Both classifications should however be treated with caution since the analyses are based on small number of glass objects and belong to diverse periods from relatively small geographical area of the Indian Subcontinent.

O.P. Agrawal and his colleagues have presented new analyses of glasses from Hulaskhera. Inspite of a sizable number of analyses, it appears that the colours of glasses can not be assigned with certainty to a particular element or a group of elements. The colourless glasses also show presence of some colouring agents (elements) such as copper. The orange colour as assigned to the presence of lead stannate is worth pursuing for further study.

E.M. Stern in her paper on the glass industry of Arikamedu has projected Arikamedu as an important centre of international trade. She presents evidence of the tube drawing, the tube cutting and the polishing processes. Drawing information from the literary and archaeological sources Prof. S.B. Deo discusses the antiquity of Indian glass. He suggests that the real glass appeared in India around 8th-6th century B.C. However, the occurrence of glazed siliceous ware from Mohenjodaro and the glass bangles in black and blue colour from Period IB of Bhagwanpura contradicts this. Dr. B.B. Lal presents a panoramic view of glass objects from almost all important archaeological excavations. He observes that Kopia, Ahichchatra and Nevasa were main centres of glass manufacturing in India.

The chemical analyses of glasses from Sumatra have been reported for the first time by E. McKinnon and R.H. Brill. The glass come from six ancient sites dating approximately 7th to 17th century A.D. Although only the glass from Kota Cina have a well stratified context, the analyses have made a useful contribution to out knowledge. The influence of not only India but also China is clearly reflected from the analyses. In the non-Indian section of this volume, other important papers are on the Chinese glass. Chinese glasses are unique in their composition having high percentage of lead and barium. Meiguang and his colleagues in their papers have differentiated the chinese glass containing high potash from that of the West postualting the use of saltpeter having been used as flux rather than plant ash.

This volume gives us upto date information on the chemical analyses of ancient glasses from India, Sumatra and China. However, it may be suggested that in order to make fruitful comparisons of the ancient glasses, different laboratories engaged in this study should follow common conventions for analytical procedures. In absence of any convention, it is not possible to compare glasses of one site with anather.

Deccan College
Pune
Vishwas D. Gogate

Paintings of the Babur-nama. By M.S. Randhawa, (National Museum, New Delhi, 1983). Pp. xii +139, 20 plates in colour, 35 plates in monochrome. Rs. 240.00.

Of late Mughal paintings have been receiving considerable attention from connoisseures of art all over the world. Marked for the splash of abundant colours, accuracy of line-drawing, realism in representation, decore and finesse and laborious work, Mughal paintings make a class by themselves, distinct from all other styles of contemporary Indian art. The *Babur-nama* miniatures which are the illustrations of major events from the life of emperor Babur, as described in his Memoirs, are representatives of the middle phase of the progressing Mughal *qalam*, more or less contemporaneous as they are, with the illustrations of *Anwar-i Suhaili* (Bharat Kala Bhawan, Varanasi, dated 1596-97), *Khamsa* of Nizami (British Museum, London, dated 1598) and *Ajaib al Makhluqat* (Chester Beatty Library, Dublin, c. 1600). They were ordered to be made by Emperor Akbar, who paid special attention to the promotion of the art of book-illustration. It is important to mention that Abu-l Fazl has given in the *Ain-i Akbari* a list of manuscripts illustrated at Akbar's atelier but it does not include *Baburnama*. Since *Baburnama* was not illustrated by time of compilation of *Ain-i Akbari*, the question of its reference in the above mentioned list did not arise. The *Ain-i Akbari* was completed in 1596-97, and an addition to it was made in 1597-98.

No *Baburnama* manuscript contains the colophon. The National Museum manuscript bears a valuable note on folio 116, declaring that the painting on it was completed in the fortysecond regnal year which is equivelant to 1598. Incidentally, folio 116 was not the last to be painted; we may safely extend the time of completion of the entire work to 1600. A seal of Shah Jahan, and another of St. John's College, Agra, testify to the vicissitudes the manuscript must have passed before reaching the National Museum, Delhi.

National Museum *Baburnama* was introduced for the first time in 1955 by Rai Krishnadasa and Humayun Kabir. It was in 1971 that in a dissertation on "Paintings of *Tuzuk-i Baburi*" prepared under the supervision of Professor S. Nurul Hasan and submitted at Aligarh Muslim University, this particular manuscript alongwith other copies of *Baburnama* was taken up for study in depth. Though this piece of research yet remains unpublished, significant material on *Baburnama* appeared in the *Art and Material Culture in the Paintings of Akbar's Court* (Delhi, 1978). The most distinguished study of the *Baburnama* miniatures is the Ph. D. thesis "Paintings from the Baburnama: a study of 16th century Mughal historical manuscript illustrations", submitted by E. Smart at School of Oriental & African Studies, University of London (1977). Now though extensive work done in the recent past has considerably narrowed down the scope for fresh approach, there is still room for profitable research.

Not unexpectedly, therefore, the publi-cation of *Paintings of Baburnama* by Dr. M.S. Randhawa should arouse the curiosity of the reader seeking for illumination on a much debated subject in recent years. But the fact is otherwise. It turns out to be a monograph with little originality. Dr. Randhawa has noticed three copies of *Baburnama* known to have been preserved at the British Museum, London, State Museum of Eastern Cultures, Moscow, and National Museum, New Delhi, besides 18 astray folios lodge at the Victoria & Albert Museum, London. Several other dispersed folios of *Baburnama*, preserved at The Walters Art Gallery, Baltimore; Freer Gallery of Art, Washington; Du Musee Du Louvre, Paris; and Fogg Art Museum, Boston have escaped his notice. His work is indeed devoid of art appreciation. He has also ignored a good deal of work towards the appreciation of these miniatures of *Baburnama* already done by S.C. Welch, M.C. Beach, E. Smart, I. Stchoukine and others. It is unfortunate that he fails even to take notice of the general characteristics of the miniatures which are the representatives of the sixteenth century Mughal school. Appreciation of the work of individual artists pointing to a definite style assimilating various trends of art in vogue especially in India and Persia, would have possibly shaped the present mongraph into a excellent piece of research in the history of art.

There is a marked propensity towards naturalistic representation in *Baburnama* paintings, though the measure of success is largely determined by the artists' associations with their respective schools as well as by the commonly accepted conventions. Thus the Persian tradition makes itself emphatically felt in the aerial perspective with a deep blue sky, sprayed with stars; in the clouds with a touch of orange; in the simultaneity of vision; direct view; elaborate embellishment of costumes; in the lavish use of gold pigment and of the Persian blue and crimson. Side by side with this typical gestures introduced to characterise human figures; big elongated eyes; dense foliage of trees; long, straight tree-trunks; the saw-edge lines depicting flowing water - all these recall the various native styles of art. Incidentally, the method of shading is employed after the Ajanta paintings while the European technique also begins to show up in the deep shading technique. A similar influence may be seen in the depiction of distance by reducing the scale as the eye moves forward. But traces of these are few and far between. The general method remains more or less conventional where uniformity of scale is allowed to persist irrespective of distance.

Interestingly, features of Chinese art are not wanting in the paintings. The dragon and some of the motifs with elongated flame-like ends point to the Chinese influence.

Dr. Randhawa has rightly singled out *Baburnama* miniatures for the pictures on natural history, though other contemporary works, viz., *Anwar-i Suhaili* (School of Oriental & African Studies, London, dated 1570, and Bharat Kala Bhawan, Varanasi, dated 1597-97), *Iyar-i Danish* (Chester Beatty Library, Dublin, c. 1600) and *Ajaib al Makhluqat* (Chester Beatty Library, c. 1600) are of equal interest. The National Museum manuscript contains 43 folios representing flora and fauna of India (mainatures nos. 89-131). Originality of the author's commendation of these pictures is minimal since the text of explanatory notes (here, theme only), including identification of species, etc., preceding each entry, is lifted word for word from Beveridge's English translation of *Baburnama* (pp. 488-515).

It is disconcerting to note that Chapter III, 'Paintings of Baburnama' (pp.11-16) is a verbatim copy of the article published a decade earlier by the author (*Roopa-Lekha*, Vol. XLII, nos. 1& 2 (1973), pp. 9-16). The author has been remiss in taking into account the research material published after 1973. He has not even cared to revise the text of the paper. This paper/chapter III, has been wholly devoted to making a list of the artists responsible for the illustrations of *Akbarnama* (Victoria & Albert Museum, London) and the *Baburnama* manuscripts lodged in the British Museum, London and National Museum, Delhi, and tracing simply the names of artists found common in these manuscripts without justifying such an attempt in the present volume. Amongst the painters of the National Museum *Baburnama*, Khemkaran, Anant, Daulat, Farrukh *Chela*, Madhav, Mahesh, Miskin and Mansur are notable. Of these, Khemkaran, Madhav, Mahesh and Miskin were recognised by Abu-l Fazl as the leading painters of Akbar's court who later attained fame. Mansur, known for his animal drawings in the British Museum manuscript, has contributed the illustration 'Babur meeting his sister ' (folio 8) in Delhi manuscript. It shows Mansur's skill in portraiture as well from the beginning of his career.

While wide generalisation is in itself dangerous in historiography, Dr. Randhawa has fallen into error by passing a remark that the "portraiture of the face of Babur is uniform throughout the series [in the three copies of the *Baburnama*]" (p.15). In the portrayal of the emperor's face the artist has depended on some standard lines, the positioning of figure, costumes, ornaments, display of insignia, etc. In the National Museum copy, Babur's face does not appear entirely similar everywhere. Even his face is treated in varying shades (plates IV-V, XV and XX). The same is true of his portraits executed in other copies of *Baburnama*. However, characteristic similarity is found in most of his face drawings. Obviously, accuracy in portraiture largely depended on the skill of the individual artist. Broadly speaking, face drawings executed in the British Museum copy are superior to those seen in the Delhi manuscript and in the folios of *Baburnama* extent at The Walters Art Gallery, Baltimore and Victoria & Albert Museum, London. Illustrations of the Moscow manuscript show **cven** weaker portraits.

Names of artists written in *nastaliq* appear on the lower margin of the folios. Rarelly in one instance, the ascription containing artist's name appears on the grounds of picture (folio 137). It reads : *"Amal-i Daulat Khanazad"* (Work of Daulat *Khanazad* : [(lit.) born in the family; the child of a slave/ servant])*. It could possibly be the artist's signature. Mir Sayyid 'Ali and Khwaja 'Abdu's Samad are other painters from Akbar's aterlier who are known to have signed some of their works. However, the practice of signing the miniatures was not in vogue at the Mughal atelier and names of the artists were ascribed on their respective works by the clerk of the atelier. Thus ascriptions, in general, are 'third-person ascriptions' which possibly should not have been left out in the reporductions. Correct rendering of a few names of artists, viz., Bhag, Jagnath and Lohka is 'Payag', 'Jagannath' and 'Lohanka' resepctively.

Despite all these anomalies the present book is commendable for presenting all the miniatures of the National Museum *Baburnama*, being published for the first time, embellished with twenty full-page reproductions in colour and one hundred forty four illustrations in monochrome in a magnificently bound volume.

Aligarh Muslim University S.P. Verma
Aligarh

Iconography of Buddhist Deity Heruka. By K. Krishna Murthy, Sundeep Prakashan, New Delhi 1988, Pp. 1-60 P1.XI, Price Rs.100/-

Many researches on Buddhist iconography have been published, since the pioneering studies of illustrious preceptors like A. Foucher, Harprasad Shastri, Benoytosh Bhattacharyya. Dr. Krishna Murthy's monograph on Heruka is one such addition in the series Heruka, one of the emanations of Dhyani Buddha Aksobhya is regarded in the esoteric doctrine (Yogacara) as the personification of karuna or compassion, and his Sakti Nairatma as the personification of prajna or knowledge. In the yab-yum form, generally known as Hevajra, Heruka (compassiosn) and Nairatmah (Knowledge) collectively leads to a realization of nirvana, the enternal bliss.

This small book with sixty printed pages includes introduction, followed by tantric Buddhist iconographic sources, sculptures of Heruka and the general observations. The author has obliged us with a casual bibliography and facsimile glossary but not with an index. From the treatment of the subject, it appears that the author was in a flurry to write it. He has taken adequate note of published references but leaves unimproved knowledge about the deity. Both the *Sadhanamala* and *Abhidhanottarasadhantatra* define certain exquisite and gruesome forms of Heruka and Hevajra. Some of the very relevant sadhanas are cited in B. Bhattacharyya's and D.C. Bhattacharya's publications well known to scholars. Dr. Murthy's chapter entitled "Tantric Buddhist iconographic sources" is but a prototype of an identical book of D.C. Bhattarcharya entitled "The Tantric Buddhist iconographic Sources" published in 1974. This is visible in the introductory paras, but a number of inferences of chapter two in Dr. Murthy's book have either been drawn from B. Bhattacharyya's or D.C. Bhattacharya's published works, unmindful to attract the provisions of copy right. It is conspicuous to note that Dr. Murthy did not look into *Nispannayogavali* for various forms of Heruka, Hevajra, Sambara, etc.

The Chapter on sculptures of Heruka is bare discription of eleven illustrations taken from various known books on iconography, thereby leaving an unpleasant task of reproduction. The so-called image of Jnana Visudha from Amaravati has long been identified by R. Subramanyam as Heruka (*Indian Archaeology-A Review-1958-59*, p.5, Pl.IC). To Dr. Murthy, if the Amaravati example is Jnana Visudha form of Heruka, then, why should not Heruka of Dacca Museum (Pl.I) having same identical features be not classified as that of Amaravati example (Pl. II)?

Dr. Murthy's stand is hardldy tenable that the worship of Heruka was not known in China and Japan (Pl.41). Of late, Aksobhya and his emanations like Sambara (?) Trailokyavijaya and Raktayamari, etc. have been reported from the Kansu province of China by which a revision is necessitated. Moreover, the worship of Heruka and Hevajra is very popular in Tibet.'

The monograph also abounds in printer's devil causing detraction. Eventually the book is wanting in continuity, thereby leaving much to get the desired effect of narration. The only plus point could be the identification of a Heruka figure from Amaravati.

Archaeological Survey Amarendra Nath
of India, Nagpur

Excavations at Inamgaon. By M.K. Dhavalikar, H.D. Sankalia and Z.D. Ansari. Deccan College Post Graduate and Research Institute, Pune. Vol. I (Part i & ii), pp. 1044, Figures and Plates 679. Price Rs. 1500 (set).

It is a report of an archaeological excavations conducted at Inamgaon for as many as 12 seasons starting from 1968. The excavation was initially planned and started by Prof. H.D. Sankalia and later continued by Prof. Dhavalikar and Dr. Ansari. The main aim of the excavations was to throw light on the socio-economic conditions of chalcolithic Maharashtra. The part i of the volume contains 11 chapters mostly by Prof. Dhavalikar and Dr. Ansari. Besides, especialist chapters on geomorphology, site catchment analysis and palaeontology are contributed by Prof. S.N. Rajaguru, Dr. R.S. Pappu and Dr. G.L. Badam. Part ii has seven chapters and mostly technical in nature. These deal with Palaeobotany, archaeozoology, chemical analysis and microwear analysis, contributed by Drs. M.D. Kajale, P.K. Thomas, B.C. Deotare, V.G. Gogate, Anupama Kshirsagar and Vasant Shinde. It may be mentioned here that Vol. II (Part i) of *Inamgaon Excavations* by Dr. S.R. Walimbe has already come out and it deals with Human Skeletal material.

One of the most important things that this report brings out in sharp focus is the methods of horizontal excavations. After obtaining a clear idea of chronological, straigraphic and various phases the horizontal excavations obtaining and recording were controlled not only through the trenches and layers but also through structures, houses, huts, courtyards etc. It is because of this the excavators could talk about the findings not only in the context of layers and the trenches but also in the context of structures. Because of this contextual recording of the material the excavators successfully talk about the utility of various spaces and identify various structures like chief's house, potter's, smith's and stone bead maker's house, workshop etc. However in the chapter of cuttings and stratigraphy the published sections (Fig. 7.2, 7.4 and 7.6) have no details. They surely deserved better treatment. A clear and detail section would have helped us in understandng the overlap phase between Pd. I and II better and so also the transition from period II to Period III. The details of excavated area have also been reduced beyond recognition (Fig. 2.1.)

It is very heartening to note that with all their limitations the excavators were able to take arial photograph of the site and surrounding area from a simple toy plane at a remarkably low cost. If used extensively in the field of Indian Archaeology, this method will surely add new dimensions. On the basis of arial photography Prof. Dhavalikar and his colleagues have identified a ditch around the site and an irrigation canal. While these lines may be clear enough, what I feel is they should have cut a section across the identified ditch and canal to confirm their identification. Here I may mention our own experience at Shrinagaverpura where a big water tank was found during the course of excavations. In this tank water was brought through a canal connected to a *nala* of the Ganga. To confirm our identification of the canal we dug a cross-section in which it could be seen.

The excavation report abounds in the use of various modern techniques of data recovery and conceptual framework for the interpretation of data. The floatation technique to recover the charred grains, the detail statistical analysis of animal bones, the trace element analysis of human bones to determine the dietary patterns are a few to mention. On the basis of the size of settlement and the approximate need of the inhabitants, the excavators have developed a model of catchment area. Except for Dr. Makkhan Lal's work which is at a regional scale this is the first detail work on catchment area analysis. However, my feeling is that excavators have over-used the data available from the site and relied too much an ethnographic parallel. A note of caution is required in use of ethnographic data as we all know that it can be sometimes quite misleading.

The recovery of botanical and zoological data has been the most extensive one. As many as 33 species of plant food has been identified. A detail trench-wise, layer-wise, phase-wise and house-wise analysis and frequency of each species gives a very good idea of the various species, the time of their introduction and when they fell in disuse. Similar is the situation with the faunal remains. Thirty-five species of mammals, birds, reptiles, fishes, molluscs and crabs have been identified. Once again the detail trench-wise, layer-wise, house-wise analysis of the data has been provided. Because of very extensive data recovery and a careful analysis it could be established that in the late Jorwe period people were increasingly dependent on meat diet rather than on agriculture.

A reconstruction of dietary pattern of the chalcolithic people of Inamgaon is a further contribution to the Indian Archaeology. The analysis of human bones have been carried out to see the percentage of trace elements - copper, zinc, stroteim and mangnese on the basis of which dietary pattern has been reconstructed.

The sections on pottery, antiquities, lithic industries etc. are well written and well illustrated.

I am fully aware that a brief review like this one cannot do full justice to a report of this magnitude. However, the report under the review is highly praiseworthy and may be treated as a model report for the future excavations.

Archaeological Survey of India, New Delhi

K.N. Dikshit

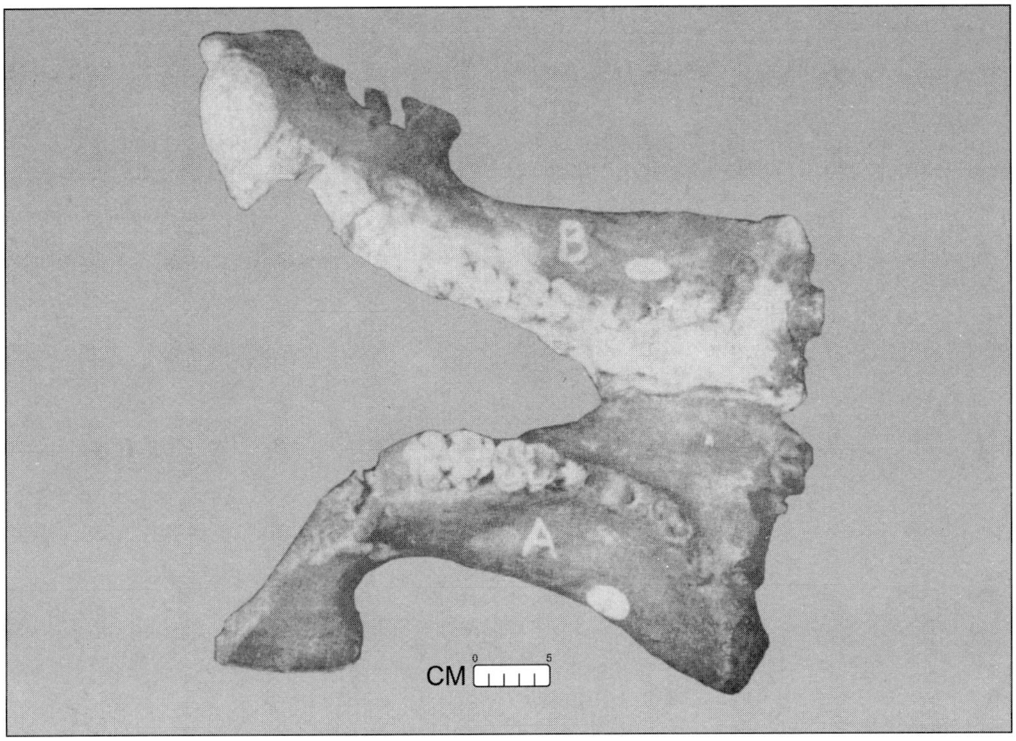

Plate I. Lower jaw of *H.namadicus* from Talayyaghat, river varurewa catalogue No. NMD/231 AB/DC. (Salahuddin).

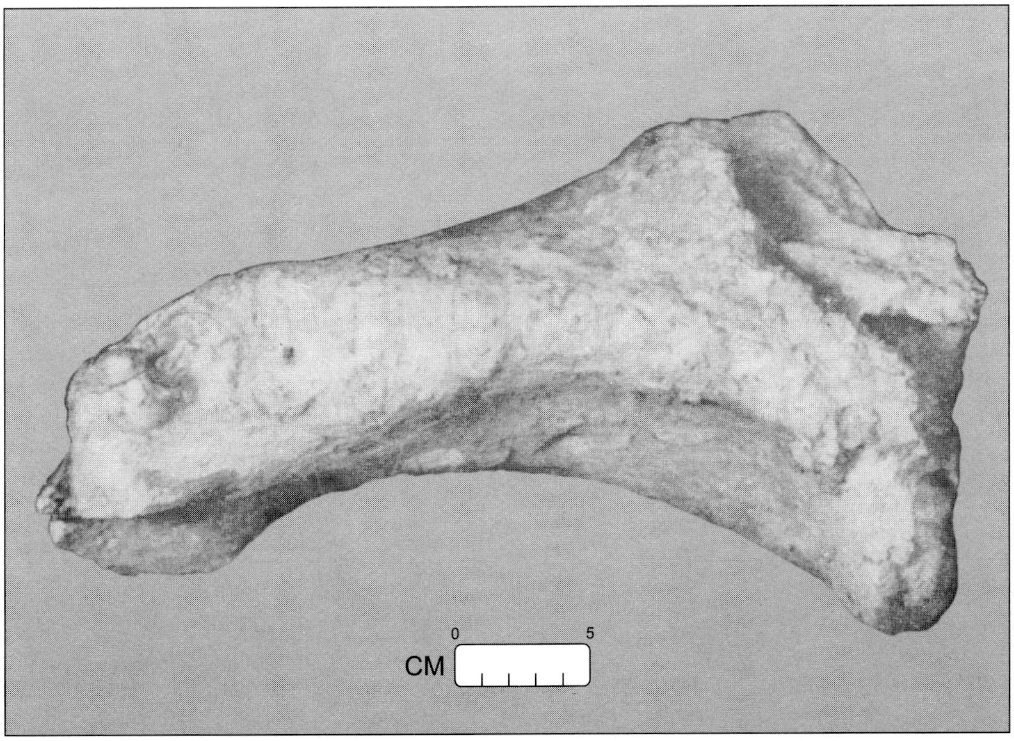

Plate II. Right ramus of *H Palaeindicus* from Talayyaghat, river Varurewa catalogue No. NMD/28/DC. (Salahuddin).

Plate III. Mandibular symphysis of *H Palaeindicus* from Devakachar, river Sher catalogue No. NMD/232/DC. (Salahuddin).

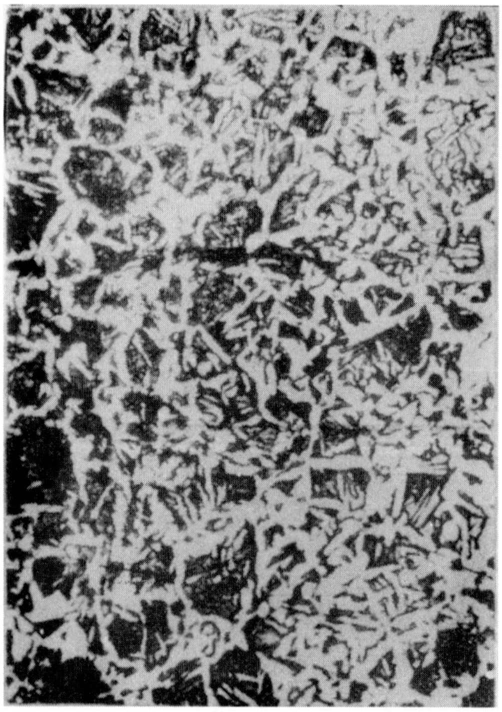

Plate I. Magnification of 100X showing pealite (black) and ferrite (white) midmastatten pattern (Ghosh *et al.*).

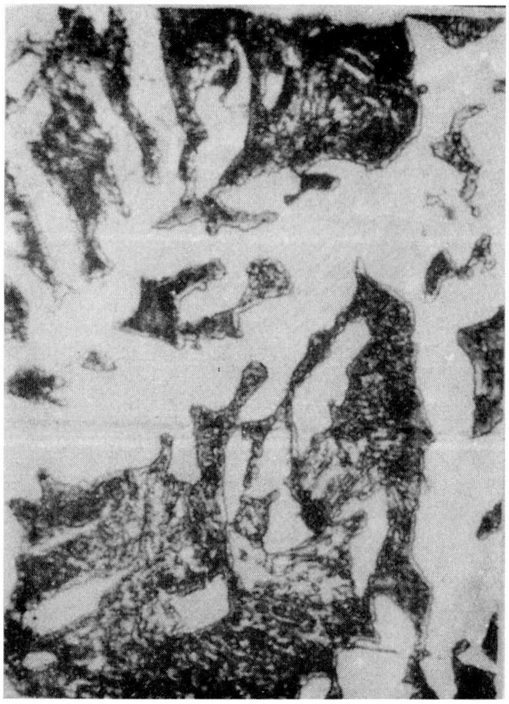

Plate II. Photomicrography at 500X pearlite broken ametter type are resolved along with midmastatten pattern (Ghosh *et al.*).

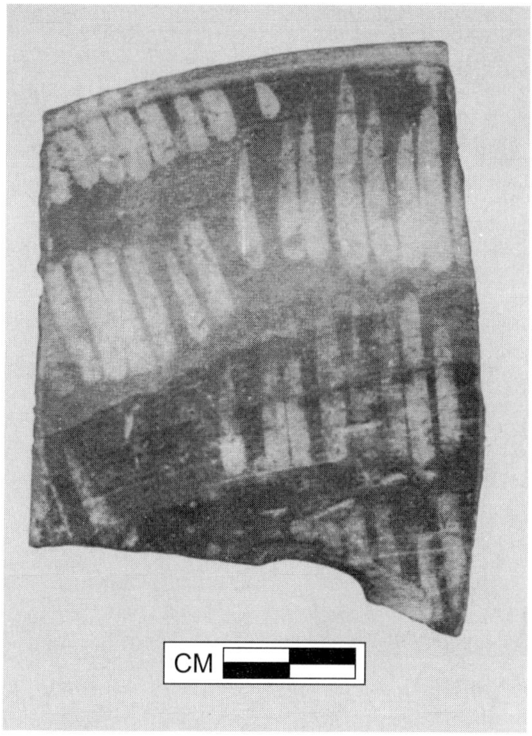

Plate I. Painted Red Ware, Pd. I (Singh).

Plate II. Socketed arrowhead of bone and Copper (Singh).

Plate III. Painted Black Slipped Ware (Singh).

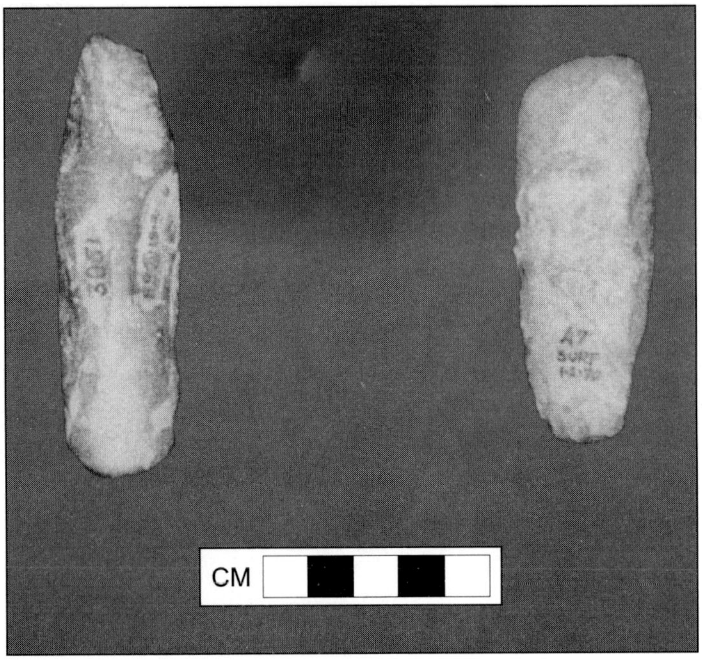

Plate I. Polished Stone Chisels (Shinde).

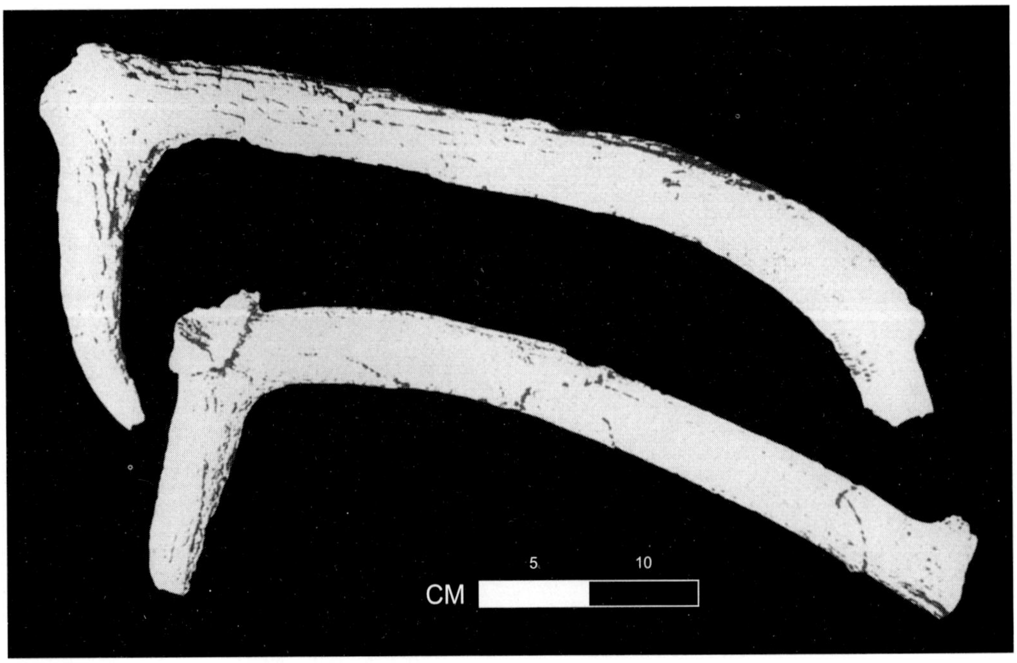

Plate II. Antler pieces from Inamgaon (Shinde).

Plate I. Megalithic Circle at Khairwada : Standard type (Walimbe).

Plate II. Megalithic Circle at Khairwada : Khairwada type (Walimbe).

Plate III. Megalithic Circle at Raipur with chamber of large boulders at its centre (Walimbe).

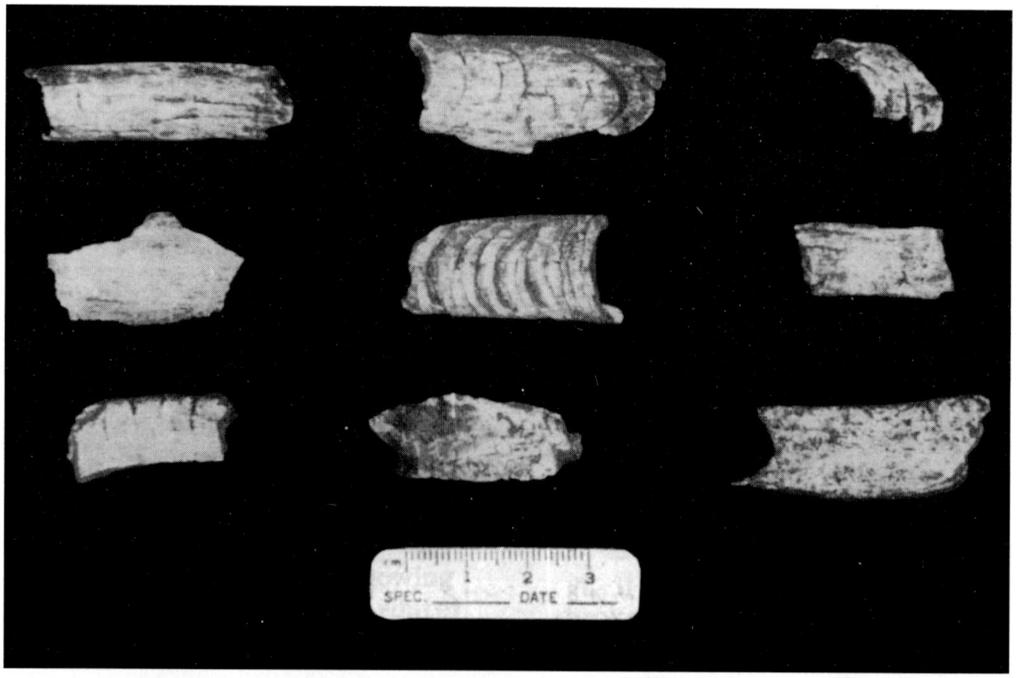

Plate IV. Khairwada specimen : Megalithic I, locality III. Cracks on long bones due to exposure to fire in flesh-on condition (Walimbe).

Plate I. Superimposition from Rock Shelter No. 2 (Fig. I:1) (Chandra Mouli).

Plate II. Pregnant deer, Rockshelter No. 6 (Fig 2:4) (Chandra Mouli).

Plate III. Deers in pairs (Fig II:7 & 10) (Chandra mouli)

Plate I. General view of Siva temple at Payer (Malla).

Plate II. Bhairva in Pediment of Siva temple south Payer (Malla).

Plate III. Lakulisha in pediment, Siva temple east Payer (Malla).

Plate IV. Nataraja in Pediment, Siva temple west Payer (Malla).

Plate V. Maheshwar in Pediment, north Payer (Malla).

Plate I. Mahamrityunjaya : Sangameshwar temple, Animala, Distt. Cuddappah, Andhra Pradesh (Gurumurthy).